New Approaches to Monetary Economics brings together presentations of innovative research in the field of monetary economics. Much of this research develops and applies newly initiated approaches to modeling financial intermediation, aggregate fluctuations, monetary aggregation, and transactions motivated monetary equilibrium.

The contents of this volume comprise the proceedings of the second in a new conference series entitled International Symposia in Economic Theory and Econometrics. This conference was held in 1985 at the IC² (Innovation, Creativity, and Capital) Institute at the University of Texas at Austin. The symposia in this series are sponsored by the IC² Institute and the RGK Foundation.

New Approaches to Monetary Economics, edited by Professors William A. Barnett and Kenneth J. Singleton, consists of five parts. Part I examines transactions motivated monetary holding in general equilibrium; Part II, financial intermediation; Part III, monetary aggregation theory; Part IV, issues in aggregate fluctuation; and Part V, theoretical issues in the foundations of monetary economics and macroeconomics.

New approaches to monetary economics

International Symposia in Economic Theory and Econometrics

Editor
William A. Barnett, *University of Texas at Austin*

New approaches to monetary economics

Proceedings of the Second International Symposium in Economic Theory and Econometrics

edited by

WILLIAM A. BARNETT
University of Texas at Austin
and
KENNETH J. SINGLETON
Carnegie-Mellon University

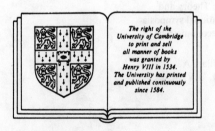

The right of the
University of Cambridge
to print and sell
all manner of books
was granted by
Henry VIII in 1534.
The University has printed
and published continuously
since 1584.

CAMBRIDGE UNIVERSITY PRESS

Cambridge
New York   New Rochelle
Melbourne   Sydney

Published by the Press Syndicate of the University of Cambridge
The Pitt Building, Trumpington Street, Cambridge CB2 1RP
32 East 57th Street, New York, NY 10022, USA
10 Stamford Road, Oakleigh, Melbourne 3166, Australia

© Cambridge University Press 1987

First published 1987
Reprinted 1988

Printed in the United States of America

Library of Congress Cataloging-in-Publication Data

International Symposium in Economic Theory and
Econometrics (2nd : 1985 : Austin, Tex.)

New approaches to monetary economics.

(International symposia in economic theory and
econometrics)

1. Monetary policy – Econometric models – Congresses.
2. Money supply – Econometric models – Congresses.
I. Barnett, William A. II. Singleton, Kenneth J.
III. Title. IV. Series.

HG205.I565 1985   332.4'0724   87-5113

British Library Cataloguing in Publication Data

International Symposium in Economic
Theory and Econometrics *(2nd)*
New approaches to monetary economics :
proceedings of the Second International
Symposium in Economic Theory and
Econometrics. – (International symposia
in economic theory and econometrics).

1. Money
I. Title II. Barnett, William A.
III. Singleton, Kenneth J. IV. Series

332.4 HG221

ISBN 0 521 33265 6

Contents

Editors' introduction   *page* vii
List of contributors   ix

**Part I: Transactions motivated monetary holdings in
general equilibrium**

    1. Monetary dynamics with proportional transaction
       costs and fixed payment periods
       Sanford J. Grossman   3

    2. A multiple means-of-payment model
       Edward C. Prescott   42

    3. Credit policy and the price level in a cash-in-advance
       economy
       Michael Woodford   52

Part II: Financial intermediation

    4. Preference shocks, liquidity, and central bank policy
       Sudipto Bhattacharya and Douglas Gale   69

    5. Banking and macroeconomic equilibrium
       Ben Bernanke and Mark Gertler   89

Part III: Monetary aggregation theory

    6. The microeconomic theory of monetary aggregation
       William A. Barnett   115

    7. Monetary asset separability tests
       Apostolos Serletis   169

    8. Money demand in open economies: a Divisia
       application to the U.S. case
       Jaime Marquez   183

v

9. Aggregation of monetary goods: a production
   model
   Diana Hancock   200

10. Money in the utility function: an empirical
    implementation
    James M. Poterba and Julio J. Rotemberg   219

11. Comment on papers in Part III
    William A. Barnett   241

Part IV: Issues on aggregate fluctuations

12. Asset prices in a time-series model with disparately
    informed, competitive traders
    Kenneth J. Singleton   249

13. Nominal surprises, real factors, and propagation
    mechanisms
    Robert G. King and Charles I. Plosser   273

14. A rational expectations framework for short-run
    policy analysis
    Christopher A. Sims   293

**Part V: Theoretical issues in the foundations of monetary economics
and macroeconomics**

15. Pricing and the distribution of money holdings in
    a search economy, II
    Peter Diamond and Joel Yellin   311

16. The optimal inflation rate in an
    overlapping-generations economy with land
    Bennett T. McCallum   325

17. Some unsolved problems for monetary theory
    Neil Wallace   340

18. Externalities associated with nominal price and
    wage rigidities
    John B. Taylor   350

Editors' introduction

The contents of this volume comprise the proceedings of a conference held at the IC^2 Institute at the University of Texas at Austin on May 23–24, 1985.[1] The conference title was "New Approaches to Monetary Economics," and it was organized to bring together presentations of some of the particularly innovative new research that recently has been under way in the field of monetary economics. Much of this research develops and applies recently initiated approaches to modeling financial intermediation, aggregate fluctuations, monetary aggregation, and transactions motivated monetary equilibrium. We believe that this conference included pathbreaking research and revealed some fundamental trends in the direction in which monetary economics research is beginning to move.

The conference that produced this proceedings volume is the second in a new conference series, called *International Symposia in Economic Theory and Econometrics.*[2] The symposia in the series are sponsored by the IC^2 Institute at the University of Texas at Austin and are cosponsored by the RGK Foundation. This second conference also was cosponsored by the Federal Reserve Bank of Dallas and by the Department of Economics and the Center for Statistical Sciences at the University of Texas at Austin. The first conference in the series was co-organized by William Barnett and Ronald Gallant, who also co-edited the proceedings volume. That volume has appeared as the volume 30, October/November 1985 edition of the *Journal of Econometrics.*

Beginning with this second symposium in the series, the proceedings of the symposia will appear as volumes in this new Cambridge University Press monograph series. The co-organizers of the second symposium and co-editors of this proceedings volume are William Barnett and Kenneth Singleton. The series is under the general editorship of William Barnett.

[1] IC^2 stands for Innovation, Creativity, and Capital.
[2] The title of the series recently was changed from the *Austin Symposia in Economics,* as a result of the increasingly international nature of the symposia in the series.

Individual volumes in the series will often have co-editors, and the series has a permanent Board of Advisory Editors.

The co-organizers of the third symposium, held on May 22–23, 1986 and entitled "Dynamic Econometric Modeling," are William Barnett and Ernst Berndt, and the co-editors of the proceedings volume for that conference will be William Barnett, Ernst Berndt, and Halbert White. That proceedings volume will be the second volume in this Cambridge series. The fourth symposium in the series currently is being organized for May 19–20, 1987 by William Barnett, John Geweke, and Karl Shell. That conference will be entitled "Economic Complexity: Chaos, Sunspots, Bubbles, and Nonlinearity." The proceedings volume for that conference will be the third volume in this monograph series.

The intention of the volumes in the proceedings series is to provide refereed journal–quality collections of research papers of unusual importance in areas of activity that currently are highly visible within the economics profession. Because of the refereeing requirements associated with the editing of the proceedings, the volumes in the series will not necessarily contain all of the papers presented at the corresponding symposia.

William A. Barnett
University of Texas at Austin

Kenneth J. Singleton
Carnegie-Mellon University

Contributors

William A. Barnett
Department of Economics
University of Texas at Austin

Ben Bernanke
Department of Economics
Princeton University

Sudipto Bhattacharya
Department of Economics
University of California at Berkeley

Peter Diamond
Department of Economics
Massachusetts Institute of Technology

Douglas Gale
Department of Economics
University of Pennsylvania

Mark Gertler
Department of Economics
University of Wisconsin at Madison

Sanford J. Grossman
Department of Economics
Princeton University

Diana Hancock
Department of Finance
University of California at Santa Clara

Robert G. King
Department of Economics
University of Rochester

Jaime Marquez
International Finance Division
Federal Reserve Bank

Bennett T. McCallum
Graduate School of Industrial
  Administration
Carnegie-Mellon University

Charles I. Plosser
Graduate School of Management
University of Rochester

James M. Poterba
Department of Economics
Massachusetts Institute of Technology

Edward C. Prescott
Department of Economics
University of Minnesota at Minneapolis

Julio J. Rotemberg
Sloan School of Management
Massachusetts Institute of Technology

Apostolos Serletis
Department of Economics
University of Calgary

Christopher A. Sims
Department of Economics
University of Minnesota at Minneapolis

Kenneth J. Singleton
Graduate School of Industrial
  Administration
Carnegie-Mellon University

John B. Taylor
Department of Economics
Stanford University

Neil Wallace
Department of Economics
University of Minnesota at Minneapolis

Michael Woodford
Department of Economics
Columbia University

Joel Yellin
Department of Environmental Studies
University of California at Santa Cruz

PART I

Transactions motivated monetary holdings in general equilibrium

CHAPTER 1

Monetary dynamics with proportional transaction costs and fixed payment periods

Sanford J. Grossman

1 Introduction

A general equilibrium model of an economy is presented where people
hold money rather than bonds in order to economize on transaction costs.
It is not optimal for individuals to instantaneously adjust their money
holdings when new information arrives. This (endogenous) delayed response to new information generates a response to a new monetary policy
which is quite different from that of standard flexible price models of
monetary equilibrium. Though all goods markets instantaneously clear,
the transaction cost causes delayed responses in nominal variables to a
change in monetary policy. This in turn causes real variables to respond
to the new monetary policy.

Earlier work by Grossman and Weiss (1983), Grossman (1982), and
Rotemberg (1984) have considered models of the above type where individuals hold money for an *exogenously* fixed amount of time – their "payment period." As in the model to be developed here, these models assume
that goods can be bought only with cash. However, unlike what we will
assume here, individuals can exchange bonds for cash only on the exogenously fixed "paydates" which occur at the beginning and end of their
payment periods. Thus an individual's money holding period is exogenously given and insensitive to the nominal interest rate. In such models,
when there is an unanticipated increase in the money supply, people can
be induced to hold the new money only by a large fall in the real rate of
interest. The fall in the real rate of interest induces people to increase
their real spending in the current payment period relative to future payment periods. They thus hold more cash in order to be able to purchase

I am grateful to Jerry Fusselman and Narayana Kocherlakota for helpful comments. The
computer simulations were generated by Narayana Kocherlakota and Chi Ki Chaing. This
research was supported by grants from the National Science Foundation and the Alfred P.
Sloan Foundation.

3

the goods. In contrast, the Baumol–Tobin model implies that *people want to exhaust their money later when the nominal interest rate falls*, so that the stock of money demanded can increase even if the rate of spending is constant.

Another aspect of the exogenously fixed money-holding period is that (with a zero interest–rate elasticity of money demand) expected inflation has almost no effect on the demand for money and hence on the current price level. In the model to be developed here the money-holding period falls when there is expected inflation, so that the price level is sensitive to announcements of monetary policy.

The model to be developed here drops the assumption of an exogenously fixed money-holding period, but retains the assumption of an exogenously fixed pay period. Though current work is underway on a model with endogenous pay periods, the model is far simpler when there is only an endogenous money-holding period. Section 2 develops a particularly simple model of the money-holding period by assuming that there is a proportional transactions cost of converting bonds into money at all dates except on a paydate.[1] On a paydate a consumer can freely transfer between bonds and money. It is shown that an optimal policy for a consumer is to withdraw an amount of cash on his paydate which is designed to finance his spending for a period of time $\bar{t}$, and to finance spending from bonds thereafter until the next paydate. The sensitivity of $\bar{t}$ to interest rates yields qualitatively and quantitatively different dynamic responses to the unanticipated monetary policy announcements than occur in the previously mentioned work, where $\bar{t}$ is exogenously fixed.

Section 3 develops the general equilibrium for the steady-state cross-sectional distribution of cash. It reemphasizes the need for a cross-sectional distribution of cash with the property that the money flowing out of consumers' hands from their spending must equal the rate at which other consumers desire to increment their cash balances.

Section 4 considers the effects of unanticipated monetary policies as a perturbation of the steady state in a perfect foresight model. It is shown how the perfect foresight model can be thought of as an approximation to a rational expectations model. This section studies unanticipated monetary policies called "price level policies," which have the effect of keeping

---

[1] See Jovanovic (1982) for an analysis of the steady state of an economy where there is a cash-in-advance constraint and a fixed cost of converting between capital and money. See Leach (1982) for an analysis of the steady state of an economy where there is a proportional transactions cost, but each consumer spends out of money for only a single period in his life.

nominal interest rates unchanged but change the path of money and the price level. For example, it is shown that there is a unique path of money which raises the price level in the long run by $\alpha\%$ without changing the nominal interest rate. This money supply path involves a gradual rise in money over a pay period until the money supply rises by $\alpha\%$. This should be contrasted with the standard flexible-price LM model where the initial money supply can simply be chosen to be $\alpha\%$ higher, and this will immediately raise prices by $\alpha\%$. In our model, if the money supply grows too rapidly then the nominal rate is driven down, because of a liquidity effect associated with it being costly for consumers to increment their cash balances. In the standard LM model [derived, say, from Sidrauski's (1967) equilibrium model], it is as if all consumers can, without paying a transaction cost, increment their cash balances at any instant of their choosing.

Section 5 considers a class of monetary policies, called interest rate policies, where the money supply is chosen to cause a particular path of interest rates to be the market-clearing rates. The first interest-rate paths to be considered involve a permanent rise in the nominal interest rate. Because of the liquidity effect mentioned earlier, this is associated with an initial contraction in the money supply, followed by a rise in the money supply to its new steady-state growth rate. Again, this differs from what would occur in the standard LM model, where a rise in the nominal rate of (say) 1% is implemented by a new monetary growth rate of 1% (with a degree of freedom involving the level of the money supply). We go on to consider temporary interest-rate changes, as well as analyzing the response of the economy to various frequencies of interest-rate movements. Section 6 contains conclusions.

2 The consumer's optimization problem

A consumer at time 0 chooses a path of consumption, money, and bond holdings. At that time he has perfect foresight about the path of prices and interest rates at all times $t > 0$. Bonds pay an endogenously determined rate of interest, while money earns no nominal interest. The consumer holds money because goods can only be purchased with money. The consumer can transfer between bonds and money according to the following transactions technology: At the end of each interval of length h (which represents the exogenously given "pay period"), a consumer has a "paydate." At that date he can freely convert his assets between bonds and cash. At dates other than paydates the consumer bears a transactions cost which is proportional to the amount of bonds converted to cash.[2] He has a continuous-time optimization problem that involves the choice of a time path (of consumption, bonds, and money) to maximize lifetime discounted utility, subject to a wealth constraint and the above transactions technology.

It will be shown that the above assumptions imply that a consumer will withdraw a stock of cash M on his paydate z, and will spend only out of cash until a time $t(z)$ that depends on the path of interest rates between z and (his next paydate) $z+h$. In the time remaining between $t(z)$ and $z+h$, the consumer will convert his bonds to money continuously to finance his consumption. That is, the consumer holds no (stock of) money for times t satisfying $t \in [t(z), z+h]$.

Assume that at each date there is a single consumption good. Let $P(t)$ be the money price of the good at date t. Let $\gamma(t)$ be the value at date t of one dollar invested at time 0. Thus $\dot{\gamma}(t)/\gamma(t) = r(t)$ is the interest rate at time t. Let M_0 and W_0 denote the money-holding and nominal wealth of the consumer at time 0. Let $m(t)$ denote the flow value of the consumption obtained from the sale of bonds at time t, and let $(k-1) > 0$ denote the transactions cost per dollar of bonds converted into cash. Finally, let $M(t)$ be the stock of money held at t. Throughout this chapter we will use the notation $x_+ = \text{Max}(0, x)$. Consider a consumer whose last paydate was at time $z \in (-h, 0)$. His optimization problem involves maximizing

$$\sum_{n=0}^{\infty} \int_{(z+nh)_+}^{z+(n+1)h} u(c(t)) e^{-\beta t} \, dt \tag{2.1}$$

subject to:

$$\int_0^{z+h} \frac{km(t)}{\gamma(t)} \, dt + \sum_{n=1}^{\infty} \left[\int_{z+nh}^{z+(n+1)h} \frac{km(t)}{\gamma(t)} \, dt + \frac{M^+(z+nh)}{\gamma(z+nh)} \right]$$

$$\leq W_0 + \frac{M^-(z+h)}{\gamma(z+h)} + \frac{D_0}{k}; \tag{2.2a}$$

$$M(t) \geq 0; \tag{2.2b}$$

$$m(t) \geq 0; \tag{2.2c}$$

$$\dot{M}(t) = m(t) - P(t)c(t) \quad t \neq z+h, z+2h, \ldots; \tag{2.2d}$$

$$M(0) = M_0 - D_0; \tag{2.2e}$$

---

[2] The proportional cost model has been chosen because of its tractability. I prefer a model without exogenously determined paydates, where a consumer can withdraw any sum of money for a *fixed* transactions cost. I have analyzed the steady states of such a model in Grossman (1982), and it is quite similar to the steady states of the proportional transactions cost model. However, the nonconvexities inherent in the fixed-cost model make the dynamics intractable except for the simplest sorts of interest rate policies.

where $\beta \in (0,1)$ is his rate of time preference, and a superscript like $M^+(t)$ indicates $\lim_{x \downarrow t} M(x)$ and $M^-(t) \equiv \lim_{x \uparrow t} M(x)$.

The left-hand side (LHS) of (2.2a) is the present value of the consumer's spending out of bonds and money. There is a stock withdrawal of $M^+(z+nh)$ at the nth paydate bearing no transactions cost, and flow withdrawals $m(t)$ at t costing $km(t)$ due to the transactions cost of converting bonds to money. The right-hand side (RHS) of (2.2a) involves the term $M^-(z+h)$, because the consumer may decide not to exhaust his initial stock of money $M(0)$ by the time of his first paydate $z+h$. We permit the consumer to make a stock deposit in his bank account of $D_0 \ge 0$ at time 0 out of his initial cash holding M_0, as indicated in (2.2e). The transactions cost of D_0 is such that wealth increases by only D_0/k in (2.2a).

The wealth constraint assumes that any money withdrawn on a paydate $z+nh>0$ will be totally spent by the next paydate. There is no loss of generality in this assumption because if $r(t)>0$, as we shall assume throughout, it is obviously never optimal for a consumer to withdraw more money than he will spend before his next paydate. However, since the economy faces a monetary policy which at time 0 is different than was anticipated at the last paydate $z<0$, M_0 may not be the money desired at $t=0$ under the new policy. Therefore $M^-(z+h)$ need not be zero and D_0 may be nonzero.

Inequality (2.2b) is the condition that consumers cannot create cash. Inequality (2.2c) requires that the consumer cannot make flow deposits into his bank account; this constraint is for notational simplicity only. The transaction cost of depositing a dollar at a date which is not a paydate is such that the bank account increases by only $1/k$ dollars. If $r(t)>0$, as we shall assume throughout, the consumer will want to make a deposit only in the interval $t \in [0, z+h]$, because at all future dates he can choose his money stock withdrawn so that a deposit is never necessary. Similarly, for the given stock M_0 at $t=0$, a consumer who desired to make a deposit during $t \in (0, z+h)$ will always find it optimal to make the deposit at $t=0$ instead, and this is captured by D_0.

Equation (2.2d) is the accounting identity that the consumer's stock of cash falls at the rate of his spending when $m(t)=0$, and otherwise is incremented by his bond withdrawals.

The maximization of (2.1) is accomplished by the controls $c(t)$, $m(t)$, and D_0, subject to (2.2), with W_0 and M_0 given. We assume that $u(\cdot)$ is concave, and it is easy to verify that this optimization problem involves a concave objective and a convex constraint set.[3] Further, it is easy to verify that

---

[3] This is the obvious benefit from using proportional rather than fixed transactions cost.

$$M(t) > 0 \text{ implies } m(t) = 0. \tag{2.3}$$

Fact (2.3) holds because, with $r(t) > 0$, if both $M(t) > 0$ and $m(t) > 0$ then the consumer can keep $c(t)$ unchanged, set $m(t) = 0$ until M reaches zero, and finance consumption out of m. This increases wealth because interest is earned over the period in which the withdrawal is delayed.

The consumer does not make withdrawals until his money is exhausted, so it is possible to simplify the problem by defining controls t_n that specify the time in the nth pay period when the consumer decides to exhaust his money holdings. Hence (2.1) and (2.2) are equivalent to maximizing

$$\sum_{n=0}^{\infty} \left[\int_{(z+nh)_+}^{t_n} u(c)e^{-\beta t}\, dt + \int_{t_n}^{z+(n+q)h} u(c)e^{-\beta t}\, dt \right] \tag{2.4}$$

subject to:

$$\sum_{n=0}^{\infty} \left[\int_{t_n}^{z+(n+1)h} k\,\frac{P(t)c(t)}{\gamma(t)}\, dt + \frac{1}{\gamma(z+(n+1)h)} \int_{z+(n+1)h}^{t_{n+1}} P(t)c(t)\, dt \right]$$

$$\leq W_0 + \frac{1}{\gamma(z+h)} \left[M_0 - D_0 - \int_0^{z+h} P(t)c(t)\, dt \right]^+ + \frac{D_0}{k}; \tag{2.5a}$$

$$\int_0^{t_0} P(t)c(t)\, dt \leq M_0 - D_0; \tag{2.5b}$$

where the maximization is with respect to the controls $\{t_n\}_{n=0}^{\infty}$ and the path of $c(t)$, with the obvious nonnegativity constraints $c(t) \geq 0$ and $t_{n+1} - t_n \geq 0$, $t_n \in [(z+nh)_+, z+(n+1)h]$.

The Appendix gives necessary and sufficient conditions for the maximization of (2.4). One important condition is that if $T(x)$ denotes the solution to

$$\frac{\gamma(T)}{\gamma(x)} = k, \tag{2.6}$$

then

$$t_n = \min[z+(n+1)h, T(z+nh)] \quad \text{for } n \geq 1. \tag{2.7}$$

This follows from the observation that if a consumer is exhausting his money holdings at $t_n < z+(n+1)h$ then, if he withdraws \$1 more at time $z+nh$, this costs $1/\gamma(z+nh)$; whereas the benefit is that he can save the conversion of bonds into money to finance his consumption, that is, save $k/\gamma(t_n)$ per dollar of consumption. Thus (ignoring the boundary possibility) if the interest rate is r, the money holding period $T-x$ implied by (2.6) is

$$T - x \approx \frac{\ln k}{r} \approx \frac{k-1}{r}. \tag{2.8}$$

So a transaction cost of 1% and an interest rate of 10% per year would imply an exhaustion interval of 1/10 of a year.

The optimal consumption path for $y \geq t_0$ must satisfy

$$e^{-\beta y} u'(c(y)) = k \frac{P(y)q}{\gamma(y)} \quad \text{for } t_n \leq y < z + (n+1)h, \ n = 0, 1, 2, 3, \ldots;$$
$$\tag{2.9}$$

$$e^{-\beta y} u'(c(y)) = \frac{P(y)q}{\gamma(z+nh)} \quad \text{for } z = nh \leq y < t_n, \ n = 1, 2, 3, \ldots; \tag{2.10}$$

where q is the Lagrange multiplier for (2.5a). The interpretation of (2.9) is that the cost of $c(y)$ when it is financed out of bonds is $kP(y)$, while the RHS of (2.10) involves the cost of $c(y)$ when it is financed out of the money withdrawn at the nth paydate [i.e., $P(y)/\gamma(z+nh)$].

The choice of t_0 (which is characterized in the Appendix) is much more complicated because M_0 is given. Our exposition is simplified by considering only the special case where $D_0 = 0$ and the consumer always chooses to exhaust his money before $z + h$. This will indeed be the case if the monetary policy is inflationary relative to what was expected. The numerical simulations for deflationary policies use the appropriate formulas from the Appendix.

It is useful to define $c(t, y)$ as the solution to

$$u(c)e^{-\beta t} = yP(t) \tag{2.11}$$

for c as a function of t and y. Under the assumption of exhaustion by $z + h$,

$$M_0 = \int_0^{t_0} P(t)c(t) \, dt. \tag{2.12}$$

Using (A.5) in the Appendix, there exists $\lambda \geq 0$, which is the Lagrange multiplier for (2.12) such that

$$M_0 = \int_0^{t_0} P(t)c(t, \lambda) \, dt, \tag{2.13}$$

$$\gamma(t_0)\lambda = qk. \tag{2.14}$$

Given the marginal utility of wealth q, (2.13) and (2.14) jointly determine t_0 and λ. The interpretation of (2.14) is straightforward: λ is the marginal utility of cash at time 0, so a reduction in the exhaust time t_0 generates cash worth λ at time 0 in utility, but costs $qk/\gamma(t_0)$ in the utility of wealth forgone from the transactions cost of maintaining consumption when money runs out.

The logarithmic utility assumption

For the remainder of the paper it will be assumed that utility is logarithmic (i.e., $u(c) = \log c$) so as to facilitate the general equilibrium calculations. Let $M(t, z)$ denote the money holdings at t of someone whose last paydate before time 0 was at z, henceforth called Mr. z. Similarly, let $S(t, z)$ represent consumer z's gross spending, given by $P(t)c(t)$ when he spends out of money and by $kP(t)c(t)$ when he spends out of bonds. Further, let $t_n(z)$ represent the t_n in (2.7) and let $t_0(z)$ represent the solution to (2.13) and (2.14) for Mr. z. Then, using (2.6), (2.7), (2.9), (2.10), and the fact that all money withdrawn at $z + nh$ is spent by t_n:

$$M(t, z) = \begin{cases} \dfrac{\gamma(t_n(z))}{kq} \dfrac{e^{-\beta t} - e^{-\beta t_n(z)}}{\beta} & \text{for } (z+nh)_+ \leq t \leq t_n(z), \\ 0 & \text{for } t_n(z) \leq t < z+(n+1)h; \end{cases} \qquad (2.15)$$

$$S(t, z) = \begin{cases} \dfrac{\gamma(t)e^{-\beta t}}{q} & \text{for } t_n(z) \leq t < z+(n+1)h, \\ \dfrac{\gamma(t_n(z))e^{-\beta t}}{kq} & \text{for } (z+nh)_+ \leq t < t_n(z).[4] \end{cases} \qquad (2.16)$$

Equation (2.13) can be used to show that

$$\lambda(z) = \frac{1 - e^{-\beta t_0(z)}}{\beta M_0(z)}, \qquad (2.17)$$

where $M_0(z) \equiv M(0, z)$ and $\lambda(z)$ is the multiplier for a person with paydate z. Substituting (2.17) into (2.14) yields

$$k = \frac{1 - e^{-\beta t_0(z)}}{q\beta M_0(z)} \gamma(t_0(z)). \qquad (2.18)$$

Substituting (2.15) and (2.16) into (2.5a), and maintaining the assumption that $D_0 = 0$ and $t_0 < z + h$, we obtain

$$q = \frac{e^{-\beta t_0(z)}}{\beta W_0}. \qquad (2.19)$$

---

[4] In (2.15) and (2.16), if $n \geq 1$ and if $T(z+nh) > z+(n+1)h$ then $\gamma(t_n(z))/k$ must be re-placd by $\gamma(z+nh)$.

Note that, given interest rates $\gamma(\cdot)$ and given W_0 and M_0 for Mr. z, (2.18) and (2.19) can be used to solve for $t_0(z)$; (2.7) gives $t_n(z)$ for $n \geq 1$; and (2.15) and (2.16) are then used to solve for $M(t,z)$ and $S(t,z)$.

3 General equilibrium and the steady state

In the previous section we took as given consumer z's paydates, his time-zero wealth $W_0(z)$, and his time-zero money stock $M_0(z)$. In order to describe the general equilibrium it is necessary to specify the cross-sectional distribution of these characteristics at time zero. By "general equilibrium" we mean a path of prices $P(t)$, money supply $M^s(t)$, and interest factors $\gamma(t)$ such that the goods, money, and bond markets clear. It is shown in Grossman (1985, Appendix B) that the only cross-sectional distribution of paydates consistent with a steady-state equilibrium is a uniform distribution. By a "steady state" we mean a time-independent cross-sectional distribution of real balances such that $r(t)$ and $\dot{P}(t)/P(t)$ are independent of time.

We will take the consumer's paydates as exogenously given and thus unchanged when the economy is surprised at time 0 by a new monetary policy. Clearly, if there is a fixed transactions cost of adjusting the paydates, then there will be a range of shocks for which this will be a reasonable approximation. However, this is not studied here.

We shall assume throughout that monetary policy is conducted by open-market operations and not by direct transfers to consumers. This is a crucial assumption; if newly issued money is hand-delivered to all consumers then the liquidity effects and monetary nonneutralities that we analyze will not appear. We shall assume that aggregate real wealth involves a claim to the exogenously given output of "stores" that produce a flow of real output $Y(t)$. This implies that when a monetary injection occurs via an open-market operation at time t, aggregate consumer nominal wealth is to rise by $\dot{M}^s(t)$ (because taxes will not have to be paid to finance interest on the debt, and an open-market operation directly reimburses holders of the debt for the capital value of the bond which they sell). Hence aggregate nominal wealth at time 0 is

$$W_0 = \int_0^\infty \left[\frac{P(t)Y(t) + \dot{M}^s(t)}{\gamma(t)} \right] dt. \tag{3.1}$$

We assume that each consumer z owns part of W_0 given by $W_0(z)$, which satisfies:

$$W_0 = \frac{1}{h} \int_{-h}^0 W_0(z)\, dz, \tag{3.2}$$

where the first paydates z are assumed to be uniformly distributed on $[-h, 0]$, where h is the exogenously given time between paydates.

I will analyze the perfect foresight market-clearing path of prices and interest rates which arise after a new money supply path $M^s(t)$ is announced at time zero, given the cross-sectional distribution of money and wealth $M_0(z)$ and $W_0(z)$.

In Grossman and Weiss (1983) we considered an economy where the only assets held by individuals were bonds, money, and claims to profit flows from the stores. Consumers also faced tax liabilities associated with the levies needed for interest payments on government bonds. Steady states were considered in which consumers had assets and tax liabilities such that they would all choose identical consumption profiles irrespective of their paydates; that is, a person's consumption depended only on how much time elapsed since his last paydate. Here we consider a generalization of this hypothesis. We shall assume that the cross-sectional distribution of initial wealth (i.e., assets net of liabilities) is such that all consumers have the same marginal utility of wealth, denoted by q in Section 2. This assumption is made to avoid having to analyze the effects of an open-market operation on the cross-sectional distribution of wealth, and any consequential effects on prices and interest rates.

Note that the consequences of a shock at time 0 on the cross-sectional distribution of wealth will be very sensitive to the types of assets people hold prior to time 0. Further, for the shocks of such magnitude that it is reasonable to keep the time between paydates a constant, the shock's effect on the cross-sectional distribution of wealth is likely to be very small. For these reasons we will assume that the postshock cross-sectional distribution of wealth always has the property that all consumers have the same marginal utility of wealth at time zero, equal to (say) q.

It may help the reader to understand the above assumption if the perfect foresight economy is imbedded in a rational expectations economy as follows. Let there be a complete set of state-contingent bond markets in the economy. That is, a consumer can buy a promise to have \$1 delivered to his bank account at any time under any contingency. He cannot contract for the delivery of state-contingent cash without paying the transactions cost described in Section 2. If all consumers are ex ante identical, then they will trade state-contingent securities to equalize their marginal utility of wealth ex post the policy announcement $M^s(t)$ and the assignment of consumers to paydates. We compute the ex post general equilibrium.

With the above remarks in mind, we can define a general equilibrium as a marginal utility of wealth q, path of prices $P(t)$, interest factors $\gamma(t)$, and money supply $M^s(t)$ such that

$$\frac{1}{h} \int_{-h}^{0} M(t,z) \, dz = M^{s}(t); \tag{3.3}$$

$$\frac{1}{h} \int_{-h}^{0} S(t,z) \, dz = P(t) Y(t); \tag{3.4}$$

where the initial cross-sectional distribution of money and the path of output are taken as given. Note that we do not specify the initial cross-sectional distribution of wealth $W_0(z)$. Given a marginal utility of wealth q, equalized across agents, and the cross-sectional distribution of money $M_0(z)$, the demand functions for money and spending $M(t,z;q), S(t,z;q)$ are well defined. A variant of Walras's Law can be used to show that if (3.3) and (3.4) are satisfied for these functions then the present value of spending [i.e., the LHS of (2.2a)], when integrated over all consumers, equals W_0. Thus, for every q, there exists a cross-sectional distribution of wealth $W_0(z)$ such that the posited prices clear markets for that wealth distribution.

Computation of the steady state

In the steady state with $r(t) \equiv r$, the holding period for money is given by (2.6) and (2.7) as

$$\bar{t} = \text{Min} \left[h, \frac{\text{Log}(k)}{r} \right]. \tag{3.5}$$

In order to compute the cross-sectional distribution of money we can use the equations derived in Section 2 for optimal consumption and money holdings. In particular, if $t > \bar{t}$ then the only people holding money are those who have had a paydate in $(t - \bar{t}, t)$. Therefore, by (3.3), aggregate money at t must satisfy

$$M^{s}(t) = \frac{1}{h} \int_{t-\bar{t}}^{t} M(t,x) \, dx, \tag{3.6}$$

when it is recalled that by time t, the people with paydates in $[t-h, t-\bar{t}]$ have already exhausted their money and are financing their consumption out of bonds. Similarly, using (2.16), aggregate spending at t must satisfy

$$P(t) Y(t) = \frac{k}{h} \int_{t-h}^{t-\bar{t}} \frac{e^{rt} e^{-\beta t}}{kq} \, dx + \frac{1}{h} \int_{t-\bar{t}}^{t} \frac{e^{rx} e^{-\beta t}}{q} \, dx, \tag{3.7}$$

where the first term on the RHS gives the total spending at t (inclusive of transactions services) by consumers who have exhausted their money balances, while the second term is the real spending of those consumers who have not exhausted their money at time t. Note that we are computing the symmetric steady state, and thus q is independent of a person's pay-date.[5]

In what follows we will assume $Y(t) \equiv Y$; then (3.7) can easily be shown to imply that

$$\beta + \pi = r, \tag{3.8}$$

because $P(t) \equiv P(0)e^{\pi t}$. This fact can then be used in (3.6) and (3.7) to show that $M^s(t)$ must be growing at rate π. Thus in a steady state we can write (3.6)–(3.7) as

$$\frac{M^s(0)}{P(0)} = \left[\frac{1-e^{-r\bar{t}}}{r} - \frac{e^{-\beta\bar{t}}-e^{-r\bar{t}}}{\pi} \right] \cdot \frac{1}{P(0)qh\beta}; \tag{3.9}$$

$$Y = \frac{h-\bar{t}}{hP(0)q} + \frac{1-e^{-r\bar{t}}}{hP(0)qr}. \tag{3.10}$$

Thus, in the steady state (with real output constant), a given money growth rate π, or equivalently an interest-rate policy r, determines π and r from (3.8) and an individual's exhaustion time $\bar{t}$ by (3.5). Equation (3.10) determines the marginal utility of real wealth $P(0)q$, and (3.9) determines the equilibrium level of real balances $M^s(0)/P(0)$. The cross-sectional distribution of real balances can be found from (2.15):

$$\frac{M(0,x)}{P(0)Yh} = \begin{cases} \left[\dfrac{1-e^{-\beta(x+\bar{t})}}{\beta} \right] e^{rx} \left[h-\bar{t}+\dfrac{1-e^{-r\bar{t}}}{r} \right]^{-1} & \text{for } x \in [-\bar{t}, 0], \\ 0 & \text{for } x \in [-h, -\bar{t}]. \end{cases} \tag{3.11}$$

If (3.9) is substituted into (3.10) to eliminate $P(0)q$, and if the interior portion of (3.5) is used to solve for $\bar{t}$ as a function of k (i.e., $r\bar{t} = \text{Log } k$), then a second-order Taylor expansion of (3.9) about $k = 1$ yields

$$\frac{M^s}{P} \cong \frac{(k-1)^2}{2} \left(\frac{3r+2\beta}{2r^2} \right) \frac{Y}{\beta h}. \tag{3.12}$$

Referring to (3.5), we see that if the transactions cost $k-1$ is .25% then $\bar{t}$ is one month when $r = \beta = 3\%$ per year. Under these parameters, if h is about 1.67 months then M^s/PY is about 3/4 of a month. That is, if each consumer chooses to hold one month's worth of his spending in money, and if there are 1.67 months between paydates, then the economy will have about 3/4 of a month's income in real balances. Note that M^s/PY

---

[5] It can be imagined that, before consumers know the paydate they will be assigned, they are ex ante identical and are capable of trading securities which are equivalent to state-contingent claims which pay (say) $1 into the bank account of the consumer, as a function of the paydate which he will be assigned ex post. The effect of this insurance will be to equalize all the consumers' marginal utility of wealth q.

will always be lower than $\bar{t}$ because consumers have spent all of their money by the end of $\bar{t}$ (their average cash holding is approximately $P\bar{Y}t/2$ dollars), and because a fraction of consumers hold no cash. Clearly, to obtain an aggregate money-holding period of 5–8 weeks of income, as is observed in the United States, each individual in our model must have a long exhaustion time. This result is an artifact of the fact that each dollar that a consumer spends at t goes immediately to the bond market and is immediately withdrawn by someone with a paydate at t. In the U.S. economy a consumer may pay a firm or another consumer, who after some delay may pay another firm or another consumer, and so forth. That is, it takes some time before a dollar spent by a consumer is used to purchase bonds (i.e., returns to the bank). Thus each "consumer" in our model should be interpreted as representing all the consumers and firms who hold a given dollar between the time it is withdrawn from a bank and the time it returns to the banking system.

Equation (3.12) can be used to compute the interest elasticity of money demand:

$$\eta \equiv \frac{\partial \operatorname{Log} M^s/P}{\partial \operatorname{Log} r} \cong -\left(\frac{3r+4\beta}{3r+2\beta}\right). \tag{3.13}$$

If $\beta = r$ the elasticity is $-7/5$, while at $r = 5\beta$ (e.g., $\beta = 3\%$ and $r = 15\%$) the elasticity is -1.1. These interest-rate elasticities are substantially higher than is predicted by the fixed-cost Baumol–Tobin model. However, it must be recalled that (3.9) is computed under the assumption that the proportional transactions cost k is sufficiently low relative to the interest rate, so that all consumers withdraw on their paydate an amount of cash that is insufficient to cover all their expenditures up to the next paydate. If instead k were sufficiently large relative to the interest rate, so that all consumers set $\bar{t} = h$ (i.e., they strictly prefer to withdraw cash only on paydates), then (3.9) will yield an interest-rate elasticity which is essentially zero.

It may well be a good approximation in the U.S. economy to assume that some agents (e.g., poor people) face a k sufficiently large so that they never make a withdrawal between paydates, while other agents (e.g., rich people) have a small k and hence make a withdrawal between paydates. Depending upon the proportions of each type, the interest-rate elasticity of money demand can be anywhere between zero and η in (3.13). It is easy to extend the general equilibrium analysis presented here to the case where there is a fixed proportion of each type of agent.

4　Liquidity effects and monetary policies

We will consider the effects of a new monetary policy $M^s(t)$ which is announced at time 0, taking as given that – previous to time 0 – consumers anticipated that the steady-state monetary policy described in Section 3 would be followed. We will compute the perfect foresight equilibrium after time 0, taking the cross-sectional distribution of cash ex ante the shock to be given by (3.11). We will ignore the ex ante cross-sectional distribution of wealth, and continue to maintain the assumption that the ex post cross-sectional distribution of wealth adjusts to keep the time-0 marginal utility of wealth equal across consumers.

It may help the reader if the perfect foresight economy is thought of as approximating a rational expectations economy with complete bond markets, as described in Section 3. Further, imagine that monetary policy can take on two values: the steady state value of Section 3, or the path $M^s(t)$ that we called the new monetary policy. Let the economy begin with the steady-state money path and let the arrival of the new policy be a Poisson event with probability of occurrence ρdt. Further, once the new policy occurs, it is the permanent state of the economy. Ex ante the shock, there will be a cross-sectional distribution of cash which will not be identical to the one described in Section 3, because consumers will have to take account of the possibility of a change in prices and interest rates associated with the new money supply $M^s(t)$. However, if ρ is close to zero then the steady state cross-sectional distribution of money derived in Section 3 will closely approximate the preshock cross-sectional distribution that arises when consumers take account of the possibility of the shock. In any case, the qualitative results to be derived will not rely on the exact form of the preshock cross-sectional distribution of cash.

One method of studying the dynamics associated with a new monetary policy is to posit a particular new money supply path $M^s(t)$ – for example, a $g\%$ increase in money growth – and then to find the $P(t), r(t)$ that clear all markets. However, a simpler approach will be taken here: The policies will be characterized by their effects on the path of market-clearing interest rates. The first type of policy will be a money supply path $M^s(t)$ that keeps the nominal interest rate unchanged, that is, at its original steady-state value. The second type of policy to be considered is one where the monetary authority picks a new interest rate path $r(t)$ and chooses $M^s(t)$ so that $r(t)$, and some $P(t)$, will clear markets. For reasons which will become clear below, we call the first type of policy a *price level* policy and the second type of policy an *interest rate* policy.

Price-level policies

Consider the standard LM model of money demand, where by holding real balances all consumers get utility that is separable from their utility of consumption [as in the Sidrauski (1967) model]. A new monetary policy will leave real output and the real interest rate unchanged. Such models imply:

$$\frac{M}{P} = L(r) = L(\beta + \dot{P}/P). \tag{4.1}$$

If the nominal rate is unchanged by the policy, then $\dot{P}/P$ and M/P must be unchanged. Hence the rate of growth in money must be unchanged. Thus, if a new monetary policy is announced at time 0, and the new policy does not change the nominal interest rate, then it can only involve a once-and-for-all jump in the level of money and the price level at time 0.

In contrast to the above scenario in the standard LM model, our model does not have equilibria involving a jump in the money supply in the presence of an unchanged, positive, nominal interest rate. This is because, in the model considered here, the money supply can only be incremented via an open-market operation, and not by the direct delivery of cash into the hands of consumers. Therefore, if the government wants to get the stock of cash up by (say) 5%, it must induce people to hold 5% more cash than they otherwise would. However, a consumer who holds a stock of cash at time 0 will not find it optimal to make a withdrawal at time 0 which increments his cash – he would do better to wait until his cash is exhausted. Further, consumers who hold no cash at time 0 do not find it optimal to withdraw a stock of cash when there is a proportional transactions cost. Hence the only type of person who will increment his cash to a higher level is a person who has a paydate at time 0. However, this consumer only holds an infinitesimal proportion of the economy's money stock.

In summary, we will show that the liquidity effect associated with staggered paydates implies that the only way the price level can be raised without changing (i.e., lowering) interest rates is by a gradual increase in the money supply. To see this it is useful to define

$$t_0^* \equiv \operatorname*{Max}_{z} t_0(z), \qquad \bar{t}_0 \equiv \operatorname{Max}(\bar{t}, t_0^*),$$

where $\bar{t}$ is the preshock, steady-state money-holding period and t_0^* gives the longest time it takes for any consumer to exhaust his cash held at time 0. Thus, for $t > \bar{t}_0$, any cash held in the economy will have been withdrawn after time 0. Note further that the exhaustion time chosen by a person at any paydate after time 0 (i.e., t_n for $n \geq 1$) will be $\bar{t}$ if interest rates are unchanged; see equation (2.6). Next, note that when $t > \bar{t}_0$, the fraction of people spending out of cash stocks is equal to its steady-state value of $\bar{t}/h$. Therefore we may use (3.6) and (3.7) for the money and goods market-clearing conditions when $t > \bar{t}_0$. It is clear from (3.7) that there is a unique path $P(t)q$ which satisfies (3.7) for each q. Hence, with r fixed, the only degree of freedom which the monetary authority has is to choose different values of q, and this changes $P(t)$ so as to keep $M^s(t)q$ and $P(t)q$ unchanged for $t > t_0$. That is, the feasible changes in money supply which keep r constant will be equivalent to changes in q.

For $t \geq \bar{t}_0$, the equilibrium caused by a price level policy in our model is identical to the equilibrium in the standard LM model. The distinction between the two models arises for $t \in (0, \bar{t}_0)$. During that time the level of real balances and $M^s(t)q$ will change under the new monetary policy even though r is unchanged. Furthermore, $M^s(t)$ will change at a rate designed just to prevent the interest rate from falling.

It is useful to define $z_0(t)$ as the inverse function of $t_0(z)$; that is, $z_0(t)$ is the paydate of the person who decides to exhaust his initial money at time t. Let $z_0(t) \equiv 0$ if $t > t_0^*$ and $L \equiv \text{Max}(0, t - \bar{t})$. We can use (2.16) to write (3.4) for $t < \bar{t}_0$ as

$$P(t)Y(t) = \frac{1}{h} \int_L^t \frac{e^{-\beta t}\gamma(x)}{q} \, dx = \frac{1}{h} \int_0^L \frac{e^{-\beta t}\gamma(t)}{q} \, dx$$

$$+ \frac{1}{h} \int_{z_0(t)}^0 \frac{e^{-\beta t}\gamma(t_0(x))}{qk} \, dx + \frac{1}{h} \int_{t-h}^{z_0(t)} \frac{e^{-\beta t}\gamma(t)}{q} \, dx, \qquad (4.2)$$

where the first term on the RHS of (4.2) is the spending (out of money) of those who have had a paydate in $[L, t]$, that is, those whose last paydate previous to 0 was in $[L-h, t-h]$; the second term is the spending (out of bonds) of people who have had a paydate in $(0, t)$ and have exhausted their cash by time t; the third term is the spending of those who have not yet exhausted their initial cash; and the fourth term is the spending of those who have exhausted their initial cash but have not yet had a paydate. We can use (2.6) and (2.15) to write (3.3) for $t < \bar{t}_0$ as

$$M^s(t) = \frac{1}{h} \int_L^t \frac{\gamma(x)}{q} \frac{e^{-\beta t} - e^{-\beta t_1(x)}}{\beta} \, dx$$

$$+ \frac{1}{h} \int_{z_0(t)}^0 \frac{\gamma(t_0(x))}{kq} \left[\frac{e^{-\beta t} - e^{-\beta t_0(x)}}{\beta} \right] dx, \qquad (4.3)$$

where the first term on the RHS is the money holdings of those who have had a paydate between 0 and t, and the second term is the money holdings at t of those who have not had a paydate in $[0, t]$.

It is now readily proved that as long as monetary policy involves keeping r unchanged, we may discuss the policy as if it were a choice of q rather than $M^s(t)$.

Theorem 4.1: *Let the economy be in a steady state, with an interest rate r at time 0, when a new monetary policy is announced. If the new monetary policy keeps the interest rate at r, then the policy generated by a particular $M^s(t)$ implies a unique $P(t)$ and q such that all markets clear. Conversely, for each choice of q there is a unique $M^s(t)$ and $P(t)$ such that all markets clear when the interest rate is r.*

Proof: We have already shown that, for $t > \bar{t}_0$, $P(t)$ and $M^s(t)$ must each grow at the (old) steady-state value of $r - \beta = \pi$, with the level of each having the property that $M^s(t)q$ and $P(t)q$ are unchanged when q changes. Therefore $M^s(\cdot)$ determines a unique q. We now study the market-clearing conditions at time $t < \bar{t}_0$, that is, before everyone has exhausted their preshock money holdings. Note from equation (2.18) that r and q determine the function $t_0(z)$; the path of prices does not enter (2.18). Similarly, from (2.6), $t_1(z)$ depends only on r. Hence (4.2) and (4.3) imply that $M^s(t)$ and $P(t)$ are uniquely determined by r and q.

Q.E.D.

We now prove that the money supply rule that implements a new price level without changing interest rates must involve a gradual change in $M^s(t)$.

Theorem 4.2: *If a monetary policy is chosen that keeps the nominal rate constant and also raises the long-run price level by $\alpha\%$, then the money supply will increase by less than $\alpha\%$ for $t < \bar{t}_0$ and then be $\alpha\%$ higher for $t \geq \bar{t}_0$; that is, if $M^{-s}(t)$ was the preshock anticipated path of the money supply, then an $\alpha\%$ price-level policy will make $M^s(t) < (1+\alpha)M^{-s}(t)$ for $t < \bar{t}_0$ and $M^s(t) = (1+\alpha)M^{-s}(t)$ for $t \geq \bar{t}_0$.*

Proof: If the monetary policy is designed to raise the price level by $\alpha\%$ and we denote the preshock q by q_0, then

$$1/q = (1+\alpha)/q_0. \qquad (4.4)$$

Recalling that $t_1(x)$ is unchanged when q changes, the first term on the RHS of (4.3) increases by $\alpha\%$ when q changes.[6] If we let $B(t)$ represent the preshock value of the first term on the RHS of (4.3), we can write (4.3) as

---

[6] Note from (2.18) that a rise in the price level (i.e., a fall in q) causes $t_0(x)$ to fall. Hence $t_0^* < \bar{t}$, and $L = 0$. If instead $\alpha < 0$, then the first integral on the RHS of (4.5) would be from L to t, rather 0 to t. The argument given can be modified in an obvious manner in this case.

$$M^s(t) = (1+\alpha)(B(t) + g(\alpha, t)),$$ (4.5)

where

$$g(\alpha, t) \equiv \frac{1}{h} \int_{z_0(t)}^0 \frac{\gamma(t_0(x))}{kq_0} \cdot \frac{e^{-\beta t} - e^{-\beta t_0(x)}}{\beta} \, dx.$$ (4.6)

Note that (2.18) can be used to show that, for each x, $t_0(x)$ is an increasing function of q and hence a decreasing function of α, by (4.4). Therefore, when α rises the integrand on the RHS of (4.6) falls. Further, since $z_0(t)$ is the inverse function of $t_0(x)$, $z_0(t)$ will rise when α rises. Hence $g(\alpha, t)$ is a decreasing function of α. Recall that $B(t) + g(0, t)$ gives the preshock anticipated money supply at t. Hence from (4.5) the postshock money supply will rise by less than $\alpha\%$ for $t \in [0, \bar{t})$. We have already shown that $M^s(t)$ rises by $\alpha\%$ for $t \geq \bar{t}_0$.   Q.E.D.

Theorem 4.2 is illustrated by Figure 1. It is assumed that $\beta = 3\%$ per year, and k is chosen so that there is a steady-state holding period of 30 days; that is, $\exp[(30/365)\beta] = k$.[7] The pay period h is chosen to be 50 days. In the steady state the economy holds approximately $30/2$ days' worth of spending in the form of money. The only role of h in these simulations is that a consumer's exhaustion interval must be less than h. If h is made smaller than $\text{Max}_z t_0(z)$ then it will affect the figure by making movement to the new steady state occur sooner. The first graph (on the top) of Figure 1 shows the money paths for which it is a general equilibrium for the interest rate to be unchanged (i.e., $r = \beta = 3\%$ per year), corresponding to various price level policies. It can be seen that when α rises, money gradually rises to its new level of $1 + \alpha$. When α falls it takes somewhat longer for money to reach the new steady state, because $t_0(z)$ rises and the persistence of the nonsteady-state behavior is determined by how long it takes those with money at time zero to exhaust that money. Another nonlinearity between positive and negative shocks is that the money stock actually jumps down at time 0 when $\alpha = -.5$, as people find it optimal to bear the transactions cost of making a deposit at a date which is not a paydate.

The effect of an $\alpha\%$ price-level policy on the price level in the short run is similar to the effect on the money supply. This is because those who have money at the time of the shock will not want to increase their spending by

---

[7] All the numerical simulations in this paper are solutions to a discrete time version of the model. In the discrete time version agents choose an integer number of periods over which to exhaust their cash. It is assumed that the new policy is announced at the end of period zero, so that consumers making a withdrawal at time zero can do so with perfect foresight about the path of prices and interest rates. The simulations reported in Figure 1 are based on a discretization of 1 period $= 1/365$ of a year.

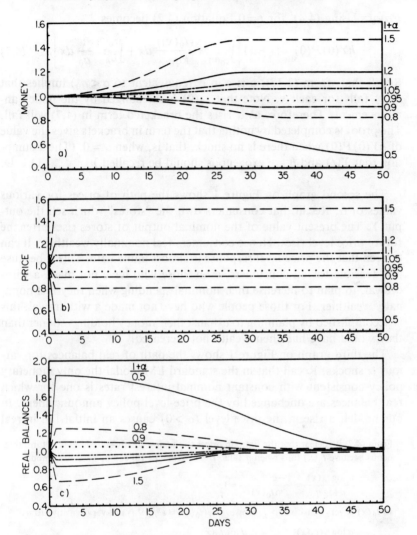

Figure 1. Price-level policies.

$\alpha\%$, since doing so would require too rapid exhaustion of cash and thus incur an excess of transactions costs. It can be shown that prices rise at first by less than $\alpha\%$.

Theorem 4.3: *If the money supply path at time 0 is chosen to keep interest rates unchanged and to lead to an $\alpha\%$ rise in the price level [i.e., (4.4) is satisfied], then $P(0^+)$ will rise by less than $\alpha\%$.*

22   **Sanford J. Grossman**

Proof: Using (4.4), for $t = 0$ Equation (4.2) becomes

$$hY(0)P(0) = (1+\alpha)\left[\int_{z_0(0)}^{0} \frac{\gamma(t_0(x))}{kq_0}\,dx + \int_{-h}^{z_0(0)} \frac{1}{q_0}\,dx\right]. \quad (4.7)$$

Recall that, from (2.18), a rise in α (equivalent to $q < q_0$) implies that $t_0(x)$ falls for each x. Note that $z_0(0)$ is unchanged by the policy announcement. Therefore, as α rises the bracketed term in (4.7) will fall. The proof is completed by noting that the term in brackets gives the value of $hY(0)P(0)$ when there is no shock, that is, when $\alpha = 0$. (The assumption that $Y(t)$ and h are exogenous should be recalled.)   Q.E.D.

The second graph on Figure 1 shows the path of prices for various values of α. Recall that consumers own the "stores" which sell the output Y. The present value of the nominal output of stores rises after the future price level rises. Hence consumers feel nominally wealthier. It can be seen that the price-level response is almost immediate. This is because it is feasible for all consumers, even those who have not made a withdrawal, to plan to increase their nominal spending when they feel nominally wealthier. For those people who have not made a withdrawal, this is accomplished by planning to exhaust their money holdings sooner than they would have had their wealth not increased.[8]

The third graph on Figure 1 shows the path of real balances for various α shocks. Recall that in the standard LM model the only monetary policy consistent with constant nominal interest rates is one for which real balances are unchanged by the price-level policy announcement. In our model, a rise in the price level ($\alpha > 0$) causes an initial fall in real

[8] From (4.7) it is clear that the jump in prices to the new steady-state level is not instantaneous because $t_0(x)$ falls when q falls. If $\beta = r$ then (2.18) can be used to compute

$$\frac{d\log t_0(x)}{d\log q} = \frac{1 - e^{-\beta t_0(x)}}{\beta t_0(x)} \approx 1,$$

so $t_0(x)$ is very sensitive to q. However $\gamma(t_0(x)) = e^{\beta t_0(x)}$ is not very sensitive to q:

$$\frac{d\log \gamma(t_0(x))}{d\log q} = \beta t_0(x)\frac{d\log t_0(x)}{d\log q} \approx \beta t_0(x),$$

which in the simulations is at most $(.03)(30/365)$. Thus spending will move very quickly to its new steady-state value. It is interesting to note why the money supply does not also move very quickly to its new steady-state value. From (4.6), the percentage change in the money held at time 0 by someone with a paydate of x is less than $1+\alpha$ by a factor of

$$\frac{d\log e^{\beta t_0(x)}}{d\log q}[1 - e^{-\beta t_0(x)}] \approx [1 + \beta t_0(x)]\frac{d\log t_0(x)}{d\log q} \approx \beta t_0(x) + 1.$$

Intuitively, the fact that spending will move proportionally with q implies that money holdings will change much less than proportionally because $t_0(x)$ falls a lot when q rises.

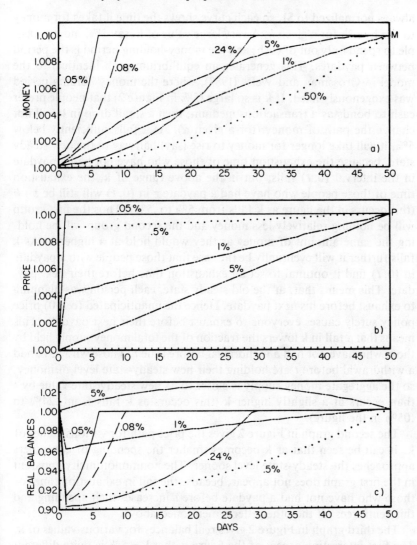

Figure 2. Effect of changing transactions cost on 1% price-level policy.

balances and then a gradual rise in real balances that returns it to the old steady-state level. This is a reflection of the fact that spending (and thus prices) responds faster to the increase in nominal wealth than does the aggregate stock of money.

Figure 2 plots the path of money prices and real balances for $\alpha = 1\%$ for various values of $\mathbf{k} = k - 1$. As k varies the preshock money supply is always normalized to $1, so each curve shows the time it takes for money to rise by $\alpha\%$ for a given k. A very large value of **k**, say 5%, induces people to spend only out of cash, and the money-holding period is the period between paydates. This generates an equilibrium path identical to the model in Grossman and Weiss (1983), where the money holding period was exogenously fixed. If **k** is so large (5% in Figure 2) that people prefer cash to bonds as a transactions medium, then a small drop in **k** will not change the path of money (for a given α). As **k** falls sufficiently below 5%, it will take longer for money to rise (say) halfway to the new steady state, because the exhaustion time of those who have not had a paydate in the interval $(0, t)$ falls; but in the above range of **k**, the exhaustion time of those people who have had a paydate z in $(0, t)$ will still be $z + h$ (this occurs in the figure as **k** falls from 5% to .5%). Thus the first group will be holding relatively less money and the second group will be holding the same amount of money as they would hold at a higher **k**. As **k** falls further it will eventually be the case that those people with a paydate in $(0, t)$ find it optimal to set an exhaustion time before their next paydate. This means that, at the old steady state, each person was planning to exhaust before his next paydate. Hence the unanticipated $(\alpha > 0)$ price policy surely causes everyone to exhaust before their next paydate. This means that a fall in **k** lowers the fraction of the total money supply held by those who have not had a withdrawal before time t. Those who have had a withdrawal before t are holding their new steady-state level of money, so the aggregate money supply is closer to its new steady state value by t than occurs at a slightly higher **k** (this occurs as **k** falls from .24% to .05% in the figure).

The second graph in Figure 2 gives the price path for various values of **k**. It can be seen that as **k** becomes smaller the spending of consumers approaches the steady-state level sooner. The nonmonotonicity apparent in the first graph does not appear, because the fall in exhaustion times of those who have not had a paydate before t increases their spending and this reinforces all the other effects mentioned above.

The third graph in Figure 2 gives real balances for various values of **k**. The first interesting aspect of the figure is that $\mathbf{k} = 5\%$ is quite different from all the other paths. When $\mathbf{k} = 5\%$, the shock at time zero does not cause any consumer to change his holding period. Real balances rise at first because the consumers who have a paydate at t hold more than their pro rata share of cash. As t rises, the fraction of consumers with a paydate since time zero rises sufficiently high that most of the money in the economy is held by those who have made a withdrawal and thus incremented their cash balances. For smaller values of **k**, a nonmonotonicity appears for the same reason as in the first graph.

5   Interest rate policies

In the standard LM model, if an interest rate $r(t) = r > \beta$ is chosen, then, in a general equilibrium, the money supply must be growing for $t > 0$. In that model consumers (correctly) expect inflation so they immediately increment their cash holdings. In contrast with the standard LM model, the model considered here can, for example, have $r - \beta > 0$ and yet the money supply will be falling. This is because consumers do not find it optimal, in the face of a rise in the inflation rate, to immediately increment their cash balances. Instead there is a liquidity effect, where a contractionary monetary policy is needed in the short run to implement a higher interest rate. A rise in interest rates will be associated with those consumers having a stock of money at the time of the announcement holding less money than before (rather than more) because of a desire to exhaust their money sooner when interest rates rise.

As is well known, any discussion of interest-rate policies must specify an additional nominal magnitude before a well-defined money-supply rule exists [see, e.g., Sargent and Wallace (1975)]. In the model developed here it is also necessary to specify a nominal magnitude, and we implement this through q. The simplest interest rate policy to analyze is one where the change in the interest rate is permanent. Note that, after at most h units of time, every consumer has exhausted his initial money stock. Further, any money held by a consumer at $t > h$ is derived from a withdrawal made after the new interest rate has been announced. Thus for $t > h$ and $r(t) \equiv r$, the money market clearing condition is

$$M^s(t) = \frac{1}{h} \int_{t-\bar{t}}^{t} M(t, z) \, dz, \tag{5.1}$$

where $\bar{t}$ satisfies [using (3.5)]

$$r\bar{t} = \log k \tag{5.2}$$

under the assumption (which we shall maintain) that $\bar{t} < h$. If $r(t) \equiv r \equiv \beta + \pi$, then (2.15) can be used to write (5.1) as

$$M^s(t) = e^{\pi t} \int_0^{\bar{t}} e^{-r\bar{t}} \left[\frac{e^{ry} - e^{\pi y}}{\beta q h} \right] dy \quad \text{for } t > h. \tag{5.3}$$

Thus, changes in q change the long-run level of the money supply in a proportional manner.

The short-run dynamics of the money supply are more complicated. This is because, by (2.18), the initial exhaust time of consumers who have money at the time of the shock depends on q as well as r. Equation (4.3) can be used to compute the rate of change in money at time 0:

$$\dot{M}^s(0^+) = \left[\frac{1-e^{-\beta t_1(0)}}{q\beta h} - \int_{z_0(0)}^0 \frac{\gamma(t_0(z))}{qkh} \, dz\right], \tag{5.4}$$

where the first term on the RHS is the money withdrawn by the person with a paydate at time 0. The second term is the spending out of money. Thus (5.4) states that the flow of money into the economy must equal the difference between the flow increases in money holdings generated by consumers with paydates, and the flow decrement in money holding by consumers spending out of money.

We will next show that if q is unchanged by the monetary policy, and if any interest rate policy is chosen for which $r(t) > \beta$ for $t \in [0, h]$, then $\dot{M}(0^+) < 0$; that is, a higher interest rate is associated with a contracting money supply. Recall that a fall in q is associated with a higher price-level policy. If the interest-rate policy is combined with a sufficiently strong price-level policy, then arbitrarily large inflation can be generated between $t = 0$ and $t = h$. In such an extreme case the liquidity effect associated with a higher interest rate is overwhelmed. If q falls only by enough to keep money withdrawn at $t = 0$ unchanged when r rises above β, then we will show that the expansionary price-level policy does not overwhelm the liquidity effect associated with a rise in $r(t)$.

Theorem 5.1: *Assume that the preshock steady state involves no inflation. Let a new interest rate policy $r(t)$ and price level policy q be chosen such that $r(t) > \beta$ for $t \in [0, h]$.*

(i) If $q < q_0$ and q satisfies

$$\frac{1-e^{-\beta t_1(0)}}{q} \leq \frac{1-e^{-\beta \bar{t}}}{q_0}, \tag{5.5}$$

where q_0 and $\bar{t}$ are (respectively) the preshock values of q and the exhaust time corresponding to $r = \beta$, then the money supply will initially contract.

(ii) If $q \geq q_0$, then the money supply will initially contract.

Proof: Recall that in the preshock steady state the money supply is constant. Thus we need only show that $\dot{M}(0^+) < 0$.

Case (i) $q < q_0$: Under condition (5.5) the first term on the RHS of (5.4) clearly is lower than its preshock value. It remains to show that the second term on the RHS of (5.4) rises. Rewrite (2.18) as

$$k\beta M_0(z) = (1-e^{-\beta t_0(z)})\frac{\gamma(t_0(z))}{q}. \tag{5.6}$$

When q falls, $\gamma(t)/q$ rises for each t. Hence $t_0(z)$ falls for each z when q falls. But $1-e^{-\beta t_0}$ is a monotone increasing function of t_0, so $\gamma(t_0(z))/q$

rises when $\gamma(\cdot)/q$ rises. Therefore the second term on the RHS of (5.4) rises.

Case (ii) $q \geq q_0$: Let $t_0(z; q)$ denote the solution to (5.6) for t_0, where q appears explicitly as a determinant of t_0. First fix q and raise $\gamma(t)$ for each t; clearly, from (5.6) this causes $t_0(z; q)$ to fall. But $1 - e^{-\beta t_0}$ is a monotone increasing function, so $\gamma(t_0(z; q))$ must rise when $\gamma(\cdot)$ rises. Next rewrite (5.4) as

$$\dot{M}(0) = \frac{1}{qh}\left[\frac{1 - e^{-\beta t_1(0)}}{\beta} + \int_{z_0(0)}^{0} \frac{\gamma(t_0(z; q))}{k}\, dz\right].$$

From (2.7), $t_1(0)$ clearly falls when γ rises; thus $\dot{M}(0)$ becomes negative as $\gamma(\cdot)$ rises for a given q. Next fix $\gamma(\cdot)$ and raise q. From (5.6), $t_0(z; q)$ is an increasing function of q. Hence $\dot{M}(0)$ becomes negative when q rises for a given $\gamma(\cdot)$. [It should be recalled that $z_0(0)$ is the paydate of someone who has just exhausted his money at time zero; and this is clearly unaffected by a change in q or $r(\cdot)$ at time zero.]   Q.E.D.

Before presenting numerical simulations of money-supply paths that implement monetary policies, it is of interest to mention one other method of choosing q. In the standard LM model, it is possible to implement a new interest-rate policy at time 0 and keep the money supply at time zero unchanged from its preannouncement value. (Of course, such a monetary policy would lead to a jump in the price level at time 0.) Further, in the LM model every interest rate $r(t)$ is given by $r(t) = \beta + \dot{P}/P$, and any $\dot{P}/P$ may be implemented by the M which satisfies (4.1).

Equation (4.1) can be solved for M at an arbitrary time T, as

$$M(T) = M(0)\gamma(T)e^{-\beta T} \cdot L(r(T))/L(r(0^+)).$$

Hence, if an interest rate policy is announced where $r(T) = r(0^+)$ then the level of money at time T should increase by a factor of $\gamma(T)e^{-\beta T}$, relative to $M(0)$.

Thus, when the change in $r(\cdot)$ is permanent so that $r(T) = r(0^+) \equiv r(t) \equiv r$, we can calibrate the price-level effect of the shock to be the same in our model as in the LM model, where $M(0)$ is unchanged. In the case where the change in r is permanent, (5.3) may be used to choose q such that at $T = h$ (by which time the short-run effect of the shock is over) $M(T) = e^{\pi T}M(0^-)$.

Figure 3a shows the effect of a permanent increase in the interest rate by 10%, – that is, from $r = \beta = .03$ to $r = .04$. Curves are drawn for 3 values of q. The first is for q_{LM} which corresponds to the long-run money-supply increase generated in the LM model when $M(0)$ is not allowed to jump; the second, denoted by q_u, corresponds to a decrease in q which just keeps unchanged the money withdrawn by those at the bank at the

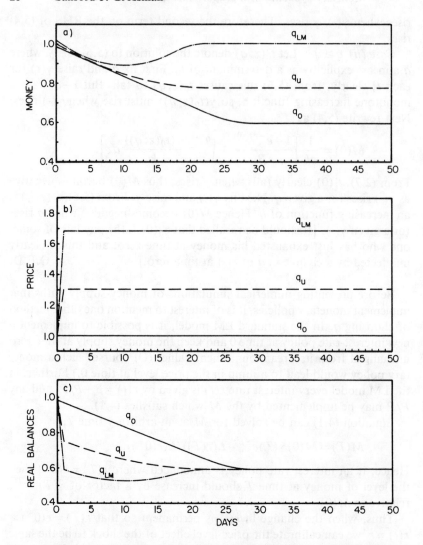

Figure 3. Consequences of a permanent increase in the interest rate for various values of q.

time of the announcement; the third sets $q = q_0$ (i.e., q is unchanged). Figures 3b and 3c show corresponding curves for the price level and real balances respectively.[9] Figure 3a shows the liquidity effect for $q = q_{LM}$

[9] Unless stated otherwise, all the plots in Section 5 are for the discretized version of the model with 1 period ≡ 1/365 years. The proportional transaction cost is chosen to generate a steady-state holding period of 30 days at an interest rate of 3%. The pay period is set equal to 50 days.

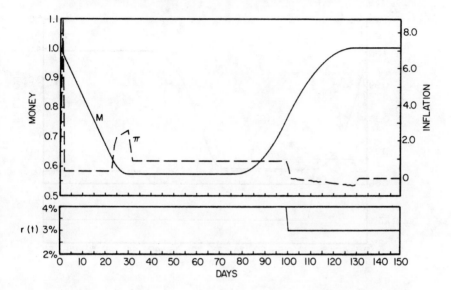

Figure 4. Consequences of a temporary but long-lived rise in the interest rate.

most clearly. There is a fall in money for 10 days to accommodate the desire of those people who have not been to the bank to reduce their money holdings. As the fraction of money held by those who have not been to the bank falls, the curve rises to its new steady-state rate of growth (which looks flat only because of the scale of the figure).

Figure 3 shows the price paths associated with various values of q. It simply reflects the fact that $q_0 > q_u > q_{LM}$. The value of the price level at time t is plotted relative to the preshock steady-state level. Note that $q = q_0$ leads to essentially no change in the price level when the new interest-rate policy is announced. Figure 3c combines the previous two figures to generate a path of real balances. In the standard LM model real balances immediately fall to their new steady-state level, while here there is a delayed response.

Discussion of Figures 4, 5, and 6

Figure 4 shows the effect of a temporary increase in the interest rate (from 3% to 4%) which lasts for 100 days. The lower section of the figure shows the path of interest rates, while the upper section shows the path of money (denoted by M) and inflation (denoted by π). For this figure and all that follow, q is set equal to q_0. The inflation rate is given by the broken line,

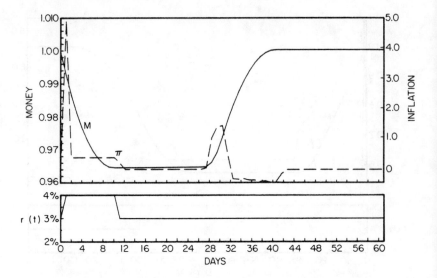

Figure 5. Consequences of short-term rise in the interest rate.

and the units (in percent per year) are given on the right-hand vertical axis in the figure. There is an initial jump in the price level indicated by a very high inflation rate at time 0. Then, for about 20 days, an inflation rate of about .5% is associated with the fact that those who have not yet had a pay date do not increase their spending rate because doing so would cause them to bear an excessive transactions cost. The period between 20 and 30 days is a transitional one in which all those people who had money stocks at date zero have just about exhausted. Indeed, at around $t = 30$, the inflation rate jumps as the spending out of money in the economy becomes generated solely from those consumers who have had a paydate after $t = 0$. Between $t = 30$ and $t = 70$ all money is held by people who know that interest rates will be 4% until their next paydate, so the economy has reached a temporary steady state associated with $r = 4\%$. The inflation rate is 1%. Note that at around $t = 80$, the money supply starts growing to accommodate the fact that those who make a money withdrawal anticipate a fall in interest rates during their pay period. In comparing Figure 3b with Figure 4, it should be noted that (for each q) prices are indeed varying over time in Figure 3b; however, the scale of the graph is such that these variations cannot be seen.

Figure 5 is similar to Figure 4 except that the interest-rate policy lasts only 10 days. This sharp rise and fall of interest rates occurs within the length of a single paydate, and more importantly, within the length of a single money-holding period. As a consequence, the inflation rate never

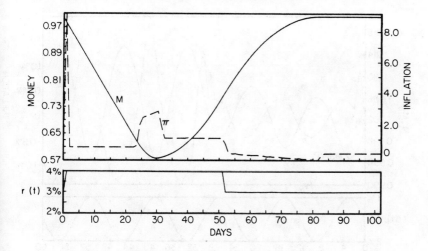

Figure 6. Consequences of an intermediate-term rise in the interest rate.

attains the 1% level even though the nominal interest rate is above the rate of time preference by 1%. Figure 6 is also similar, but the interest-rate policy lasts for 50 days, which is long enough so that at around $t = 30$ everyone in the economy faces the 4% interest rate for almost a whole money-holding period, and so that the inflation rate does rise to 1% for a short period. The figures show that the real rate of interest on bonds rises in the short run when there is a monetary policy designed to raise the nominal rate of interest. It also is clear that the nominal interest rate is not highly correlated with the expected rate of inflation when these rates are measured over periods of length equal to the average holding period of money in the economy.

Discussion of Figures 7, 8, 9, and 10

The next set of numerical simulations concerns permanent monetary policies. Here we are interested in the economy's response to oscillatory interest rate policies. In these figures ω denotes the frequency of oscillation in interest rates relative to the preshock steady state. In the preshock steady state the money-holding period is 30 days, and thus $\omega = 2$ denotes an interest rate sine curve that has a period of 15 days.[10] As we move from

[10] More precisely, the figures are drawn using the function $r(t) = .03 + .01 \sin(2T\pi t/30)$ to give the annual interest rate at day t. Further, because of numerical noise, the plots of the inflation rate were generated by using a discretization of four periods per day and then using the average price per day to compute the inflation rate.

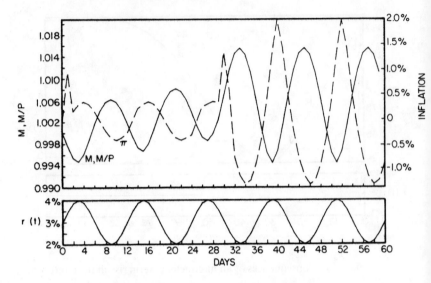

Figure 7. Response to high-frequency rate policy: $\omega = 2.5$.

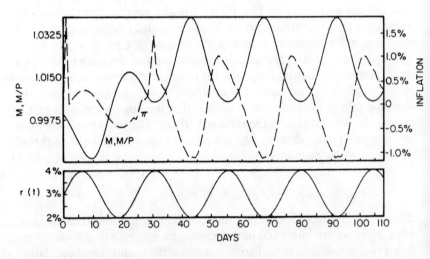

Figure 8. Response to interest-rate policy: $\omega = 1.2$.

Figure 7 to Figure 10, the period for one interest-rate cycle rises from 12 days ($\omega = 2.5$) to 120 days ($\omega = .25$). Though the money-supply path is qualitatively the same in all the figures, there are important quantitative differences. The first thing to note is that the money scale is different on each of the figures. As ω falls, the size of the money-supply movement

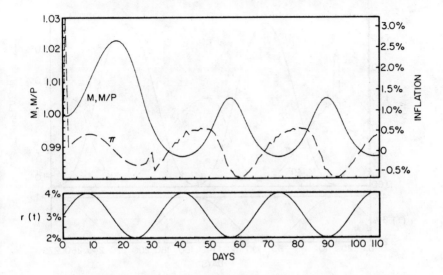

Figure 9. Response to interest-rate policy: $\omega = 0.9$.

consistent with the interest-rate path rises. When $\omega = 2.5$ (Figure 7) the money-supply oscillations are on the order of 1%. However, by Figure 10 the money-supply oscillations are on the order of 50%. In all cases interest rates are oscillating by as much as 33%. When the interest rate oscillates very rapidly around the steady state of $r = 3$%, the optimal money exhaustion time changes very little relative to the case where $r = 3$%. This is because the accumulated interest over a given period of time determines the money-holding period, and if interest rates vary quite rapidly around 3% then the accumulated interest will be very close to the value it would have if interest rates were constant at 3%. These figures thus illustrate the fact that rapidly varying interest rates will have very little effect on money demand.

The next interesting aspect of the figures is that money and interest rates are negatively correlated. A rise in the nominal interest rate lowers the desired money-holding period, and also lowers money demand. Note that in the figures M and M/P are plotted together. This is because prices are measured relative to the preshock steady state, and are thus sufficiently close to 1 that (given the scale of the figures) M is sufficiently close to M/P to be indistinguishable.

Another interesting aspect of the figures is that, although interest rates and inflation are roughly in phase, it is false that $\pi(t) = r(t) - \beta$ even after the economy reaches the new steady state. This is because the spending of consumers is varying with time due to the fact that the money-exhaustion

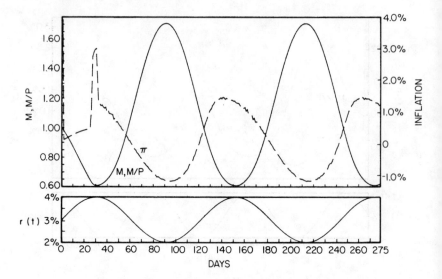

Figure 10. Response to interest-rate policy: low-frequency $\omega = 0.25$.

period is time-varying. This effect is in addition to the effect that consumers desire a rate of growth in nominal spending of $r(t) - \beta$ for a given money-holding period. Furthermore, at any point in time different consumers have spending determined by interest rates over different periods, so there is a time-averaging of the interest rate which determines nominal spending growth for a given money-holding period.

Further note should be made of the initial effect of the new interest-rate policy. The interest-rate policy is designed so that interest rates initially rise. In all the figures this leads to a jump in the price level and a fall in the money supply. Thus a rise in interest rates is associated with a contractionary monetary policy.

It is interesting to note that, if $\omega = 1$, then each consumer who makes a withdrawal will choose the same money-holding period under the oscillatory policy as he would have chosen under $r = 3\%$ in the old steady state. If we had included such a figure it would have shown the money supply equal to 1 (the old steady state) for $t > \bar{t}_0$ and a small liquidity effect for earlier values of t. Some of this is apparent in Figures 8 and 9, where the average level of the money supply changes after $\bar{t}_0$. In each case the fact that ω is not equal to 1 changes the long-run average holding period. For example, in Figure 9 the long-run average money supply falls below the preshock steady state because the average person is choosing a lower exhaustion time at $\omega = .9$ than at $\omega = 1$.

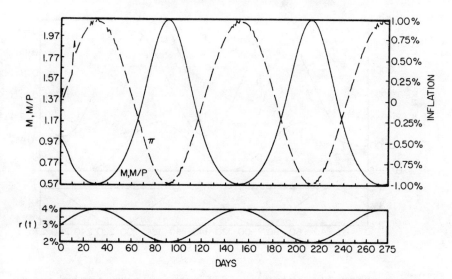

Figure 11. Response to $\omega = 0.25$ interest-rate policy: very low transactions cost.

Discussion of Figures 11 and 12

Figure 11 shows the path of money and inflation when the transactions cost is sufficiently low that people exhaust their money in one day ($k = 1 + 8 \cdot 10^{-4}$) and $\omega = .25$. It can be seen that the short-run effects described earlier are absent, and more importantly that $\pi(t) = r(t) - \beta$. Figure 12 incorporates a transactions cost so high that people never find it optimal to exhaust their cash between pay periods ($k = $ infinity). This corresponds to the Grossman–Weiss (1983) model. As we noted in Section 3, there is virtually zero interest elasticity of the demand for money in this case, so movements in money are extremely small relative to Figure 11, as is clear from the scale of the money axis. Note that the price level does not jump, so that M/P diverges from M. In addition the inflation rate is damped relative to $r(t) - \beta$ because at t the spending rate of a consumer who had a paydate at z is $\gamma(z) e^{-\beta t}/q$ by (2.16). Hence aggregate spending at t is determined by an average of interest rates over a period from $t - \bar{t}$ to t. In particular, it can be shown that

$$\pi(t) = -\beta + \frac{\gamma(t) - \gamma(t - \bar{t})}{\int_{t - \bar{t}}^{t} \gamma(z)\, dz}.$$

Thus the inflation rate at t depends on interest rates from $t - \bar{t}$ to t.

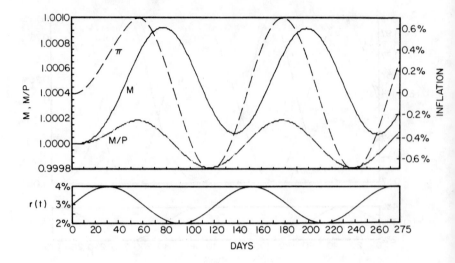

Figure 12. Response to $\omega = 0.25$ interest-rate policy: very high transactions cost.

6   Conclusions

The two classes of monetary policies analyzed here are price-level policies and interest-rate policies. We have shown that the money supply must rise gradually to its new steady-state level if the price level is to be raised without causing nominal interest rates to fall. The money supply cannot jump immediately by $g\%$ if it desired to raise the price level by $g\%$ without changing interest rates. Further, the real rate of interest must fall in the transition period.

When interest-rate policies are analyzed, it becomes clear that aggregate money demand at time t depends on the path of interest rates, not just on the instantaneous interest rate at time t. This is because the aggregate money holding at time t is composed of the money holdings of various consumers, each of whom has a different but overlapping holding period. The staggering of money-holding periods is a necessary condition for general equilibrium; general equilibrium requires that some consumers must be incrementing their cash when other consumers are decrementing their cash via spending.[11] (If all consumers decrement their cash at the same time then where does the money go?)

---

[11] Thus our model should be distinguished from models that use one-period Clower cash-in-advance constraints such as Grandmont and Younes (1972). In such models *all* consumers decrement their cash during a period, and markets only clear at the end of each period.

Some results of our analysis highlight this point. First, high-frequency movements of the interest rate cause a much smaller change in money demand than low-frequency movements, because it is the *integral* of the interest rate over a holding period that determines money demand. Second, at high frequencies the rate of inflation is not the difference between the nominal interest rate and the rate of time preference. This is because different consumers face different relevant paths of interest rates when the interest rate oscillates within the length of a pay period. Our theoretical results are consistent with the empirical relation presented in Cochraine (1985): There is a negative correlation between interest-rate movements and money-supply movements at frequencies of about four weeks. He also finds that higher-frequency movements produce an effect too small to measure, and very low-frequency movements produce a positive correlation between money-supply changes and interest rates; all of which is consistent with the results of Section 5. A model that distinguishes between low-frequency and high-frequency interest-rate movements is also necessary to explain the money-supply announcement effects [documented in, e.g., Cornell (1983)], though clearly a stochastic version of our model must be developed for this purpose.

In contrast to my previous work on monetary dynamics with overlapping pay periods and exogenous money-holding periods (where the interest-rate elasticity of money demand is almost zero), the aggregate demand for money here is very interest-rate elastic.[12] In those earlier models the low interest-rate elasticity implied that a very small open-market operation, say of about 5% per year, is sufficient to drive the nominal interest rate to zero. The monetary velocity and aggregate interest-rate elasticity observed in the United States is probably generated by a combination of the two models. That is, in our model the consumers with high interest-rate elasticity are firms in our economy for whom the fixed transactions cost of converting between bonds and cash may be negligible, but for whom the proportional transactions cost is important. For households in the U.S. economy the fixed and proportional transactions costs are much higher, and it is probably a satisfactory approximation to take their money-holding period as fixed over a large range of interest rates. Hence aggregate money demand probably responds to shocks as if it is composed of a convex combination of consumers with a small proportional transactions cost, and another group of consumers with a transactions cost sufficiently high for their money-holding period to be fixed.

The model clearly needs to be extended to deal with a fixed transactions cost as well as a proportional cost. The nonconvexities associated

---

[12] See Lucas and Stokey (1983) for a cash-in-advance constraint model where the demand for money depends on the nominal rate of interest, but in which the money-holding period is exogenous.

with a fixed cost make this difficult, except for very simple interest-rate policies. Another problem with the model is that it is not explicitly stochastic, so that it is impossible to understand the effects of high-frequency innovations to the money supply. The proportional transactions cost model may be far simpler to develop in a stochastic framework than the fixed-cost model.

Appendix

Characteristics of optimal money exhaustion times

Assume $u'(0) = \infty$, $u' > 0$, $u'' < 0$, $r(t) > 0$, and $P(t)$ has at most a finite number of discontinuities in any finite interval of time. If $P(t) > 0$ and $k > 1$, then there exist multipliers $q > 0$ for the wealth constraint (2.5a) and $\lambda \geq 0$ for (2.5b) such that the optimal $c(t) \geq 0$, $D_0 \geq 0$, and t_n satisfy:

$$e^{-\beta y} u'(c(y)) = \frac{kP(y)q}{\gamma(y)} \quad \text{for } t_n \leq y < z + (n+1)h, \ n = 0, 1, 2, 3, \ldots;$$

(A.1)

$$e^{-\beta y} u'(c(y)) = \frac{P(y)q}{\gamma(z + nh)} \quad \text{for } z + nh \leq y < t_n, \ n = 1, 2, 3, \ldots;$$ (A.2)

$$\text{if } t_n < z + (n+1)h \text{ then } \frac{\gamma(t_n)}{\gamma(z + nh)} = k, \quad \text{for } n = 1, 2, 3, \ldots;$$ (A.3)

$$\text{if } M_0 - D_0 > \int_0^{z+h} P(t)c(t)\, dt \text{ then}$$ (A.4)

$$u'(c(y))e^{-\beta y} = q \frac{P(y)}{\gamma(z+h)} \quad \text{for } y \in [0, z+h],$$ (A.4a)

$$\frac{1}{k} \leq \frac{1}{\gamma(z+h)} \quad \text{and} \quad D_0\left[\frac{1}{\gamma(z+h)} - \frac{1}{k}\right] = 0;$$ (A.4b)

$$\text{if } M_0 - D_0 \leq \int_0^{z+h} P(t)c(t)\, dt \text{ then}$$ (A.5)

$$\gamma(t_0)\lambda \leq qk \quad \text{and} \quad [qk - \gamma(t_0)\lambda][z + h - t_0] = 0 \quad \text{if } t_0 > 0,$$

$$\lambda \geq qk \qquad \qquad \text{if } t_0 = 0,$$ (A.5a)

$$u'(c(y))e^{-\beta y} = \lambda P(y) \quad \text{for } y \in [0, t_0),$$ (A.5b)

$$\lambda \geq q/k \quad \text{and} \quad D_0[\lambda - q/k] = 0,$$ (A.5c)

if there is equality in (A.5) then $\lambda \geq q/\gamma(z+h)$. (A.5d)

The derivation of these inequalities is standard. Note that (A.3) is derived by observing that a small increase in t_n yields net benefit

$$q\left[\frac{kP(t_n^+)c(t_n^+)}{\gamma(t_n)} - \frac{P(t_n^+)c(t_n^+)}{\gamma(z+nh)}\right],$$

and a small decrease in t_n yields the same expression except that t_n^+ is replaced by t_n^-. Hence (A.3) holds even if $P(t)$ jumps at $t = t_n$. Note that (A.5d) holds because, when (A.5) is an equality (i.e., $t_0 = z + h$), it is always possible to reduce consumption a little at $t < z + h$, and hold the money for spending at $t_0 = (z + h)_+$. The net benefit of such a decrement in spending before $t = z + h$ is $q/\gamma(z+h) - \lambda$, and this leads to (A.5d).

The analysis of the initial exhaust time t_0 is complicated by the fact that the consumer may choose to make a deposit at time 0, or to not exhaust his initial money holdings. The following theorem characterizes the optimal choice of his initial exhaustion policy. Let $F(x, y) \equiv \int_0^x P(t)c(t, y)\, dt$, where $c(t, y)$ is as defined in (2.11).

Theorem A1: *Let $q > 0$ be given and $M_0 > 0$, then:*
Case (a) *if $\gamma(z+h) > k$, then (A.5) holds; additionally,*
Case (a1) *if $F(z+h, qk/\gamma(z+h)) < M_0$ and $F(z+h, q/k) \geq M_0$ then $t_0 = z + h$, $D_0 = 0$, and λ is the solution to*

$$F(z+h, \lambda) = M_0; \tag{A.6}$$

Case (a2) *if $F(z+h, qk/\gamma(z+h)) < M_0$ and $F(z+h, q/k) < M_0$, and if $\gamma(z+h) \leq k^2$, then $t_0 = z + h$, $D_0 = M_0 - F(z+h, q/k)$, and $\lambda = qk$; if $\gamma(z+h) > k^2$ then t_0 is given by the solution to*

$$\gamma(t_0) = k^2, \tag{A.7}$$

$$\lambda = qk/\gamma(t_0), \text{ and} \tag{A.8}$$

$$D_0 = M_0 - F(t_0, qk/\gamma(t_0)); \tag{A.9}$$

Case (a3) *if $F(z+h, qk/\gamma(z+h)) \geq M_0$, then let t^* solve*

$$F(t^*, qk/\gamma(t^*)) = M_0 \tag{A.10}$$

and let

$$\bar{\lambda} = qk/\gamma(t^*); \tag{A.11}$$

if $\bar{\lambda} > q/k$ then $D_0 = 0$, $t_0 = t^*$, and $\lambda = \bar{\lambda}$; if $\bar{\lambda} \leq q/k$ then t_0, λ, and D_0 are given by (A.7)–.(A.9). Also:
Case (b) *If $\gamma(z+h) \leq k$ then it is impossible for $D_0 > 0$ and $t_0 \in (0, z+h)$.*
Case (b1) *In addition, if $F(z+h, qk/\gamma(z+h)) < M_0$ then consider the λ^* which solves (A.6). If $\lambda^* < q/\gamma(z+h)$ then $t_0 = z + h$, $c(t)$ is given by (A.4a), and $D_0[k - \gamma(z+h)] = 0$. If $\lambda^* \geq q/\gamma(z+h)$ then $c(t)$ is given by (A.5b), $t_0 = z + h$, and $D_0[k - \gamma(z+h)] = 0$.*

Case (b2) *In addition, if $F(z+h, qk/\gamma(z+h)) \geq M_0$ then* (A.5) *holds,* $t_0 = t^*$ *[where t^* is given by* (A.10) *and* $\lambda = \bar{\lambda}$ *as defined in* (A.11)*], and* $D_0 = 0$.

Proof: Note that $F(x, y)$ is increasing in x and decreasing in y.

Case (a) From (A.4b) we are sure that (A.5) must hold.

Case (a1) The inequalities involving $F(\cdot)$ imply that $k^2 > \gamma(z+h)$. If $t_0 \in [0, z+h)$ then $F(z+h, qk/\gamma(z+h)) < M_0$ implies that $D_0 > 0$. Thus [using (A.5a) and (A.5c)] $k^2 \leq \gamma(t_0)$, which is impossible because $\gamma(\cdot)$ is nondecreasing. Since $t_0 = z+h$, if $D_0 > 0$ then (A.5c) implies that $F(z+h, q/k) = M_0 - D_0$, contradicting $F(z+h, q/k) \geq M_0$.

Case (a2) Note that for $t_0 \in (0, z+h)$ and $D_0 > 0$, (A.5a) and (A.5c) imply that (A.7) and (A.8) must hold. Hence, if $\gamma(z+h) \leq k^2$, we have $t_0 = z+h$, $D_0 = M_0 - F(z+h, q/k)$, and $\lambda = q/k$ as the only solution to (A.5) [recall that $\lambda \leq qk/\gamma(z+h)$ since this inequality is equivalent to $\gamma(z+h) \leq k^2$ when $\lambda = q/k$]. If $\gamma(z+h) > k^2$ then there is a $t_0 \in (0, z+h)$ such that (A.7) holds.

Case (a3) Here there is exhaustion at a $t_0 \in (0, z+h)$. If (A.10) holds and $\bar{\lambda}$ in (A.11) satisfies $\bar{\lambda} > q/K$, then we must have $D_0 = 0$ by (A.5c). However, if $\bar{\lambda} < q/k$ then we must have $D_0 > 0$, so the solution must instead be given by (A.7)–(A.9). Note that $\bar{\lambda} \leq q/k$ implies $\gamma(t^*) \geq k^2$, so there will be a solution to (A.8).

Case (b) Here we must have $\gamma(z+h) < k^2$, so there is no solution to (A.5a) and (A.5c) with both as equalities. Thus $D_0 > 0$ implies $t_0 = z+h$ and that (A.5) must be an equality if it holds at all.

Case (b1) If $t_0 \in (0, z+h)$ then $D_0 = 0$, and consumption would be governed by λ such that $\lambda = qk/\gamma(t_0)$ and $F(t_0, qk/\gamma(t_0)) = M_0$. But

$$F(t_0, qk/\gamma(t_0)) < F(z+h, kq/\gamma(z+h)),$$

which contradicts $F(z+h, qk/\gamma(z+h)) < M_0$. Hence $t_0 = z+h$, since $t_0 = 0$ implies $D_0 = M_0 > 0$ and (A.5a) contradicts (A.5c). Note that $t_0 = z+h$ means that if (A.5) holds at all then it must hold as an equality. Furthermore, if (i) $\gamma(z+h) < k$ then (A.5) is impossible because $D_0 > 0$ implies $\gamma = q/k$, which contradicts (A.5d), and $D_0 = 0$, $t_0 = z+h$ implies that $\lambda = \lambda^*$ and $\lambda^* < q/\gamma(z+h)$ contradicts (A.5d); whereas if (ii) $\gamma(z+h) = k$, it is impossible for (A.5) to hold with $\lambda < q/k$ by (A.5d), while $\lambda > q/k$ would imply $D_0 = 0$ and thus $\lambda = \lambda^*$, which contradicts $\lambda^* < q/\gamma(z+h)$ and $k = \gamma(z+h)$. Thus the optimal solution involves $\lambda = q/k = q/\gamma(z+h)$ and $D_0 = M_0 - F(z+h, q/k)$. It is also optimal to be in case (A.4) and have $D_0 < M_0 - F(z+h, q/\gamma(z+h))$ when $k = \gamma(z+h)$; of course (A.4a) and (A.5b) coincide in that case. If $\lambda^* \geq q/\gamma(z+h)$ then $F(z+h, q/\gamma(z+h)) > M_0$, so case (A.4) is impossible. Hence (A.5) holds with $\lambda = \lambda^*$.

Case (b2) Note that

$$F(z+h, q/\gamma(z+h)) > M_0 \quad \text{because} \quad F(z+h, qk/\gamma(z+h)) \geq M_0;$$

hence we cannot be in case (A.4). Under the hypothesis of case (b2), $t^* \leq z+h$. Furthermore, we cannot have $D_0 > 0$ because (i) t_0 interior is ruled out in case (b), and (ii) $t_0 = z+h$ is ruled out by the fact that $\gamma(z+h) \leq k$ and $\gamma(z+h)\lambda \leq qk$ imply $F(z+h, \lambda) > M_0 - D_0$, which contradicts (A.5) holding as an equality. Hence $D_0 = 0$. Q.E.D.

REFERENCES

Cochrane, J. "The Return of the Liquidity Effect." Unpublished Ph.D. dissertation, Department of Economics, University of California–Berkeley.
Cornell, B. 1983. "The Money Supply Announcements Puzzle: Review and Interpretations." *American Economic Review* 73: 644–57.
Grandmont, J. M., and Y. Younes. 1982. "On the Role of Money and the Existence of a Monetary Equilibrium." *Review of Economic Studies* 39: 355–72.
Grossman, S. 1982. "A Transactions Based Model of the Monetary Transmission Mechanism Part 2." Working Paper No. 973, *National Bureau of Economic Research*.
1982. "Class Notes on the Transactions Demand for Money." Unpublished mimeo.
1985. "Monetary Dynamics with Proportional Transaction Costs and Fixed Payment Periods." Working Paper No. 1663, *National Bureau of Economic Research*.
Grossman, S., and L. Weiss. 1983. "A Transactions Based Model of the Monetary Transmission Mechanism." *American Economic Review* 73: 871–80.
Leach, J. 1983. "Monetary Adjustment in an Intergenerational Economy." Unpublished mimeo, Department of Economics, McMaster University.
Lucas, R., and N. Stokey. 1983. "Optimal Fiscal and Monetary Policy in an Economy Without Capital." *Journal of Monetary Economics* 12: 55–93.
Rotemberg, J. 1984. "A Monetary Equilibrium Model with Transactions Costs." *Journal of Political Economy* 92: 40–58.
Sargent, T., and N. Wallace. 1975. "Rational Expectations, the Optimal Monetary Instrument, and the Optimal Money Supply Rule." *Journal of Political Economy* 83: 241–54.
Sidrauski, M. 1967. "Inflation and Economic Growth." *Journal of Political Economy* 75: 798–810.

CHAPTER 2

A multiple means-of-payment model

Edward C. Prescott

In this chapter we study an economy in which there are two technologies for making payments. The first is currency; the second, bank drafts drawn on interest-bearing demand deposits. The interest-bearing asset does not dominate the noninterest-bearing currency because there is a fixed recordkeeping cost incurred whenever a bank draft is used as the means of payment. The steady-state equilibrium is characterized. It is found that the value of the good or (more precisely) package of goods purchased at a given location determines which means of payment is used. Bank drafts are used for large purchases and currency for small purchases.

In the environment studied, the highly centralized Arrow–Debreu competitive equilibrium is impractical, because the number of date-, event-, and location-contingent commodities is so large that the resources required for information collection and processing would be prohibitive. In this sense we follow Brunner and Meltzer (1971) and consider as the chief role of money economizing on costly information collection and processing.

The approach is close in spirit to that of Townsend (1980), who views the payment system as a communication system.[1] It differs in that no effort is made to find the best arrangement. The arrangement studied, however, is sufficiently explicit that one can calibrate the model and then examine the costs and benefits associated with modifying the scheme – say, by imposing reserve requirements or interest-rate ceilings. Upper bounds for the gains that can be realized from alternative systems can

Prepared for the Second Annual Austin Symposium in Economics, Austin, Texas, May 1985. This paper evolved from an earlier paper entitled "Money as a Means of Payment," delivered at the Foundation of Monetary Policy and Government Finance Symposium at Rice University, April 1982. I thank Jack Kareken and Gary D. Hansen for helpful comments and thank the National Science Foundation and the Minneapolis Federal Reserve Bank for financial support.
[1] Other related models are those of Lucas (1980) and Gale and Hellwig (1984).

be computed. A system that is simple and implementable and nearly optimal-independent of the exact specification of the environment: This is the most that economic theory can provide.

The scheme studied requires collective actions, which are virtually necessary for any payment system which uses fiat money. The question of what would develop absent any collective action besides enforcement of contracts is not addressed.[2] In this environment there are no gains from credit arrangement, as the interest-bearing debit account dominates. In fact, credit is often used, particularly when there are ongoing relations. An important extension of this research would be to introduce some feature into the environment that would give rise to the use of credit as well as the use of currency and bank drafts.

The model is close to the growth model, a structure that has proven useful in public finance and macroeconomics. This, I think, is desirable; the closer a specification is to those used in other economic applications, the greater the prior knowledge that can be used to restrict the model's parameters. A second desirable feature of the construct is that the record keeping costs associated with using a bank draft as the means of payment can and have been measured. The number obtained is not small – nearly a half dollar per draft – and would be larger if the value of the transactor's time associated with writing a check and verifying the payee's identity were taken into account. The number of transactions also can be measured and then used to restrict the theory. To summarize, the hope is that this line of research will lead to the development of a theory that can be used to quantitatively evaluate alternative payment systems and aid in the design of better payment arrangements.

The chapter is organized as follows. In Section 1 the environment is specified. The means-of-payment decisions of an agent, given the market interest rate and that agent's total expenditures, is solved in Section 2. In spite of the fixed cost per bank draft, standard convex analysis is applicable. This is possible because each purchase is a negligible fraction of an individual's total expenditures. Others have previously assumed a finite number of transactions, and the resulting nonconvexity held back the development of a transaction-based general equilibrium theory of money. In Section 3 the saving–consumption expenditure decision is considered. It is found that the resulting behavior is essentially the same as for the neoclassical growth model. The steady-state capital stock equates the marginal product of capital to the sum of the depreciation rate of capital and the subjective time discount rate. This steady-state capital

[2] See King (1983) for an insightful discussion of the economics of the private provision of money.

stock is invariant to the inflation rate for this model. The steady-state equilibrium is determined in Section 4, and Section 5 contains some illustrative uses of the construct.

1   The economy

There is a continuum of agents and products. Time is discrete, with half the agents allocating their time to production in odd periods and to shopping–consumption in even periods. The other half of the population produce goods in even periods and shop in odd periods. The shoppers purchase many different goods at different locations – indeed, a continuum of them. For an individual, the goods can be categorized into a finite number of equivalence classes, which are indexed by θ belonging to a finite set of positive reals $\Theta = \{\theta_1, \ldots, \theta_n\}$. The classes of goods are ordered so that $\theta_i < \theta_{i+1}$. Element π_θ is the fraction of goods of type θ. Within an equivalence class of goods, all goods enter the individual's utility function symmetrically. Letting e name the goods within an equivalence class, the utility function used has the form

$$\sum_{t,\theta} \beta^t \int_0^{\pi_\theta} u[\theta x_{\theta t}(e)] \, de, \tag{1.1}$$

where $x_{\theta t}(e)$ is the quantity of good e in class θ that is consumed in period t, and $0 < \beta < 1$ is the subjective time discount factor. The function u is continuously differentiable, strictly increasing and strictly concave, and is defined on the nonnegative reals. Furthermore, $u(0) = 0$.

Rather than keeping track of the quantities of every good consumed by every person, I will (and need only) monitor the distribution of quantities of goods consumed in the various goods' equivalence classes. The quantity of a good consumed is indexed by x belonging to some finite set of positive real numbers. Indirect utility functions will be defined over arrays $z_{\theta x t}$ for $\theta \in \Theta$, $x \in X$, and $t \in \{0, 1, 2, \ldots\}$. Element $z_{\theta x t}$ is the number (or more precisely the measure) of goods of type θ consumed in quantity x in period t. The utility function defined on z has the form

$$U(z) = \sum_{t,\theta,x} \beta^t u(\theta x) z_{\theta x t}.$$

The sets Θ and X are assumed (for expository – not technical – reasons) to have a finite number of elements. In the following arguments, the only property needed is that the cross product of Θ and X be a compact separable metric space. Since Θ and X are subsets of the real line, their cross product is compact if the sets are closed and bounded. Sets of measures that are defined on the Borel sigma algebra of a separable compact metric space and that are closed and bounded are compact with respect to the weak* topology.[3] At points in the analysis we will proceed as if X were a continuum and differentiate with respect to x. Implicitly we are assuming the points in X are so closely spaced that the derivative and the finite difference are the same for all practical purposes.

Producers are located at spatially distinct points or islands and shoppers visit a random sample of islands. At each location there is precisely one type (not class) of goods sold by a number of producer-sellers and as a result prices are determined competitively. The sample of purchasing opportunities is large. Consequently, a shopper receives a representative sample of purchase opportunities. Letting λ denote the number (measure) of purchase opportunities, $\pi_\theta \lambda$ is the number of opportunities for the purchase of different goods in class θ. A given good is of type θ for fraction π_θ of the population. Thus some goods are more highly valued by a given individual (i.e., have higher θ), but the fraction of the population which values a given good at a given level is the same for all goods. This introduces symmetry in both the goods and agent space, which simplifies the subsequent analysis. Because of this symmetry, in equilibrium all goods will have the same price and the same distribution of purchase quantities.

There is the additional restriction that a given good, if purchased, is purchased only once, using either currency or a draft. This constraint greatly simplifies the formulation and is nonbinding. Using currency, there is no gain from making five one-dollar purchases of a given good rather than one five-dollar purchase. If drafts are used, it is wasteful to make multiple purchases of the same good because the fixed cost would be unnecessarily incurred more than once.

2   Means of payment and quantity purchased

The decisions first considered are the means of payment and the quantity purchased. By symmetry, the price of all goods must be the same in equilibrium. Units are selected so that this price is one unit of currency. Let M denote currency holdings and B bank deposits at the beginning of a shopping period. Letting $m = (m_{\theta x})$ be the measure of cash purchases and $d = (d_{\theta x})$ the measure of debit purchases, wealth at the end of the period is

$$W' = (1+r)B + M - \sum_{\theta, x} x m_{\theta x} - \sum_{\theta, x} x d_{\theta x} - \gamma \sum_{\theta, x} d_{\theta x}. \qquad (2.1)$$

---

[3] For the development of general equilibrium theory with signed measures used as the commodity point, see Mas-Colell (1975) and Jones (1984). They exploit them for the case of a continuum of differentiated products.

The first summation is the value of all cash purchases, the second is the value of all credit transactions, and the third is sum of the fixed costs of credit transaction (γ is the cost per transaction and $\sum d_{\theta x}$ is the number of transactions).

Let

$$M = \sum_{\theta,x} xm_{\theta x}, \tag{2.2}$$

$$D = \sum_{\theta,x} xd_{\theta x}, \tag{2.3}$$

$$S = \gamma \sum_{\theta,x} d_{\theta x}. \tag{2.4}$$

As $W = M + B$ it follows that

$$W' = (1+r)W - Y,$$

where

$$Y = (1+r)M + D + S. \tag{2.5}$$

Variable Y is total expenditures on goods and bank services plus forgone interest earnings on currency holdings.

The program facing the individual with these definitions is

$$U(Y,r) = \max_{m,d \geq 0} \sum_{\theta,x} u(\theta x)(m_{\theta x} + d_{\theta x}), \tag{2.6}$$

subject to

$$\sum (m_{\theta x} + d_{\theta x}) \leq \lambda \pi_\theta \quad \text{for all } \theta \tag{2.7}$$

(purchases of a given class of good are constrained by the number of goods in that class found while searching), and subject also to

$$(1+r) \sum_{\theta,x} xm_{\theta x} + \sum_{\theta,x} xd_{\theta x} + \gamma \sum_{\theta,x} d_{\theta x} \leq Y. \tag{2.8}$$

This is a linear program. The constraint set is closed and bounded and is nonempty. Consequently an optimum exists.

The first-order conditions are

$$u(\theta x) \leq \mu_\theta + (1+r)x\phi \quad \text{with equality if } m_{\theta x} > 0 \tag{2.9}$$

and

$$u(\theta x) \leq \mu_\theta + (\gamma + x)\phi \quad \text{with equality if } d_{\theta x} > 0, \tag{2.10}$$

where μ_θ are the Lagrange multipliers associated with constraints (2.7) and ϕ is the multiplier associated with constraint (2.8).

If purchases are made using currency, the quantity purchased satisfies

$$\theta u'(\theta x) = (1+r)\phi, \tag{2.11}$$

whereas, if a draft is the means of payment, the quantity purchased satisfies

$$\theta u'(\theta x) = \phi. \tag{2.12}$$

Let $x_m(\theta, \phi)$ and $x_d(\theta, \phi)$ be the solutions to (2.11) and (2.12), respectively. Currency will be used if

$$u[\theta x_m(\theta, \phi)] - (1+r)\phi x_m(\theta, \phi) > u[\theta x_d(\theta, \phi)] - \theta x_d(\theta, \phi) - \gamma\phi; \tag{2.13}$$

drafts will be used if the inequality is in the opposite direction. With equality, it is optimal to use either means of payment for purchase of goods of that marginal type. The fraction of purchases of that type good using the two alternative means of payment is, however, determined, so there is a unique solution to the program. For θ less than some critical value $\theta(Y, r)$, currency is the means of payment. For θ greater than $\theta(Y, r)$ bank drafts are used.

The larger is Y, the smaller is the marginal utility ϕ of additional expenditures. The smaller is ϕ, the larger are the purchase quantities $x_m(\theta, \phi)$ and $x_d(\theta, \phi)$. And as θ increases, drafts are used for the purchases of more goods; that is, $\theta(Y, r)$ is decreasing in Y. Consequently the value of purchases using drafts increases as Y increases. Because

$$M = (Y - D - S)/(1+r), \tag{2.14}$$

a one-unit increase in Y results in a change in M that is bounded from above by $(1+r)^{-1}$. Thus the optimal currency holding $M(Y, r)$ has slope less than 1 with respect to Y.

It is readily verifiable that increases in r decrease the use of currency and therefore increase the use of bank drafts.

3   The dynamic problem

The production function of an individual is

$$f(k), \tag{3.1}$$

where f is increasing, strictly concave, and continuously differentiable, with $f'(0) = \infty$ and $f'(\bar{k}) = 0$. Because all goods enter symmetrically, all goods have the same equilibrium price, which we normalize to be 1. Then, if k units of capital are rented and W is wealth at the beginning of the production period, end-of-period wealth is

$$W' = (1+r)W + f(k) - rk \tag{3.2}$$

as sales, $f(k)$, are realized and capital rental payments, rk, made at the end of the period.

Letting $v_1(W)$ and $v_2(W)$ be the dynamic programming value functions for (respectively) beginning-of-production and purchase periods, one optimality condition is

$$v_1(W) = \max_k \{\beta v_2[(1+r)W + f(k) - rk]\}. \tag{3.3}$$

Given that v_2 is increasing, the first-order condition is

$$f'(k) = r, \tag{3.4}$$

which is the usual steady-state condition for the optimal growth model.

Another result is that if v_2 is concave then v_1 is concave, given that f is concave.

Using the indirect utility function derived in Section 2, the optimality condition requires that

$$v_2(W) = \max_Y \{U(Y, r) + \beta v_1[(1+r)W - Y]\}. \tag{3.5}$$

As U is concave in Y, v_2 is concave if v_1 is concave. By standard discounted dynamic programming results, functional equations (3.3) and (3.5) have unique solutions which are concave and continuous. These solutions are the optimal value functions for this discounted dynamic program.

4   Steady-state equilibrium

In order to determine the steady-state equilibrium, the interest rate r must be determined. An individual shopper at date t can transform Y_t into Y_{t+2} via borrowing or lending at rate $(1+r)^2$. The marginal rate of substitution between Y_t and Y_{t+2} relative to the indirect utility function U is $1/\beta^2$. Consequently, the steady-state interest rate is

$$r = \beta^{-1} - 1. \tag{4.1}$$

Given r, steady-state k is determined by condition (3.4).

A unique steady-state wealth for an individual is determined not by the interest rate r, but rather by equilibrium in the goods market. In particular, equilibrium in the goods and service markets requires that

$$f(k) = M(Y, r) + D(Y, r) + S(Y, r). \tag{4.2}$$

Because purchases of goods and services are increasing in Y, equation (4.2) can be solved for Y given r and k.

Letting W_1 and W_2 denote (respectively) beginning-of-production and shopping-period wealth,

$$k = W_1 + (W_2 - M). \tag{4.3}$$

Further, from (3.2),

$$W_2 = (1+r)W_1 + f(k) - rk. \tag{4.4}$$

Given M, k, r, these equations, linear in W_1 and W_2, determine W_1 and W_2.

The one remaining variable to be determined is the price level. The steady-state price level P satisfies

$$\frac{M(Y,r)}{2} = \frac{M^s}{P}, \tag{4.5}$$

where M^s is the per capita money supply and $M(Y,r)/2$ is the average real cash balance of agents. Thus, the quantity theory holds for this economy.

5   Illustrated uses of the construct

The purpose of this discussion is to indicate the type of questions that can be addressed within models of this type. Before such a model is confronted with data it will be necessary to incorporate many additional features. For example, one reason for using drafts as a means of payment is that they provide a record of payment necessary for tax purposes. Similarly, currency may be used so that there is no record of the payment – in order to facilitate illegitimate economic activities or to avoid taxation – or not be used as much as it might otherwise be, in order to reduce the risk of loss by theft or fire. Still another possibly important feature is that income allocated to bank services is not taxable when it is financed by lower interest payments on deposits. A final caveat before discussing applications is that the model is a steady-state model. Such models are not designed for studying fluctuations in interest rates and various monetary aggregates. It is suited only for the study of smoothed data series for a given economy or for cross-country, time-averaged data. Given these caveats, the illustrative uses are as follows.

Suppose there are two economies alike in every way except that, for one, the marginal product of capital is uniformly higher. Steady-state capital and output are greater for the more productive economy. Checks will be used for more purchases and these purchases will be larger in the rich country. One implication is that more banking services are used in the rich country. Predictions with respect to the use of currency are ambiguous, as they depend upon the distribution of goods by types. In the high-income country, goods using currency as the means of payment are purchased in greater quantities, leading to a greater use of currency. This effect is offset by the use of checks for a greater fraction of the purchases.

A second application is the question of the optimal growth rate of money. Suppose injections of money are in the form of lump-sum transfers of money to agents at the time they are selling their goods. Withdrawals of money are accomplished by lump-sum taxes, also at the times when households–firms sell their products. Assuming the money supply grows (declines) at a constant rate ϕ, prices will grow at rate ϕ and the nominal interest rate paid on demand deposits will be $i = \phi + r$. The larger is ϕ, the greater is the use of checks and the smaller is the steady-state consumption (output less banking services). For $\phi = -r$, the nominal interest rate i is zero. This minimizes the amount of resources allocated to banking services and maximizes steady-state consumption. In this sense the model supports the view of Freidman and Samuelson: because currency is costless to produce, it is optimal to deflate at the real interest rate. This, of course, assumes lump-sum taxes and no private information, features which are needed for taxation to have no deadweight loss. Optimal taxation implies a zero tax on liquidity only if other taxes are distortion-free. However, having a zero nominal interest rate does eliminate incentives to economize upon currency holdings for this economy.

The economy considered has zero reserve requirements, but they are easily introduced. Suppose then there is a reserve requirement, that interest is not paid on reserves, and that currency is supplied perfectly elastically. This is closer to the U.S. payment system than is the model. The quantity theory would still hold, but for currency plus reserves rather than (as in the model considered) for currency alone. If ρ is the reserve requirement, the interest on demand deposits would be $(1 - \rho)r$ rather than r. Deposits would be just large enough to insure zero deposits after payments were made. The banks would finance only part of capital investment and would charge interest rate r. In summary, the steady-state behavior of this economy is very much like the static, textbook models of money and banking.

One final use is to consider what happens as the cost of record keeping approaches zero. In the limit, currency is not used and there is no numeraire; consequently, the price level is indeterminate. In such an environment, a reserve requirement along with a fixed supply of reserves is an arrangement for which the price level is determined.

REFERENCES

Brunner K., and A. Meltzer. 1971. "The Use of Money: Money in the Theory of an Exchange Economy." *American Economic Review* 61: 784–805.
Gale, D., and M. Hellwig. 1984. "A General-Equilibrium Model of the Transaction Demand for Money." CARESS Working Paper #85-07, University of Pennsylvania.
Jones, L. E. 1984. "A Competitive Model of Commodity Differentiation." *Econometrica* 52: 507–30.
King, R. G., 1983. "On the Economics of Private Monies." *Journal of Monetary Economics* 12: 127–58.
Lucus, R. E., Jr. 1980. "A Pure Currency Economy." In N. Wallace (ed.), *Models of Monetary Economics,* pp. 131–46. Minneapolis, MN: Federal Reserve Bank.

Mas-Collel, A. 1975. "A Model of Equilibrium with Differentiated Commodities." *Journal of Mathematical Economics* 2: 693–5.
Townsend, R. 1980. "Models of Money with Spatially Separated Agents." In N. Wallace (ed.), *Models of Monetary Economics,* pp. 265–304. Minneapolis, MN: Federal Reserve Bank.

CHAPTER 3

Credit policy and the price level in a cash-in-advance economy

Michael Woodford

This chapter considers the determination of interest rates and prices in a simple intertemporal general equilibrium framework. The resulting theory is used to examine the short- and long-run consequences of a policy of credit expansion through inside money creation.

The intertemporal equilibrium framework used here combines the demographic structure of an overlapping-generations model with a cash-in-advance constraint. The cash-in-advance constraint allows valued fiat money to co-exist in equilibrium with debt, yielding a positive nominal interest rate. The specific structure considered here allows a traditional account of the "liquidity effect" of open market operations upon the nominal interest rate in the short run to be rigorously connected with a long-run equilibrium analysis. The absence of such a theoretical connection has led to a certain amount of confusion in the literature about whether or not the liquidity effect of credit expansion, generally agreed to exist in the short run, can be maintained in the long run.[1] It is shown that for the model economy considered here, open market operations can keep both the nominal and the real rate of interest low forever; and, whereas a lower interest rate is achieved in the short run only at the cost of a rise in the price level, in the long run different interest rates may be equally compatible with price-level stability.

I would like to thank Guillermo Calvo, Roger Farmer, Meir Kohn, Bennett McCallum, Edmund Phelps, Neil Wallace, and two anonymous referees, for helpful comments on earlier drafts.
[1] For example, Friedman (1968) argues that monetary policy cannot keep interest rates low forever. Cagan (1972) argues that it is theoretically possible for continuing expansion of bank loans to keep interest rates low forever, but that the conditions under which this could occur are extremely restrictive and empirically disconfirmed, and that even in the ideal case a permanent "credit effect" would require perpetual inflation.

1 An overlapping-generations model with a market for loanable funds

The model considered here[2] is a stationary overlapping-generations economy. There exists one consumption good each period, which is produced directly using the labor power with which agents are endowed. The good is assumed not to be storable. All agents live for three periods. Agents supply labor power in the first period of life only, but consume in each of the three periods of life. All agents have preferences described by the utility function

$$u(c_1, c_2, c_3, n) = a \log c_1 + b \log c_2 + d \log c_3 - n, \qquad (1.1)$$

where c_j is the quantity of the good consumed in the jth period of life ($j = 1, 2, 3$) and n is the amount of labor power supplied during the first period of life. Units are chosen so that one unit of labor power produces one unit of the consumption good, in the same period as the labor power is supplied. The number of agents in each generation is assumed to be the same.

It is assumed that all consumption goods must be purchased with money, and that wages are paid in money rather than directly in consumption goods; agents cannot produce for their own immediate consumption, but must sell their labor power in one market and buy consumption goods in another. Furthermore, it is assumed that any consumption during period t must be paid for using money held at the beginning of period t, so that wages earned during period t can be spent only in period $t + 1$. The liquidity services provided by money are thus modeled by assuming a *cash-in-advance constraint*. However, the money spent in a given period need not have been accumulated in the previous period by exactly the same agents in the same amounts. Each period is divided into two subperiods. In the first subperiod, competitive trading in one-period money loans occurs. In the second subperiod, consumption goods are purchased using funds on hand at the end of the first subperiod. Wages are paid during the second subperiod, and so can be lent or spent only in the following period.

Let c_{jt} denote the consumption during period t by each agent in the jth period of life ($j = 1, 2, 3$), n_t the labor supply of each young agent in period t, and p_t the money price of the consumption good. Let R_t denote one plus the nominal interest rate on money loans between the first

---

[2] Extensions of this simple model are treated in Woodford (1985). Kohn and Karacaoglu (1985) present an open-economy version of the model.

subperiod of period t and the first subperiod of period $t+1$. Then an agent born in period t chooses $(n_t, c_{1t}, c_{2t+1}, c_{3t+2})$ to maximize (1.1), subject to the lifetime budget constraint[3]

$$R_t p_t c_{1t} + p_{t+1} c_{2t+1} + R_{t+1}^{-1} p_{t+2} c_{3t+2} \leq p_t n_t.$$

Agents therefore choose $n_t = a+b+d$, and $c_{1t} = a/R_t$, regardless of the prices or interest rates expected in subsequent periods. They hold money balances

$$M_{2t+1} = (b+d)p_t \tag{1.2}$$

in the first subperiod of period $t+1$, after repayment of period-t loans but before new loans are made. They supply period-$t+1$ loans in the amount of $(d/(b+d))M_{2t+1}$, and purchase $c_{2t+1} = (b/(b+d))M_{2t+1}/p_{t+1}$. They hold money balances

$$M_{3t+2} = (d/(b+d))M_{2t+1}R_{t+1} \tag{1.3}$$

in the first subperiod of period $t+2$, after repayment of period $t+1$ loans, and use them to purchase $c_{3t+2} = M_{3t+2}/p_{t+2}$.

Hence in period t, given money balances (M_{2t}, M_{3t}), the condition for market cleaning of goods is

$$ap_t/R_t + (b/(b+d))M_{2t} + M_{3t} = (a+b+d)p_t. \tag{1.4}$$

Loan market clearing requires $(d/(b+d)) \cdot M_{2t} \geq ap_t/R_t$, $R_t \geq 1$, with at least one relation holding with equality. (When the nominal interest rate is zero, the supply of loanable funds may exceed the demand for transaction purposes, as there is no cost to holding idle balances.) These conditions may equivalently be rewritten

$$M \geq (a+b+d)p_t, \tag{1.5a}$$

$$R_t \geq 1, \tag{1.5b}$$

where M is the constant total money stock. Equations (1.4)–(1.5) determine a unique temporary competitive equilibrium[4] (p_t, R_t) for a given

---

[3] Agents are subject to a single linear budget constraint, despite the fact that bonds earn a higher rate of return than fiat money. Hence the reason for optimal financing of a government deficit to involve some government borrowing (see Section 4) is not the same in this model as in Bryant and Wallace (1984). Their argument depends upon agents whose optimal consumption plan lies at a kink in their budget set.

[4] The fact that expectations of future prices and interest rates nowhere enter these equilibrium conditions is a very special feature of the example presented here. If labor is supplied in periods later than the first, or if more general preferences are considered, then expectations do matter and multiple perfect foresight equilibria may exist, as shown in Woodford (1985).

distribution of the total money stock between middle-aged and old agents. The equilibrium conditions are seen to have the form of a flexible-price IS-LM model, with (1.4) playing the role of the IS equation and (1.5) the role of the LM equation. (Note that while the LM equation has the standard quantity-theoretic form, the IS equation depends upon the *distribution* of money balances between agents with different propensities to consume. This is crucial for price level determinacy when the nominal interest rate is pegged, as discussed in Section 2.)

Given a temporary equilibrium for period t, the initial money balances for the following period, (M_{2t+1}, M_{3t+1}), are given by (1.2)–(1.3). Then the temporary equilibrium for period $t+1$ is determined, and so on. Since $M_{2t} + M_{3t} = M$ in all periods, it suffices to trace the dynamics of M_{2t}. One finds

$$M_{2t+1} = \begin{cases} \dfrac{b+d}{a+b+d}M & \text{if } M_{2t} \leq \dfrac{a(b+d)}{(a+b+d)d}M, \\[2ex] M - \dfrac{d}{b+d}M_{2t} & \text{if } M_{2t} \geq \dfrac{a(b+d)}{(a+b+d)d}M. \end{cases}$$

The long-term behavior of M_{2t} is then easily determined.

When $a \geq d$, regardless of the initial distribution of money balances, one finds that $M_{2t+j} = M_2^*$ for all $j \geq 2$, where

$$M_2^* = M(b+d)/(a+b+d).$$

The economy converges to a steady state in which there are no idle balances, the constant price level is $p^* = M/(a+b+d)$, and the constant nominal interest rate is $R = a/d$. When $a < d$, one finds that M_{2t} converges asymptotically to M_2^{**} regardless of the initial distribution, where $M_2^{**} = M(b+d)/(b+2d)$. The economy converges to a steady state in which $R = 1$, idle balances exist, and the constant price level is $p^{**} = M/(b+2d)$. Note that in both cases there is a unique long-run distribution of real balances, independent of the initial distribution.

Hence the "quantity theory" holds in the long run in this model, in the sense discussed by Archibald and Lipsey (1958). That is, if one hands out new (outside) money at some date, in such a way as to alter the existing distribution of money holdings, one finds that both nominal and real interest rates are affected by the intervention. But if there are no further monetary interventions thereafter, the distribution of real balances returns to its unique steady-state equilibrium pattern; the price level converges to a new constant level greater than its original level, in proportion to the increase in the total quantity of money; and the real rate of interest converges to its unique steady-state equilibrium value.

However, this result does not imply that in a long-run steady state the real interest rate and the distribution of money balances cannot be affected by monetary policy. A continuing intervention in the market for loanable funds can permanently affect the real interest rate by altering the steady-state distribution of money balances, as shown in Section 2.

2   Credit expansion by a government bank

Banking and inside money may now be introduced in the following manner. We consider first the case in which the banking system consists of a government-owned central bank that supplies all money loans in the economy. (The case of a privately owned banking system is taken up in Section 3.) Let us suppose that the central bank can create or destroy money in any quantities that it wishes. Let us suppose, furthermore, that the central bank intervenes only through *open-market operations* – exchanging money for debt at the competitive interest rate. [Other possible monetary policies are considered in Woodford (1985).] The central bank operates in the market for loanable funds each period, as either a net lender or a net borrower. If net bank lending in period t is L_t then condition (1.5a) becomes

$$M_t \geq (a+b+d)p_t, \tag{2.1}$$

where now the quantity of money $M_t = M_{2t} + M_{3t} + L_t$. Notice that L_t represents the quantity of "inside money" each period (i.e., money backed by private-sector debt), and $M_{2t} + M_{3t}$ the quantity of "outside money."

Otherwise, the equilibrium conditions are unchanged. One finds a unique temporary equilibrium for every $M_{2t} > 0$, $M_{3t} > 0$, and $L_t > -(d/(b+d))M_{2t}$. Thus, as in the textbook model, an open-market operation (purchase of debt with newly issued money by the government bank, increasing L_t) shifts the LM curve outward in proportion to the increase in the total quantity of money M_t, while the IS curve remains in its previous position. In the case of an equilibrium with $R_t > 1$, an increase in L_t lowers the nominal interest rate and increases the price level in proportion to the increase in the total quantity of money.

Thus far, the analysis of short-run effects of an open-market operation on interest and prices remains quite traditional. The advantage of the framework developed here is that it also allows one to determine the effects of a given monetary policy over time, into the indefinite future. For example, suppose the monetary authority seeks to keep nominal interest rates low by means of a liberal supply of inside money by the government bank. Can such a policy be continued forever? And if so, what happens to the price level?

Given an initial distribution of cash balances (M_{20}, M_{30}), a unique intertemporal equilibrium is easily found to exist for each possible sequence of interest rates $\{R_t\}_{t=0}^{\infty}$. The price level p_t in each period is determined by (1.4), given M_{2t} and M_{3t}; the evolution of M_{2t} and M_{3t} is determined by (1.2)–(1.3).

As long as M_{2t} and M_{3t} are both positive, (1.4) yields a positive price level; this in turn implies that M_{2t+1} and M_{3t+1} will both be positive. Hence a solution may be constructed with a positive price level in all periods. The quantity of inside money L_t that must be supplied in each period to achieve the desired sequence of interest rates may then be determined from (2.1).

Note that there is no indeterminacy of the price level associated with a policy that pegs the nominal rate of interest. Sargent and Wallace (1975) obtain their indeterminacy result because money enters the equilibrium conditions of their model only through total real balances M_t/p_t. Here, as noted above, the distribution of real balances also matters. An increase of the money supply through expansion of the inside money supply L_t does not only increase M_t; it also changes the ratios M_{2t}/M_t and M_{3t}/M_t, and hence is not neutral. It is this nonneutrality that renders the price level determinate. (It is easily seen that this result is not dependent upon the special preferences assumed here; quite generally, an inside money expansion must have real effects in a model of this type.)

This does not mean that there may not be multiple perfect foresight equilibria in a model of this sort. As shown in Woodford (1985), for alternative specifications of preferences or endowments there may exist continua of perfect foresight equilibria corresponding to a given sequence of interest rates.[5] However, the multiplicity is not due to a homogeneity property of the sort that exists in the Sargent–Wallace model. In the terminology of McCallum (1984), this is an example of "multiplicity" as distinguished from "indeterminacy" of equilibrium; the alternative equilibria involve alternative allocations of resources and not simply different paths for the price level. And the possibility of multiple equilibria is not special to the type of monetary policy that seeks to peg nominal interest rates; it is shown in Woodford (1985) that there may equally well exist a continuum of perfect foresight equilibria corresponding to a given sequence of money supply targets $\{M_t\}_{t=0}^{\infty}$. Let us consider in particular policies that peg the interest rate at a constant level $R \geq 1$. It follows from (1.2)–(1.4) that the evolution of money holdings over time will be given by

---

[5] This should not be surprising. The choice of a sequence of interest rates $R_t = 1$ for all t reduces the model to the standard overlapping generations model of fiat money of Wallace (1980), and it is well known that continua of equilibria may exist for that model.

$$\begin{bmatrix} M_{2t+1} \\ M_{3t+1} \end{bmatrix} = \begin{bmatrix} \dfrac{b}{b+d+a\left(\dfrac{R-1}{R}\right)} & \dfrac{b+d}{b+d+a\left(\dfrac{R-1}{R}\right)} \\ \dfrac{dR}{b+d} & 0 \end{bmatrix} \begin{bmatrix} M_{2t} \\ M_{3t} \end{bmatrix}. \qquad (2.2)$$

The matrix in (2.2) has two eigenvalues, which are the two roots of

$$(b+d+a(R-1/R))\lambda^2 - b\lambda - dR = 0. \qquad (2.3)$$

Equation (2.3) has two real roots, one positive and one negative, for each value of $R \geq 1$. The sum of the roots is positive, so that the positive root has the larger absolute value. Hence the asymptotic rate of expansion of the money supply, for arbitrary initial money holdings, is given by the positive root λ^+. This positive root equals 1 for $R = 1$. When $a < d$ (i.e., when $R = 1$ in the long-run steady state without banking), $\lambda^+ > 1$ for all $R > 1$. When $a > d$ (i.e., when $R = R^* = a/d$ in the long-run without banking), $\lambda^+ < 1$ for $1 < R < R^*$, $\lambda^+ = 1$ for $R = R^*$, and $\lambda^+ > 1$ for $R > R^*$. We find that any desired level of the nominal interest rate ($R \geq 1$) can be maintained forever through open-market operations, and furthermore that the long-run rate of money growth (and hence of inflation) is low in the case of a low nominal interest rate.

Thus the Wicksell–Friedman proposition – that a sustained attempt to hold interest rates at a low level causes unending "cumulative inflation" that eventually must prevent the continuation of such a policy – does not hold. If (in the case $a > d$) one interprets R^* as the "natural rate" of interest, then pegging R at a lower level leads to deflation in the long run,[6] or (when $R = 1$) to a constant price level. The Wicksell–Friedman doctrine assumes that the short-run effect of moving to a lower interest rate requires a greater volume of bank loans being repaid each period, so that a greater rate of growth of the money supply is not implied.

It is easy to show that an equilibrium of the above model is Pareto optimal if and only if the nominal interest rate is zero in all periods.[7] Hence –

---

[6] Deflation occurs because the profits from government lending are never spent, resulting in a contraction of the money supply. In the case of privately owned banks (Section 3), all these steady states have a constant price level.

[7] If $R_t > 1$, the marginal rate of substitution between period t leisure and period t consumption on the part of young agents will not equal the marginal rate of transformation between these two "goods" allowed by the technology. Hence $R_t = 1$ is necessary for Pareto optimality. Conversely, if $R_t = 1$ for all t, the equilibrium is an equilibrium of the corresponding overlapping-generations model without a cash-in-advance constraint, and the welfare theorem of Balasko and Shell (1980) can be applied.

assuming that open-market operations are the only available policy instrument – the monetary policy that pegs the nominal interest rate at zero forever is the unique policy leading to a Pareto optimal allocation of resources. The zero nominal rate requirement for efficiency agrees with the analysis of Friedman (1969). But Friedman's conclusion is that welfare would be increased by a lower rate of expansion of the money supply. This would be true in the present model as well, if monetary expansion through lump-sum transfers were considered. But in the case of expansion through open-market operations, one finds that it is impossible to have too great a rate of monetary expansion. For if (in any period) L_t exceeds the quantity necessary to reduce the nominal interest rate to zero, then idle balances are held without any effect upon either prices or the allocation of resources.[8] Continuing inflation can occur only if there are constant additions to the money incomes of agents (rather than merely to the quantity of loanable funds), and this results only when the government pays interest to the private sector on government debt that is rolled over forever – that is, only in the case of a tight credit policy.

Of course, the mere fact that one allocation is Pareto optimal and others are not need not mean that the one must be preferred by policymakers. The equilibrium with $R_t = 1$ forever does not Pareto-dominate the other equilibria; it is obvious that welfare of the initial old is greater the higher is the nominal interest rate in the initial period, since a high interest rate means a low price level and hence a greater value for their accumulated cash. But it is also interesting to note that the equilibrium with $R_t = 1$ forever converges asymptotically to the optimal stationary allocation – that is, to that stationary allocation which achieves the highest stationary level of utility (the "golden rule" allocation). Any monetary policy under which the nominal interest rate asymptotically approaches a level $R > 1$ will result in an asymptotic utility that remains forever below the golden-rule level; hence such a policy cannot even be constrained-optimal (i.e., optimal among the class of policies that involve open-market operations) unless the policymaker discounts the welfare of future generations.

At this point a comment is appropriate on the extent to which the results rely upon special features of the example considered here. It can be shown, for a very general overlapping-generations model with cash-in-advance constraints (general preferences, multiple agents per generation, many periods of life, multiple goods per period, and production), that at least one steady-state equilibrium exists with a zero nominal interest

---

[8] A similar result is obtained by Sargent and Wallace (1982) in a different but related model.

rate and zero rate of inflation.[9] Hence, with the right initial distribution of money balances (and, in the case of a production economy, the right initial capital stocks) a policy that pegs the nominal interest rate at zero is consistent with a constant price level. It can also be proved for the general model that $R_t = 1$ in all periods is necessary and sufficient for equilibrium to be Pareto optimal, and that if there is a single agent per generation then the optimal stationary allocation of resources is achieved by the (unique) steady-state equilibrium with a zero nominal interest rate and a constant price level. What is not known in general is whether adoption of a cheap money policy, when the initial distribution of money balances is not consistent with a zero-inflation steady state, results in convergence to such a steady state (as occurs above). There may be more than one steady-state equilibrium with a zero nominal interest rate, and some may involve steady inflation (or deflation). In such a case, for at least some initial conditions, at least some possible equilibria consistent with a cheap money policy do not involve a constant price level in the long run. [Examples are given in Section 6 of Woodford (1985).] But it is certainly not true in general that cheap money policies necessarily lead to inflation that continues until the policy is abandoned, as has often been claimed.

3   Credit expansion by commercial banks

It is interesting to compare the results of the previous section with those obtained in the case where inside money is supplied by privately owned, competitive, profit-seeking banks. In this case, the monetary authority regulates the supply of money by fixing the reserve ratio that must be maintained by commercial banks. Let us assume that all money to be spent in the second subperiod of period t is held, at the end of the first subperiod, in the form of demand deposits at one or another of the private banks, and let us also assume that each of the private banks' "reserves" in period t are calculated as the excess of demand deposits at the end of the first subperiod over the quantity of loans made during the first subperiod. Then if the reserve ratio requirement in period t is set at ϕ_t ($0 < \phi_t \leq 1$), the total quantity of bank loans L_t in period t can be no greater than $(1-\phi_t)\cdot M_t$. Hence, given a stock of outside money $M_{2t}+M_{3t}$, the total quantity of money M_t in period t can be no greater than $(M_{2t}+M_{3t})/\phi_t$.

---

[9] This follows from the general existence of a monetary steady state with a constant price level for the overlapping-generations model without finance constraint. This is proved for a general production economy by Muller and Woodford (1983).

As a result of the reserve ratio requirement, demand deposits are valuable to the bank that receives them, with the result that banks will wish to compete for deposits. Let us assume here that there are no legal restrictions upon the payment of interest on deposits. [The case of a restriction forbidding the payment of interest on deposits is treated in Woodford (1985).] Let us suppose that interest on deposits is paid by the bank at the end of the second subperiod, when loans are repaid. Then competition for deposits will result in a relation

$$r_{Dt} = (1 - \phi_t) r_{Lt} \tag{3.1}$$

between the nominal interest rate paid on deposits r_{Dt} and the nominal interest rate charged for loans r_{Lt}. Profit-seeking banks will always grant the maximum number of loans allowed by the reserve requirement. Hence, in equilibrium,

$$r_{Dt} M_t = r_{Lt} L_t. \tag{3.2}$$

Assuming the same preferences as in Section 1, but now allowing for the payment of interest on demand deposits, the optimizing supply and demand functions become

$$c_{1t} = \frac{a}{R_{Lt} - r_{Dt}},$$

$$c_{2t} = \frac{b}{b+d} \frac{M_{2t}}{p_t} \frac{R_{Lt}}{R_{Lt} - r_{Dt}},$$

$$c_{3t} = \frac{M_{3t}}{p_t} \frac{R_{Lt}}{R_{Lt} - r_{Dt}},$$

$$n_t = a + b + d,$$

where $R_{Lt} = 1 + r_{Lt}$. Hence the goods market clearing relation (1.4) becomes

$$ap_t + ([b/(b+d)]M_{2t} + M_{3t})R_{Lt} = (a+b+d)p_t(R_{Lt} - r_{Dt}). \tag{3.3a}$$

The LM relation analogous to (1.5) is

$$r_{Lt} \geq r_{Dt}, \tag{3.3b}$$

$$M_t \geq (a+b+d)p_t, \tag{3.3c}$$

where one must have $r_{Lt} = r_{Dt}$ if any idle balances exist. But since $\phi_t > 0$ is assumed, (3.3b) is equivalent to

$$r_{Lt} \geq 0 \tag{3.3d}$$

and one must have $r_{Lt} = 0$ if any idle balances exist. Finally, (3.2) and (3.3b)–(3.3c) imply

$$(a+b+d)p_t(r_{Lt}-r_{Dt}) = (M_{2t}+M_{3t})r_{Lt}.$$

Hence (3.3a) may be rewritten as

$$(b+d)p_t+(d/(b+d))M_{2t}r_{Lt} = (b/(b+d))M_{2t}+M_{3t}. \qquad (3.3e)$$

The system of equations (3.3c)–(3.3e) can now be manipulated as was the system (1.4)–(1.5) in Section 2. Equation (3.3e) gives a downward-sloping relationship between r_{Lt} and p_t, the location of which depends upon M_{2t} and M_{3t} but is not affected by changes in the supply of inside money L_t. Equations (3.3c)–(3.3d) give an L-shaped relationship between r_{Lt} and p_t, the location of which depends only upon the total quantity of money M_t. The system determines a unique temporary equilibrium (p_t, r_{Lt}) for any $M_{2t}>0$, $M_{3t}>0$, and $L_t \ge 0$. The value of r_{Dt} is then given by (3.2). Furthermore, a credit expansion (increase in L_t, via a reduction of ϕ_t) increases p_t while reducing r_{Lt}, as before, up to the point where $r_{Lt}=0$; beyond this point, further increases in the money supply have no effect on either the price level or interest rates. The only difference is in the amount of inside money required to achieve a given reduction in the interest rate r_{Lt}. For example, if one considers a small credit expansion, starting from an initial position of the zero inside-money steady state with $R=a/d$ (in the case $a>d$), one finds that in the case of a government bank

$$\frac{\partial R_t}{\partial (\log M_t)} = -\left(\frac{a+b}{d}\right)\frac{a}{d},$$

whereas, in the case of commercial banks,

$$\frac{\partial R_{Lt}}{\partial (\log M_t)} = -\left(\frac{b+d}{d}\right).$$

Thus the effect of a small credit expansion on the loan rate is larger in the case of a government bank, as argued by Cagan (1972) on different grounds.

The evolution of the beginning-of-period money balances is again given by (1.2)–(1.3), where now R_t in (1.3) should be replaced by R_{Lt}. Using (3.3e), it follows that $M_{2t+1}+M_{3t+1}=M_{2t}+M_{3t}$. Thus the total outside money supply remains constant over time, regardless of the degree of inside money creation by the banking system. Let this constant quantity be $M^\circ = M_{20}+M_{30}$. Then we need only keep track of the evolution of M_{2t}.

In the case of a monetary policy that chooses ϕ_t each period so as to peg R_{Lt} at a constant level $R>1$, (1.3) implies

$$M_{2t+1}=M^\circ - M_{2t}dR/(b+d). \qquad (3.4)$$

It follows that there exists a steady-state equilibrium with $R_{Lt} = R$ forever, with M_{2t} always equal to $M_2^* = M^°(b+d)/(b+(1+R)d)$ and a constant price level $p^* = M^°/(b+(1+R)d)$. This steady state requires a nonnegative supply of inside money by the commercial banks if and only if $R \leq a/d$. Hence, in the case that $a > d$, there exists a continuum of nominal interest rates $1 \leq R \leq a/d$, all equally consistent with a constant price level.

It is evident from (3.4) that a policy of pegging $R_{Lt} = R$ results in an equilibrium that converges to the steady state, for any initial distribution of money holdings (M_{20}, M_{30}) close enough to the steady-state distribution, if and only if $R < (b+d)/d$. On the other hand, if $R > (b+d)/d$, the policy cannot be maintained forever for any initial distribution other than that associated with the steady state. For in a finite number of periods, one will obtain $M_{2t} > M^° a(b+d)/(a+b+d)dR$. With such a distribution of money holdings, it is impossible to make R_{Lt} as high as R with $L_t \geq 0$; hence a lower interest rate will be necessary. Thus there is no problem in pegging the nominal interest rate forever by manipulating ϕ_t, as long as the desired level is sufficiently low.

4   Financing a government deficit

One can easily introduce government expenditures into the above framework, and compare the effects of money creation and borrowing as ways of financing a government deficit. Let us consider again the case of a government bank, treated in Section 2. Let g_t be the quantity of goods purchased by the government in period t. Then (1.4) becomes

$$\frac{ap_t}{R_t} + \frac{M_{2t}b}{(b+d)} + M_{3t} + p_t g = (a+b+d)p_t,$$

while equilibrium conditions (1.5) remain the same. Thus an increase in the government deficit g_t shifts the IS curve, as in the standard textbook account. If there is no change in M_t (i.e., the deficit is financed by borrowing, and the government bank does not "accommodate" the increased borrowing), the LM curve is not shifted. If M_t is increased at the same time as g_t (representing finance by money creation, or, equivalently, purchase of government debt by the government bank), then the LM curve is shifted to the right due to the increase in the money supply. Hence the present model yields the traditional results: Government borrowing means a higher nominal interest rate but less of an increase in the price level than would occur if the deficit were financed by printing money.

What are the long-run effects of a government deficit? If the deficit exists only for a finite number of periods, the analysis of Section 2 is unchanged. It remains possible to peg the nominal interest rate forever at any desired level, and the long-run rates of inflation associated with alternative interest rates are those derived in Section 2. A zero nominal interest rate in all periods remains necessary and sufficient for Pareto optimality, and such a policy results in an equilibrium allocation that converges asymptotically to the optimal stationary allocation.

On the other hand, if a constant real level of deficit expenditure $g > 0$ is continued forever, these conclusions do not go through. It is still possible to maintain any $R \geq 1$ forever, as long as the government deficit satisfies $g < b + d$. When $g \geq b + d$, then it is not possible to maintain forever a nominal interest rate $R \leq \underline{R}$, where $\underline{R} = a/(a+b+d-g)$. In the case of $g > 0$, equation (2.7) becomes

$$(b + d + a((R-1)/R) - g)\lambda^2 - b\lambda - dR = 0. \tag{4.1}$$

When $g < b + d$ (or $R > \underline{R}$), equation (4.1) still has one positive root and one negative, and the positive root is still larger in absolute value. Hence the positive root still indicates the asymptotic rate of growth of the money supply and of prices. If the interest rate were pegged at zero forever, it is possible that maintaining a higher nominal interest rate (incomplete accommodation of government borrowing by the central bank) can reduce the long-run rate of inflation; this occurs if $a > d$.

Although $R_t = 1$ in all periods is still necessary for equilibrium to be Pareto optimal, it is no longer sufficient. Thus none of the equilibria that can be achieved through open-market operations alone are Pareto optimal. The equilibrium with $R_t = 1$ forever (which exists as long as $g < b + d$) is "weakly Pareto optimal" in the sense of Balasko and Shell (1980), but displays an inefficiency of the Malinvaud–Koopmans–Cass type because the real rate of interest is negative in the long run. The highest level of long-run steady-state utility is achieved when $R = 1 + r^*$, where $r^* = g/(a+b+d-g)$.[10]

The result continues to hold when one considers a banking system with both a government bank and commercial banks. Suppose that a fraction s of the total inside money creation in each period results from lending by the government bank, and the remainder represents lending by commercial banks, where $0 < s \leq 1$. Then, for a given choice of the loan rate $r_{Lt} = r$, the asymptotic rate of growth of the money supply is given by the positive root of

$$(asr + (b + d - g)(1 + sr))\lambda^2 - b(1 + r)\lambda - d(1 + r)^2 = 0,$$

which generalizes (4.1). The asymptotic stationary value of the reserve ratio is $\phi = s$. In this case, the choice of r that achieves the maximum level

---

[10] See Woodford (1985), pp. 74–8.

of stationary utility is $r = r^*/s$.[11] Thus the greater the proportion of growth in the money supply that comes through inside money creation by commercial banks, the higher the nominal interest rate that maximizes long-run average utility.

Hence, in the case of a constant real government deficit, a policy of maintaining moderately high nominal interest rates may be preferable to a cheap money policy;[12] the increase in the long-run real rate of return has beneficial effects on the pattern of life-cycle consumption that more than make up for the inefficiency associated with the binding cash-in-advance constraint. But the results of Sections 2 and 3 suggest that a cheap money policy need not have undesirable long-run consequences, in a world committed to responsible fiscal policy.

REFERENCES

Archibald, C., and R. Lipsey. 1958. "Monetary and Value Theory: A Critique of Lange and Patinkin." *Review of Economic Studies* 26: 1–22.

Balasko, Y., and K. Shell. 1980. "The Overlapping Generations Model, I: The Case of Pure Exchange Without Money." *Journal of Economic Theory* 23: 281–306.

Bryant, J. 1980. "Nontransferable Interest-Bearing National Debt." *Journal of Finance* 35: 1027–31.

Bryant, J., and N. Wallace. 1979. "The Inefficiency of Interest-Bearing National Debt." *Journal of Political Economy* 87: 365–81.

——— 1984. "A Price Discrimination Analysis of Monetary Policy." *Review of Economic Studies* 51: 279–88.

Cagan, P. 1972. *The Channels of Monetary Effects on Interest Rates.* New York: NBER.

Friedman, M. 1968. "The Role of Monetary Policy." *American Economic Review* 58: 1–17.

---

[11] In fact, it is found that only the product rs affects the long-run stationary allocation of resources, so that any choice of r and s such that $rs = r^*$ achieves the same (constrained-optimal) stationary allocation.

[12] This result contrasts with that of Bryant and Wallace (1979), who find that financing a government deficit entirely by printing money achieves the highest possible stationary level of utility. They also challenge the conventional wisdom that "financing a given deficit by money is more inflationary than financing it by bond sales and, perhaps, so inflationary that the financing cannot be accomplished by money issue." We find, instead, that increasing the steady-state nominal interest rate may indeed bring down the steady-state rate of inflation (for low interest rates, when $a > d$ and $g < b + d$), and that in some cases $(g > b + d)$ a nominal interest rate that is too low cannot be maintained forever. Their results are thus less robust than is suggested in the conclusion to their paper; for the present model, like theirs, assumes zero intermediation costs for the government and positive costs for private parties. The result also contrasts with that of Bryant (1980), who finds, for a different model, that the optimal mix of money and bond finance is the one that leads to a zero nominal interest rate.

1969. "The Optimum Quantity of Money." In *The Optimum Quantity of Money and Other Essays*. Chicago: Aldine.

Kohn, M., and G. Karacaoglu. 1985. "A New, Classical Model of Balance of Payments Adjustment." Mimeo, University of Western Ontario.

McCallum, B. T. 1984. "Some Issues Concerning Interest Rate Pegging, Price Level Determinacy, and the Real Bills Doctrine." Working Paper No. 1294, NBER.

Muller, W. J., and M. Woodford. 1983. "Stationary Overlapping Generations Economies with Production and Infinite Lived Consumers: I. Existence of Equilibrium." Working Paper No. 325, Massachusetts Institute of Technology.

Sargent, T. J., and N. Wallace. 1975. "Rational Expectations, the Optimal Monetary Instrument, and the Optimal Money Supply Rule." *Journal of Political Economy* 83: 241-54.

1982. "The Real Bills Doctrine versus the Quantity Theory." *Journal of Political Economy* 90: 1212-36.

Wallace, N. 1980. "The Overlapping Generations Model of Fiat Money." In J. Kareken and N. Wallace (eds.), *Models of Monetary Economies*. Minneapolis, MN: Federal Reserve Bank.

Woodford, M. 1985. "Interest and Prices in a Cash-in-Advance Economy." Discussion Paper No. 281, Department of Economics, Columbia University.

Financial intermediation

CHAPTER 4

Preference shocks, liquidity, and central bank policy

Sudipto Bhattacharya and Douglas Gale

Abstract: We characterize the role of a central bank as a mechanism designer for risk-sharing across banks that are subject to privately observed "liquidity shocks." The optimal mechanism involves borrowing/lending from a "discount window." The optimal discount rate and the induced distortions in holdings of liquid assets suggest a rationale for subsidized lending and reserve requirements on the observable part of liquid asset holdings.

1 Introduction

Several recent papers have examined the micro-theoretic foundations for a theory of financial intermediation. The role of intermediaries as agents who provide delegated monitoring services has been developed in Leland and Pyle (1977) and Diamond (1984). More recently, Bryant (1980) and Diamond and Dybvig (1983) have considered issues pertaining to the optimal form of intermediary (deposit) contracts. They examine intertemporal models in which depositors are subject to privately observed preference shocks and the returns to investments depend on their time to maturity (liquidity). Within this framework, Bryant, Diamond–Dybvig and Jacklin (1986) have demonstrated the superiority of deposit contracts over Walrasian (mutual fund) trading mechanisms in providing agents with insurance for risks connected with preference shocks.[1]

The work on banking contracts has also served to focus attention on problems of coordination across agents who have private information on (risky) investments undertaken by the depository intermediaries or mutual

The authors would like to thank Douglas Diamond, Stanley Fischer, Joe Haubrich, Charles Jacklin, Hayne Leland, John Parsons, and particularly Philip Dybvig and Franco Modigliani for helpful discussions and comments, while retaining responsibility for all errors.

[1] As Jacklin (1986) has noted, with the specific "corner" parameterization employed in Diamond and Dybvig (1983) – and given the socially optimal production decision – their optimal (first-best) allocation is indeed achievable through a mutual-fund trading mechanism. However, this is not true with more general smooth preferences.

funds. The pioneering study of Bryant (1980) considered the instabilities (panics) and imperfect risk-sharing that would arise if bank depositors (with fixed commitment contracts) make earlier withdrawals based on information about asset returns. Jacklin and Bhattacharya (1985) have analyzed the implications of such phenomena for the welfare-optimal choice over depository and mutual-fund (Walrasian) intermediation mechanisms. Diamond and Dybvig (1983) have shown that, even in the absence of private information about asset returns, deposit contracts are subject to a coordination problem across agents (multiple Pareto-ordered Nash equilibria). In essence, the insurance aspect of deposit contracts leads to the possibility of panics. Agents who conjecture that other agents will panic and make early withdrawals are then led to make early withdrawals themselves because excessive early withdrawals make their promised second-period payoffs infeasible.

While the Diamond–Dybvig analysis of "banking panics" provides a useful starting point, its implications for optimal policies to improve coordination are somewhat sparse. As noted in their paper, when (privately observed) preference shocks are statistically independent across a large number of agents, panics are easily eliminated by a policy of precommitment not to liquidate more than a certain proportion of investments early. Such a policy, which they term "suspension of convertibility," serves to ensure that agents who conjecture that others might withdraw early nevertheless perceive no impact on the feasibility of their later contractual payoffs. Thus, no agent who truly wishes to consume later is induced to join the panic; that is, the Pareto-superior Nash equilibrium is uniquely attained. Diamond and Dybvig also consider the case in which the proportion of agents who (truly) wish to consume early is stochastic in aggregate, owing to correlations among agents' preference shocks. In this case, suspension of convertibility is an imperfect measure which leads to second-best distortions in optimal risk-sharing, unless intermediary contracts can respond to the realized proportion of early diers.

Diamond and Dybvig consider a role for central bank policy, in the case of aggregate preference shocks, arising from the central bank's assumed superior ability to make payoffs to depositors contingent on realized aggregate outcomes. But we find this explanation less than compelling (cf. Section 5). Instead, we focus on a setting in which individual intermediaries are subject to privately observed shocks affecting the proportion of their depositors wishing to make early withdrawals. In addition to these shifts in their demand for liquidity, intermediaries have private information about the mix of liquid (short-term) and illiquid (longer-term) investments in their portfolios. The liquidity shocks, which may be regional in nature, are imperfectly correlated across intermediaries. Thus there is a need for a borrowing–lending mechanism across banks to insure depositors partially against variations in their liquidity requirements.

By developing a model of such an interbank coordination problem, we are able to show that the optimal mechanism design problem is subject to inherent second-best distortions, even in the absence of aggregate liquidity shocks over (a large number of) intermediaries as a whole. In addition, we are able to provide fairly sharp characterizations of the extent and terms of the optimal quantity-constrained borrowing–lending program across banks. We also show that, in many cases involving plausible restrictions on preferences, banks are induced to underinvest in liquid assets at the second-best optimum, relative to a setting with representative intermediaries or (equivalently) informationally unconstrained coordination across banks. Our results here provide a promising start to a research program, one that seriously examines the implications of the recent micro-theoretic modeling of intermediation for detailed and realistic aspects of optimal (governmental) policy.

This paper is organized as follows. In Section 2, we first discuss the underlying framework developed in Diamond and Dybvig (1983), and then proceed to the detailed development of our model of interbank coordination. The characteristics of our second-best optimal interbank contract are analyzed in Section 3, and further interpreted in terms of the role and function of a central bank in Section 4. In Section 5, which concludes the paper, we suggest avenues for further research and integration with related literature, particularly on models with aggregate shocks and fiat money.

2   The model of interbank coordination

Since the Diamond–Dybvig framework is used as a basis for the subsequent analysis, it is worth sketching the outlines here. There are three dates indexed $T = 0, 1, 2$ and a single commodity at each date. Agents are identical ex ante and observe (privately) an idiosyncratic preference shock at date 1. Their preferences are given by

$$U(C_0, C_1, C_2) = \begin{cases} U(C_1) & \text{with probability } t, \\ U(C_2) & \text{with probability } (1-t), \end{cases} \tag{2.1}$$

where U is a von Neumann–Morgenstern utility function and C_T denotes consumption at date $T = 0, 1, 2$. Agents who realize the utility function $U(C_1)$ [respectively, $U(C_2)$] at date 1 are called early [late] diers.

Each agent has an initial endowment of one unit of the consumption good at date 0 and none at subsequent dates. The agent deposits this endowment with the intermediary at date 0 in return for consumption at dates 1 and 2. The intermediary has access to two investment technologies. The first, corresponding to investment in the short-term asset, yields one unit of consumption at date 1 for every unit of investment at the beginning of that period. The second, corresponding to investment in the long-term asset, yields $R > 1$ units of consumption at date 2 for every unit of investment at date 1. Individuals are also able to store consumption between date 1 and date 2.

It is assumed that the number of agents is large and that there is no aggregate uncertainty. The cross-sectional distribution of preference shocks realized at date 1 is the same as the probability distribution of these shocks for an individual agent at date 0. Thus t is the proportion of early diers realized at date 1 and $(1-t)$ the proportion of late diers. A representative intermediary accepts a deposit of one unit from each depositor and knows that a fraction t of them will be early diers. In exchange for the deposit, the intermediary offers each agent a contract which allows him to withdraw either C_1 units of consumption at date 1 or C_2 units at date 2. In order to finance withdrawals, the intermediary liquidates L units per capita at date 1 and hence receives $R(1-L)$ units per capita at date 2.

The intermediary chooses (C_1, C_2, L) to maximize the ex ante expected utility of individual agents. Then it solves the problem:

$$\underset{(C_1, C_2, L)}{\text{Max}} \ \{tU(C_1) + (1-t)U(C_2)\} \tag{2.2}$$

$$\text{subject to} \quad t_1 C_1 = L, \tag{2.3a}$$

$$(1-t)C_2 = R(1-L). \tag{2.3b}$$

Assuming U is differentiable, strictly increasing, and strictly concave, any interior optimum must satisfy:

$$U'(C_1^*) = RU'(C_2^*), \tag{2.4}$$
$$C_1^* = L^*/t \quad \text{and} \quad C_2^* = (1-L^*)R/(1-t).$$

Clearly $C_2^* > C_1^*$ is implied by (2.4) and the condition $R > 1$. A sufficient condition for C_2^*/C_1^* to be less than R is that $CU'(C)$ be decreasing in C. Thus if U has a coefficient of relative risk aversion greater than unity, early diers will share in the higher returns on illiquid assets. In what follows it will always be assumed that this condition holds.[2]

In attempting to implement the first-best allocation (C_1^*, C_2^*, L^*) defined by (2.4), the intermediary faces a coordination problem. In defining the first-best allocation problem above, it was assumed that only early diers consumed C_1 and only late diers consumed C_2. Since preference shocks are privately observed the intermediary may not be able to guar-

---

[2] This assumption about the Arrow–Pratt relative risk-aversion coefficient of the "representative investor" is an empirically plausible one, in the light of recent (and past) studies [e.g., Hansen and Singleton (1983)].

antee this. In fact, the late dier's decision whether to withdraw C_1 at date 1 and store it or to withdraw C_2 at date 2 is a strategic one, depending on what other agents do. Diamond and Dybvig find that there are two, Pareto-ranked, Nash equilibria. In the first (Pareto-dominant) equilibrium, only those agents who have a genuine preference for early consumption choose to make an early withdrawal. In the second (Pareto-dominated) equilibrium, agents who actually prefer late consumption, fearing withdrawal by others of the same type, also choose to withdraw early. The inefficiency of these "bank runs" arises directly from the premature and unnecessary disinvestment of the higher yielding assets.

Another way to solve the problem of bank runs is to treat the intermediary as a mutual fund. That is, the intermediary chooses L^* as its investment in short-term assets and provides each depositor with an income stream $(L^*, (1-L^*)R)$ over the remaining two periods. At date 1 a market opens on which agents can trade shares in these income streams. The optimal consumption plan (C_1^*, C_2^*) can be implemented through such a market, but the resulting share price does not make L^* a value-maximizing decision for the intermediary. To see this, note that the ex dividend share price at date 1 is $(1-t)L^*/t$. Each shareholder receives a dividend of L^* at the beginning of date 1. Early diers supply their shares inelastically and late diers supply consumption goods inelastically. The supply of shares is t and the supply of consumption is $(1-t)L^*$, so the market-clearing price is $(1-t)L^*/t$. Then the share price at date 1 *per unit of period 2 payoff* R is $(1-t)L^*/t(1-L^*)$. At this price, an intermediary choosing L to maximize its own realizable value at date 1 would solve

$$\text{Max}\{L+(1-L)P[R]\},$$
$$L$$

where $P[R] \equiv (1-t)L^*/t(1-L^*) = RC_1^*/C_2^* > 1$. The solution is $L=0$. The apparent liquidity created by the market in shares leads to underinvestment in the short-term asset.

In this paper we have tried to shift the focus away from the Diamond–Dybvig coordination problem. Instead we focus on the problems faced by the intermediaries themselves when their demand for liquidity is uncertain. We make three basic changes in the Diamond–Dybvig model. First, we assume that while there is no aggregate uncertainty, individual intermediaries are uncertain at date 0 about what proportion of their depositors will be early diers at date 1. Second, we assume that the intermediary's investment decision is made (irrevocably) at date 0.[3] Third,

---

[3] It should be noted that this irreversibility of investment allocations, where illiquid assets cannot be realized earlier, removes the Diamond–Dybvig bank runs problem. This assumption is also more consistent with a context where intermediaries can signal the value of their well-diversified *aggregate* portfolios, but are subject to a Lemons problem [Akerlog (1970)] in liquidating individual elements (loans) in their portfolios.

we assume that the intermediaries have incomplete information. Each intermediary observes its own investment decision and the proportion of early diers among its own depositors but not those of the other intermediaries.

Under these assumptions there is clearly scope for intermediaries to provide themselves with insurance against unexpected liquidity needs. Because L is fixed at date 0, an intermediary cannot provide itself with extra liquidity by changing L once the demand for liquidity is realized. On the other hand, the intermediaries can collectively provide extra liquidity by borrowing and lending after their liquidity needs are known. In other words, they have an incentive to set up an interbank market at date 1. However, setting up a Walrasian interbank market creates a free-rider problem. Individual intermediaries will rely on the ex post market to provide them with liquidity and will underinvest in the liquid asset. In the aggregate however, the liquidity of the market is limited by the investments of individual intermediaries in the liquid asset. For this reason we should not expect an interbank market to perform very well. We are thus led to consider the design of an optimal insurance scheme and the distortions that result from its implementation.

In our model, as in the Diamond–Dybvig model, depositors have one unit of the good at date 0 and none at subsequent dates. They are identical ex ante, but ex post discover themselves to be early or late diers. Their preferences are given by (2.1). Intermediaries are also assumed to be identical ex ante, discovering ex post that they are one of two types. These types are distinguished by the proportion of early diers. Let t_i denote the proportion of early diers in the ith type of intermediary ($i = 1, 2$) and assume $0 < t_1 < t_2 < 1$. Intermediaries have probability p_i of being type i and, in the aggregate, the proportion of intermediaries of type i is $p_i (p_1 + p_2 = 1)$. The aggregate proportion of early diers is constant and equal to $t = \sum p_i t_i$.

What we have in mind is that the intermediaries are banks, distinguished by geographical location. Depositors attach themselves to particular banks by locational proximity. Then local economic conditions in the area where the bank operates will have a marked impact on the demand for liquidity. For example, when unemployment is high (the proportion of early diers is high), the demand for liquidity is high also as the unemployed draw down their savings.

We can represent the choice of an optimal insurance contract among the banks as a planning problem. The hypothetical planner chooses an allocation to maximize the ex ante expected utility of the representative bank/depositor. The planner, like the typical intermediary, knows the stochastic structure of the model but cannot observe either the type or the investment decision of an intermediary.[4] He therefore relies on the individual bank to choose the correct level of investment in the liquid asset at date 0 and to reveal his true type (demand for liquidity) at date 1. The planner is therefore constrained to choose an *incentive-compatible* allocation. It must not give the bank an incentive to lie or deviate from the correct investment decision.

The choice variables for the planner are the per capita investment in the liquid asset (L), and the consumption of early diers (C_{1i}) and of late diers (C_{2i}) in type-i banks[5] $(i = 1, 2)$. The expected utility of a representative depositor at date 0, given the choice of $\{C_{1i}, C_{2i}\}_{i=1}^{2}$, is

$$V = \sum_{i=1}^{2} p_i\{t_i U(C_{1i}) + (1-t_i) U(C_{2i})\}. \qquad (2.5)$$

With probability p_i the depositor is in a type-i bank and, given that he finds himself in a type-i bank, the probability that he receives C_{1i} [respectively, C_{2i}] is t_i $[(1-t_i)]$.

The resource-balance constraints for the first period are implicit in the assumption that investment in the longer-term asset equals $(1-L)$. The resource-balance constraints for the second and third periods are, respectively,

$$\sum_{i=1}^{2} p_i t_i C_{1i} = L, \qquad (2.6a)$$

$$\sum_{i=1}^{2} p_i(1-t_i)C_{2i} = (1-L)R. \qquad (2.6b)$$

---

[4] This assumption is the most extreme form of allowing intermediaries to have superior ex ante information about their withdrawal pattern and liquidity needs. We also do not allow interbank contracts to respond to public information, if any, about realized preference shocks. Considerations outside our model (e.g., the effect of enhanced liquidity on the elimination of panics by depositors) provide additional justification for this assumption. Although it is not clear that our qualitative results would be affected by altering this assumption (when banks have imperfect private information about their local liquidity shocks), it would be interesting to consider extensions in which there are other liquidity effects, such as timing effects in liquid asset returns when intermediaries have asymmetric information about realized returns.

[5] This dependence on payments of early and later diers on the realized $\{t_i\}$ may to some extent be viewed as an adjustment of "implicit interest" paid to depositors, as documented by Startz (1979). More realistically, such adjustments should probably be viewed as erosions/additions to the shareholder equity in a bank. Under the latter interpretation, questions of aggregation of preferences across depositors and shareholders (in each bank) arise quite naturally, if simplicity in modeling preference shocks is to be preserved. Our two-point support assumption about $\{t_i\}$ may allow for some sort of Chipman aggregation if $U(\cdot)$ is homothetic (but possibly different across depositors and shareholders), because income-expansion paths are necessarily linear in this case.

The total per capita supply of goods is L at date 1 and $(1-L)R$ at date 2. A fraction p_i of the banks are in state i and the per capita demand for consumption in a type-i bank is $t_i C_{1i}$ at date 1 and $(1-t_i)C_{2i}$ at date 2. So the aggregate requirement for goods is $\sum p_i t_i C_{1i}$ at date 1 and $\sum p_i(1-t_i)C_{2i}$ at date 2.

The incentive-compatibility constraints are complicated by the mixture of moral hazard and adverse selection problems implicit in the model. An intermediary that wishes to deviate from the plan laid down by the planner can do so in two different ways. It can choose an investment in the liquid asset $\ell \neq L$ or it can report a realized state $s(i) \neq i$. Thus the action of a deviant intermediary can be represented by an ordered pair (ℓ, s), where ℓ is the choice of investment in the liquid asset and s is a signalling strategy. A type-i bank receives a net transfer of $(t_i C_{1i} - L)$ at date 1 and $((1-t_i)C_{2i} - (1-L)R)$ at date 2. These transfers are simply the difference between the per capita consumption level chosen by the planner and the per capita supply of goods available to the bank from its own investments. A deviant bank that chooses (ℓ, s) will therefore be able to give every early dier

$$\frac{t_{s(i)} C_{1s(i)} - L + \ell}{t_i}$$

units of consumption in state i. Similarly, in state i it can give every late dier

$$\frac{(1-t_{s(i)})C_{2s(i)} - (1-L)R + (1-\ell)R}{1-t_i}.$$

In order for the plan to be implemented there must be no incentive for any intermediary to deviate. That means that for any deviant action (s, ℓ) the expected utility of the representative depositor in the deviating intermediary must not exceed the expected utility of the representative depositor in an intermediary that does not deviate. Incentive-compatibility requires that, for any (ℓ, s),

$$\sum_{i=1}^{2} p_i\{t_i U(C_{1i}) + (1-t_i)U(C_{2i})\}$$

$$\geq \sum_{i=1}^{2} p_i\left\{t_i U\left[\frac{t_{s(i)} C_{1s(i)} + \ell - L}{t_i}\right]\right.$$

$$\left. + (1-t_i)U\left[\frac{(1-t_{s(i)})C_{2s(i)} + (L-\ell)R}{1-t_i}\right]\right\}. \quad (2.7)$$

Definition 2.1: The second-best optimal risk-sharing problem is solved by choosing $\{L, (C_{1i}, C_{2i})_{i=1}^{2}\}$ to maximize (2.5) subject to (2.6) and (2.7).

It is helpful, for analytical purposes as well as for the interpretation of the problem, to reformulate (2.5), (2.6), and (2.7) in terms of borrowing and lending. Let

$$B \equiv t_2 C_{12} - L \tag{2.8}$$

denote the net transfer to a type-2 bank at date 1. Resource balance (2.6a) implies that the net transfer to a type-1 bank is $-Bp_2/p_1$. We can interpret B as the net amount borrowed by a type-2 bank or lent by a type-1 bank. Of course, B may be positive or negative. Next let

$$DB \equiv R(1-L) - (1-t_2)C_{22} \tag{2.9}$$

denote the amount repaid by a type-2 bank at date 2, that is, the net transfer from the bank to the insurance system. Again, resource balance (2.6b) implies that the net transfer to a type-2 bank at date 2 is $-DBp_2/p_1$. The variable D implicitly defined by equation (2.9) can be interpreted as the (gross) borrowing (lending) rate. To simplify notation we deal explicitly only with the case $p_1 = p_2$. However, *all propositions are valid for the more general case $p_1 \neq p_2$*. Using equations (2.8) and (2.9), the planner's problem can be equivalently expressed as

$$V^* = \underset{\{B,D,L\}}{\text{Max}} \sum_{i=1}^{2} \left\{ t_i U\left[\frac{(-1)^i B + L}{t_i} \right] + (1-t_i) U\left[\frac{(-1)^{i+1} DB + (1-L)R}{1-t_i} \right] \right\} \tag{2.10}$$

subject to:

$$V^* \geq \sum_{i=1}^{2} \left\{ t_i U\left[\frac{(-1)^{s(i)} B + \ell}{t_i} \right] + (1-t_i) U\left[\frac{(-1)^{s(i)+1} DB + (1-\ell)R}{1-t_i} \right] \right\}$$

for any (s, ℓ). $\tag{2.11}$

The resource-balance constraints (2.6a) and (2.6b) have been subsumed in (2.10) using (2.8) and (2.9); (2.11) is the reformulated incentive-compatibility constraint.

3   Analysis of the optimal interbank contract

In this section we wish to examine the qualitative properties of the second-best optimal contract. We focus on the relationship between the return on interbank lending D and the return on the illiquid asset R, as well as on the relationship between the second-best optimal investment in liquid assets (reserves) L and the first-best investment L^*.

The constrained maximization problem stated in (2.10) and (2.11) is a rather complicated one. The incentive-compatibility constraint (2.11) does not lend itself to ordinary Lagrangean techniques because it contains a discrete variable s. One way to deal with the problem would be to re-place (2.11) with four separate constraints, one corresponding to each possible choice of s. Fortunately, there is an easier way: The problem can be further simplified so that it reduces to a standard Lagrangean prob-lem. The successive steps in this reduction are presented as a sequence of propositions. The proofs that are not given here can be found in the Ap-pendix to Bhattacharya and Gale (1986). The first thing to note is that, under the maintained assumptions, we have the following.

Proposition 1: *The first-best optimum is not attainable as a solution to the second-best risk-sharing problem defined by* (2.10) *and* (2.11) *when* $(t_2 - t_1)$ *is not too large.*

The next step is to note that the second-best optimum involves giving a net transfer (loan) to the intermediaries with a higher proportion of early diers at date 1.

Proposition 2: *If* (B, D, L) *is the second-best optimum contract, then* $B > 0$.

The next result shows that we do not need to consider all possible sig-naling strategies. Strictly speaking, incentive compatibility requires that (2.11) is satisfied for all possible deviations (s, ℓ). What matters, how-ever, is the deviations for which (2.11) is binding – that is, values of (s, ℓ) such that (2.11) is satisfied as an equation. Let $V(B, D, s, \ell)$ denote the expected utility ex ante of an intermediary who plans to use the deviation (s, ℓ). $V(B, D, s, \ell)$ is just the right-hand side of (2.11). We are concerned, therefore, with deviations that satisfy $V^* = V(B, D, s, \ell)$; these deviations are called *optimal* deviations. The next result tells us that we need not consider all possible signaling strategies. If (s, ℓ) is an optimal deviation then the signaling strategy s makes the same report in both states.

Proposition 3: *If* (s, ℓ) *is an optimal deviation – that is,* $V^* = V(B, D, s, \ell)$ *– then* $s(1) = s(2)$.

Thus, in considering deviations from the social optimum, one need only consider two possible signaling strategies: either the deviant always claims to be in type 1 or he always claims to be in type 2. Let j denote the re-ported type, now known to be independent of the true type. The incen-tive-compatibility constraint (2.11) can be written, without loss of gen-erality, as

$$V^* \geq \sum_{i=1}^{2} \left\{ t_i U\left[\frac{(-1)^j B + \ell}{t_i} \right] + (1 - t_i) U\left[\frac{(-1)^{j+1} DB + R(1 - \ell)}{1 - t_i} \right] \right\} \quad (3.1)$$

for any (ℓ, j). Note that since the right-hand side of (3.1) is strictly concave in ℓ, there is a unique optimal deviation corresponding to each choice of $j = 1, 2$.

Proposition 4: *Suppose that $V(B, D, j, \ell) = V^*$. Then $D < R$ implies $j = 2$ and $D > R$ implies $j = 1$.*

If the interbank rate is less than the rate of return of illiquid assets, a deviant bank will always claim to have a high proportion of early diers. It will borrow at date 1 whether it actually has a high proportion or a low proportion of early diers. Conversely, if the interbank rate is greater than the return on illiquid assets, a deviant bank will always lend to the system. These results are quite intuitive and, in fact, the proof follows from a straightforward dominance argument.

Proposition 4 does not tell us what happens when $D = R$. One might expect this to be a boundary case at which two constraints, corresponding to two optimal deviations, were just binding. In fact, there is no binding incentive-compatibility constraint in this case.

Proposition 5: *If (B, D, L) is an optimal contract and $D = R$, then there is no binding incentive-compatibility constraint; that is, the first-best is achieved.*

Thus, in the cases of interest, Proposition 4 applies and there is a unique optimal deviation for any optimal contract (B, D, L). [The value of j is given by Proposition 4 and, given j, there is a unique ℓ such that $V^* = V(B, D, j, \ell)$.] This means that there is a single incentive-compatibility constraint of the standard form, from which we can form a standard Lagrangean.

Proposition 6: *Let (B, D, L) be a second-best optimal contract that does not implement the first best. Then there is a Lagrangean multiplier λ and an optimal deviation (j, ℓ) such that (B, D, L, ℓ, λ) is an extreme point of the Lagrangean:*

$$\sum_{i=1}^{2} \left\{ t_i U\left[\frac{(-1)^i B + L}{t_i} \right] + (1 - t_i) U\left[\frac{(-1)^{i+1} DB + (1 - L)R}{1 - t_i} \right] \right\}$$
$$+ \lambda \left\{ V^* - \sum_{i=1}^{2} \left\{ t_i U\left[\frac{(-1)^j B + \ell}{t_i} \right] + (1 - t_i) U\left[\frac{(-1)^{j+1} DB + (1 - \ell)R}{1 - t_i} \right] \right\} \right\},$$

where $j = 1, 2$ as $D \gtreqless R$.

The analysis of this Lagrangean leads immediately to a characterization of the optimal consumption allocation $\{(C_{1i}, C_{2i})_{i=1}^{2}\}$.

Proposition 7: *Let (B, D, L) be a second-best optimal contract that does not implement the first best. Let $\{(C_{1i}, C_{2i})\}$ be the corresponding consumption allocation. Then*

$$U'(C_{1i}) = RU'(C_{2i}) \quad (i = 1, 2)$$

and

$$C_{11} \gtreqless C_{12} \quad as \quad D \lesseqgtr R.$$

There is a partial decentralization of the optimal consumption allocation, according to Proposition 7. For each $i = 1, 2$, the consumption pattern (C_{1i}, C_{2i}) solves the problem

$$\text{Max } t_i U(C_{1i}) + (1 - t_i) U(C_{2i}) \tag{3.2a}$$

$$\text{Subject to } t_{i1} C_{1i} + (1 - t_i) C_{2i}/R = W_i. \tag{3.2b}$$

It is as if the type-i bank were given a shadow income and allowed to allocate it, at the shadow prices $(1, R^{-1})$, to maximize the ex ante expected utility of its members conditional on the bank's type. Furthermore, the shadow income of a type-1 bank is greater (respectively, less) than that of a type-2 bank as D is less (greater) than R. The intuition behind this is quite straightforward. Suppose that $D > R$. Then Proposition 4 tells us that the optimal deviation from truth-telling always involves claiming to be a type-1 bank. In order to discourage deviations and hence relax the incentive-compatibility constraint, the planner reduces the planned utility of a type-1 bank and increases the planned utility of a type-2 bank. If $D < R$ the situation is simply reversed.[6]

The preceding discussion leaves open the question of whether D is greater than or less than R at the second-best optimum. Our intuition about the free-rider problem, presented in Section 2, suggests that deviant banks will want to borrow too much and invest too little in the liquid asset. In other words, $D < R$ so that $j = 2$ and $L < L^*$. The next proposition shows that this intuition is indeed justified when the preference shocks (t_1, t_2) do not differ very greatly.

Proposition 8: *Let (B, D, L) be a second-best optimal contract. Then $D < R$ if $t_2 - t_1$ is not too large.*

The proposition follows from an application of the envelope theorem at the point where $t_2 = t_1$. It can be shown that if t_2 rises slightly relative to

---

[6] Thus our results generalize to situations in which banks can locally reverse their two-period investment decisions at date 1, as in Diamond and Dybvig (1983), provided mechanisms for dealing with coordination problems across depositors are in place in each bank.

t_1, the ex ante expected utility of type-2 banks falls relative to that of type-1 banks. From Proposition 7 it follows that $D < R$. Thus, within some region next to the diagonal $\{t_1 = t_2\}$, the free-rider problem determines the outcome. Farther from the diagonal, the case $D > R$ may conceivably arise. It is worth noting that Proposition 8 does depend on the assumption that $U'(C)C$ is decreasing. If $U'(C)C$ were assumed increasing then the result could be reversed. For a particular class of utility functions the result in Proposition 8 can be shown to hold globally.

Proposition 8A: *Let $U(C) = (1/a)C^a$ ($a < 1$) and let (B, D, L) be an optimal, second-best contract. Then $D \lessgtr R$ as $a \lessgtr 0$.*

Note that the limiting case $a = 0$ corresponds to the logarithmic utility function, for which the first best is attainable and $D = R$.

Proposition 8B: *Let $U(C) = (1/a)\exp(aC)$ and let (B, D, L) be an optimal, second-best contract (i.e., not the first best). Then $D < R$ as $a < 0$.*

Finally we come to the question of how much investment in the liquid asset takes place at the second-best optimum. Is it greater or less than L^*? Here again the relationship between D and R appears to be crucial. In order to obtain a determinate result we have had to restrict our attention to a special class of utility functions. We assume that, for some constants α and β which depend on the utility function U,

$$RU'(\alpha + \beta x) = U'(x) \tag{3.3}$$

for all $x \geq 0$. Strictly speaking, (3.3) need only hold for $x \in \{C_{11}, C_{12}\}$, but we cannot guarantee this without assuming that (3.3) holds globally. Note that (3.3) is satisfied by such familiar examples as the quadratic utility function, logarithmic and power utility functions, and the exponential utility function.[7]

Proposition 9: *Let (B, D, L) be an optimal, second-best contract and suppose that U satisfies (3.3). Then $L \lessgtr L^*$ as $D \lessgtr R$.*

To summarize, we have shown that when the "normal case" (which arises in the neighborhood of the first-best solution) holds, $D < R$. Furthermore, when $D < R$, $L < L^*$. The optimal mechanism thus involves banks borrowing (and being forced to lend) at a subsidized rate, but results in

---

[7] Equation (3.3) is satisfied by all utility functions in the Hyperbolic Absolute Risk-Aversion (HARA) class, functions satisfying $U'(C)/U''(C) = a + bC$ for all C and for some a and b.

underinvestment in reserves relative to the first-best level that obtains in the absence of asymmetric information.

4   Preference shocks, adverse selection, and central banks

Our model with heterogeneous intermediaries above suggests a multiplicity of roles for a centralized institution, with respect to monitoring the values of key economic variables as well as permitting the date-0 commitment that our mechanism design formulation assumed. The first, and most obvious, role for a centralized (unduplicated) entity in our setting is that of improving the external observability of the date-0 investment allocation. Given our underinvestment (relative to the first-best) results above, even noisy imperfect monitoring is likely to be welfare-improving.[8] Of course, if $L = L^*$ could be perfectly enforced (i.e., "moving-support" monitoring) then free trading across intermediaries ex post would implement the first-best in our simple setup, along the lines of Section 2. This is unrealistic, however, given that the abstractions of asymmetric observability of L, as well as the illiquidity of longer-term investments, represent in reality asymmetric knowledge of the quality of a continuum of assets in overall bank portfolios.

Our results for borrowing/lending at $D < R$ (Proposition 8) may be combined with the above observation to yield a date-0 *reserve requirement* on which the full rate of interest is not paid, coupled with date-1 access to a "discount-window" (at a subsidized interest rate) that is made use of to a greater extent by type-2 banks. Note, however, that the right comparison to a market rate of interest is unclear, since free trading of intermediary claims to date-2 payoffs at date 1 may produce an interest rate that is strictly lower than R, as in the representative intermediary case of Section 2. In addition, our model does not account for voluntary reserves that are maintained because of risky loan assets (i.e., portfolio choice), nor for ongoing liquid reserve requirements (mandated or otherwise) beyond date 1. Making realistic connections to existing institutions and policies requires, in our opinion, further enrichment of (our type of) modeling to incorporate intertemporal and portfolio tradeoffs, as well as the juxtaposition of market versus nonmarket contracting in assets and liabilities.

Even within our simplified framework, however, it is possible to make the case for a nonmarket entity which acts as the planner (mechanism designer) that solves the second-best risk-sharing problem. This is the

---

[8] The proof of such a result will differ from that of Shavell (1979), given the essential interaction between heterogeneity and moral hazard in our model, where the first-best is achieved if either problem is absent.

case because both the problems of ex post state revelation and ex ante moral hazard must be dealt with.[9] As a result, while intermediaries which are ex ante identical may themselves design the allocation process analyzed above, at $T = 1$ there may be incentives for some to reverse themselves and propose alternative allocations. Knowing that such proposals might arise would, in turn, dilute the (second-best) optimal ex ante incentives. For example, given $D < R$ and the characterization in Proposition 7, type-1 intermediaries would not wish to lend as much at date 1 as the ex ante optimal mechanism calls for because $[-U'(C_{11}) + DU'(C_{21})] < 0$.

Some (limited) analyses of such "durability" problems have been carried out in the literature, in a market context by Rothschild and Stiglitz (1976) and Miyazaki (1977), and in a more explicitly strategic setting by Myerson (1983). Their results suggest that, in general, the ex ante optimum we have characterized cannot be attained by unfettered strategic interactions across privately motivated agents. Only a welfare-maximizing agent (such as a central bank), acting subject to resource and incentive constraints but with ex ante commitment, will suffice.

5   Concluding remarks

In contrast to our focus on central bank policy as a cross-sectional coordination device, several recent models have focused on the implications of aggregate shocks for various aspects of banking and monetary policy. Diamond and Dybvig (1983) have suggested that when the aggregate proportion of early-diers t is stochastic, central bank or governmental policy is (more) able to make depositors' real consumption payoff responsive to the realized value of t, even though individual (representative) banks are unable to do so. While their claim lacks a sound foundation in the form of an explicit model of fiscal or monetary allocation mechanisms, it is possible that further refinement of themes such as those developed in Bhattacharya (1982) – which suggest that monetary mechanisms for risk-sharing may be able to elicit information regarding heterogeneous agents with lower communication costs – may provide some justification for such a role for policy in an intertemporal overlapping-generations setting. Other models of banking with more explicit aggregate shocks, in the form of depositors' information about banks' asset returns, have been analyzed by Bryant (1980) and by Jacklin and Bhattacharya

[9] Essentially, agents' preference functionals are defined over a larger-dimensional commodity space than what is commonly observable – e.g., $(L^* - B)/t_1$ versus B. Given this, and a more general support for the distribution of the preference shock variable $\tilde{t}$, non-linear loan contracts across intermediaries (with some centralized monitoring of quantities) may be required.

(1985). These models suggest that governmental deposit insurance, possibly backed by powers of intergenerational taxation, may improve ex ante welfare by discouraging agents from collecting information about asset returns.

Without an explicit incorporation of fiat money into models of banking, it is clearly difficult to provide detailed monetary interpretations of results such as ours on underinvestment in liquid assets by banks and the resulting need for central-bank reserve requirements. Recently, Siegel (1981) has considered the role of optimal monetary reserve requirements in a model of banks which postulates demand and supply functions for banks' and depositors' portfolio choices across different classes of assets and liabilities. By considering exogenously given (aggregate) shocks to these functions, Siegel is able to develop a theory of price-level fluctuations and show that there exists an optimal reserve requirement that minimizes price-level variability. Furthermore, such an optimal reserve requirement does not minimize the variability of the usual ad hoc "money stock" measures aggregated across currency and deposits. These results are related to those of Weiss (1980), who shows that an active monetary policy responsive to realized investment return shocks may improve the information content of nominal prices by removing the portfolio reactions of agents who have superior information about asset returns.

The lines of enquiry pursued in the work of Siegel and Weiss ought to be incorporated in greater detail in richer models of banking, models that incorporate the roles of interbank coordination as well as aggregate shocks. In particular, the explicit modeling of preference-shocks in agents' objective functions – characteristic of the latter type of models – should be preserved. As Polemarchakis and Weiss (1977) and Muench (1977) have noted in the context of the Lucas (1972) model, plausible derivative goals such as those optimized in the models of Siegel and Weiss may not be welfare-optimal in models that explicitly incorporate (market incompleteness arising from) privately observed preference shocks. Our understanding of the role of and interactions among contractual and market-mediated allocation processes (e.g., banks and mutual funds), and the resulting implications for government policy, is likely to be greatly enhanced by the process of integrating these diverse types of models.

Appendix

Proof of Proposition 7: Differentiate the Lagrangean in Proposition 6 with respect to B, D, L, and ℓ and set the partial derivatives equal to zero. Using the notation $U'_{Ti} \equiv U'(C_{Ti})$ for $T, i = 1, 2$ and

$$\hat{U}'_{1i} \equiv U'\left[\frac{(-1)^j B + \ell}{t_i}\right], \qquad \hat{U}'_{2i} \equiv U'\left[\frac{(-1)^{j+1} DB + (1-\ell)R}{1-t_i}\right]$$

for $i = 1, 2$, this gives us the following equations:

$$\sum_{i=1}^{2} \{U'_{1i}(-1)^i + U'_{2i}(-1)^{i+1}D\} - \lambda \sum_{i=1}^{2} \{\hat{U}'_{1i}(-1)^j + \hat{U}'_{2i}(-1)^{j+1}D\} = 0,$$

$$\tag{A.1}$$

$$\sum_{i=1}^{2} \{U'_{2i}(-1)^{i+1}B - \lambda \hat{U}'_{2i}(-1)^{j+1}B\} = 0, \tag{A.2}$$

$$\sum_{i=1}^{2} \{U'_{1i} - U'_{2i}R\} = 0, \tag{A.3}$$

$$\sum_{i=1}^{2} \lambda\{\hat{U}'_{1i} - \hat{U}'_{2i}R\} = 0. \tag{A.4}$$

Because $B > 0$, equation (A.2) implies that

$$\sum_{i=1}^{2} \{U'_{2i}(-1)^{i+1}D - \lambda \hat{U}'_{2i}(-1)^{j+1}D\} = 0, \tag{A.5}$$

and substituting this equation into (A.1) gives

$$\sum_{i=1}^{2} U'_{1i}(-1)^i - \lambda \sum_{i=1}^{2} \hat{U}'_{1i}(-1)^j = 0. \tag{A.6}$$

From (A.4) and (A.2) (recalling $B > 0$) we obtain

$$\sum_{i=1}^{2} \{\lambda \hat{U}'_{1i}(-1)^j - U'_{2i}(-1)^i R\} = 0. \tag{A.7}$$

Substituting (A.7) into (A.6) gives us

$$\sum_{i=1}^{2} \{U'_{1i}(-1)^i - U'_{2i}(-1)^i R\} = 0. \tag{A.8}$$

But (A.3) and (A.8) together imply that

$$U'_{1i} - RU'_{2i} = 0 \tag{A.9}$$

for $i = 1, 2$.

From (A.6) it is clear that

$$\sum_{i=1}^{2} U'_{1i}(-1)^i \lessgtr 0 \quad \text{as } j = 1, 2.$$

Thus $j = 2$ implies $U'_{12} > U'_{11}$ and $j = 1$ implies $U'_{11} > U'_{12}$. In view of (A.9) this means that $(C_{12}, C_{22}) \ll (C_{11}, C_{21})$ if $j = 2$ and $(C_{11}, C_{21}) \ll (C_{12}, C_{22})$ if $j = 1$.   Q.E.D.

Proof of Proposition 8A: We give the proof when $a < 0$. The other case is similar. From Proposition 7,

$$\left(\frac{L-B}{t_1}\right)^{a-1} = R\left(\frac{R(1-L)+DB}{1-t_1}\right)^{a-1} \tag{A.10}$$

and

$$\left(\frac{L+B}{t_2}\right)^{a-1} = R\left(\frac{R(1-L)-DB}{1-t_2}\right)^{a-1} \tag{A.11}$$

Rearranging (A.10) and (A.11), we obtain

$$\left(\frac{L-B}{t_1}\right) = R^\gamma(R(1-L)+DB)+(L-B), \tag{A.12}$$

$$\left(\frac{L+B}{t_2}\right) = R^\gamma(R(1-L)-DB)+(L+B), \tag{A.13}$$

where $\gamma = 1/(a-1)$. Subtracting (A.13) from (A.12) gives

$$\left(\frac{L-B}{t_1}\right)-\left(\frac{L+B}{t_2}\right)=(R^\gamma D-1)2B.$$

If (contrary to what we wish to prove) $D \geq R$ then $R^\gamma D > 1$, contradicting Proposition 7. So $D < R$ as required.   Q.E.D.

Proof of Proposition 8B: From (A.9) we have

$$\exp[-a(L-B)/t_1] = R\exp[-a\{R(1-L)+DB\}/(1-t_1)].$$

Taking logarithms and rearranging gives us:

$$C_{11} = (L-B)/t_1 = -(\ln R)/a + \{R(1-L)+DB+L-B\}. \tag{A.14}$$

Similarly, it can be shown that

$$C_{12} = (L+B)/t_2 = -(\ln R)/a + \{R(1-L)-DB+L+B\}. \tag{A.15}$$

Subtracting (A.16) from (A.15) yields:

$$C_{11}-C_{12} = 2B(D-1).$$

If $D > R > 1$ then $C_{11}-C_{12} > 0$, contradicting Proposition 7, so we must have $D < R$.   Q.E.D.

Proof of Proposition 9: From Proposition 7 and condition (13), $C_{1i} = \alpha+\beta C_{2i}$ for $i = 1, 2$. Then

$$\tfrac{1}{2}(t_1 C_{11}+t_2 C_{12}) = \alpha t + \beta(\tfrac{1}{2}t_1 C_{21}+\tfrac{1}{2}t_2 C_{22}). \tag{A.16}$$

Because $t_1 < t_2$ and $C_{21} \leq C_{22}$ as $D \geq R$ (Proposition 7), it follows that

$$\frac{t_1 C_{21} + t_2 C_{22}}{t_1 + t_2} \gtreqless \frac{(1-t_1)C_{21} + (1-t_2)C_{22}}{(1-t_1) + (1-t_2)} \quad \text{as } D \gtreqless R. \qquad \text{(A.17)}$$

From the feasibility conditions (2.6a) and (2.6b), the left-hand side of (A.16) is L and the right-hand side of (A.17) is $R(1-L)/(1-t)$. Then (A.16) and (A.17) together imply that

$$L/t \gtreqless \alpha + \beta R(1-L)/(1-t) \quad \text{as } D \gtreqless R. \qquad \text{(A.18)}$$

Now condition (3.3) and the first-best optimal condition (2.4) imply that L^* satisfies $L^*/t = \alpha + \beta R(1-L^*)/(1-t)$. Comparison with (A.18) yields the desired result.   Q.E.D.

REFERENCES

Akerlof, George. 1970. "The Market for Lemons: Quality Uncertainty and the Market Mechanism." *Quarterly Journal of Economics* 84: 488–500.

Bhattacharya, S. 1982. "Aspects of Monetary and Banking Theory and Moral Hazard." *Journal of Finance* 37: 371–84.

Bhattacharya, S., and D. Gale. 1986. "Preference Shocks, Liquidity, and Central Bank Policy." CARESS Working Paper #86-01, University of Pennsylvania.

Bryant, J. 1980. "A Model of Reserves, Bank Runs and Deposit Insurance." *Journal of Banking and Finance* 4: 335–44.

Diamond, D. W. 1984. "Financial Intermediation and Delegated Monitoring." *Review of Economic Studies* 51: 393–414.

Diamond, D. W., and P. H. Dybvig. 1983. "Bank Runs, Deposit Insurance, and Liquidity." *Journal of Political Economy* 91: 401–19.

Hansen, L. P., and K. J. Singleton. 1983. "Stochastic Consumption, Risk Aversion, and the Temporal Behavior of Asset Returns." *Journal of Political Economy* 91: 249–65.

Holmstrom, B. 1979. "Moral Hazard and Observability." *Bell Journal of Economics* 10: 74–91.

Jacklin, C. 1986. "Demand Deposits, Trading Restrictions and Risk Sharing." In E. C. Prescott and N. Wallace (eds.), *Contractual Arrangements for Intertemporal Trade*, University of Minnesota Press.

Jacklin, C., and S. Bhattacharya. 1985. "Distinguishing Panics and Information-Based Bank Runs: Welfare and Policy Implications." Unpublished manuscript, University of Chicago.

Leland, H., and D. Pyle. 1977. "Informational Asymmetrics, Financial Structure and Financial Intermediation." *Journal of Finance* 32: 371–87.

Lucas, R. E., Jr. 1972. "Expectations and the Neutrality of Money." *Journal of Economic Theory* 4: 103–24.

Miyazaki, H. 1977. "The Rat Race and Internal Labor Markets." *Bell Journal of Economics* 8: 394–418.

Muench, T. 1977. "Optimality, the Interaction of Spot and Futures Markets, and the Nonneutrality of Money in the Lucas Model." *Journal of Economic Theory* 15: 325–44.

Myerson, R. B. 1983. "Mechanism Design by an Informed Principal." *Econometrica* 51: 1767–97.

Polemarchakis, H. M., and L. Weiss. 1977. "On the Desirability of a Totally Random Monetary Policy." *Journal of Economic Theory* 15: 345–50.

Rothschild, M., and J. E. Stiglitz. 1976. "Equilibrium in Competitive Insurance Markets." *Quarterly Journal of Economics* 90: 629–49.

Shavell, S. 1979. "Risk Sharing and Incentives in the Principal-Agent Model." *Bell Journal of Economics* 10: 55–73.

Siegel, J. J. 1981. "Bank Reserves and Financial Stability." *Journal of Finance* 36: 1073–84.

Startz, R. 1979. "Implicit Interest on Demand Deposits." *Journal of Monetary Economics* 5: 515–34.

Weiss, L. M. 1980. "The Role for Active Monetary Policy in a Rational Expectations Model." *Journal of Political Economy* 88: 221–33.

CHAPTER 5

Banking and macroeconomic equilibrium

Ben Bernanke and Mark Gertler

1 Introduction

The Miller–Modigliani theorem asserts that, in a setting of perfect capital
markets, economic decisions do not depend on financial structure. An
implication is that the addition of financial intermediaries to this type of
environment has no consequence for real activity.

A number of recent papers [e.g., Bernanke (1983), Blinder and Stiglitz (1983), Boyd and Prescott (1983), Townsend (1983), and Williamson
(1985)] have questioned the relevance of this proposition, even as an approximation, for macroeconomic analysis. Instead, they revive the view
of Gurley and Shaw (1956), Patinkin (1961), Brainard and Tobin (1963),
and others that the quality and quantity of services provided by intermediaries are important determinants of aggregate economic performance.
The basic premise is that, in the absence of intermediary institutions, informational problems cause financial markets to be incomplete. By spe-
cializing in gathering information about loan projects, and by permitting
pooling and risk-sharing among depositors, financial intermediaries help
reduce market imperfections and improve the allocation of resources.
Thus, changes in the level of financial intermediation due to monetary
policy, legal restrictions, or other factors may have significant real effects
on the economy. For example, Bernanke (1983) argued that the severity
of the Great Depression was due in part to the loss in intermediary services suffered when the banking system collapsed in 1930–33.

The objective of this paper is to provide an additional step toward understanding the role of financial intermediaries (hereafter, simply "banks")
in aggregate economic activity. We employ a model of the banking sector

We would like to thank Darrel Duffie, Nobu Kiyotaki, Arnold Kling, David Romer, Bruce
Smith, Rob Townsend, Steve Williamson and two anonymous referees for reading an ear-
lier draft of this paper and providing helpful comments. Financial support from the Alfred
P. Sloan Foundation and the National Science Foundation is gratefully acknowledged.

that is highly simplified, but rich enough to motivate several character-istic features of banks. When embedded in a general equilibrium setting, this model implies that banks play an important role in real allocation and are not merely financial veils. A key premise is that, due to a cost advantage in project evaluation, banks provide the only available conduit between savers and certain types of investments. Thus, factors which affect the ability of banks to provide intermediary services, or which directly affect the costs of intermediation, will have real effects.

Our specific results focus on the critical importance for the macro-economy of the financial health of the banking sector itself. We show that (1) the adequacy of bank capital and (2) a measure of the perceived quality of the bank's potential investments (specifically, the lower support of the distribution of possible returns) affect the proportions of bank deposits allocated between illiquid risky investments with high mean returns and safe assets with low yields; and that when there exists an alternative to the banking sector, that these factors also affect the quantity of deposits that banks can attract. This behavior has direct implications for aggregate investment, output, and interest rates. As we discuss briefly, our model is potentially useful for understanding the macroeconomic effects of phenomena such as financial crises, banking regulation, and certain types of monetary policy.

The paper is organized as follows. In Section 2, we outline some features of banking relevant to macroeconomic behavior. Section 3 develops a simple general equilibrium model with consumers and banks. Steady-state equilibria are characterized in Section 4. In Section 5, we analyze how the equilibrium is affected by the addition of an alternative investment sector (in which there are none of the information problems that exist in the banking sector). Section 6 discusses some applications.

2   Modeling banks: some basic assumptions

A voluminous and growing literature analyzes the banking firm and its relations with borrowers, depositors, and the government; many subtle issues in the economics of information, incentives, and insurance have been raised. It is, however, far beyond the scope of the present paper to attempt to develop a model of banking that fully reflects the insights of this literature. Instead, our approach is to make a number of strong simplifying assumptions that may be used to motivate, in an internally consistent way, the features of banking relevant to macroeconomic performance.[1]

---

[1] An additional important feature of banks, which we will not however emphasize in this paper, is their role in facilitating transactions. For a model of banking that focuses on their transactions role, see Fischer (1983).

Obviously, such an exercise can be useful if one believes (as we do) that the character of the results would remain essentially unchanged under more realistic assumptions.

As a preliminary to the analysis, this section states some of the key simplifying assumptions and provides some discussion. All assumptions are restated in the more formal setup of the model in Section 3.

1. It will be assumed throughout that there are certain investment projects in the economy in which consumers can invest only through the intermediation of the banking system. To motivate this, we postulate that there exist projects which require specialized evaluation and monitoring; that these evaluations can be performed only via a technology with a large fixed cost; and that because of this fixed cost the evaluation technology is accessible to banks but not to individuals. It will also be assumed that the postulated technology is used by banks for ex post monitoring of returns as well as for ex ante evaluation. This last assumption, which may be rationalized as arising from an informational economy of scope, may be used to explain why the institutions which initiate loans also hold them as assets.

The specialness of bank assets, due to the exclusive access of banks to a class of projects, is obviously going to be an important reason why changes in the level of intermediation will have real effects in this analysis. What is important here, however, is not that the banking system has unique access to certain projects; rather, only that specialization gives banks some cost advantage, perhaps only a temporary one, in making certain types of loans. There is considerable evidence that this lending advantage, reflected in the imperfect substitutability between certain types of bank loans and open market credit, is an important characteristic of banking. [See, e.g., Fama (1985).]

2. A second assumption we make is that any information gained from project evaluation and monitoring remains private to the bank. As with Diamond (1984) and Williamson, the purpose of this assumption is to motivate simply – but in a manner consistent with agency theory – the heavy reliance of banks on (noncontingent) debt as a source of funds. The argument for debt from this assumption is direct: If returns to bank investments are not publicly observable, then it will not be incentive-compatible for payoffs to the bank's suppliers of funds to be contingent on those returns.

We view the assumption that bank asset returns are not publicly observable to be a stand-in for more complex informational and agency problems that in the real world lead to bank reliance on debt. Nonetheless, it is worth noting that the assumption of nonobservability of returns is frequently made in the banking literature and is taken fairly seriously as a literal description. For example, Cone (1982) and Diamond (1984) give excellent expositions of the close relationship between banks and loan customers, especially long-term customers with complex credit needs: Banks need the privileged information gained via these relationships in order to ensure that loan covenants are observed and to decide whether these lending relationships should be continued. Because the information about the current status of loans is costly to obtain and highly idiosyncratic, it is not easily observed by depositors or other outsiders.[2]

3. So that the model may include potential risk to bank depositors, it will be assumed that bank investment projects are large, and that the evaluation and monitoring technology permits an individual bank to handle only a number of projects that is too small to permit perfect diversification of the risk to bank assets.[3] The potential depositor risk will imply in our analysis that factors affecting the soundness of bank liabilities (i.e., bank capital and the quality of bank assets) will determine the scale of banking, which in turn will have macroeconomic consequences.

4. Because bank portfolios are risky and depositors cannot observe the returns, it is necessary to consider how bank liabilities can be made incentive-compatible. In practice, an important way that banks secure debt is by the holding of insider bank capital.[4] The latter is equity that is either obtained directly from the owner/managers or from retained earnings.[5] So that our analysis may include this important factor, we assume below that bank owner/managers have capital that yields dividends each period. Since greater amounts of insider capital allow banks to issue more deposits, ceteris paribus, we will conclude that this quantity is very important in the determination of resource allocation between bank investment and other uses. Similarly, the quality of bank investment projects is also relevant, because it affects the quantity of deposits that can be supported per unit of insider capital.

---

[2] Indeed, Peltzman (1970) notes that even professional bank examiners typically focus on the quantity of bank capital relative to the quantities of certain broad categories of loans, since individual bank assets are so difficult to value.

[3] Banks appear to specialize in certain types of loans (e.g., energy, agricultural, or regional loans) rather than hold portfolios which completely diversify independent risk. The assumptions just made in the text can be viewed as attempting to motivate behavior consistent with this observation.

[4] When government deposit insurance does exist, it is usually accompanied by regulations that establish minimum capital requirements for a given amount of intermediation. We briefly discuss government intervention in banking in Section 6, and expect to address this issue more directly in later research.

[5] Roughly 50 percent of bank equity can be viewed as "insider" [cf. Table 1 of *Bank Operating Statistics* (1983, p. 2)]. We focus on inside equity because – as discussed in Section 5 – outside equity, which is raised by issuing securities to the general public (i.e., nonmanagers), is not useful in solving the agency problem arising between the bank and its depositors.

5. Finally, a factor traditionally cited as relevant to banking stability is that bank liabilities are mostly short-term and highly liquid relative to bank assets. To explore the effect of this additional complexity, we introduce demand deposits into our model by assuming that consumers face private liquidity risks, as in Bryant (1980) and Diamond and Dybvig (1983). This assumption serves to motivate a liquidity management problem; banks must adjust their portfolios so that the pattern of asset returns can support short-term debt obligations. We differ from the other authors by exploring the implications for resource allocation rather than for "sunspot" bank runs, as we discuss.

3 Setup of the basic model with consumers and banks

We consider an intertemporal economy with the following production possibilities. There is one type of output, a consumption good. The consumption good is perishable and must be consumed in the same period that it is produced. The only input is an endowment good, which cannot be consumed immediately. There exist two technologies for converting endowment to consumption, which we refer to as the liquid and illiquid investments. The former involves storing endowment for one period; one unit of endowment stored at t yields one unit of consumption at $t+1$. The latter involves investing endowment in a project which yields a stochastic amount of output in two periods. The gross return per unit of endowment invested is given by the random variable $\tilde{R}$, which is supported on the closed interval $[R^\ell, R^h]$, with $R^\ell < R^h$. The lower bound of the support R^ℓ is meant to reflect the sum of the minimum possible output yield and the scrap value measured in terms of the consumption good. We may think of R^ℓ as the per unit collateral value of an illiquid project. All illiquid investments have the same expected return R and collateral value R^ℓ, per unit of endowment invested. However, realized project returns are independent.

We will assume that no information problems attach to the liquid investment. In contrast, an information-gathering technology is necessary to "find" illiquid projects and to monitor their ex post returns.

The consumer sector of this economy consists of overlapping generations of identical agents, each of whom lives three periods. The population of consumers is represented as a continuum of constant length. Each newly born agent receives W units of the endowment good, but does not consume until either the second or third period of life. Individuals face idiosyncratic liquidity risks. A fraction α of the population born at time t are type I's who receive utility from consumption only in $t+1$; conversely, $(1-\alpha)$ are type II's who receive utility only in $t+2$. (A specific utility function is later assumed.) An individual agent's type is private information. However, consumers must decide how to allocate their endowment before they learn their respective types. Their options are storage (i.e., direct investment in the liquid asset) and lending to the banking system, described below. A consumer cannot directly invest in illiquid projects because evaluating and auditing of the projects is prohibitively costly for individuals.

The banking sector, upon which we will focus most of our attention, has the following properties. There exist a fixed number of agents distinct from consumers, termed bankers, who are infinitely lived and risk-neutral.[6] Each banker has access to the project evaluation and monitoring technology, and also owns a non-marketable physical asset which yields a fixed stream of the endowment good each period. As discussed earlier, insider bank capital is postulated as a source of collateral to overcome the agency problems that arise in this model.

Having access to the banking technology enables a banker to locate one potentially profitable illiquid project each period, in which an arbitrary amount of endowment can be invested. As discussed in Section 2, we assume technology constrains the number of illiquid investments a bank can process, so that it is not possible to completely diversify the nonsystematic risk: Otherwise, the agency problem between depositors and the bank would disappear. Given this restriction, there is no loss in generality from assuming that unity is the maximum number of projects per period which technology permits the bank to handle. The same technology enables the bank to observe the true realization of the investment project's return, so that a single institution performs both evaluation and monitoring functions. We postulate that the endowment required as input for the technology (the marginal intermediation cost) is proportional to the size of the project.[7] For each unit of endowment used as input in the illiquid investment, the intermediation cost is δ units of endowment.

Let L_t (for liabilities) be the flow of new endowment the bank borrows from others at time t, W_b the yield in endowment from bank capital each period, S_t the amount of endowment the bank invests in the liquid asset (storage), and I_t the amount invested in the illiquid project. The representative bank's resource constraint is given by

[6] The risk-neutrality assumption plays no critical role but is adopted for convenience. It is also possible to conduct the analysis with finite-lived bankers; however, in this case certain inefficiencies arise in equilibrium which we do not consider to be fundamentally interesting. The exogenous division of the population into bankers and nonbankers is a weakness of our model; see Boyd and Prescott (1983) for a model in which this division is endogenous.

[7] See Williamson (1984) for framework which explicitly motivates intermediation costs and scale economies in intermediation arising from costly state verification of loan contracts. We believe Williamson's analysis could be integrated with ours without affecting our basic conclusions.

$$L_t + W_b = (1 + \delta)I_t + S_t. \tag{3.1}$$

Banks acquire deposits during each time interval from newly born agents who, as just described, expect to receive utility from consumption in either the subsequent period or the one after. Since depositors cannot observe the returns to the banks' illiquid investments, equity contracts are inadmissible. However, at least three basic types of debt-type deposit contracts are possible (plus linear combinations). These are: (1) "storage contracts" that pay the depositor a fixed sum in the second period of life, one period after the initial deposit; (2) "time deposits" T that pay a fixed sum two periods after the deposit, in the depositor's third period of life; and (3) "demand deposits" D which, as in Diamond and Dybvig, the depositor may redeem at his volition, but in an amount that depends on whether he withdraws in the second or third period of life. Because depositors are uncertain about the timing of their desire to withdraw, it is straightforward to demonstrate that in equilibrium they will always prefer demand deposit contracts to storage and/or time deposits, as long as the former are incentive-compatible. We show subsequently (in a footnote) that the environment we postulate precludes incentive problems with demand deposits.

We therefore take all bank deposits made by consumers to be representable as demand deposits. In addition, it will be convenient for exposition to allow banks to buy and sell time deposits among themselves. Since banks are identical, the equilibrium quantity of these financial instruments is zero; however, allowing them to be traded permits us to characterize the behavior of the time deposit rate, which will prove useful. Accordingly, we can disaggregate the net flow of new deposits as follows:

$$L_t = D_t + T_t - T_{b,t}, \tag{3.2}$$

where (again) L_t is new bank liabilities at t, D_t is new demand deposits from consumers, T_t is new time deposits issued to other banks, and $T_{b,t}$ is the bank's new holdings of time deposits at other banks.

Let r_t be the rate of return on time deposits acquired at t. Let r_t^1 and r_t^2 be the rates of return on demand deposits acquired at t and redeemed after one and two periods, respectively. The expression for the bank's profit each period $\tilde{\Pi}_t$ is

$$\tilde{\Pi}_t = \tilde{R}_t I_{t-2} + S_{t-1} - \alpha r_{t-1}^1 D_{t-1} - (1-\alpha)r_{t-2}^2 D_{t-2} - r_{t-2}(T_{t-2} - T_{b,t-2}). \tag{3.3}$$

The first term on the right-hand side reflects gross returns from the bank's illiquid investment, made two periods earlier. The second is the return from storing endowment, that is, from the liquid investment. The last three terms represent the bank's net obligations at t. Depositors will withdraw the fraction α (representing the percentage of type I's in each generation) of deposits made one period earlier, and the fraction $1-\alpha$ (reflecting the percentage of type II's) of deposits made two periods ago. Also, all time deposits either issued or acquired by the bank two periods earlier come due.

Since bank liabilities are potentially risky, it is necessary to consider how these debt contracts can be made incentive-compatible.[8] A potentially interesting type of contract involves making payments contingent on default versus nondefault states. Such an arrangement would specify a fixed return the bank would pay its depositors, as long as it continues to operate. Not meeting this obligation implies the bank is in default; the contract in this case specifies another payment. Making this scheme incentive-compatible requires either imposing some form of punishment on bankers who default [as in Diamond (1984)], or having lenders undertake costly auditing [as in Townsend (1979) or Williamson (1984)]. For our purposes, this approach has two limitations (besides the problem of tractability in our setting). First, forming this type of contract requires that depositors have more information about bank assets than we feel is plausible; they must know the distribution of the returns to the bank's illiquid projects.[9] Second, collateral such as bank capital has no role, even though empirically it appears highly relevant.

Instead of a contract with default contingencies, we will consider an arrangement where a bank uses its supply of insider capital to perfectly collateralize its debt. This contract involves the bank planning its illiquid and liquid investments so as to be able to meet its deposit obligations in each period, even under the worst possible set of outcomes on its risky projects. (As will become obvious, the bank's base of insider capital may restrict its portfolio choice under this scheme.) Recall that we have postulated the collateral value of an illiquid project to be publicly observable. Hence, if we also assume that the quantities of bank deposits, illiquid

---

[8] Even though our model is dynamic, there is no scope for reputation building to induce honest reporting by banks. The reason for this is that for each period banks are identical ex ante. (Differences arise only because of the ex post returns to their portfolios, which are realized independently.) Hence, honest reporting (which is not verifiable by depositors) does not enhance a bank's reputation. An interesting extension of this analysis would be to introduce some form of heterogeneity that would allow a meaningful role for reputation building.

[9] Usually, one appeals to rational expectations to justify agents knowing the relevant objective probability distributions. However, this assumption may be overly strong in this case, given the highly idiosyncratic nature of many bank loan projects and the fact that (in the real world) projects are not identical over time. We feel it plausible to restrict depositors' knowledge to the collateral value of bank assets.

investment, and storage are observable, then the deposit contract is clearly incentive-compatible.

We conjecture that allowing for default would not affect our basic conclusions, so long as default is costly. If the latter is true, then banks will still rely heavily on collateral arrangements to secure their debt, as we describe. Further, even though our model does not allow for bank failure, there can be sharp contractions of the banking system, as we discuss in Section 6. For the purpose of macroeconomic analysis, such a contraction is essentially equivalent to a wave of bank failures.

For bank debt contracts to be incentive-compatible, we therefore require the following condition to hold for all $t > 0$:

$$R^\ell I_{t-1} + S_t \geq \alpha r_t^1 D_t + (1-\alpha) r_{t-1}^2 D_{t-1} + r_{t-1}(T_{t-1} - T_{b,t-1}).   \qquad (3.4)$$

We refer to (3.4) as the bank's liquidity constraint. The left-hand side of the inequality is the sum the bank will be able to pay at $t+1$ in the event that all its illiquid investments pay the minimum possible gross return R^ℓ. The right-hand side is the bank's net obligation at $t+1$. In the initial period zero, when the bank has neither investments nor deposits from the past, the relevant constraint is

$$S_0 \geq \alpha r_0^1 D_0.   \qquad (3.5)$$

Each banker's objective is to choose the sequence of assets and liabilities $\{I_t, S_t, D_t, T_t, T_{b,t}\}_{t=0}^\infty$ to maximize the intertemporal sum of expected profits, that is,

$$E_0 \left\{ \sum_{t=1}^\infty \tilde{\Pi}_t \right\},   \qquad (3.6)$$

subject to the constraints (3.1)–(3.5), and where E_0 is the mathematical expectation operator conditional on information at time zero. Recall that bank profits come in the form of the output good which cannot be reinvested. This assumption greatly simplifies the analysis by making the bank's sequential decisions independent of the returns to earlier investments. It also makes it unnecessary to introduce an arbitrary discount factor in (3.6) to bound the accumulation of wealth.

To solve the bank's optimal control problem, we may use the resource constraint (3.1) and the deposit relation (3.2) to eliminate total deposits L_t and demand deposits D_t from the problem. Let λ_t be the multiplier associated with the constraint (3.4). Then, the first-order necessary conditions for illiquid investment I_t and storage S_t are, respectively,

$$[R + \lambda_{t+1} R^\ell]/(1+\delta) \leq [(1+\lambda_t)\alpha r_t^1 + (1+\lambda_{t+1})(1-\alpha) r_t^2],   \qquad (3.7)$$

$$(1+\lambda_t) \leq [(1+\lambda_t)\alpha r_t^1 + (1+\lambda_{t+1})(1-\alpha) r_t^2].   \qquad (3.8)$$

Equation (3.7) holds with equality when I_t is greater than zero, and the same is true for (3.8) when S_t is positive.

The first-order conditions for T_t and $T_{b,t}$ together imply an arbitrage relationship between the expected returns on demand and time deposits, as follows:

$$r_t(1+\lambda_{t+1}) = [(1+\lambda_t)\alpha r_t^1] + [(1+\lambda_{t+1})(1-\alpha)r_t^2]. \tag{3.9}$$

According to (3.9), the bank's valuations of the respective returns on time and demand deposits must be equal. This condition eliminates the bank's incentive to take an infinitely long or short position in either of the instruments.

Finally, we impose the following pair of conditions on the return to the illiquid project:

$$R/(1+\delta)>1, \qquad R^\ell<1. \tag{3.10}$$

The conditions ensure the following behavior. First, when the liquidity constraint is not binding, banks will desire to invest exclusively in illiquid projects because the expected return to illiquid projects [equal to $R/(1+\delta)$] exceeds the return on liquid investments (equal to unity). Second, when the liquidity constraint is binding, banks may prefer to hold at least some liquid assets because the minimum return to the illiquid investment R^ℓ is less than the return to storage. We elaborate in Section 4.

4   Equilibrium with consumers and banks

We are now in a position to determine the equilibrium allocation between illiquid and liquid projects, and the corresponding behavior of the rates of return on demand and time deposits. A point we will emphasize is that, because of private information about bank assets, the equilibrium is highly sensitive to the availability of insider bank capital and the collateral value of illiquid projects.

So as to avoid keeping track of population parameters, we normalize the number of consumers in each generation at unity and also normalize the number of banks at unity. Thus, for each period, the total endowment received by consumers is W and the yield that bankers receive from bank capital is W_b.

We recall from an earlier discussion that we need only consider equilibria in which consumers invest all their endowment in demand deposits. In equilibrium, therefore, we have

$$D_t = W. \tag{4.1}$$

The relation between demand and time deposit rates

To calculate the equilibrium, it is first necessary to characterize the behavior of deposit rates. In this section we establish the link between the demand and time deposit rates. Subsequently we will describe the relation between the time deposit rate and the expected rate of return on the bank's portfolio.

At time t, the bank offers newly born agents demand deposit contracts yielding r_t^1 if withdrawn one period later or r_t^2 if held for two periods. From the discussion at the end of Section 3 it is clear that (given r_t) the bank is indifferent at the margin among combinations of r_t^1 and r_t^2 satisfying the arbitrage relation (3.9) between the returns to time and demand deposits. Therefore, the pair which survives in the marketplace should be the one which maximizes consumer's utility, subject to the relation (3.9), and also subject to an incentive-compatibility condition discussed below.

Assume that $\ln[c_{t+1}^I]$ and $\ln[c_{t+2}^{II}]$ are the ex post utility functions for agents born at t who become (respectively) type I's and type II's, where c_j^i is consumption by a type i ($i = I, II$) at time j. The representative newly born agent at t then has the following expected utility function:

$$E_t\{U(c_{t+1}^I, c_{t+2}^{II})\} = \alpha \ln[c_{t+1}^I] + (1 - \alpha) \ln[c_{t+2}^{II}]. \qquad (4.2)$$

Further, since agents allocate all their endowment to demand deposits,

$$c_{t+1}^I = r_t^1 D_t = r_t^1 W, \qquad (4.3)$$

$$c_{t+2}^{II} = r_t^2 D_t = r_t^2 W. \qquad (4.4)$$

The equilibrium pair (r_t^1, r_t^2) is the one that maximizes (4.2), subject to (3.9), (4.3), and (4.4). Solving this problem yields

$$r_t^1 = [(1 + \lambda_{t+1})/(1 + \lambda_t)]r_t, \qquad (4.5)$$

$$r_t^2 = r_t. \qquad (4.6)$$

As demonstrated in Bernanke and Gertler (1985) (hereafter, "B/G"), λ_{t+1} is always less than or equal to λ_t. It follows that r_t^1 is always less than or equal to r_t^2.

As noted, (4.5) and (4.6) give true equilibrium values for deposit rates only if the deposit contract is incentive-compatible. Specifically, it must be verified that, given (4.5) and (4.6), it will not be in the interest of a consumer who learns he is a type II (a "late dier") to mimic type I behavior and withdraw early; otherwise the candidate equilibrium will unravel.

Given the simplifying assumptions that we have made, it is easy to show that the incentive compatibility condition will hold.[10]

Investment and interest rates in the steady state

We now derive the steady-state allocation of investment and the time-deposit rate. Once the time-deposit rate is known it is then possible to use (4.5) and (4.6) to calculate the associated demand-deposit rates. All the results depend in an important way on the liquidity constraint (3.4).

To obtain the equilibrium, we use the steady-state versions of the following relations: the two first-order necessary conditions for investment in the illiquid and liquid assets, the liquidity constraint, and the arbitrage condition between the time- and demand-deposit rates. Omit the time subscript to denote a variable's steady-state value. Then an expression linking the time-deposit rate r to the expected return on the illiquid investment R, to the minimum possible return R^ℓ, and to the shadow price for the liquidity constraint λ follows from the steady-state analogues of (3.7) and (3.9):

$$r = [R + \lambda R^\ell]/[(1+\delta)(1+\lambda)] \quad \text{if } I > 0. \tag{4.7}$$

The equation holds with equality only if I is positive, since it was obtained in part from the first-order necessary condition for illiquid investment. According to (4.7), r varies positively with R and R^ℓ and inversely with λ. Intuitively, the time-deposit rate is sensitive to the expected return on bank assets. The latter depends on the allocation of the bank's portfolio between liquid and illiquid projects. The proportion of liquid assets varies positively with λ (which reflects the tightness of the liquidity constraint); hence, r varies inversely with λ. When the liquidity constraint is not binding, so that λ equals zero, the time-deposit rate attains its maximum value $R/1+\delta$. Since banks need not hold liquid assets in this case, the time-deposit rate simply equals the expected return on illiquid projects.

---

[10] Note first that, since consumption is assumed to be neither storable nor reinvestable, and since Type II consumers born in t get utility only from consumption in $t+2$, a Type II cannot get direct utility from withdrawing in $t+1$; he will withdraw early only if he can trade it on favorable terms for claims to consumption in $t+2$. Indeed, since $r_t^2/r_t^1 \geq 1$, the Type II consumer will be induced to withdraw early only if he can trade $t+1$ consumption at one-for-one or better. However, at that price there will be no net suppliers of consumption futures in $t+1$; in particular, since bankers value $t+1$ and $t+2$ consumption precisely equally, no banker can make a positive profit by attempting to induce the Type II depositors of other banks to withdraw early. Thus the utility-maximizing deposit rates defined in (4.5) and (4.6) are also incentive-compatible. See Jacklin (1985) for a general discussion of incentive-compatibility issues in these types of frameworks.

If there is storage in the steady state (resulting from a binding liquidity constraint), the bank's first-order condition for liquid investment holds with equality. Combining the steady-state versions of (3.8) and the arbitrage condition (3.9) yields

$$r = 1 \quad \text{if } S > 0. \tag{4.8}$$

The time-deposit rate equals unity since in this case the liquidity constraint permits banks to invest at the margin only in liquid assets.

From (3.4), (4.1), (4.5), and (4.6), we obtain an expression for the steady-state version of the liquidity constraint:

$$R^{\ell} I + S \geq rW, \tag{4.9}$$

where, in analogy to (3.4), the left-hand side reflects bank earnings under the worst outcome on its portfolio and the right-hand side reflects its per-period obligations to depositors. Furthermore, because I equals $(W + W_b - S)/(1 + \delta)$,

$$R^{\ell} (W + W_b)/(1 + \delta) \geq rW \quad S = 0, \tag{4.10}$$

$$R^{\ell} [(W + W_b - S)/(1 + \delta)] + S = rW \quad \text{if } S > 0. \tag{4.11}$$

Equation (4.11) holds with equality since the liquidity constraint is binding when storage is positive.

One more result is necessary to proceed.

Lemma 1: *The time deposit rate cannot remain below unity indefinitely.*

Remark: This lemma is proved in a slightly more general form in B/G. The intuition is straightforward: When $r < 1$ persistently, it is possible for a "storage intermediary" (i.e., a bank that holds only one-period liquid assets) to play an infinite Ponzi game in which new deposits are used to pay off old obligations. However, the feasibility of such a Ponzi game could not be consistent with equilibrium, since it would imply (among other things) an infinite demand for deposits by storage intermediaries. Thus, r must not be less than 1.

We can now characterize the conditions under which various steady-state behaviors of investment and the time-deposit rate arise. What is critical is whether the incentive constraint binds. This outcome depends on the value of the dividend from bank capital W_b and the minimum return on the illiquid investment R^{ℓ}.

Proposition 1: *If $R^{\ell}(1 + W_b/W)/(1 + \delta)$ is:*

(i) $\geq R/(1+\delta)$, then $I=(W+W_b)/(1+\delta)$, $S=0$, $r=R/(1+\delta)$, and $\lambda=0$;

(ii) $<R/(1+\delta)$ but ≥ 1, then $I=(W+W_b)/(1+\delta)$, $S=0$, $r=R^\ell(1+W_b/W)/(1+\delta)$, and $\lambda=[R-r(1+\delta)]/[r(1+\delta)-R^\ell]$;

(iii) <1, then $I=W_b/(1+\delta-R^\ell)$, $S=W+W_b-(1+\delta)I$, $r=1$, and $\lambda=[R-(1+\delta)]/(1+\delta-R^\ell)$.

Proof: Equation (4.10) defines the liquidity constraint in the steady state for the case with no liquid investment (storage). Rearranging (4.10) yields the following condition, which must apply if banks are not holding liquid assets:

$$R^\ell(1+W_b/W)/(1+\delta) \geq r. \tag{4.12}$$

If (4.12) is satisfied, then banks have sufficient revenues from previous illiquid investments to perfectly guarantee new liability issues without having to resort to storage. Since this restriction applies in (i) and (ii), it follows that all the endowment is used for illiquid projects in these cases. Furthermore, if the left-hand side exceeds $R/(1+\delta)$ (the maximum value of r), as in case (i), then (4.12) is not binding. Hence, in case (i) λ equals zero; it follows from (4.9) that $r=R/(1+\delta)$. When the left-hand side of (4.12) is less than $R/(1+\delta)$, as in (ii), then $r=R/(1+\delta)$ would violate the liquidity constraint. In this case, (4.10) is binding: The time deposit rate r adjusts to satisfy this restriction, so long as the resulting value is greater than or equal to unity (as required by Lemma 1). Here, even though $R/(1+\delta)$ exceeds r, banks cannot invest more in illiquid projects because they are liquidity constrained. In this case (4.9) and (4.10) jointly determine r and λ, which gives the expressions in (ii).

When case (iii) applies, the requirement that r not fall below one (Lemma 1) implies that banks must invest in the liquid asset in the steady state. The liquidity constraint is thus binding in this case. Furthermore, r equals unity, according to (4.8). The level of investment in the liquid asset adjusts to satisfy the liquidity constraint (4.11), given the restriction that $r=1$. This is the value of S given in (iii).   Q.E.D.

According to Proposition 1, investment in illiquid projects is a nondecreasing function of the dividend from bank capital and the minimum return (the collateral value). The same is true for the time-deposit rate. When the liquidity constraint is binding, increases in W_b or R^ℓ reduce the need for storage; this allows the bank to invest more in illiquid projects and hence offer depositors a higher return.

We have treated insider bank capital exogenously. What are the implications of permitting this quantity to be endogenous? The results stated in Proposition 1 should remain qualitatively intact as long as the supply curve for capital facing banks is not perfectly elastic at a moment in time; otherwise, capital would always flow instantaneously to preclude the liquidity constraint from binding. The constraint would remain potentially relevant if supply were imperfectly elastic, at least over a temporary time interval. We conjecture that this latter case is applicable to insider equity, the supply of which is constrained by the owner/manager's net wealth and retained earnings. We emphasize that although outside equity (capital raised from individuals who are not managers) may be obtained quickly, it is not useful for solving the incentive problem. That is, outside equity holders face the same agency problem vis-a-vis the bank as do depositors.[11] We plan to consider endogenous bank capital explicitly in future work.

Finally, it is possible that a non-banking steady-state equilibrium, in which banks invest no depositor funds in illiquid projects, might arise. Whether this happens depends critically on the values of W_b and R^ℓ.

Proposition 2: *If either W_b or R^ℓ is zero, then there will be no investment of depositor funds in illiquid projects.*

Proof: If either W_b or R^ℓ is zero, then (4.12) cannot be satisfied because, according to Lemma 1, r cannot be less than unity. Thus there must be storage in the steady state, with S determined by condition (iii) of Proposition 1. However, if the dividend from bank capital or the minimum return on an illiquid project (i.e., collateral value) equals zero, $S = W$. Thus all deposits are invested in the liquid asset.   Q.E.D.

The result is straightforward. Without W_b, bankers cannot insure liabilities backed by investments in the risky illiquid project. If illiquid bank projects do not have any collateral value (if R^ℓ equals zero) then perfectly guaranteeing bank liabilities requires backing them with the completely safe asset, storage.

Dynamics: The dynamics of the model outside the steady state are of some interest, but space constraints preclude a discussion here (see B/G).

---

[11] In practice, outside bank equity can be viewed as another form of debt, where holders accept the role of residual claimants in case of default and in return receive a promised yield in nondefault states higher than all other types of bank debt. Like debt, this yield is not automatically sensitive to current earnings. The recent experience of Bank of America (where federal examiners had to intervene to execute a change in the dividend payment) seems to confirm this view of outside bank capital.

We only note here that the model of this section, and the one developed in Section 5, are dynamically stable.

5   Equilibrium with an alternative, publicly observable, technology

We now explore the implications of adding a productive technology which does not require bank evaluation and monitoring. All aspects of projects using this technology are observable; as a result, investment in this alternative project may be financed by directly issuing securities on the open market.

We assume that the alternative technology has the following characteristics: An input at time t of $\hat{I}_t$ units of endowment yields $f(\hat{I}_t)$ units of consumption two periods later. The function f is concave and increasing. Further, the output of consumption per unit of endowment invested, $g(\hat{I}) = f(\hat{I})/\hat{I}$, obeys the following restrictions:

$$g(0) > 1, \qquad g(W) < 1. \tag{5.1}$$

The restrictions in (5.1) ensure an interior solution for investment in the alternative technology.

Assume that there exist a fixed number of firms that each independently operate the technology. For convenience, normalize the number of firms at unity. The firm's economic decisions are trivial. It simply accepts endowment and issues securities which are claims to the subsequent yield. It uses the endowment to produce consumption output two periods later and then distributes all the revenue to its creditors, based on their respective contributions to the investment. The key point is that, because its production activity is publicly observable, the firm can directly issue securities without the need of a monitoring intermediary.

Since there is no agency problem, it is also true that the securities issued by the firm may have returns contingent on its earnings if they are random. This potential dependence on earnings is in practice an important distinction between equity-like securities and (adequately backed) demand deposits issued by banks. In the present analysis, however, we will avoid dealing with random security yields by assuming that the alternative technology is purely deterministic. We make this assumption for two reasons. First, this approach results in considerable simplification, without affecting the nature of the main results. Second, as will be seen in a moment, in our model determinacy of security returns implies that securities may be repackaged as assets that are perfect substitutes for bank demand deposits; consumers prefer these repackaged assets for the same reason they prefer demand to time deposits. This perfect substitutability between the principal financial assets available to savers will permit us to shift the focus of the analysis from traditional issues concerning the special role of bank liabilities to the question that concerns us most here: the special role of bank-intermediated credit.[12]

As we have noted, because consumers need flexibility they will desire to have securities repackaged into demand deposits. In B/G we introduced a new class of intermediaries, called brokers, to perform this repackaging function. Brokers were assumed to have no capital and no monitoring technology, and earned zero profits from the repackaging of securities. It turns out, however, that the addition of brokers complicates the analysis but yields a real equilibrium no different from that which arises when we simply allow the banks to repackage securities. Thus, we choose the latter assumption here. However, since bank credit is unnecessary to finance input into the alternative technology (in contrast with funding for illiquid projects) and since the security repackaging function can be separated from banking, we will refer to $\hat{I}$ as "investment in the alternative sector."

To analyze the model, we note that the resource constraint (3.1), the definition of profits (3.3), and the liquidity constraint (3.4) must be expanded to include the possibility of investment in the alternative sector, as well as the illiquid and liquid projects. The bank's first-order necessary conditions for illiquid and liquid investments are the same as before. [See equations (3.7) and (3.8).] Further, the arbitrage condition (3.9) between demand and time deposits remains, as do the relations between the demand- and time-deposit rates [equations (4.5) and (4.6), respectively]. However, because the bank – unlike before – now has the option of investing in securities (claims to investment in the alternative sector), the following additional first-order condition arises in this case:

$$\hat{R}_t = r_t, \tag{5.2}$$

where $\hat{R}_t$ is the (two-period) rate of return on a security purchased at t. According to (5.2), an interior solution requires that the return on securities equals the return on time deposits. Since $\hat{R}_t$ equals $g(\hat{I}_t)$ by definition, it follows from (5.2) that

$$g(\hat{I}_t) = r_t. \tag{5.3}$$

Equation (5.3) relates the level of investment in the alternative technology to the time-deposit rate. For example, a decline in the time-deposit rate will induce banks to acquire securities, which in turn increases the level

---

[12] The emphasis of most analyses on bank liabilities rather than bank assets derives from the traditional concern with the quantity of the medium of exchange. For further discussion see Section 6.

of investment in the alternative technology. Because of diminishing returns, the security rate declines. The process continues until, once again, $\hat{R}$ equals r. Hence, investment in the alternative technology varies inversely with the time-deposit rate.

We are now in a position to characterize behavior in the steady state. Define $\hat{I}(r) \equiv g^{-1}(\hat{I})$. It follows from (5.3) that $\hat{I}'(r) < 0$. Next define $\phi(r) \equiv r - [r - R^{\ell}/[1+\delta]]\hat{I}(r)/W$. It follows from Lemma 1 and (3.10) and (5.1) that $\phi(r), \phi'(r) > 0$.

Proposition 3: *If $R^{\ell}[1+W_b/W]/[1+\delta]$ is*

   (i) $\geq \phi(R/[1+\delta])$, *then* $I = [W + W_b - \hat{I}(R/[1+\delta])]/[1+\delta]$, $S=0$, $r = R/[1+\delta]$, *and* $\lambda = 0$;

  (ii) $< \phi(R/[1+\delta])$ *but* ≥ 1, *then* $I = [W + W_b - \hat{I}(r)]/[1+\delta]$, $S=0$, $r = \phi^{-1}(R^{\ell}[1+W_b/W]/[1+\delta])$, *and* $\lambda = [R - [1+\delta]r]/[r(1+\delta) - R^{\ell}]$;

 (iii) $\leq \phi(1)$, *then* $I = W_b/[1+\delta-R^{\ell}]$, $S = W + W_b - (1+\delta)I - \hat{I}(1)$,   *and* $\lambda = [R - [1+\delta]]/[1+\delta-R^{\ell}]$.

The proof of Proposition 3 parallels that of Proposition 1. (An explicit proof is provided in B/G.) Analogous to the previous case, the critical issue is whether the liquidity constraint is binding. As before, steady-state investment and interest rates depend on the quantity of insider bank capital and the lower bound on the return to illiquid projects. The only difference from the previous case is that banks have the option of acquiring securities. Before, acquiring liquid assets was the only way banks could relax the liquidity constraint. Now, banks can invest in the alternative technology. This activity relaxes the liquidity constraint because demand deposit liabilities backed by securities need not be collateralized; agency problems do not arise in this case because security returns are publicly observable.

Investment in the illiquid technology is here potentially more sensitive to movements in W_b and R^{ℓ} than in the case without the alternative technology. In the previous case, when the liquidity constraint was binding and all endowment was invested in illiquid projects, a small decline in either W_b or R^{ℓ} precipitated a fall in the time-deposit rate, but otherwise had no allocative effects. [See part (ii) of Proposition 1.] In this setting, a fall in W_b or R^{ℓ} leads banks to reduce the percentage of their portfolio devoted to illiquid investment and, correspondingly, increase the percentage devoted to securities. Hence, associated with the decline in the time-deposit rate is a shift in allocation in favor of the alternative technology. In an environment where repackaging securities is decoupled from banking, deposits would flow from banks to brokers (see B/G). In either case, there is a decline in the funding of projects explicitly requiring bank credit.

Finally, analogous to Proposition 2 in the previous case, we have the following.

Proposition 4: *If W_b or R^ℓ equals zero, then in the steady state*

$$I = W_b/(1+\delta), \quad \hat{I} = \hat{I}(1), \quad S = W + W_b - \hat{I}(1), \quad r = 1, \quad and$$

$$\lambda = [(R - (1+\delta))/(1+\delta - R^\ell)].$$

(The proof is omitted.) That is, deposits will be divided only between the alternative technology and storage; there will be no investment of consumers' savings in illiquid projects.

6   Some applications

The relationship of financial stability to macroeconomic performance

In a descriptive historical paper, Bernanke argued that the collapse of the financial system in the 1930s, and the resulting loss of intermediary services, played an important role in the general decline in output and employment. One also hears considerable conjecture that the precariousness of international or domestic credit markets poses a significant threat to the contemporary economy. Yet there has been little substantive economic analysis of how or whether a financial collapse could have large real effects, or of how such effects could be averted.

Though considerable work remains, the model of this chapter seems to provide insight into this problem. We have already shown, for example, that the quantity of bank capital and the minimum gross return to illiquid bank assets (which we interpret as the collateral value) play a key role in banking activity. Let us define financial collapse as a sharp reduction in the level of funds banks are able to intermediate for projects requiring bank credit. (Thus a collapse does not necessarily involve a bank run.) Then a financial crisis would emerge if there were either a large deterioration of bank capital or a significantly unfavorable change in the collateral value of illiquid bank assets. As follows from the analysis of Sections 4 and 5, either of these occurrences would force a contraction of bank illiquid investment projects, with resources being shifted to liquid assets and the alternative technology. As actually happened in the 1930s, the cost of funds to firms in the "safe" alternative sector would fall (i.e., the rate of return on securities would decline), while information-intensive projects which rely on bank credit might not be able to obtain funds at all. Overall, the marginal efficiency of investment would decline. With endogenous labor supply in place of the fixed consumer endowments assumed in the model's present version, the decline in safe rates of return might have second-round effects on output, as agents find the return to work is lower.

Our model is currently not rich enough to explain why the quantity of insider bank capital or the collateral value of illiquid projects might change unfavorably. We would expect both these variables to bear a relation to aggregate economic activity, as was clearly the case in the Great Depression. Conceivably, the analysis can be extended to a setting where W_b and R^ℓ are endogenous. (We are currently exploring this issue.) This extension would show how fundamental factors can explain major contractions in the availability of bank credit. This approach contrasts with Diamond and Dybvig, who emphasize market psychology. Our framework may allow for synthesizing the two explanations, especially given that it has already incorporated much of the Diamond–Dybvig structure.

The effects of banking regulation and deregulation

There is currently much deregulation of the banking system, most of it in the name of microeconomic efficiency. However, most of the original regulation was imposed on macroeconomic, not microeconomic grounds. How does banking regulation relate to the performance of the macroeconomy? The discussion of financial stability above suggests that certain regulations, such as deposit insurance and the associated minimum capital requirements and public auditing, may be macroeconomically justified. Our model, as it stands, does not explicitly justify government intervention in banking. However, imposing an alternative information structure – for example, one in which the government has a cost advantage in monitoring bank portfolios – might change this result. Whether this could motivate policies like deposit insurance seems to be a question worth pursuing.

Some other legal restrictions (e.g., interest rate ceilings) are (were) probably not justified, since they distort the allocation of investment without visibly contributing to financial stability.[13] With minor modification, our model would be potentially useful for studying these questions.

The monetary transmission mechanism

The relation between central bank policy and real activity is one of the basic questions of macroeconomics. Researchers have addressed this ques-

---

[13] For an opposing view, see Smith (1984).

tion in a number of ways. The traditional, and most familiar, analysis of central bank policy focuses on the quantity of the medium of exchange, arguing that the central bank can affect the economy only insofar as it affects this quantity. The liability side of the bank balance sheet receives special attention in this approach, because demand deposits are a large part of conventionally defined money.

We certainly do not wish to claim that the quantity of the medium of exchange is without significance. However, as originally argued by Gurley and Shaw, the traditional approach becomes less relevant as the number of substitutes for conventionally defined money increases in consumers' portfolios.[14] An alternative to the traditional approach, the alternative approach of this paper, is to take into account bank assets as well as bank liabilities. In particular, as discussed in Section 5, our model eliminates any "specialness" of bank liabilities, permitting us to focus on the implications of possible nonsubstitutability between bank and nonbank credit. [Our model is thus in the spirit of, e.g., Blinder and Stiglitz (1983).] In this alternative framework, monetary policy (e.g., the manipulation of reserve requirements) matters to real activity primarily because it affects the extent of financial intermediation, not because it affects the quantity of the medium of exchange. This distinction may be of practical importance – for example, in the choice of intermediate targets or in the implications for monetary policy of changing bank regulations.

It should be emphasized that there are several ways to introduce monetary policy into our framework, and that the conclusions drawn may depend heavily on the chosen specification. A particularly important modeling decision is whether to treat the central bank as controlling the nominal or the real quantity of bank reserves. Nominal reserve control means that the central bank issues a fixed number of "dollars" to be held as legal reserves against nominal quantities of deposits. In this case, changes in the aggregate price level can make the existing quantity of reserves consistent with any level of real deposits or loans. Under these circumstances, open-market operations (for example) will have no significant real effects.[15] Alternatively, under a regime of real reserve control, the central bank is to be thought of as issuing a fixed number of "permits" that a bank is required to hold before accepting a unit of deposit in real (resource) terms. Real reserve control may be the appropriate assumption in (for example) a Keynesian setting with imperfect price adjustment, or when deposits and loans are issued in nominal terms and are not indexed;

---

[14] Hester (1981) argues that the numerous money substitutes that have resulted from ongoing financial innovation have made dubious the notion that regulating monetary aggregates is useful or even feasible.

[15] See Lacker (1985) for an analysis of reserve requirements and monetary policy in an otherwise frictionless neoclassical setting.

it is also isomorphic to a policy of direct control of bank credit, which has been experienced in recent episodes in the United States and United Kingdom. With real reserve control, open-market operations will affect the real size of the banking sector and, as should be obvious by now, will change real allocations in the economy.

Ultimately, whether monetary policy works primarily through bank assets or bank credit is an empirical issue. The early returns are mixed. Stephen King (1984) found stronger reduced-form correlations between demand deposits and output than between commercial and industrial loans made by banks and output. However, because both demand deposits and bank credit presumably have large endogenous components [see R. King and Plosser (1984)], this finding does not definitely settle how an exogenous shock to deposits or credit will affect the economy. By imposing some limited structure on the vector autoregressions and working with a broader measure of intermediary credit than King, Bernanke (1985) found some support for the credit hypothesis.

REFERENCES

Bernanke, Ben S. 1983. "Nonmonetary Effects of the Financial Crisis in the Propagation of the Great Depression." *American Economic Review* 73: 257-76.
_____. 1985. "Alternative Explanations of the Money/Income Correlations." Mimeo, Princeton University.
Bernanke, Ben S., and Mark Gertler. 1985. "Banking in General Equilibrium." Working Paper #1647, National Bureau of Economic Research.
Blinder, Alan S., and Joseph E. Stiglitz. 1983. "Money Credit Constraints, and Economic Activity." *American Economic Review* 73: 297-302.
Boyd, John H., and Edward C. Prescott. 1983. "Financial Intermediaries." Mimeo, Minneapolis Federal Reserve Bank and University of Minnesota.
Brainard, William, and James Tobin. 1963. "Financial Intermediaries and the Effectiveness of Monetary Control." *American Economic Review* 53: 383-400.
Bryant, John. 1980. "A Model of Reserves, Bank Runs, and Deposit Insurance." *Journal of Banking and Finance* 4: 335-44.
Cone, Kenneth. 1982. "Regulation of Depository Financial Intermediaries." Ph.D. Thesis, Stanford University.
Diamond, Douglas. 1984. "Financial Intermediation and Delegated Monitoring." *Review of Economics Studies* 51: 393-414.
Diamond, Douglas, and Philip Dybvig. 1983. "Bank Runs, Deposit Insurance, and Liquidity." *Journal of Political Economy* 91: 401-19.
Fama, Eugene F. 1985. "What's Different About Banks?" *Journal of Monetary Economics* 15: 29-40.
Fischer, Stanley. 1983. "A Framework for Monetary and Banking Analysis." *Economic Journal* 93: 1-16.
Gurley, John G., and E. S. Shaw. 1956. "Financial Intermediaries and the Savings-Investment Process." *Journal of Finance* 11: 259-75.
Hester, Donald. 1981. "Innovations and Monetary Control." *Brookings Papers on Economic Activity* 1: 141-89.

Jacklin, Charles. 1985. "Essays in Banking." Ph.D. Thesis, Stanford Graduate School of Business.

King, Robert, and Charles Plosser. 1984. "Money, Credit, and Prices in a Real Business Cycle." *American Economic Review* 74: 363–80.

King, Stephen R. 1985. "Monetary Transmission: Through Bank Loans, or Bank Liabilities?" Mimeo, Stanford University.

Lacker, Jeff. 1985. "Inside Money and Real Output." Mimeo, Purdue University.

Patinkin, Don. 1961. "Financial Intermediaries and the Logical Structure of Monetary Theory." *American Economic Review* 51: 95–116.

Peltzman, Sam. 1970. "Capital Investment in Commercial Banking and Its Relation to Portfolio Regulation." *Journal of Political Economy* 78: 1–26.

Smith, Bruce D. 1984. "Private Information, Deposit Insurance Rates, and the 'Stability' of the Banking System." *Journal of Monetary Economics* 14: 293–317.

Townsend, Robert. 1979. "Optimal Contracts and Competitive Markets with Costly State Verification." *Journal of Economic Theory* 21: 265–93.

1983. "Financial Structure and Economic Activity." *American Economic Review* 73: 895–911.

Williamson, Stephen. 1984. "Costly Monitoring, Financial Intermediation, and Equilibrium Credit Rationing." Mimeo, Queens University.

1985. "Financial Intermediation, Business Failures, and Real Business Cycles." Mimeo, University of Western Ontario.

PART III

Monetary aggregation theory

CHAPTER 6

The microeconomic theory of monetary aggregation

William A. Barnett

In recent decades there has been a resurgence of interest in index numbers resulting from discoveries that the properties of index numbers can be directly related to the properties of the underlying aggregator functions that they represent. The underlying functions – production functions, utility functions, etc. – are the building blocks of economic theory, and the study of relationships between these functions and index number formulas has been referred to by Samuelson and Swamy (1974) as the economic theory of index numbers.[1]

1 Introduction

The use of economic index number theory was introduced into monetary theory by Barnett (1980a, 1981a). His merger of economic index number theory with monetary theory was based upon the use of Diewert's approach to producing "superlative" approximations to the exact aggregates from consumer demand theory.[2] As a result, Barnett's approach produces a Diewert-superlative measure of the monetary service flow perceived to be received by consumers from their monetary asset portfolio. However, aggregation and index number theory are highly developed in production theory as well as in consumer demand theory. Substantial literatures exist on aggregation over factor inputs demanded by firms, aggregation over multiple product outputs produced by firms, and aggregation over individual firms and consumers. In addition, substantial literatures exist on exact measurement of value added by firms and of technical

This research was partially supported by National Science Foundation grant SOC 8305162.
[1] Caves, Christensen, and Diewert (1982, p. 73).
[2] For empirical applications, see Barnett (1980b, 1981b, 1982b, 1983a, 1984); Barnett, Offenbacher, and Spindt (1984); Barnett and Spindt (1979, 1982); Serletis (1984a, b, 1986); Ewis and Fisher (1984, 1985); Barnett, Hinich, and Weber (1986); Cockerline and Murray (1981); Serletis and Robb (1986); Marquez (1986); Ishida (1984); and Swofford and Whitney (1986). For a survey of the theory, see Barnett (1982a, 1983b) and Barnett, Offenbacher, and Spindt (1981).

change by firms. All of these literatures are potentially relevant to closing a cleared money market in an exact aggregation-theoretic monetary aggregate. In this paper, we establish the relationship between monetary theory and all of the above listed areas of aggregation and index number theory. These results are relevant to building and using theoretical or empirical macroeconomic models possessing an aggregated money market.

The demand for money is both by firms and consumers. Hence we present the aggregation and index number theory relevant to demand by firms as well as by consumers. The supply of money is partially produced by financial intermediaries. As a result, we present the aggregation and index number theory relevant to aggregation over the multiple outputs of such financial firms. Because there has been considerable technological change in the industry in recent years, a theory relevant to measuring technological change within a financial firm is presented. In addition, because the impact of changes in outside money on the economy is likely to depend upon value added by financial intermediaries, the theoretical and approximation approaches relevant to measuring value added by such firms are also presented.

In this paper, the models of monetary asset demand by consumers and by firms, as well as the model of monetary asset supply by financial intermediaries, are based upon commonly used neoclassical formulations. In addition, the results in aggregation and index number theory used in this paper are well established and widely known in their respective literatures. Besides surveying the relevant results from those literatures, the primary objective of this paper is algebraically to formulate and manipulate the presented theories of monetary consumption, factor demand, and production in a manner that provides immediate direct relevancy to the existing results in the literatures on aggregation and index number theory.

Because a government sector is not introduced, the financial firm, the consumer, and the manufacturing firm modeled herein are not imbedded in a macroeconomic model. The reason is that the results surveyed and developed here are applicable to macroeconomic modeling regardless of the nature of the model's transmission mechanism or of any policy implications that might be suggested by a full macroeconomic model. There are as many ways to imbed these results into a macroeconomic model as there are ways to build a macroeconomic model.

2   Consumer demand for monetary assets

In this section we formulate a consumer's decision problem over consumer goods and monetary assets. The decision will be structured in a manner that provides immediate applicability of the relevant literature on economic aggregation over consumer goods. Hence the existing results in economic aggregation and index number theory will be directly usable.

Two versions of the decision problem will be provided. The first version will use a finite planning horizon and will be an extension of Barnett's (1978, 1980a, 1981a) formulation. The second version will use an infinite planning horizon and will be shown to produce the same aggregation theoretic results as the finite-horizon version. The reason is that both versions produce the same current period aggregator function over monetary assets, and both versions produce the same user cost formulas for monetary assets.

2.1   Finite planning horizon

The following variables are used in consumer c's decision problem, formulated in period t for periods $t, t+1, \ldots, s, \ldots, t+T$, where T is the number of periods in the consumer's planning horizon:

$\mathbf{x}_s$ = vector of planned consumption of goods and services during period s;

$\mathbf{p}_s$ = vector of goods' and services' expected prices and of durable goods' expected rental prices during period s;

$\mathbf{m}_s$ = vector of planned real balances of monetary assets during period s;

$\mathbf{r}_s$ = vector of expected nominal holding period yields of monetary assets;

A_s = planned holdings of the benchmark asset during period s;

R_s = the expected one-period holding yield on the benchmark asset during period s;

L_s^c = planned labor supply during period s;

$\bar{L}_s = k - L_s^c$ = planned leisure demand during period s, where k = total hours available per period;

w_s = the expected wage rate during period s;[3] and

I_s = other expected income (government transfer payments, profits of owned firms, etc.) during period s.

The benchmark asset is defined to provide no services other than its yield R_s, which motivates holding of the asset solely as a means of accumulating wealth. As a result, R_s is the maximum expected holding period yield

---

[3] If the expected demand for the consumer's labor is not equal to planned supply, then w_s is the expected shadow price of leisure. See Barnett (1980a, 1981a).

in the economy in period s; and the benchmark asset is held to transfer wealth between multiperiod planning horizons, rather than to provide liquidity or other services.

The consumer's intertemporal utility function in period t is[4]

$$u_t = u_t(\mathbf{m}_t, \ldots, \mathbf{m}_{t+T}; \bar{L}_t, \ldots, \bar{L}_{t+T}; \mathbf{x}_t, \ldots, \mathbf{x}_{t+T}; A_{t+T}). \qquad (2.1)$$

We assume that u_t is blockwise weakly separable as follows.

$$u_t = U_t(u(\mathbf{m}_t), u_{t+1}(\mathbf{m}_{t+1}), \ldots, u_{t+T}(\mathbf{m}_{t+T}); \bar{L}_t, \ldots, \bar{L}_{t+T};$$

$$v(\mathbf{x}_t), v_{t+1}(\mathbf{x}_{t+1}), \ldots, v_{t+T}(\mathbf{x}_{t+T}); A_{t+T}). \qquad (2.2)$$

The functions $u, u_{t+1}, \ldots, u_{t+T}, v, v_{t+1}, \ldots, v_{t+T}$ are called category sub-utility functions. Then, dual to the functions v and v_s ($s = t+1, \ldots, t+T$), there exist current and planned true cost of living indexes, p_t^* and p_s^* ($s = t+1, \ldots, t+T$), that can be used to deflate nominal to real values.[5]

Assuming continuous replanning at each t, the consumer's decision is to choose $(\mathbf{m}_t, \ldots, \mathbf{m}_{t+T}, \bar{L}_t, \ldots, \bar{L}_{t+T}; \mathbf{x}_t, \ldots, \mathbf{x}_{t+T}; A_{t+T})$ to maximize u_t subject to the $T+1$ budget constraints

$$\mathbf{p}_s' \mathbf{x}_s = w_s L_s^c + \sum_{i=1}^{n} [(1+r_{i,s-1})p_{s-1}^* m_{i,s-1} - p_s^* m_{is}]$$

$$+ [(1+R_{s-1})p_{s-1}^* A_{s-1} - p_s^* A_s] + I_s \qquad (2.3)$$

for $s = t, t+1, \ldots, t+T$ and with $\bar{L}_s = k - L_s^c$. The consumer's initial nominal wealth in period t is $\sum_{i=1}^{n}(1+r_{i,t-1})p_{t-1}^* m_{i,t-1} + (1+R_{t-1})p_{t-1}^* A_{t-1}$.

Let $(\mathbf{m}_t^*, \ldots, \mathbf{m}_{t+T}^*, \bar{L}_t^*, \ldots, \bar{L}_{t+T}^*; \mathbf{x}_t^*, \ldots, \mathbf{x}_{t+T}^*; A_{t+T}^*)$ be the solution to that constrained optimization problem. Following the procedures in Barnett (1980a, 1981a), it then can be shown that $\mathbf{m}_t^*$ is also the solution for $\mathbf{m}_t$ to the following current period conditional decision:

$$\text{maximize } u(\mathbf{m}_t) \quad \text{subject to } \boldsymbol{\pi}_t' \mathbf{m}_t = y_t, \qquad (2.4)$$

where $\boldsymbol{\pi}_t = (\pi_{1t}, \ldots, \pi_{nt})'$ is the vector of monetary asset nominal user costs

$$\pi_{it} = p_t^* \frac{R_t - r_{it}}{1 + R_t} \qquad (2.5)$$

and $y_t = \boldsymbol{\pi}_t' \mathbf{m}_t^*$. We could convert from the nominal user costs $\boldsymbol{\pi}_t$ to the real user costs $\boldsymbol{\pi}_t^*$ by dividing the budget constraint of (2.4) by p_t^* to obtain

$$\text{maximize } u(\mathbf{m}_t) \quad \text{subject to } \boldsymbol{\pi}_t^{*'} \mathbf{m}_t = y_t^*, \qquad (2.6)$$

---

[4] Regarding the existence of this derived utility function, into which the consumer's transactions technology has been absorbed, see Arrow and Hahn (1971), Phlips and Spinnewyn (1979), and Samuelson and Sato (1984).

[5] See Barnett (1980a, 1981a).

where $y_t^* = y_t/p_t^*$ and $\pi_t^* = \pi_t/p_t^*$. The function u is assumed to be mono-tonically increasing and strictly concave. Decision problem (2.6) is in the form of a conventional consumer decision problem, and hence the litera-ture on aggregation theory and index number theory for consumers is immediately available.

2.2   Infinite planning horizon

In this section, we reformulate the consumer's decision problem using an infinite planning horizon. We show that the same current-period condi-tional decision problem, (2.6), is acquired. As a result, the existing liter-ature on aggregation and index number theory will remain relevant.

We replace the finite planning horizon intertemporal utility function (2.2) by the infinite horizon intertemporally separable utility function

$$u_t = \sum_{s=t}^{\infty} \left(\frac{1}{1+\xi}\right)^{s-t} U(u(\mathbf{m}_s), \bar{L}_s, \mathbf{x}_s), \tag{2.7}$$

where ξ is the consumer's subjective rate of time preference, assumed to be constant to assure Strotz consistent planning.[6] The consumer selects the sequence $(\mathbf{m}_s, \bar{L}_s, \mathbf{x}_s)$, $s = t, t+1, \ldots$, to maximize (2.7) subject to the sequence of constraints (2.3) for $s = t, t+1, \ldots$. The upper limit $t+T$ to the planning horizon no longer exists. Again R_s must exceed r_{is} for all i, because A_s^c is not in the utility function and hence would not otherwise be held.

Construct the Lagrangean, Λ, and differentiate with respect to A_t, $\mathbf{x}_t$, and $\mathbf{m}_t$ to acquire the following first-order conditions for constrained maximization at t:

$$\partial\Lambda/\partial A_t = -\lambda_t + \lambda_{t+1}(1+R_t) = 0, \tag{2.8}$$

$$\partial\Lambda/\partial x_{it} = \partial U/\partial x_{it} - \lambda_t p_{it} = 0, \tag{2.9}$$

$$\partial\Lambda/\partial m_{it} = \partial U/\partial m_{it} - \lambda_t p_t^* + \lambda_{t+1} p_t^* = 0, \tag{2.10}$$

where λ_t and λ_{t+1} are two of the Lagrange multipliers in the sequence $(\lambda_t, \lambda_{t+1}, \lambda_{t+2}, \ldots)$ of Lagrange multipliers in Λ. Substituting (2.8) into (2.10) to eliminate λ_{t+1}, we obtain

$$\partial U/\partial m_{it} = \lambda_t \pi_{it}, \tag{2.11}$$

where π_{it} is as in (2.5).

---

[6] The same current-period conditional decision would result if ξ were not constant. As a result, Strotz consistency produces no loss in generality in our aggregation-theoretic re-sults. If intertemporal separability were not assumed, expectations could be endogenized through rational expectations, as in Attfield and Browning (1985).

Hence, from (2.11), we have that

$$\frac{\partial U/\partial m_{it}}{\partial U/\partial m_{jt}} = \frac{\pi_{it}}{\pi_{jt}}, \tag{2.12}$$

or

$$\frac{\partial u/\partial m_{it}}{\partial u/\partial m_{jt}} = \frac{\pi_{it}^*}{\pi_{jt}^*}. \tag{2.13}$$

Now for $s = t, t+1, \ldots$ let $(\mathbf{m}_s^*, \bar{L}_s^*, \mathbf{x}_s^*)$ maximize (2.7) subject to (2.3), and let

$$y_t^* = \boldsymbol{\pi}_t^{*\prime} \mathbf{m}_t^*. \tag{2.14}$$

Then the first-order conditions for the solution to problem (2.6) are (2.13) and (2.14). Hence $\mathbf{m}_s^*$ solves problem (2.6). As a result, we again find that we can use the conventional neoclassical decision (2.6), and thereby all of the existing literature on aggregation over goods consumed.

2.3   *Income taxes*

The results in Sections 2.1 and 2.2 do not explicitly incorporate taxes. Nevertheless all of those results would remain valid if we convert to after-tax yields as follows. Let τ_t be the consumer's marginal tax rate on interest earned from the benchmark asset, and let τ_{it} be the consumer's marginal tax rate on monetary asset i. Then the nominal user cost (2.5) becomes

$$\pi_{it} = p_t^* \frac{R_t(1-\tau_t) - r_{it}(1-\tau_{it})}{1 + R_t(1-\tau_t)}, \tag{2.5a}$$

which in turn becomes

$$\pi_{it} = p_t^* \frac{(R_t - r_{it})(1-\tau_t)}{1 + R_t(1-\tau_t)} \tag{2.5b}$$

if $\tau_{it} = \tau_t$ for all i.

In the latter case, we can return to using (2.5) instead of (2.5b) to acquire $\pi_{it}^* = \pi_{it}/p_t^*$, when π_t^* is to be used in decision (2.6). To do so, we need only replace y_t^* by $[1 + R_t(1-\tau_t)]y_t^*/[(1-\tau_t)(1+R_t)]$, since we then would only have divided both sides of the budget constraint of (2.6) by $[1 + R_t(1-\tau_t)]/[(1-\tau_t)(1+R_t)]$.

3   Supply of monetary assets by financial intermediaries

Monetary assets are generally either primary securities, such as currency or Treasury bills, or assets produced through the financial intermediation of financial firms. In this section, we develop a model of production by financial intermediaries under perfect certainty.[7] It will be shown that the model can be manipulated into the conventional neoclassical form of production by a multiproduct firm. As a result, the existing literature on output aggregation becomes immediately applicable to the construction of a neoclassical money supply function for aggregated money.

Consider a financial intermediary which makes only one kind of loan, yielding R_t, and produces (through financial intermediation) a vector μ_t of real balances of monetary assets.[8] The firm uses c_t real units of excess reserves, in the form of currency, as a factor of production in producing μ_t during period t.[9] Real balances such as μ_t and c_t are defined to equal nominal balances divided by p_t^*, which was defined in Section 2.1. The firm also uses the vector L_t of labor quantities and the vector z_t of other factor quantities. The vector of reserve requirements is k_t, where k_{it} is the reserve requirement applicable to μ_{it} and $0 \leq k_{it} \leq 1$ for all i.

The firm's efficient production technology is defined by the transformation function $F(\mu_t, z_t, L_t, c_t; k_t) = 0$. The firm's technology can be equivalently defined by its efficient production set (also called the production possibility efficient set)

$$S(k_t) = \{(\mu_t, z_t, L_t, c_t) \geq 0: F(\mu_t, z_t, L_t, c_t; k_t) = 0\} \tag{3.1}$$

or by its production correspondence F, defined such that

$$G(z_t, L_t, c_t; k_t) = \{\mu_t \geq 0: (\mu_t, z_t, L_t, c_t) \in S(k_t)\}. \tag{3.2}$$

If $(z_t, L_t) = 0$ then no financial intermediation takes place, no value added exists, and no loans are made. In short, in that case the firm is acting as a vault, so that all of $\sum_i p_t^* \mu_{it}$ is reserves, and hence excess reserves are $p_t^* c_t = \sum_i \mu_{it}(1 - k_{it})p_t^*$.

The transformation function F is strictly quasiconvex in (μ_t, z_t, L_t, c_t). In addition, $\partial F/\partial L_{it} < 0$, $\partial F/\partial z_{it} < 0$, and $\partial F/\partial c_t < 0$, because L_t, z_t, and c_t are inputs. Conversely, $\partial F/\partial \mu_{it} > 0$ because μ_t are outputs.[10] All factors

---

[7] Because risk premia will be left in all yields, a certainty equivalence assumption could be viewed as implicit. The explicit incorporation of expected profit maximization would greatly complicate the analysis to follow.

[8] In practice, R_t should be "the marginal cost of borrowing an additional dollar for one period" [see Diewert (1980a, pp. 476-7)].

[9] We treat monetary assets produced by financial intermediation to be outputs of financial intermediaries, and we thereby implicitly assume that the user costs of such assets are positive. Hancock (1985, 1986) postulates that some such assets can be inputs to financial intermediaries if the corresponding user costs are negative. That possibility is not excluded by the formulation presented below, although we shall not explicitly discuss the probably unusual case of negative user costs.

[10] If the user cost of μ_{it} were negative for some $i = j$, then $\partial F/\partial \mu_{jt}$ would become nonpositive because μ_{jt} would become an input. In that probably rare case, μ_{jt} could be removed from μ_t and treated as a component of z_t.

z_t are purchased at the start of period t for use during period t, and the firm must pay for those factors at the start of the period. The exception is labor L_t, which receives its wages at the end of period t for labor quantities supplied to the firm during period t. Interest on produced monetary assets μ_t is paid at the end of the period, and interest on loans outstanding during period t is received at the end of period t.

Because our model contains only one kind of primary market loan, yielding R_t, the federal funds rate must therefore also equal R_t. However, the discount rate, being regulated, can differ from R_t. Let R_t^d be the discount rate during period t, and define $\bar{R}_t = \min\{R_t, R_t^d\}$. We assume that required reserves are never borrowed from the Federal Reserve, but could be borrowed in the federal funds market.[11] Excess reserves can be borrowed from either source. As a result, if $R_t^d < R_t$ then all excess reserves will be borrowed from the Federal Reserve and there are no free reserves. If $R_t^d > R_t$, then there is no borrowing from the Federal Reserve and free reserves equal excess reserves. In addition, in that case the percentage of excess reserves borrowed from the federal funds market is indeterminate, because the opportunity cost of not lending free reserves at R_t is equal to the cost of borrowing free reserves from the federal funds market at R_t. For the same reason, the percentage of required reserves borrowed in the federal funds market is indeterminate in both cases. If $R_t^d = R_t$, then all of the following are indeterminate: the percentage of required reserves or of excess reserves borrowed in the federal funds market, the percentage of excess reserves borrowed from the Federal Reserve, and the level of free reserves.

We now proceed to determine the level of variable profits at the end of period t. Suppose that $R_t \le R_t^d$, so that $\bar{R}_t = R_t$. Then variable revenue from loans is

$$\left(\sum_i \mu_{it} p_t^* - \sum_i k_{it} \mu_{it} p_t^* - c_t p_t^* - \mathbf{q}_t' \mathbf{z}_t \right) R_t, \tag{3.3}$$

where $\mathbf{q}_t$ is the price of the factors $\mathbf{z}_t$. If z_{it} is a durable variable factor, then $\mathbf{q}_t$ is its user cost. However, if $R_t > R_t^d$, so that $\bar{R}_t = R_t^d$, then variable revenue from loans is

$$\left(\sum_i \mu_{it} p_t^* - \sum_i k_{it} \mu_{it} p_t^* - \mathbf{q}_t' \mathbf{z}_t \right) R_t - c_t p_t^* R_t^d. \tag{3.4}$$

Hence, in either case, variable revenue from loans is

$$\left[\sum_i (1 - k_{it}) \mu_{it} p_t^* - c_t p_t^* - \mathbf{q}_t' \mathbf{z}_t \right] R_t + c_t p_t^* (R_t - \bar{R}_t). \tag{3.5}$$

---

[11] This assumption of "perfect moral suasion" could easily be weakened or removed.

Variable cost that must be paid out of variable revenue is

$$\sum_i \mu_{it} p_t^* \rho_{it} + q_t' z_t + w_t' L_t, \tag{3.6}$$

where w_t is the vector of wage rates corresponding to labor quantities L_t, and ρ_t is the vector of yields paid by the firm on μ_t. Observe that $w_t' L_t$ appears in (3.6), but not in (3.5), because $w_t' L_t$ is not paid until the end of the period and therefore is not subtracted out of loan quantities placed at the beginning of the period.

Variable profit received at the end of period t is acquired by subtracting (3.6) from (3.5).[12] If we then divide by $1 + R_t$ in order to discount variable profits to the beginning of period t, we find that the present value of period t variable profits is

$$P(\mu_t, z_t, L_t, c_t; p_t^*, q_t, R_t, R_t^d, \rho_t, w_t, k_t)$$
$$= \mu_t' \gamma_t - q_t' z_t - L_t' w_t / (1 + R_t) - \gamma_{ot} c_t, \tag{3.7}$$

where the nominal user cost price of produced monetary asset μ_{it} is

$$\gamma_{it} = p_t^* \frac{(1 - k_{it}) R_t - \rho_{it}}{1 + R_t} \tag{3.8}$$

and the nominal user cost price of excess reserves (real balances of currency) is

$$\gamma_{ot} = p_t^* \frac{\bar{R}_t}{1 + R_t}. \tag{3.9}$$

The corresponding real user costs are γ_t / p_t^* and γ_{ot} / p_t^*.[13]

If we write the vector of all variable factor quantities as $\alpha_t = (z_t', L_t', c_t)'$ and the vector of corresponding factor prices as $\beta_t = (q_t', w_t'/(1 + R_t), \gamma_{ot})'$, it becomes evident that variable profits take the conventional form

$$P_t = \mu_t' \gamma_t - \alpha_t' \beta_t, \tag{3.10}$$

and the firm's variable profit maximization problem takes the conventional form of selecting $(\mu_t, \alpha_t) \in S(k_t)$ to maximize (3.10). Hence the existing literature on output aggregation for multiproduct firms becomes immediately applicable to aggregation over the produced monetary assets μ_t and to measuring value added and technological change in financial intermediation.

---

[12] Observe that fixed factors, including financial capital, are not relevant to the determination of variable profit.

[13] Observe that those derived user cost formulas, after some manipulation, become equivalent to those used by Hancock (1985, 1986), although her method of measuring the discount rate is not consistent with the above theory that produced results (3.8) and (3.9). She also incorporated explicit transactions costs into the formula.

3.1   *Properties of the model*

Observe that variable revenue can be written in the form

$$\mu_t' \gamma_t = \mu_t' \pi_t^b - \frac{p_t^* R_t \mathbf{k}_t' \mu_t}{1+R_t}, \tag{3.11}$$

where

$$\pi_{it}^b = p_t^* \frac{R_t - \rho_{it}}{1+R_t} \tag{3.12}$$

has the same form as the monetary asset user cost formula (2.5) for consumers' π_{it}. Clearly π_{it}^b in (3.12) would equal γ_{it} if $\mathbf{k}_t = \mathbf{0}$. As a result, it is evident that $p_t^* R_t \mathbf{k}_t' \mu_t / (1+R_t)$ is the present value (at the beginning of the period) of the tax $p_t^* R_t \mathbf{k}_t' \mu_t$ "paid" by the financial intermediary (at the end of the period) as a result of the existence of reserve requirements. The tax is the forgone interest on uninvested required reserves.

The solution to the firm's variable profit-maximization problem is its factor demand functions for $\alpha = (\mathbf{z}_t', \mathbf{L}_t', c_t)'$ and its supply functions for its multiple products μ_t. Derived demand is thereby produced for high-powered (base) money. That derived demand, in real terms, is

$$h_t = c_t + \sum_i k_{it} \mu_{it}. \tag{3.13}$$

The financial firm's nominal demand for high-powered money is $p_t^* h_t$.

Stockholder capital (net worth) is a fixed factor during period t and hence does not enter the variable cost function. Since stockholder capital is not reservable, all stockholder capital will go into loans at yield R_t. If capital is paid the competitive rate of return, then all of the yield on the investment of stockholder capital will be paid to stockholders as dividends and hence will not affect either total or variable economic profits. However, the investment of stockholder capital will augment total accounting profits and will contribute to the total stock of loans in the economy.

3.2   *Separability of technology*

If the user costs γ_t all moved proportionally, then we could use Hicksian aggregation to aggregate over the firm's joint monetary supplies μ_t. But since that proportionality assumption is not typically reasonable for monetary asset user costs, aggregation over outputs is possible only if outputs are separable from inputs in the financial firm's technology. Hence, in order to establish the existence of an output aggregate, we shall assume that there exist functions f and H such that[14]

---

[14] For the theoretical implications of that assumption for technology, see Denny and Pinto (1978), Hall (1973), and Shephard (1970, p. 275).

$$F(\mu_t, \mathbf{z}_t, \mathbf{L}_t, c_t; \mathbf{k}_t) = H(f(\mu_t; \mathbf{k}_t), \mathbf{z}_t, \mathbf{L}_t, c_t). \tag{3.14}$$

It seems likely that $\mathbf{k}_t$ would enter F only through f, as in (3.14). However, this analysis could easily be extended to the case in which $\mathbf{k}_t$ also enters H as independent arguments.

There will exist a function g such that

$$f(\mu_t; \mathbf{k}_t) = g(\mathbf{z}_t, \mathbf{L}_t, c_t) \tag{3.15}$$

is the solution for $f(\mu_t; \mathbf{k}_t)$ to[15]

$$H(f(\mu_t; \mathbf{k}_t), \mathbf{z}_t, \mathbf{L}_t, c_t) = 0. \tag{3.16}$$

The function $f(\mu_t; \mathbf{k}_t)$ is called the factor requirements function because it equals the right-hand side of (3.15), which is the minimum amount of aggregate input required to produce the vector μ_t. The function $g(\mathbf{z}_t, \mathbf{L}_t, c_t)$ is the production function because it equals the left-hand side of (3.15), which is the maximum amount of aggregate output that can be produced from the inputs $(\mathbf{z}_t, \mathbf{L}_t, c_t)$. Hence f is both the factor requirements function and the outputs aggregator function, while g is both the output production function and the inputs aggregator function.

We assume that f is convex and linearly homogeneous in μ_t. In addition, it follows – from our assumptions on the derivatives of the transformation function F – that g is monotonically increasing in all of its arguments and that f is monotonically increasing in μ_t. We assume that g is locally strictly concave in a neighborhood of the solution to the first-order conditions for variable profit maximization. In addition, it follows – from the strict quasiconvexity of the transformation function F – that g is globally strictly quasiconcave.

4   Demand for monetary assets by manufacturing firms

In addition to consumer demand for monetary assets, there also is demand for monetary assets by manufacturing firms. In this section we formulate the decision problem of such a manufacturing firm when monetary assets enter the firm's production function.[16] The firm is assumed to

---

[15] The existence of g follows from the implicit function theorem and our assumptions on the transformation function F. See footnote 2 of Brown, Caves, and Christensen (1979).

[16] Since manufacturing technology does not depend upon money balances, our production function is actually a derived production function acquired by absorbing the firm's transactions technologies in factor markets into the production function. The existence of such a derived production function follows from the same analysis used to prove the existence of a derived utility function containing monetary balances. See Arrow and Hahn (1971), Phlips and Spinnewyn (1979), and Samuelson and Sato (1984). For explicit derivations of the derived production function based upon a Baumol–Tobin transactions model or a vending-machine model, see Fischer (1974). Fischer (1974, p. 532) concludes

maximize the present value of its profit flow subject to its technology. The firm's intertemporal technology, over its T-period planning horizon, is defined by its transformation function

$$\Omega(\delta_t, ..., \delta_{t+T}, \epsilon_t, ..., \epsilon_{t+T}, \kappa_t, ..., \kappa_{t+T}) = 0, \qquad (4.1)$$

where, for $t \le s \le t + T$:

δ_s = vector of planned production of output quantities during period s;

ϵ_s = vector of planned real balances of monetary assets held during period s; and

κ_s = vector of planned use of other factors during period s.

The firm's technology can be equivalently defined by its efficient production set

$$\Gamma = \{(\delta_t, ..., \delta_{t+T}, \epsilon_t, ..., \epsilon_{t+T}, \kappa_t, ..., \kappa_{t+T}):$$

$$\Omega(\delta_t, ..., \delta_{t+T}, \epsilon_t, ..., \epsilon_{t+T}, \kappa_t, ..., \kappa_{t+T}) = 0\}. \qquad (4.2)$$

The transformation function Ω is assumed to be strictly quasiconvex. In addition, $\partial\Omega/\partial\delta_{is} > 0$, $\partial\Omega/\partial\epsilon_{is} < 0$, and $\partial\Omega/\partial\kappa_{is} < 0$.

The firm's decision problem is formulated in period t for periods $t, t+1, ..., s, ..., t+T$, where T is the number of periods in the firm's planning horizon. During period s, the firm's profits are

$$\Psi_s = \delta_s' \nu_s - \kappa_s' \zeta_s + \sum_i [(1 + r_{i,s-1}) p_{s-1}^* \epsilon_{i,s-1} - p_s^* \epsilon_{is}], \qquad (4.3)$$

where

ν_s = vector of output expected prices, and

ζ_s = vector of expected prices of the factors κ_s.

To simplify the notation, we assume that consumers and manufacturing firms have access to the same monetary assets, so the expected nominal holding period yields on ϵ_s can be viewed as being r_s (defined in Section 2.1). Real balances ϵ_t are defined to equal nominal balances divided by p_t^* (also defined in Section 2.1).[17]

---

that real balances can be entered into production or utility functions unless a "deeper explanation of the demand for money" is needed. Since we are not seeking to explain why people demand money, but rather how they behave when money has value, we have no need for deeper explanation for motives.

[17] This definition is greatly simplifying because it permits use of the same price index, p_t^*, for the manufacturing firm as for the consumer. We shall do the same thing with the financial firm's output in the next section. Thus the same price deflator applies to consumer monetary asset demand, manufacturing firm monetary factor demand, and financial firm output demand. Unfortunately this assumption is not based upon solid theoretical foundations; in principle, a different price deflator should be used in each of the

The discounted present value of the firm's profit flow during the $T+1$ periods plus the discounted present value of the firm's monetary asset portfolio at the end of the planning horizon is

$$\Psi^* = \sum_{s=t}^{t+T} (\Psi_s/\theta_s) + (1/\theta_{t+T+1}) \sum_i p^*_{t+T}\epsilon_{i,t+T}(1+r_{i,t+T}), \quad (4.4)$$

where the discount factor is θ_s, such that $\theta_s = 1.0$ for $s = t$ and

$$\theta_s = \prod_{a=t}^{s-1} (1+R_a) \quad \text{for } t+1 \le s \le t+T+1.$$

We now substitute (4.3) into (4.4) and rearrange the terms, grouping together those terms with common time subscripts. The result is

$$\Psi^* = \sum_{s=t}^{t+T} \delta'_s \bar{\nu}_s - \sum_{s=t}^{t+T} \kappa'_s \bar{\zeta}_s - \sum_{s=t}^{t+T} \epsilon'_s \eta_s + \sum_{i=1}^{n} (1+r_{i,t-1})p^*_{t-1}\epsilon_{t-1}, \quad (4.5)$$

where $\bar{\nu}_s = \nu_s/\theta_s$ and $\bar{\zeta}_s = \zeta_s/\theta_s$ are the discounted present values of the prices ν_s and ζ_s respectively, and where the user cost of ϵ_{is} is

$$\eta_{is} = (p^*_s/\theta_s) - (1+r_{is})p^*_s/\theta_{s+1}. \quad (4.6)$$

Because $\sum_{i=1}^{n}(1+r_{i,t-1})p^*_{t-1}\epsilon_{t-1}$ is wealth endowed from the previous planning horizon, that contribution to present wealth is fixed. Hence the discounted present value of variable profits is

$$\Psi^*_v = \sum_{s=t}^{t+T} \delta_s \bar{\nu}_s - \sum_{s=t}^{t+T} \kappa'_s \bar{\zeta}_s - \sum_{s=t}^{t+T} \epsilon'_s \eta_s, \quad (4.7)$$

which is in conventional form. In addition, the user cost η_{is} in the current period $s = t$ is

$$\eta_{it} = p^*_t \frac{(R_t - r_{it})}{1+R_t}, \quad (4.8)$$

which is in familiar form [see equations (2.4) and (3.12)]. With the conventional decision problem of maximizing variable profit (4.7) subject to (4.1), we have immediate access to the existing literature on aggregation over factors of production, enabling us to aggregate over monetary assets ϵ_t demanded by the manufacturing firm.

The approach used above to derive the user cost formula η_{is} is analogous to that used for physical capital by Diewert (1980a, p. 47). The same result would be acquired from the approach of Coen and Hickman (1970, p. 298), because the first-order conditions for maximization of (4.7) subject to (4.1) include the condition that the marginal rate of substitution

three cases. Our only defense is that perhaps the three theoretically correct deflators may not differ that much. However, our deflator is theoretically correct only for the consumer, since we produced p^*_t from consumer duality theory. For rigorous treatment of firm input and output deflators, see Fisher and Shell (1972, essay 2; 1979; 1981).

between ϵ_{is} and ϵ_{js} be $-\eta_{is}/\eta_{js}$. Using the observations of Diewert (1980a, pp. 478–9), extension of the above results to include taxes is straightforward. See Coen and Hickman (1970, p. 299) for discussion of the approaches to dealing with such further potential complications as differences between borrowing and lending rates, the existence of more than one lending rate, differences in taxation rates, risk-induced dependency upon debt/equity ratios, and so on. The extension of the above result to an infinite planning horizon is immediate by allowing $T \to \infty$ in (4.5).

4.1   *Separability of technology*

For the same reason discussed in (3.2), we shall require that technology be separable, although here separability will be assumed in current monetary assets used as inputs (by the manufacturing firm) rather than in monetary assets produced as outputs (by the financial intermediary). In particular, we assume that there exist functions a and B such that

$$\Omega(\delta_t, \ldots, \delta_{t+T}, \epsilon_t, \ldots, \epsilon_{t+T}, \kappa_t, \ldots, \kappa_{t+T})$$

$$= B(\delta_t, \ldots, \delta_{t+T}, a(\epsilon_t), \epsilon_{t+1}, \ldots, \epsilon_{t+T}, \kappa_t, \ldots, \kappa_{t+T}). \qquad (4.9)$$

In that case, the function $a(\epsilon_t)$ is called a category subproduction function.

Let $(\delta_t^*, \ldots, \delta_{t+T}^*, \epsilon_t^*, \ldots, \epsilon_{t+T}^*, \kappa_t^*, \ldots, \kappa_{t+T}^*)$ be the solution to maximizing (4.7) subject to (4.1), and let $b_t = \epsilon_t^{*\prime} \eta_t$. Then it follows that ϵ_t^* must also be the solution for ϵ_t to the current period conditional decision:

$$\text{maximize } a(\epsilon_t) \quad \text{subject to } \eta_t' \epsilon_t = b_t, \qquad (4.10)$$

which is in the same form as (2.4) for the consumer. In addition, if we divide both sides of the constraint in (4.10) by p_t^* then we obtain the following decision, which is in the same form as (2.6):

$$\text{maximize } a(\epsilon_t) \quad \text{subject to } \eta_t^{*\prime} \epsilon = b_t^*, \qquad (4.11)$$

where $\eta_t^* = \eta_t/p_t^*$ and $b_t^* = b_t/p_t^*$. The function $a(\epsilon_t)$ is assumed to be monotonically increasing and strictly concave in ϵ_t. The large literature in aggregation and index number theory based upon the conventional consumer decision, of form (2.6), is immediately applicable to decision (4.11) and hence to aggregation over ϵ_t.

Numerous simplifying assumptions were made in Sections 2, 3, and 4. Although these assumptions are common in the conventional neoclassical literature, extension of these results to include (for example) uncertainty and differences in taxation rates would be useful. A list of areas needing such extensions in the conventional approach can be found in Diewert (1980b, p. 265).

5   Aggregation theory under homogeneity

The theory of aggregation over goods directly produces unique, exact results when the aggregator function is linearly homogeneous. In that case, the growth rates of the aggregation-theoretic price and quantity aggregates are independent of selected reference levels for utility, prices, or quantities. In addition, the dual quantity and price aggregates then behave in a manner indistinguishable from that of an elementary good. In this section, we discuss that most elegant of situations. In Section 6, we present recent theory relevant to aggregation in the nonhomothetic case.

5.1   *The consumer*

Here we seek to produce the exact aggregation theoretic aggregate over the monetary asset quantities $\mathbf{m}_t$ of Section 2. As shown in Barnett (1980a, 1981a), the exact quantity aggregate is the level of indirect (i.e., optimized) utility

$$M_t^c = \max\{u(\mathbf{m}_t): \boldsymbol{\pi}_t' \mathbf{m}_t = y_t\}, \tag{5.1}$$

so u is the aggregator function that we assume to be linearly homogeneous in this section. Dual to any exact quantity aggregate, there exists a unique price aggregate, one that aggregates over the prices of the goods. Hence there must exist an exact nominal price aggregate over the user costs $\boldsymbol{\pi}_t$, and there must also exist the corresponding real (user cost) price aggregate over $\boldsymbol{\pi}_t^*$. As shown in Barnett (1980a, 1981a), the consumer behaves relative to the dual pair of exact quantity and price aggregates as if they were the quantity and price of an elementary good. As a result, the exact aggregate is empirically indistinguishable from an elementary good.

One of the properties that an exact dual pair of price and quantity aggregates satisfies is Fisher's "factor reversal" test, which states that the product of an exact quantity aggregate and its dual exact price aggregate must equal actual expenditure on the components. Hence if $\Pi^c(\boldsymbol{\pi}_t)$ is the exact user cost aggregate dual to M_t^c, then $\Pi^c(\boldsymbol{\pi}_t)$ must satisfy

$$\Pi^c(\boldsymbol{\pi}_t) = y_t/M_t^c. \tag{5.2}$$

Since (5.2) produces a unique solution for $\Pi^c(\boldsymbol{\pi}_t)$, we could use (5.2) to define $\Pi^c(\boldsymbol{\pi}_t)$. In addition, if we replace M_t^c by the indirect utility function that is defined by (5.1) and use the linear homogeneity of u, we can show that $\Pi_t^c = \Pi^c(\boldsymbol{\pi}_t)$ defined by (5.2) does indeed depend only upon $\boldsymbol{\pi}_t$, and not upon $\mathbf{m}_t$ or y_t. See Barnett (1983b) for a version of that proof. The conclusion produced by that proof can be written in the form

$$\Pi^c(\pi_t) = \left[\max_{\mathbf{m}_t}\{u(\mathbf{m}_t): \pi_t'\mathbf{m}_t = 1\}\right]^{-1},\qquad(5.3)$$

which clearly depends only upon π_t.

Although (5.2) provides a valid definition of Π_t^c, a direct definition (not produced indirectly through M_t^c and Fisher's factor reversal test) is more informative and often more useful. The direct definition depends upon the cost (or expenditure) function E, defined by

$$E(u_0, \pi_t) = \min_{\mathbf{m}_t}\{\pi_t'\mathbf{m}_t: u(\mathbf{m}_t) = u_0\},\qquad(5.4)$$

which equivalently can be acquired by solving the indirect utility function equation (5.1) for y as a function of $u_0 = M_t^c$ and π_t. It can be proved [see, e.g., Shephard (1970, p. 144)] that

$$\Pi^c(\pi_t) = E(1, \pi_t) = \min_{\mathbf{m}_t}\{\pi_t'\mathbf{m}_t: u(\mathbf{m}_t) = 1\},\qquad(5.5)$$

which is often called the unit cost or price function. The unit cost function is the minimum cost of attaining unit utility level for $u(\mathbf{m}_t)$ at given user cost prices π_t. Clearly, (5.5) depends only upon π_t. Hence by (5.2) and (5.5), we see that $\Pi^c(\pi_t) = y_t/M_t^C = E(1, \pi_t)$.

Equation (5.5) is the most informative expression for Π_t^c. For example, it is immediately evident from (5.5) that Π^c is linearly homogeneous in π_t. Hence the real user cost aggregate is $\Pi_t^{c*} = \Pi^c(\pi_t/p_t^*) = \Pi^c(\pi_t)/p_t^*$. In addition, we can see from (5.5) that (M_t^c, Π_t^c) must satisfy Fisher's factor reversal test. The demonstration of that result follows. Observe first that

$$M_t^c\min_{\mathbf{m}_t}\{\pi_t'\mathbf{m}_t: u(\mathbf{m}_t) = 1\} = \min_{\mathbf{m}_t}\{\pi_t'(M_t^c\mathbf{m}_t): M_t^c u(\mathbf{m}_t) = M_t^c\}$$

$$= \min_{\mathbf{m}_t}\{\pi_t'(M_t^c\mathbf{m}_t): u(M_t^c\mathbf{m}_t) = M_t^c\},\qquad(5.6)$$

where the last equality follows from the linear homogeneity of u. If we let $\hat{\mathbf{m}}_t = M_t^c\mathbf{m}_t$, then

$$M_t^c\min_{\mathbf{m}_t}\{\pi_t'\mathbf{m}_t: u(\mathbf{m}_t) = 1\} = \min_{\hat{\mathbf{m}}_t}\{\pi_t'\hat{\mathbf{m}}_t: u(\hat{\mathbf{m}}_t) = M_t^c\}.\qquad(5.7)$$

Hence, by (5.5), we obtain from (5.7) that

$$M_t^c\Pi_t^c = \min_{\hat{\mathbf{m}}_t}\{\pi_t'\hat{\mathbf{m}}_t: u(\hat{\mathbf{m}}_t) = M_t^c\}.\qquad(5.8)$$

However, expenditure minimization (at the optimized value M_t^c of utility) is a necessary condition for utility maximization. Hence the right-hand side of (5.8) will be actual expenditure on the services of $\mathbf{m}_t$, and therefore (5.8) is Fisher's factor reversal test. A more formal proof, not explicitly including monetary assets, is available in Shephard (1970, p. 93).

In addition, (5.1) and (5.5) provide easy interpretations of (M_t^c, Π_t^c). From (5.1), we see that M_t^c is the consumer's optimized utility level from monetary assets held during period t. Hence M_t^c is the consumer's perceived service flow from his selected $\mathbf{m}_t$. In order similarly to interpret Π_t^c, observe from (5.4) and (5.8) that $E(M_t^c, \boldsymbol{\pi}_t) = M_t^c \Pi_t^c$. Differentiating both sides with respect to M_t^c, we see immediately that

$$\Pi_t^c = \partial E(M_t^c, \boldsymbol{\pi}_t) / \partial M_t^c. \tag{5.9}$$

Hence Π_t^c is the marginal cost to the consumer of consuming another unit of aggregate monetary services, M_t^c.

It is interesting to observe that we could work in reverse to derive (5.5) from Fisher's factor reversal test, (5.8). In particular, if we *define* Π_t^c by (5.8), we could then use (5.7) to acquire (5.5) as a conclusion. Alternatively, we could start with (5.8) and simply let $M_t^c = 1$ to acquire (5.5) immediately.

The duality between M_t^c and Π_t^c is evident from (5.1) and (5.5), which use dual decision problems. In addition, the duality between M_t^c and Π_t^c permits us to get back and forth between them easily. The indirect method would be through (5.2). But we also can derive either M_t^c or Π_t^c directly in terms of the other. As can be seen from (5.1), the quantity aggregator function is u, because M_t^c is equal to $u(\mathbf{m}_t^*)$ when $\mathbf{m}_t^*$ is the consumer's chosen (constrained utility-maximizing) choice for $\mathbf{m}_t$. Hence we see immediately that we can derive the user cost price aggregate directly from the corresponding quantity aggregator function from either (5.3) or (5.5). Conversely, the quantity aggregate $M_t^c = u(\mathbf{m}_t^*)$ can be derived directly from the price aggregator function Π^c, because

$$u(\mathbf{m}_t^*) = \left[\max_{\boldsymbol{\pi} \geq 0} \{ \Pi^c(\boldsymbol{\pi}) : \boldsymbol{\pi}' \mathbf{m}_t^* = 1 \} \right]^{-1}. \tag{5.10}$$

See Diewert (1978).

We now have the fundamental aggregation-theoretic tools for aggregating over goods within the decision of a consumer. The reason that M_t^c and Π_t^c are called exact aggregates is that (M_t^c, Π_t^c) can be used to decompose the consumer's decision into a two-stage budgeting process. In the first stage, M_t^c is treated as an elementary good with price Π_t^c within the intertemporal utility maximization decision. In particular, M_t^c appears in place of $u(\mathbf{m}_t)$ within the intertemporal utility function U_t. Having solved for M_t^c in the first stage, the consumer then solves for $\mathbf{m}_t$ from the second-stage decision (2.4), with y_t determined from $M_t^c \Pi_t^c$. For all possible nonnegative values of prices and wealth, the two-stage decision will produce the same solution as the original complete decision defined in Section 2.1 or 2.2. Hence (M_t^c, Π_t^c) are behaviorally indistinguishable from the quantity and price of an elementary good. The details of the two-stage budgeting theorem are available in Barnett (1980a, 1981a) and Green (1964, Theorem 4).

5.2   *The manufacturing firm*

Since the decision problems (2.6) and (4.11) are in the same form, the aggregation theory in Section 5.1 for consumer demand for monetary assets is immediately applicable to aggregation over monetary assets demanded by a manufacturing firm. The only change is in the interpretation of the quantity aggregator function. With a consumer, the quantity aggregator function is the category subutility function u. With a manufacturing firm, the quantity aggregator function is the category subproduction function $a(\epsilon_t)$. Clearly, the quantity aggregator function in both cases is the objective function of the corresponding conditional decision problem, (2.6) or (4.11).

In the case of demand by a manufacturing firm, however, a particularly interesting interpretation of the derivable two-stage budgeting process is available, as has been observed by Blackorby, Primont, and Russell (1978, p. 210). Restating their interpretation of separable factor demand in terms of monetary asset demand, the following becomes available under our assumptions. Instead of maximizing profits directly in a single joint decision, the firm can produce the same optimum solution by decentralizing its monetary portfolio decisions to a financial "division" or department, which is instructed to maximize its financial services with a fixed allocated budget b_t. In other words, the financial division is asked to select its monetary portfolio ϵ_t by solving decision problem (4.10). In order for that decentralized decision to be solvable, the firm's corporate office must be able to determine the optimal level of monetary expenditure b_t to be supplied to the financial division before it solves problem (4.10). It can be shown that the firm can produce that correct prior solution for b_t from its first-stage decision problem. That first-stage decision requires knowledge of the firm's exact monetary user cost aggregate $\Pi_t^f = \Pi^f(\eta_t)$, which can be acquired by the financial division from the right-hand side of (5.3) or of (5.5) when the symbols (functions or variables) from the consumer's decision are replaced in the obvious manner by the corresponding symbols from the firm's decision. That correspondence between symbols is the one acquired by replacing decision (2.6) with decision (4.11).

In summary, the firm could operate in the following decentralized manner. The financial division uses (5.3) or (5.5) to acquire Π_t^f, which the financial division supplies to the firm's corporate office. The corporate office then solves the firm's first-stage decision to acquire the profit-maximizing budget b_t to be allocated to financial services. Having received b_t, the financial division then selects the optimal portfolio of monetary assets ϵ_t by solving problem (4.10) to maximize monetary services M_t^f available from the fixed budget. The result is exact profit maximization by the firm. The resulting exact monetary quantity aggregate, as with the consumer, is (5.1) (with the obvious change of symbols between consumers and firms). Observe that the monetary quantity aggregate M_t^f is the optimized level of the financial division's objective function, and hence is the optimized monetary asset service flow.

In the above decentralized two-stage decision, we have identified the second-stage decision to be decision problem (4.10), which is solved conditionally upon b_t. However, we have not formally defined the first-stage ("corporate office") decision, which is needed to determine the profit maximizing portfolio services budget b_t. That first-stage decision is to select $(\delta_t^*, ..., \delta_{t+T}^*, M_t^f, \epsilon_{t+1}^*, ..., \epsilon_{t+T}^*, \kappa_t^*, ..., \kappa_{t+T}^*)$ to maximize the discounted present value of variable profits

$$\Psi_v^* = \sum_{s=t}^{t+T} \delta_s \bar{\nu}_s - \sum_{s=t}^{t+T} \kappa_s' \bar{\zeta}_s - \sum_{s=t+1}^{t+T} \epsilon_s' \eta_s - M_t^f \Pi_t^f, \tag{5.11}$$

subject to

$$B(\delta_t, ..., \delta_{t+T}, M_t^f, \epsilon_{t+1}, ..., \epsilon_{t+T}, \kappa_t, ..., \kappa_{t+T}) = 0. \tag{5.12}$$

Having solved that decision, involving the aggregated quantity M_t^f and price Π_t^f, the optimal budget for financial services is immediately available as $b_t = M_t^f \Pi_t^f$.

The consumer's two-stage decision can be interpreted in an analogous manner, but with the quantity aggregator function u viewed as the consumer's transactions technology.

5.2.1   The two-stage decentralized decision
The fact that two-stage decentralization is possible, and that it always produces the firm's profit-maximizing solution for all values, is easily proved when the two-stage decision is restated in a different form. Since that result previously has been proved only for single-output firms, we now provide the proof for multiple-output firms. The proof is a straightforward extension of Shephard's (1970, pp. 144–6) result with a single-output technology. In this section, we assume that the second-stage decision (the financial division's decision) is to minimize cost at fixed output of monetary services. Hence the corporate office, after solving the first-stage decision, supplies M_t^f to the financial division, which then minimizes cost subject to $a(\epsilon_t) = M_t^f$. In our previous equivalent interpretation, the

corporate office supplies $b_t = M_t^f \Pi_t^f$ to the financial division, which then maximizes $a(\epsilon_t)$ subject to the condition that cost cannot exceed b_t.

We shall need the firm's full intertemporal variable cost function

$$C(\delta_t, \ldots, \delta_{t+T}, \bar{\zeta}_t, \ldots, \bar{\zeta}_{t+T}, \eta_t, \ldots, \eta_{t+T})$$

$$= \min_{(\kappa_t, \ldots, \kappa_{t+T}, \epsilon_t, \ldots, \epsilon_{t+T})} \left\{ \sum_{s=t}^{t+T} \kappa_s' \bar{\zeta}_s + \sum_{s=t}^{t+T} \epsilon_s' \eta_t : B(\delta_t, \ldots, \delta_{t+T}, \right.$$

$$\left. a(\epsilon_t), \epsilon_{t+1}, \ldots, \epsilon_{t+T}, \kappa_t, \ldots, \kappa_{t+T}) = 0 \right\}. \qquad (5.13)$$

Observe that (5.13) is acquired by minimizing all of the firm's variable factor costs. In contrast, the subcost function $E(a_0, \eta_t)$, defined by the production analog to (5.4), is acquired by minimizing only the firm's monetary service costs. In particular, that subcost function is

$$E(a_0, \eta_t) = \min_{\epsilon_t} \{ \eta_t' \epsilon_t : a(\epsilon_t) = a_0 \}. \qquad (5.14)$$

Let

$$\delta = (\delta_t', \ldots, \delta_{t+T}')', \qquad \bar{\zeta} = (\bar{\zeta}_t', \ldots, \bar{\zeta}_{t+T}')', \qquad \eta = (\eta_t', \ldots, \eta_{t+T}')',$$

$$\kappa = (\kappa_t', \ldots, \kappa_{t+T}')', \qquad \epsilon = (\epsilon_t', \ldots, \epsilon_{t+T}')', \quad \text{and} \quad \bar{\nu} = (\bar{\nu}_t', \ldots, \bar{\nu}_{t+T}')'.$$

We now prove the following theorem, which is needed to prove the consistency of the two-stage decision.

Theorem 5.1:

$$C(\delta, \bar{\zeta}, \eta) = \min_{(\kappa, a_0, \epsilon_{t+1}, \ldots, \epsilon_{t+T})} \left\{ \kappa' \bar{\zeta} + E(a_0, \eta_t) \right.$$

$$\left. + \sum_{s=t+1}^{t+T} \epsilon_s' \eta_s : B(\delta, a_0, \epsilon_{t+1}, \ldots, \epsilon_{t+T}, \kappa) = 0 \right\}.$$

Proof: Define (κ^*, ϵ^*) to solve the minimization problem in (5.13), so that

$$C(\delta, \bar{\zeta}, \eta) = \kappa^* \bar{\zeta} + \epsilon^{*\prime} \eta \qquad (5.15)$$

with

$$B(\delta, a(\epsilon_t^*), \epsilon_{t+1}^*, \ldots, \epsilon_{t+T}^*, \kappa^*) = 0; \qquad (5.16)$$

and define $(\hat{\kappa}, \hat{a}_0, \hat{\epsilon}_{t+1}, \ldots, \hat{\epsilon}_{t+T})$ such that

$$\min_{(\kappa, a_0, \epsilon_{t+1}, \ldots, \epsilon_{t+T})} \left\{ \kappa' \bar{\zeta} + E(a_0, \eta_t) + \sum_{s=t+1}^{t+T} \epsilon_s' \eta_s : B(\delta, a_0, \epsilon_{t+1}, \ldots, \epsilon_{t+T}, \kappa) = 0 \right\}$$

$$= \hat{\kappa}' \bar{\zeta} + E(\hat{a}_0, \eta_t) + \sum_{s=t+1}^{t+T} \hat{\epsilon}_s' \eta_s \qquad (5.17)$$

with

$$B(\delta, \hat{a}_0, \hat{\epsilon}_{t+1}, \ldots, \hat{\epsilon}_{t+T}, \hat{\kappa}) = 0; \qquad (5.18)$$

but suppose that

$$\kappa^{*\prime}\bar{\zeta} + \epsilon^{*\prime}\eta \neq \hat{\kappa}\bar{\zeta} + E(\hat{a}_0, \eta_t) + \sum_{s=t+1}^{t+T} \hat{\epsilon}_s'\eta_s. \qquad (5.19)$$

Define $\hat{\epsilon}_t$ to solve the minimization problem in (5.14) when $a_0 = \hat{a}_0$, so that

$$E(\hat{a}_0, \eta_t) = \eta_t' \hat{\epsilon}_t \qquad (5.20)$$

with

$$a(\hat{\epsilon}_t) = \hat{a}_0. \qquad (5.21)$$

Then, by (5.18) and (5.21), we have that

$$B(\delta, a(\hat{\epsilon}_t), \hat{\epsilon}_{t+1}, \ldots, \hat{\epsilon}_{t+T}, \hat{\kappa}) = 0, \qquad (5.22)$$

so $(\hat{\kappa}, \hat{\epsilon}_t, \hat{\epsilon}_{t+1}, \ldots, \hat{\epsilon}_{t+T})$ is feasible for the minimization problem in (5.13). Hence, by the definition of (κ^*, ϵ^*), we see that

$$\kappa^{*\prime}\bar{\zeta} + \epsilon_t^{*\prime}\eta_t + \sum_{s=t+1}^{t+T} \epsilon_s^{*\prime}\eta_s < \hat{\kappa}'\bar{\zeta} + \hat{\epsilon}_t'\eta_t + \sum_{s=t+1}^{t+T} \hat{\epsilon}_s'\eta_s. \qquad (5.23)$$

Let $a_0^* = a(e_t^*)$. Then, by (5.16), we have that

$$B(\delta, a_0^*, \epsilon_{t+1}^*, \ldots, \epsilon_{t+T}^*, \kappa^*) = 0,$$

so $(\kappa^*, a_0^*, \epsilon_{t+1}^*, \ldots, \epsilon_{t+T}^*)$ is feasible for the minimization problem in (5.17). But by (5.13), ϵ_t^* must minimize $\eta_t' \epsilon_t$ subject to

$$B(\delta, a(\epsilon_t), \epsilon_{t+1}^*, \ldots, \epsilon_{t+T}^*, \kappa^*) = 0. \qquad (5.24)$$

Also, by the monotonicity of B in $a(\epsilon_t)$ and by (5.16), it follows that (5.24) is true if and only if $a(\epsilon_t) = a_0^*$. Hence ϵ_t^* must minimize $\eta' \epsilon_t$ subject to $a(\epsilon_t) = a_0^*$, which is the minimization problem in (5.14). So

$$E(a_0^*, \eta_t) = \eta_t' \epsilon_t^*. \qquad (5.25)$$

By the feasibility of $(\kappa^*, a_0^*, \epsilon_{t+1}^*, \ldots, \epsilon_{t+T}^*)$ in the minimization problem in (5.17) and by the definition of $(\hat{\kappa}, \hat{\epsilon}_t, \hat{\epsilon}_{t+1}, \ldots, \hat{\epsilon}_{t+T})$, it follows that

$$\hat{\kappa}'\bar{\zeta} + E(\hat{a}_0, \eta_t) + \sum_{s=t+1}^{t+T} \hat{\epsilon}_s'\eta_s < \kappa^{*\prime}\bar{\zeta} + E(a_0^*, \eta_t) + \sum_{s=t+1}^{t+T} \epsilon_s^{*\prime}\eta_s.$$

Combining that result with (5.20) and (5.25), we contradict (5.23).

Q.E.D.

Producing the firm's decentralized two-stage decision problem is now straightforward. First observe from the production analog of (5.8) that

$$\Pi_t^f(\eta_t)a_0 = E(a_0, \eta_t),$$

which is just Fisher's factor reversal test. From Theorem 1 we therefore have that

$$C(\delta, \bar{\zeta}, \eta) = \min_{(\kappa, a_0, \epsilon_{t+1}, \ldots, \epsilon_{t+T})} \left\{ \kappa' \bar{\zeta} + \Pi_t^f(\eta_t)a_0 + \sum_{s=t+1}^{t+T} \epsilon_s' \eta_s : \right.$$
$$\left. B(\delta, a_0, \epsilon_{t+1}, \ldots, \epsilon_{t+T}, \kappa) = 0 \right\}. \qquad (5.26)$$

The firm maximizes profits by solving for the output levels δ to maximize $\delta \nu - C(\delta, \bar{\zeta}, \eta)$. Hence it follows from (5.26) that the firm can maximize profits by selecting $(\delta^*, \kappa^*, a_0^*, \epsilon_{t+1}^*, \ldots, \epsilon_{t+T}^*)$ to

$$\text{maximize } \delta \nu - \kappa' \bar{\zeta} - \Pi_t^f(\eta_t)a_0 - \sum_{s=t+1}^{t+T} \epsilon_s' \eta_s$$

$$\text{subject to } B(\delta, a_0, \epsilon_{t+1}, \ldots, \epsilon_{t+T}, \kappa) = 0, \qquad (5.27)$$

which is the first-stage decision.

In the second stage, the firm's corporate office instructs the financial division to purchase a_0^* quantity units of monetary services at minimum cost. The financial division then selects the monetary asset portfolio ϵ_t^* to solve the decision problem on the right-hand side of (5.14) with a_0 set at a_0^*. At this point the firm has optimally solved its full profit-maximization problem, because $(\delta^*, \kappa^*, \epsilon_t^*, \epsilon_{t+1}^*, \ldots, \epsilon_{t+T}^*)$ is the profit-maximizing input–output vector.

Recall that a necessary condition for profit maximization is that ϵ_t^* solve problem (4.2). Hence it follows from the production analog of (5.1) that the firm's solution value for $a_0^* = a(\epsilon_t^*)$ must equal its exact monetary quantity aggregate

$$M_t^f = \max\{a(\epsilon_t): \eta_t' \epsilon_t = b_t\}. \qquad (5.28)$$

The corresponding exact economic price aggregate clearly is $\Pi_t^f(\eta_t)$.

The above two-stage decomposition of the firm's profit-maximization decision provides the reason for defining M_t^f and $\Pi_t^f(\eta_t)$ to be the firm's exact monetary quantity and price aggregates. However, that decomposition can also be used as a means for estimating the firm's technology in two stages. See Fuss (1977).[18]

5.3   *The financial intermediary*

The aggregation theory relevant to aggregating over the outputs of the multiproduct financial firm is analogous to that for aggregation over the

---

[18] Fuss's procedure also requires use of the fact that homogeneous separability of a production function implies corresponding homogeneous separability of the cost function.

financial inputs of the manufacturing firm, but with the manufacturing firm's cost function replaced by the financial firm's revenue (or "benefit") function. In this manner we can produce a two-stage decision for the financial intermediary. In the first stage the firm solves for profit-maximizing factor demands and the profit-maximizing level of aggregate financial assets produced. In the second stage, the revenue-maximizing vector of individual financial asset quantities supplied is determined at fixed aggregate financial asset quantity supplied.

To display that decomposition of the firm's profit-maximization decision, we start by defining the relevant revenue functions. The financial firm's revenue function is

$$R^*(\alpha_t, \gamma_t; \mathbf{k}_t) = \max_{\mu_t}\{\mu_t'\gamma_t : f(\mu_t; \mathbf{k}_t) = g(\alpha_t)\}, \tag{5.29}$$

which is the revenue function analog of the manufacturing firm's cost function (5.13). The firm selects α_t to maximize variable profits

$$P_t = R^*(\alpha_t, \gamma_t, \mathbf{k}_t) - \alpha_t'\beta_t. \tag{5.30}$$

However, by Shephard's (1970, p. 251) Proposition 83, it follows that there exists a linearly homogeneous output price aggregator function Γ such that [19]

$$R^*(\alpha_t, \gamma_t; \mathbf{k}_t) = \Gamma(\gamma_t)g(\alpha_t). \tag{5.31}$$

Hence the financial firm's variable profits can alternatively be written as

$$P_t = \Gamma(\gamma_t)g(\alpha_t) - \alpha_t'\beta_t. \tag{5.32}$$

The firm's first-stage decision is to select α_t^* to maximize (5.32). Substituting the optimized input vector α_t^* into $g(\alpha_t)$, the firm can compute the optimum aggregate monetary asset quantity supplied, M_t^b. In stage two of the decentralized decision, M_t^b is substituted into (5.29) to replace $g(\alpha_t)$, and the maximization problem in (5.29) is solved to acquire the optimum vector of individual monetary assets μ_t produced. Observe that the intermediary's supply function for its monetary aggregate is produced from stage one alone.

Clearly, the exact economic output quantity aggregate for the financial firm is

$$M_t^b = f(\mu_t^*; \mathbf{k}_t), \tag{5.33}$$

when μ_t^* is the profit-maximizing vector of monetary assets produced; the corresponding output price aggregate is

---

[19] An analogous result exists for the firm's inputs. Under our assumptions of separability and homogeneity of the output aggregator function, Hall (1973) has shown that the firm's cost function is separable, such that $C(\mu_t, \beta_t; \mathbf{k}_t) = f(\mu_t, \mathbf{k}_t)P(\beta_t)$, where $P(\beta_t)$ is the factor price aggregate.

$$\Gamma_t^b = \Gamma(\gamma_t). \tag{5.34}$$

Fisher's output reversal test states that $M_t^b \Gamma_t^b$ must equal actual revenue from production of μ_t^*. That condition is satisfied as a result of (5.29), (5.31), and the fact that $f(\mu_t^*; \mathbf{k}_t)$ must equal $g(\alpha_t)$ at $\alpha_t = \alpha_t^*$. Also observe from (5.29) and (5.31), with $g(\alpha_t)$ set equal to 1.0, that the output price aggregate is equal to

$$\Gamma(\gamma_t) = \max_{\mu_t}\{\mu_t' \gamma_t : f(\mu_t; \mathbf{k}_t) = 1\}, \tag{5.35}$$

which is the unit revenue function. The unit revenue function is the maximum revenue that can be acquired from the production of one unit of the output monetary aggregate, $M_t^b = f(\mu_t; \mathbf{k}_t)$. The linear homogeneity of Γ is clear from (5.35). In addition, the unit revenue function is convex and increasing in γ_t.

It is easily shown that – instead of maximizing $\mu_t' \gamma_t$ subject to

$$f(\mu_t; \mathbf{k}_t) = g(\alpha_t^*)$$

to acquire the stage-two solution for μ_t^* – we could equivalently define the stage-two decision to be the selection of μ_t^* to minimize the aggregate factor requirement $f(\mu_t; \mathbf{k}_t)$ subject to

$$\mu_t' \gamma_t = \Gamma(\gamma_t) g(\alpha_t^*).^{[20]}$$

As a result, we can rewrite (5.33) to obtain

$$M_t^b = \min_{\mu_t}\{f(\mu_t; \mathbf{k}_t) : \mu_t' \gamma_t = \Gamma(\gamma_t) g(\alpha_t^*)\}, \tag{5.36}$$

while our earlier statement of the stage-two decision produces the equivalent result that

$$M_t^b \Gamma(\gamma_t) = \max_{\mu_t}\{\mu_t' \gamma_t : f(\mu_t; \mathbf{k}_t) = g(\alpha_t^*)\}. \tag{5.37}$$

Comparing (5.35) and (5.36), we can see the clear duality between the decision problems. As usual, the exact quantity and price aggregates of economic theory are true duals.

Equation (5.35) defines the unit revenue (output price aggregator) function in terms of the factor requirement (output quantity aggregator) function. The converse is also possible as a result of the fact that

$$\mathbf{f}(\mu_t^*; \mathbf{k}_t) = \left[\max_{\gamma_t \geq 0}\{\Gamma(\gamma_t) : \mu_t^{*'} \gamma_t = 1\}\right]^{-1},$$

which is the output analog to (5.10).

---

[20] The proof uses (5.31) to equate the first-order conditions for both decisions.

5.4   Summary of aggregator functions

The aggregation theory presented above demonstrates that a unique correct monetary quantity and price aggregator function exists for each of the three economic agents (the consumer, the manufacturing firm, and the financial intermediary) when the aggregator function is linearly homogeneous. We summarize below the aggregator function found in each case.

In the consumer case, the monetary quantity aggregate is given by (5.1). If $\mathbf{m}_t^*$ is the consumer's optimal portfolio that solves the decision problem on the right-hand side of (5.1), we see that the exact monetary quantity aggregate is $M_t^c = u(\mathbf{m}_t^*)$, so u is the monetary quantity aggregator function. The corresponding dual user-cost price aggregate is given by $\Pi^c(\boldsymbol{\pi}_t)$, defined in (5.5), where Π^c is the unit cost function dual to the category utility function u. So the price aggregator function is the unit cost function.

In the case of the manufacturing firm, the exact monetary quantity aggregate is given by (5.28). Hence if $\boldsymbol{\epsilon}_t^*$ is the firm's optimal portfolio that solves the decision problem on the right-hand side of (5.28), then the firm's exact monetary quantity aggregate is $M_t^f = a(\boldsymbol{\epsilon}_t^*)$, so the category production function a is the monetary quantity aggregator function. The corresponding dual user-cost price aggregate is given by $\Pi^f(\boldsymbol{\eta}_t)$, where Π^f is the unit cost function dual to the category production function a. So the price aggregator function again is the unit cost function.

In the case of the financial intermediary, the exact monetary quantity aggregate is given by (5.33), (5.36), or (5.37). Hence if $\boldsymbol{\mu}_t^*$ is the firm's profit-maximizing vector of monetary assets produced, then $M_t^b = f(\boldsymbol{\mu}_t^*; \mathbf{k}_t)$ is the firm's exact monetary supply quantity aggregate, so the input requirement function f is the firm's monetary quantity aggregator function. The corresponding dual monetary price aggregate is $\Gamma(\boldsymbol{\gamma}_t)$, defined in (5.35). So the financial intermediary's output price aggregator function is its unit revenue function Γ.

5.5   Subaggregation

In Section 5.4 we provided a single monetary quantity aggregator function for each economic agent. This quantity aggregate in each case aggregates over all of the monetary assets demanded or supplied by the economic agent. However, exact subaggregates also exist if the quantity aggregator functions in Section 5.4 are weakly separable in a subvector of the monetary assets demanded or supplied, and if those subfunctions are linearly homogeneous. The resulting weakly separable subfunction is an exact aggregator function over its subvector of monetary asset components, and the corresponding unit cost or unit revenue function is the dual user-cost price aggregate. By nesting weakly separable blocks within weakly separable blocks, a hierarchy of nested exact aggregates can be produced. See Barnett (1980a, 1981a) for the construction of such a hierarchy of exact monetary assets for a representative consumer.

The two-stage decision described above can be extended into an n-stage decision for an n-level hierarchy of nested monetary aggregates. The fact that the n-stage decision produces the optimal solution for the economic agent can be proved from induction, using the results for the corresponding two-stage decision. The theory of multistage recursive aggregation has been developed in detail by Blackorby, Primont, and Russell (1978).

By nesting weakly separable blocks within weakly separable blocks to produce recursive subaggregation, the consumer's utility function produces a "utility tree" [see, e.g., Barnett (1980a, 1981a)]. The analogous structure for the manufacturing firm's production function is a "production tree." In that case, the firm can optimize factor intensities within branches and then optimize between subset intensities conditionally upon the fixed preselected intensities within branches. [See, e.g., Berndt and Christensen (1973).] Whenever a quantity aggregator function is itself weakly separable into subfunctions, the subfunctions are themselves quantity aggregator functions at a lower level of aggregation. If those subfunctions are linearly homogeneous, then the price (unit cost or unit revenue) function is also correspondingly weakly separable. The resulting subfunctions of the price function are the price (unit cost or unit revenue) functions dual to the corresponding quantity aggregator functions.[21] See Diewert (1970). Hence all of the quantity and price aggregator functions are easily produced at all applicable levels of aggregation.

6   Index number theory under homogeneity

The results in Section 5 provide unique exact economic aggregator functions for aggregating over monetary assets demanded or supplied by each of the three classes of economic agents. Each of the resulting monetary quantity aggregates depends only upon the component monetary asset quantities and the form of the aggregator function. To use such an aggregate, it is necessary to select a parameterized econometric specification

---

[21] In addition, for a consumer the indirect utility function – written in terms of expenditure normalized prices – is also correspondingly weakly separable. The subfunctions are the indirect utility functions dual to the corresponding quantity aggregator functions.

for the aggregator function and estimate its parameters. Estimating aggregator functions and exploring their properties plays an important role in the aggregation theory literature. For many purposes, however, the most useful aggregates are those produced without the need to estimate unknown parameters. In that case, nonparametric approximations to the unknown aggregator functions are needed. The production of such nonparametric approximations is the subject of index number theory.

Index number theory eliminates the need to estimate unknown parameters by using both prices and quantities simultaneously, along with approximation techniques often resembling revealed preference theory, in order to estimate economic quantity aggregates that depend only upon quantities and not prices. Similarly, index number theory uses both prices and quantities simultaneously in order to approximate economic price aggregates that depend only upon prices and not quantities.

6.1   The consumer and the manufacturing firm

Solution of the decision problem (2.6) is a necessary condition (with the appropriate selection of notation) for optimal portfolio choice for either the consumer or the manufacturing firm, and the exact monetary aggregate is the optimized value of the objective function in either case. Hence the approximation theory relevant to producing a nonparametric approximation to the exact aggregate is the same in both. Therefore, we present the index number theory only for the consumer in this section. The corresponding results for the manufacturing firm could be acquired immediately by changing notation in the obvious way.

If $\mathbf{m}_t^*$ is acquired by solving (2.6), then $u(\mathbf{m}_t^*)$ is the exact monetary aggregate M_t^c. In continuous time, $M_t^c = u(\mathbf{m}_t^*)$ can be tracked without error [see Barnett (1983b) for a proof] by the Divisia index, which provides M_t^c as the solution to the differential equation

$$d \log M_t^c/dt = \sum_i s_{it} d \log m_{it}^*/dt, \qquad (6.1)$$

where $s_{it} = \pi_{it} m_{it}^*/y_t = \pi_{it}^* m_{it}^*/y_t^*$ is the ith asset's share in expenditure on the total portfolio's service flow. Note that $\mathbf{m}_t^*$ in (6.1) must continually solve (2.6) for (6.1) to hold.

In continuous time, under our assumptions the Divisia index is perfect. There is no remainder term in its approximation [see, e.g., Hulten 1973)], regardless of the form of the unknown function u. In discrete time, however, many different approximations to (6.1) are possible, because $\mathbf{s}_t = (s_{1t}, ..., s_{nt})'$ need not be constant during any given time interval. With annual data, differences between such approximations can be substantial. The most popular discrete time approximation to the Divisia index is the Törnqvist–Theil approximation (often called the Törnqvist index), which is just the Simpson's rule approximation:

$$\log M_t^c - \log M_{t-1}^c = \sum_i \bar{s}_{it}(\log m_{it}^* - \log m_{i,t-1}^*), \qquad (6.2)$$

where $\bar{s}_{it} = \frac{1}{2}(s_{it} + s_{i,t-1})$. By using the Simpson's rule average shares, $\mathbf{s}_t^* = (\bar{s}_{it}, \ldots, \bar{s}_{nt})'$, the index (6.2) has obvious appeal as a discrete time approximation to the Divisia index (6.1). Hence in discrete time we shall call (6.2) simply the Divisia index.

Recently, a very compelling reason has appeared for using (6.2) as the discrete time approximation to the Divisia index. Diewert (1976) has defined a class of index numbers, called "superlative" index numbers, which have particular appeal in producing discrete time approximations to $M_t^c = u(\mathbf{m}_t^*)$. Diewert defines a superlative index number to be one that is exactly correct for some quadratic approximation to u. The discrete Divisia index (6.2) is in the superlative class because it is exact for the translog specification for u. The translog is quadratic in the logarithms. As a result, if the translog specification is not exactly correct then the discrete Divisia index (6.2) has a third-order remainder term in the changes, since quadratic approximations possess third-order remainder terms. With weekly or monthly monetary asset data, the Divisia index (6.2) is accurate to within three decimal places, which is smaller than the data's roundoff error [see Barnett (1980a)].[22]

The Fisher ideal index is another popular element of Diewert's superlative class, and was proposed for use with monetary data, along with the Divisia index, by Barnett (1980a, 1981a). The Fisher ideal index is exact for the square root of the quadratic specification for u. Usually the Fisher ideal and Divisia index are identical (to within roundoff error) with monetary data.[23] Nevertheless, on theoretical grounds the Divisia index is now the preferred selection from the superlative class by index number theorists, largely as a result of its uniquely attractive properties in the nonhomothetic case (to be discussed in Section 8 below).

When the quantity aggregate M_t^c is acquired from the Divisia index, the dual user-cost price index, called the implicit Divisia price index, is acquired from Fisher's factor reversal test $\Pi_t^c = y_t/M_t^c$. Since relative user

---

[22] In addition, Star and Hall (1976) derived an analytic expression for the error in the discrete Divisia approximation to the exact continuous time Divisia index. He found that the error is always small if the shares do not fluctuate wildly.

[23] An exception is when a new asset is introduced. Special procedures, involving the imputation of a reservation price, are needed in that case. See Diewert (1980a, sec. 8.6). In addition, special procedures are needed to deal with seasonality. See Diewert (1980a, sec. 8.7).

costs usually vary more than relative quantities, use of the Divisia index to produce the quantity aggregate, with the price aggregate produced from factor reversal, is preferable to the converse. See Allen and Diewert (1981). When M_t^c is produced from the discrete Divisia index, it is easily shown that the implicit Divisia price index, produced from factor reversal, is superlative in the Diewert sense.

6.2   The financial intermediary

The financial intermediary's output aggregation is produced from a decision which does not have the same form as the decision that produced the Divisia index for the consumer or manufacturing firm. Monetary output aggregation is produced by solving the financial intermediary's second-stage decision for μ_t^* and substituting it into f to acquire $M_t^b = f(\mu_t^*; \mathbf{k}_t)$. That second-stage decision is to select μ_t to

$$\text{maximize } \mu_t' \gamma_t \quad \text{subject to } f(\mu_t; \mathbf{k}_t) = M_t^b. \tag{6.3}$$

The following theorem proves that the Divisia index tracks M_t^b without error in continuous time, so long as μ_t^* is continually selected to solve (6.3) at each instant, t.

Theorem 6.1: *If μ_t^* solves (6.3) continually at each instant $t \in T_0$, then for every $t \in T_0$*

$$d \log M_t^b / dt = \sum_i s_{it}^b \, d \log \mu_{it}^* / dt,$$

where the ith asset's share in the financial intermediary's revenue from production of monetary services is $s_{it}^b = \gamma_{it} \mu_{it}^* / \gamma_t' \mu_t^{*'}$.

Proof: The first-order conditions for solution to (6.3) are

$$\gamma_{it} = -\lambda \partial f / \partial \mu_{it} \tag{6.4}$$

and $f(\mu_t^*; \mathbf{k}_t) = M_t^b$, where λ is the Lagrange multiplier.

Compute the total differential of f to acquire

$$df(\mu_t; \mathbf{k}_t) = \sum_i \frac{\partial f}{\partial \mu_{it}} d\mu_{it}.$$

Substitute (6.4) to find, at $\mu_t = \mu_t^*$, that

$$\lambda df(\mu_t^*; \mathbf{k}_t) = -\sum_i \gamma_{it} d\mu_{it}^*. \tag{6.5}$$

But by summing (6.4) over i and solving for λ, we have that

$$\lambda = -\frac{\mu_t^{*\prime}\gamma_t}{\mu_t^{*\prime}\partial f/\partial \mu_t}.$$ (6.6)

Substitute (6.6) into (6.5) and rearrange to obtain

$$d\log f(\mu_t^*;\mathbf{k}_t) = \frac{\mu_t^{*\prime}\partial f/\partial \mu_t}{f(\mu_t^*;\mathbf{k}_t)} \sum_i \frac{\gamma_{it}}{\mu_t^{*\prime}\gamma_t} d\mu_{it}.$$ (6.7)

But since f is linearly homogeneous in μ_t, we have from Euler's equation that

$$\mu_t^{*\prime}\partial f/\partial \mu_t = f(\mu_t^*;\mathbf{k}_t).$$ (6.8)

Substituting (6.8) into (6.7), we obtain

$$d\log f(\mu_t^*;\mathbf{k}_t)/dt = \sum_i s_{it}^b d\log \mu_{it}^*/dt,$$

where $s_{it}^b = \gamma_{it}\mu_{it}^*/\gamma_t'\mu_t^*.$ Q.E.D.

Hence the Divisia index is equally as applicable to aggregating over the monetary assets produced by the financial intermediary as over the monetary assets purchased by the consumer or manufacturing firm. In addition, Simpson's rule again produces the Törnqvist–Theil discrete time approximation

$$\log M_t^b - \log M_{t-1}^b = \sum_i \bar{s}_{it}^b(\log \mu_{it}^* - \log \mu_{i,t-1}^*),$$ (6.9)

where $\bar{s}_{it}^b = \frac{1}{2}(s_{it}^b + s_{i,t-1}^b)$. Furthermore, if the input requirement function f is translog, then the discrete Divisia index (6.9) is exact in discrete time [see Diewert (1976, p. 125)]. Hence (6.9) is a superlative index number. The reason for preferring the Divisia index over the other superlative indexes will be evident from the nonhomothetic case below.

While the Divisia monetary quantity index takes the same form for all three economic agents, the financial firm's monetary output aggregate nevertheless is distinguishable from the monetary aggregates for the consumer or manufacturing firm, because only the financial intermediary's aggregate depends upon reserve requirements $\mathbf{k}_t$. The financial intermediary's monetary asset user costs γ_t each depend directly in (3.8) upon the "reserve requirement tax" produced by nonzero $\mathbf{k}_t$ with no interest paid on required reserves. But the financial intermediary's monetary quantity aggregator function f also depends upon $\mathbf{k}_t$. Hence the Divisia quantity index for the financial intermediary depends upon $\mathbf{k}_t$ both through the effect on γ_t and also upon $f(\mu_t^*;\mathbf{k}_t)$, which the Divisia index seeks to track. As a result, the Divisia monetary quantity index for the financial intermediaries tends to internalize the effects of changes in reserve requirements.

Having produced the output quantity aggregate from the Divisia index, the dual price aggregate is produced from output reversal,

$$\Gamma_t = \mu_t^{*\prime} \gamma_t / M_t^b. \tag{6.10}$$

The user-cost price index produced in that manner is called the implicit Divisia price index. The resulting price index is superlative in the Diewert sense, as is easily shown from (6.10) and the fact that M_t^b is superlative.

7 Aggregation theory without homotheticity

As we have seen in Sections 4 and 5, aggregation theory and index number theory provide readily derived results when aggregator functions are linearly homogeneous. However, linear homogeneity is a strong assumption, especially for a consumer.[24] As a result, despite the elegance of the theory produced under linear homogeneity, extension of aggregation and index number theory to the nonhomothetic case can be very important empirically. As concluded by Samuelson and Swamy (1974, p. 592):

Empirical experience is abundant that the Santa Claus hypothesis of homotheticity in tastes and in technical change is quite unrealistic. Therefore, we must not be bemused by the undoubted elegances and richness of the homothetic theory. Nor should we shoot the honest theorist who points out to us the unavoidable truth that in nonhomothetic cases of realistic life, one must not expect to be able to make the naive measurements that untutored common sense always longs for; we must accept the sad facts of life, and be grateful for the more complicated procedures economic theory devises.

This section deals with the most promising of those more complicated procedures devised by economic theory.

The quantity and price aggregates presented in previous sections were produced from duality theory under the assumption that the category utility (or production) function defined over the component quantities is linearly homogeneous. However, in recent years it has been shown in the literature on duality theory that the quantity and price aggregates produced under that homogeneity assumption are special cases of a more general pair of dual functions that are applicable without any homotheticity assumptions on tastes or technology. In this section we provide the more general aggregation theory, as it applies to the three economic agents postulated in Sections 2, 3, and 4.

---

[24] It can be shown that an aggregator function is linearly homogeneous if and only if the elasticity of substitution – between a given good outside the separable block and a good within the block – is independent of the good within the block.

7.1 *The consumer and the manufacturing firm*

As we have seen in the homogeneous case, the monetary aggregation theory applicable to the manufacturing firm is identical to that of the consumer, since the decision problems producing the aggregates are identical. All of the monetary aggregation theory for both economic agents is produced by the second-stage decision problem (2.4): The conditional portfolio decision (2.4) for the consumer is converted to the manufacturing firm's conditional portfolio decision (4.10) by a simple change of notation. Hence, in this section we shall use (2.4) with the understanding that the appropriate change of notation would be used if our results were applied to the manufacturing firm rather than the consumer. However we now no longer assume that u is linearly homogeneous, or even homothetic.

As we have seen, under linear homogeneity of u, the quantity aggregator function is the category subutility function u itself. However, if u is not linearly homogeneous, u clearly cannot serve the role of the quantity aggregator function because a quantity aggregator function that is not linearly homogeneous does not make sense. If every component quantity is growing at the same rate, then any sensible quantity aggregate would have to grow at that same rate. But that is the definition of linear homogeneity. Hence the theoretically appropriate quantity aggregator function should be linearly homogeneous in the component quantities $\mathbf{m}_t$, and should reduce to the category subutility function u in the special case of linearly homogeneous u. The corresponding price aggregator function should be the true dual to the quantity aggregator function, should be linearly homogeneous in the component prices, and should reduce to the unit cost function (5.5) in the case of linearly homogeneous category subutility u. It has been shown in recent literature that the duals that best serve those purposes are the distance function at fixed utility level (as the quantity aggregate) and the cost function at fixed utility level (as the dual price aggregate). When normalized to equal one at base-period prices and utility, the result is the aggregation-theoretic Malmquist quantity index and the Konüs true-cost-of-living index, respectively.

Before we can present these results, we must define the distance function, $d(u_0, \mathbf{m}_t)$, at u_0. That function can be defined in implicit form to be the solution to the equation

$$u(\mathbf{m}_t/d(u_0, \mathbf{m}_t)) = u_0 \tag{7.1}$$

for preselected fixed reference utility level u_0.[25] Equation (7.1) has an interesting geometric interpretation. We see that $d(u_0, \mathbf{m}_t)$ is the factor

---

[25] The equivalent direct definition is $d(u_0, \mathbf{m}_t) = \max_\kappa \{\kappa : u(\mathbf{m}_t/\kappa) \geq u_0\}$.

by which $\mathbf{m}_t$ must be deflated to reduce (or increase) the utility level to the fixed reference level u_0. In other words, we move along the direction of the $\mathbf{m}_t$ vector until we intersect the isoquant $u(\mathbf{m}_t) = u_0$; then $d(u_0, \mathbf{m}_t)$ measures how far that intersection point is from the point $\mathbf{m}_t$. While (7.1) defines the distance function in terms of the utility function, we also can do the converse, since the utility function is the solution for u to $d(u, \mathbf{m}_t) = 1$.

The distance function (at fixed u_0) is indeed linearly homogeneous, monotonically increasing, and strictly concave in $\mathbf{m}_t$, even when u is not linearly homogeneous. Hence, when u is linearly homogeneous, u has exactly the same properties that d always has, regardless of whether or not u is linearly homogeneous. In addition, when u actually is linearly homogeneous, the distance function becomes proportional to the utility function. Hence, when u is linear homogeneous, the quantity aggregate produced from the distance function will always grow at exactly the same rate as the quantity aggregate $u(\mathbf{m}_t^*)$ that we already have derived in the case of linearly homogeneous u. This fact is easily seen by observing that linear homogeneity of u implies that $u(\mathbf{m}_t)/d(u_0, \mathbf{m}_t) = u(\mathbf{m}_t/d(u_0, \mathbf{m}_t))$, which equals u_0 by (7.1). Hence $d(u_0, \mathbf{m}_t) = u(\mathbf{m}_t)/u_0$, which is proportional to $u(\mathbf{m}_t)$ at fixed u_0.

In order to acquire the dual price aggregate, we need only observe the following two relationships, which follow from equations (7.4) and (7.5) in Deaton and Muellbauer (1980, p. 55):

$$d(u_0, \mathbf{m}_t) = \min_{\boldsymbol{\pi}_t} \{\boldsymbol{\pi}_t' \mathbf{m}_t : E(u_0, \boldsymbol{\pi}_t) = 1\} \tag{7.2}$$

and

$$E(u_0, \boldsymbol{\pi}_t) = \min_{\mathbf{m}_t} \{\boldsymbol{\pi}_t' \mathbf{m}_t : d(u_0, \mathbf{m}_t) = 1\}. \tag{7.3}$$

Equations (7.2) and (7.3) demonstrate that the distance function d and the cost function E are duals.[26] As we therefore might expect, the price aggregate in general is the cost function, as a function of $\boldsymbol{\pi}_t$, at fixed reference utility level u_0.

At fixed reference u_0, the cost function has all of the correct properties for a price aggregator function, including linear homogeneity in $\boldsymbol{\pi}_t$. In addition, the cost function is monotonically increasing and concave in $\boldsymbol{\pi}_t$. Hence, regardless of whether or not u is linearly homogeneous, the cost function has all of the same properties that the unit cost function has when u is linearly homogeneous. In addition, if category subutility really is linearly homogeneous, we get the same price aggregate growth

---

[26] Also, d and E have some interesting and useful derivative properties. See Deaton (1979, p. 394).

rates by using the cost function as we did in Section 5 when we used the unit cost function, since the two functions are then proportional to each other. That result follows from (5.7) by setting M_t^c equal to u_0; the proportionality constant becomes u_0. Observe that both the exact quantity aggregate produced by the distance function and the exact price aggregate produced by the cost function are entirely ordinal, because each is invariant to monotonic transformations of utility.

In order for the duality defined in (7.2) and (7.3) to be perfect, we also need the distance and cost functions to satisfy factor reversal, when consumer decisions are made optimally. Gorman (1976) has shown this to be the case.[27] Following earlier work by Afriat, Gorman defines the price vector π_t and the quantity vector $\mathbf{m}_t$ to be "conjugate" at category subutility level u_0, if the cheapest way to reach u_0 at prices π_t is a vector proportional to $\mathbf{m}_t$. Gorman proved that if $\tilde{\pi}_t$ and $\tilde{\mathbf{m}}_t$ are conjugates in that sense, then

$$M^c(\tilde{\mathbf{m}}_t; u_0)\Pi^c(\tilde{\pi}_t; u_0) = \tilde{\mathbf{m}}_t' \tilde{\pi}_t, \tag{7.4}$$

where the exact monetary aggregate is

$$M^c(\mathbf{m}_t; u_0) = d(u_0, \mathbf{m}_t) \tag{7.5}$$

and the exact dual monetary user-cost aggregate is

$$\Pi^c(\pi_t; u_0) = E(u_0, \pi_t). \tag{7.6}$$

Clearly, (7.4) is factor reversal at $(\tilde{\mathbf{m}}_t, \tilde{\pi}_t)$.[28]

In aggregation theory, exact economic *aggregates* are converted to exact economic *indexes* by dividing by a base period value of the aggregate. The natural ways thereby to convert (7.5) and (7.6) into exact economic indexes are

$$M^{mc}(\mathbf{m}_{t_2}, \mathbf{m}_{t_1}; u_0) = d(u_0, \mathbf{m}_{t_2})/d(u_0, \mathbf{m}_{t_1}) \tag{7.7}$$

and

$$\Pi^{kc}(\pi_{t_2}, \pi_{t_1}; u_0) = E(u_0, \pi_{t_2})/E(u_0, \pi_{t_1}). \tag{7.8}$$

The price index $\Pi^{kc}(\pi_{t_2}, \pi_{t_1}; u_0)$ is the famous Konüs (1924) true-cost-of-living index. The dual quantity index $M^{mc}(\mathbf{m}_{t_2}, \mathbf{m}_{t_1}; u_0)$ is the Malmquist index, proposed in consumer theory by Malmquist (1953) and later in producer theory by Moorsteen (1961).

At this point, it is clear why the case of linear homogeneity of u is so important. Without linear homogeneity of utility, the exact quantity and price aggregator functions M^{mc} and Π^{kc}, although unique and based upon

[27] Also see Deaton (1979) for a clear presentation of the relevant theory.
[28] In addition, Malmquist (1953, p. 234) has shown that a reference utility level u_0 always exists such that the Malmquist and Konüs indexes satisfy factor reversal. The proof is reproduced in Diewert (1981, p. 177).

very elegant duality theory, nevertheless depend upon a reference utility level u_0; and the index provides no information about how to choose the reference utility level. The base period need not be t_1, or t_2. Hence the aggregation theory is equally applicable for any selection of u_0. It can be shown that M^{mc} and Π^{kc} are independent of u_0 if and only if category utility is linearly homogeneous [see Diewert (1981, sec. 3)]. Otherwise the exact economic monetary quantity and price aggregates depend upon the reference utility surface relative to which the indexes are defined.

Although the Konüs true-cost-of-living index has long been recognized to be the correct price index in economic aggregation theory, recognition that the Malmquist quantity index is the correct dual quantity index has been more recent. Previously, the quantity index commonly viewed to be exact was the Allen index

$$M^{ac}(\mathbf{m}_{t_2}, \mathbf{m}_{t_1}; \pi_0) = E(u(\mathbf{m}_{t_2}); \pi_0)/E(u(\mathbf{m}_{t_1}); \pi_0). \tag{7.9}$$

whereas the Malmquist quantity index depends upon an undefined value for u_0, the Allen quantity index depends upon an undefined value for the reference user-cost price vector π_0, which need not be the prices at either t_2 or t_1. Although the Allen index is now primarily of historical interest only, we nevertheless shall see that our choice of a statistical (nonparametric) quantity index number will be the same, regardless of whether it is viewed to be an approximation to the exact parametric Malmquist index or to the Allen index.[29] It is also interesting to observe that in the case of linearly homogeneous utility, the Malmquist and Allen indexes are equal.

7.2 The financial intermediary

As may be expected from our results in the homogeneous case, the results in Section 7.1 for the consumer and manufacturing firm apply also to aggregation of financial intermediary output with a nonhomogeneous factor requirement function, if we replace the cost function by its output analogue, the revenue function, and if we replace the category subutility function u [or $a(\epsilon_t)$ for the manufacturing firm] by its output analogue, the factor requirements function.

By analogy to (7.1), define the financial firm's output distance function implicitly to be the value of $D(\mu_t, \alpha_t, \mathbf{k}_t)$ that solves

$$f(\mu_t/D(\mu_t, \alpha_t; \mathbf{k}_t); \mathbf{k}_t) = g(\alpha_0), \tag{7.10}$$

for preselected reference input vector α_0.[30] Then the exact monetary quantity output aggregate for the financial intermediary is

[29] The primary defect of the Allen index is the fact that it is not linearly homogeneous in $\mathbf{m}_t$. Diewert (1981, p. 174).
[30] The equivalent direct definition is $D(\mu_t, \alpha_t; \mathbf{k}_t) = \min_\kappa \{\kappa: f(\mu_t/\kappa; \mathbf{k}_t) \le g(\alpha_0)\}$.

$$M^b(\mu_t; \alpha_0, \mathbf{k}_t) = D(\mu_t, \alpha_0; \mathbf{k}_t), \tag{7.11}$$

and the corresponding Malmquist economic output quantity index is

$$M^{mb}(\mu_{t_2}, \mu_{t_1}; \alpha_0, \mathbf{k}_t) = D(\mu_{t_2}, \alpha_0; \mathbf{k}_t)/D(\mu_{t_1}, \alpha_0; \mathbf{k}_t). \tag{7.12}$$

The corresponding dual Konüs monetary output price index is produced by replacing the cost function in Section 7.1 by its output analogue, the revenue function (5.29). Hence the true output price aggregate is

$$\Gamma(\gamma_t; \alpha_0, \mathbf{k}_t) = R^*(\alpha_0, \gamma_t; \mathbf{k}_t), \tag{7.13}$$

and the corresponding Konüs true financial output price aggregate is

$$\Gamma^k(\gamma_{t_2}, \gamma_{t_1}; \alpha_0, \mathbf{k}_t) = R^*(\alpha_0, \gamma_{t_2}; \mathbf{k}_t)/R^*(\alpha_0, \gamma_{t_1}; \mathbf{k}_t). \tag{7.14}$$

Again we find that, in the case of nonhomogeneity (of f), the exact economic output price and quantity aggregates and indexes depend upon an undefined choice. In this case, that choice is of the reference input vector α_0. The dependency upon α_0 disappears if and only if the factor requirement function is linearly homogeneous, in which case the results above reduce to those in Section 5.3.

The duality results analogous to (7.2) and (7.3) are

$$D(\mu_t, \alpha_0; \mathbf{k}_t) = \max_{\gamma_t}\{\gamma_t'\mu_t : R^*(\alpha_0, \gamma_t; \mathbf{k}_t) = 1\} \tag{7.15}$$

and

$$R^*(\alpha_0, \gamma_t; \mathbf{k}_t) = \max_{\mu_t}\{\gamma_t'\mu_t : D(\mu_t, \alpha_0; \mathbf{k}_t) = 1\}. \tag{7.16}$$

8   Index number theory under nonhomogeneity

There are a number of published approaches to producing nonparametric approximations to the Malmquist or Allen quantity index. Yet virtually all of them result in selection of the discrete (Törnqvist) Divisia index. In fact, it is the nonhomogeneous case in which the Divisia index stands out as being the uniquely best element of Diewert's superlative class. When Denny asked whether it is possible to acquire superlative indexes other than the Divisia in the nonhomothetic case, Diewert (1980c, p. 538) replied: "My answer is that it may be possible, but I have not been able to do it." More recently, Caves, Christensen, and Diewert (1982b, p. 1411) have proved that the (discrete) Divisia index "is superlative in a considerably more general sense than shown by Diewert. We are not aware of other indexes that can be shown to be superlative in this more general sense."

8.1   *The consumer and the manufacturing firm*

Perhaps the first rigorously proved theoretical results on nonparametric approximation in the nonhomothetic case are those of Theil (1968) and Kloek (1967). Their result produces the following conclusion in our case. Suppose that $\mathbf{m}_{t_i}$ is the consumer's utility-maximizing monetary asset portfolio at user-cost prices π_{t_i} and at expenditure $\pi'_{t_i}\mathbf{m}_{t_i}$ (with $i = 1$ or 2), and let π_0 be the vector having $(\pi_{t_1 k}\pi_{t_2 k})^{1/2}$ as its kth component. Then the (discrete) Divisia index provides a second-order approximation to the Allen quantity index (7.9).

More recently Diewert (1976, pp. 123–4) has proved that the discrete Divisia index is exact for the Malmquist quantity index (7.7) under a specific choice for the distance function and the reference utility level. In our case, those assumptions would be that: the distance function d is non-homogeneous translog; $\mathbf{m}_{t_i}$ is the consumer's utility-maximizing monetary asset portfolio at user-cost prices π_{t_i} and at expenditure $\pi'_{t_i}\mathbf{m}_{t_i}$ (with $i = 1$ or 2); and the reference utility level u_0 is $(u_1 u_2)^{1/2}$, where $u_1 = u(\mathbf{m}_{t_1})$ and $u_2 = u(\mathbf{m}_{t_2})$. Since the translog specification can produce a second-order approximation to any distance function, we see that the Divisia index produces a second-order approximation to any Malmquist quantity index if the reference utility level is selected in accordance with Diewert's theorem.

In addition, it has recently been shown that the Divisia index is not only exact for a nonhomothetic translog aggregator function, but remains appropriate even when tastes or technology are changing over time. The Divisia index is a chained index which measures changes relative to the previous period, rather than relative to a fixed base period. As a result, it has always been believed that the Divisia index would work well with shifting tastes or technology, since chained indexes adjust rapidly to the latest form of a shifting aggregator function.[31] However, Caves, Christensen, and Diewert (1982a, b) have recently found a precise relationship between the Divisia quantity index and a shifting aggregator function. In particular, their result shows that if u shifts between periods t_1 and t_2 then the Divisia index accurately produces the log change in aggregate consumption (or factor demand, for the manufacturing firm) of monetary services by the consumer, if the distance function is nonhomothetic translog in both periods t_1 and t_2 such that the second-order terms in $\mathbf{m}_t$ have the same coefficients in both periods. The result does not require constancy of the remaining coefficients or homotheticity of u.

Any of the above results can be used to prove that the implicit Divisia user-cost price index, produced from the Divisia quantity index and

---

[31] See, e.g., Samuelson and Swamy (1974, p. 587) and Diewert (1976, footnote 16).

factor reversal, possesses the same approximation properties relative to the Konüs true-cost-of-living index that the Divisia quantity index possesses relative to the Malmquist (or Allen) quantity index. Also, the results imputed above to consumer monetary portfolio aggregation clearly are immediately applicable to manufacturing firm monetary portfolio demand. We need only replace the consumer's category subutility function u with the manufacturing firm's category subproduction function a.

8.2   The financial intermediary

All of the results described in Section 8.1 are equally applicable to providing nonparametric ("statistical") approximations to the financial intermediary's monetary asset output Malmquist quantity index (7.12) and its dual Konüs user-cost price aggregate, (7.14). All that is needed is to replace the input distance function d by the output distance function D, and the cost function E by the revenue function R^*. See Diewert (1976, p. 125; 1980, p. 463) and Caves, Christensen, and Diewert (1982b, sec. 3).

8.3   Subaggregation

In Section 5.5, we discussed the theory of exact subaggregation in economic aggregation theory. The resulting utility or production tree can produce recursive aggregation over increasingly broad aggregates – for example, from Divisia M1, to Divisia M2, to Divisia M3, to Divisia L. However, the aggregation theory is in terms of exact aggregator functions, recursively nested. The question naturally arises as to whether statistical index numbers, such as the Divisia index, can be nested within each other to produce Divisia indexes of Divisia indexes at successively higher levels of aggregation.

If, for example, Divisia indexes of Divisia indexes are Divisia indexes of the original components, then the Divisia index would be called consistent in aggregation. A statistical index that has the property of consistency in aggregation is the Vartia (1976) index. However, the Vartia quantity index has the extremely unattractive property of not being invariant to rescaling of the prices in either period. Similarly, the Vartia price index does not increase at the same rate as second-period prices, when all second-period prices are inflated by a common rate. The Vartia index is also not a superlative index. However, the Divisia index is almost consistent in aggregation, since the Divisia index of Divisia indexes differs from the Divisia index over the original components only by an error of the third order. These results apply in discrete time, regardless of whether the category subutility or category subproduction function is linearly homogeneous.

Of course, in continuous time the Divisia index is exactly consistent in aggregation in the homogeneous case, because the Divisia index then is exact at all levels of aggregation for any aggregator function. There are no remainder terms.

9   Aggregation over consumers and firms

The aggregation theory presented above is for individual decision makers: either one consumer, one manufacturing firm, or one financial intermediary. We have not discussed aggregation over individual decision makers, although a large literature exists on the subject. In this section we cite a few of the more useful results in that literature, and present one particularly interesting result that is specific to the Divisia index.

The subject of aggregation over consumers has been heavily researched, and the results are well known. The most important of those results are surveyed in Barnett (1983a, 1983b) and will not be repeated here. Two different literatures exist on aggregation over firms. One literature resembles that for aggregation over consumers, but a more specialized literature exists on the derivation of production transformation surfaces for an industry or the entire economy. Sato (1975) has provided an excellent survey of that literature.[32] One of his more interesting results (1975, p. 283) is that a constant-returns-to-scale economy-wide production function exists if there is a social utility function. As a result, aggregation over consumers can itself produce perfect aggregation over firms. Other results on aggregation over firms are surveyed in Diewert (1980a, pp. 464–70). Particularly useful results are those of Bliss (1975, p. 146) and Debreu (1959, p. 45), who found that if all firms are competitive profit maximizers, then the group of firms can be treated as a single firm maximizing profits subject to the sum of the individual firm's production sets. That result provides a very simple means of aggregating over firms.

All of the theory presented above is directly linked to deterministic microeconomic and aggregation theory. However, the Divisia index can be acquired in another manner, one that easily permits aggregation over goods, consumers, and firms jointly. This approach, called the *atomistic* approach and championed by Theil (1967) and Clements and Izan (1984), treats the expenditure weights in the Divisia index as the probabilities of drawing the corresponding quantity log changes. Then the Divisia quantity index is just the mean of the distribution of log changes. To see how easily we can thereby also aggregate jointly over economic agents, consider the case of demand for monetary assets by the consumer and the

---

[32] He derives an industry production transformation surface on p. 282.

manufacturing firm. In continuous time, the consumer's Divisia monetary quantity index can be written in differential form as

$$d \log M_t^c = \sum_i s_{it}^c d \log m_{it}^*, \tag{9.1}$$

where $s_{it}^c = \pi_{it} m_{it} / \pi_t' \mathbf{m}_t$ can be interpreted as the probability of drawing $d \log m_{it}^*$ in a random sampling from the population of monetary asset growth rates at t by consumer i. The analogous Divisia index for the manufacturing firm is

$$d \log M_t^f = \sum_i s_{it}^f d \log \eta_{it}, \tag{9.2}$$

where $s_{it}^f = \eta_{it} \epsilon_{it} / \eta_t' \epsilon_t$.

Now let Π_t^c be the implicit Divisia user-cost aggregate produced from M_t^c and factor reversal, and let Π_t^f be the implicit Divisia user-cost aggregate produced from M_t^f and factor reversal. Let $W_t^f = \Pi_t^f M_t^f / (\Pi_t^f M_t^f + \Pi_t^c M_t^c)$ and $W_t^c = \Pi_t^c M_t^c / (\Pi_t^f M_t^f + \Pi_t^c M_t^c)$. Then the shares (W_t^f, W_t^c) can be interpreted as probabilities, so that we can find the Divisia quantity M_t^{fc} aggregated over both the firm and consumer by

$$d \log M_t^{fc} = W^f d \log M_t^f + W^c d \log M_t^c. \tag{9.3}$$

Substituting (9.1) and (9.2) into (9.3), we find that

$$d \log M_t^{fc} = \sum_i \frac{\eta_{it} \epsilon_{it}}{\Pi_t^f M_t^f + \Pi_t^c M_t^c} d \log \eta_{it}$$
$$+ \sum_i \frac{\pi_{it} m_{it}}{\Pi_t^f M_t^f + \Pi_t^c M_t^c} d \log m_{it}. \tag{9.4}$$

Clearly (9.4) is itself a Divisia index, since

$$\sum_i \frac{\eta_{it} \epsilon_{it}}{\Pi_t^f M_t^f + \Pi_t^c M_t^c} + \sum_i \frac{\pi_{it} m_{it}}{\Pi_t^f M_t^f + \Pi_t^c M_t^c} = 1,$$

so (9.4) is a share-weighted average of log change. But (9.4) aggregates *simultaneously* over monetary assets demanded by both the consumer and the manufacturing firm. This procedure is equally applicable to aggregation over monetary assets demanded by many consumers and firms. The approach is most advantageously used to aggregate over monetary assets demanded by different pre-aggregated groups of asset holders (e.g., firms, rich consumers, other consumers, etc.) when the ability to decompose the aggregate into the group subaggregates could be useful. Prior aggregation over the groups could be in accordance with the methods mentioned earlier in this section.

10   Technical change

It has frequently been argued that substantial technical change occurred
in the banking industry over the past decade. The potential existence of
technological innovation in that industry has sometimes been viewed as a
complicating factor in financial modeling and in monetary policy. However, aggregation theory and index number theory are directly relevant
to measuring technical change. In fact, a long literature exists on that
subject. In this section, we discuss some of those results that are most
relevant to measuring technical change in the banking industry. We shall
do so in terms of the technology of our financial intermediary.

When technical change is possible, the financial intermediary's production function is

$$M_t^b = g(\alpha_t, t),\tag{10.1}$$

where α_t is the vector of factor inputs and

$$M_t^b = f(\mu_t; k_t)\tag{10.2}$$

is the exact economic quantity aggregate over monetary asset outputs μ_t.
Technical change in production of aggregate monetary output is thereby
equivalent to a shift in technology in (10.1) over time, so $g(\alpha_t, t)$ must
have time as an argument. In accordance with Ohta's (1974) definition,
the primal (as opposed to dual) rate of total factor productivity is

$$\partial \log g(\alpha_t, t)/\partial t \,|_{\alpha_t},$$

which measures the rate of disembodied technical change.[33]

Consider first the simplest case, which is neutral technological progress. Then there must exist a function $\phi(t)$ of time such that (10.1) can
be written

$$M_t^b = \phi(t)g(\alpha_t),\tag{10.3}$$

with variation in $\phi(t)$ producing parallel translations of isoquants. In discrete time, according to Ohta's definition, the rate of disembodied technical change is the log change of (10.3) with α_t held constant:

$$(\log M_{t+1}^b - \log m_t^b)\,|_{\alpha_t} = \log(\phi(t+1)/\phi(t)).\tag{10.4}$$

Substituting (10.3) into (10.4), we obtain

[33] Also see Berndt and Khaled (1979). The dual rate of total cost diminution is

$$-\partial \log C^b(\mu_t, \beta_t, t)/\partial t \,|_{\mu_t, \beta_t},$$

which is used in Diewert (1980b, sec. III).

$$(\log M_{t+1}^b - \log M_t^b)\,|_{\alpha_t} = \log(M_{t+1}^b/M_t^b) - \log(g(\alpha_{t+1})/g(\alpha_t)). \quad (10.5)$$

If the input aggregator function (or output production function) g is linearly homogeneous, then

$$\log(g(\alpha_{t+1})/g(\alpha_t)) = \log g(\alpha_{t+1}) - \log g(\alpha_t) \quad (10.6)$$

can be measured by the discrete Divisia index over input quantities α_t. Since the index is superlative, the error is third-order. If the output aggregator function f is also linearly homogeneous, then

$$\log(M_{t+1}^b/M_t^b) = \log M_{t+1}^b - \log M_t^b \quad (10.7)$$

can be measured by the discrete Divisia index over output quantities μ_t. Hence we can see from (10.5), (10.6), and (10.7) that the rate of technical change can be measured by the difference between two Divisia indexes, one aggregating over output quantities and the other aggregating over input quantities. In continuous time, the result measures the total rate of disembodied technical change exactly.[34] If f and g are both translog, then the result is also exact in discrete time.[35]

Since we explicitly assumed output separability when we defined the technology of the financial intermediary in Section 3, we do so in the above derivation as well. However, it is worth observing that the result can be adapted to the case of nonseparability [see Diewert (1976, pp. 127-9)]. The results also can be generalized to the case of nonhomothetic g and f; see Caves, Christensen, and Diewert (1982a, b). In that case, technical progress is defined in terms of Malmquist input and output indexes. When the distance functions used to define the Malmquist input and output indexes are translog, the rate of technological change again is measured exactly in terms of Divisia input and output indices.

For a discussion of nonneutral technical change, see Jorgensen and Lau (1975). In that case, the Divisia index still measures aggregate monetary output by the financial intermediary (regardless of the technical progress), but measurement of the technical progress itself requires estimation of the firm's technology, containing an index of technological change.

11   Value added

In monetary theory, outside money plays an important role because outside (or high-powered, or base) money is not wealth, whereas the potential

---

[34] For a proof, see Diewert (1981, p. 20) or Diewert (1980b, pp. 261-2).

[35] Sometimes $\phi(t)-1$ is treated as the rate of technical progress. In that case, there is said to be technical progress if $\phi(t)>0$ or technical regress if $\phi(t)<0$. Clearly for (10.3), we see that $\phi(t)$ can be computed from the ratio of the output Divisia index to the input Divisia index.

wealth effect of inside money is often viewed as offset by equal liabilities corresponding to each such asset. Although outside money certainly is uniquely important in many ways, it seems worth observing that there is value added produced by the banking industry. So long as primary factors of production other than base money are employed in that industry, the banking industry produces net services that were not embodied in the industry's employment of outside money. In this section we discuss the measurement of value added for our financial intermediary.

Partition the financial intermediary's input vector α_t so that $\alpha_t = (\alpha'_{1t}, \alpha'_{1t})'$, where α_{1t} is quantities of primary inputs (such as labor, capital, and land), and α_{2t} is quantities of intermediate inputs (such as materials).[36] Partition the factor-price vector correspondingly so that $\beta_t = (\beta'_{1t}, \beta'_{2t})'$. Then the financial intermediary's technology can be written as

$$M_t^b = g(\alpha_{1t}, \alpha_{2t}).\tag{11.1}$$

Let the firm's maximum variable profit level at given α_{1t} be

$$V_t = V(\alpha_{1t}, \beta_{2t}, \gamma_t),\tag{11.2}$$

which is the firm's variable profit function conditional upon α_{1t}. As a function of α_{1t} at fixed prices, V has all of the usual properties of a neoclassical production function. Sato (1975) calls

$$V_{t_0, t_1} = V(\alpha_{1t_0}, \beta_2^*, \gamma^*)/V(\alpha_{1t_1}, \beta_2^*, \gamma^*)\tag{11.3}$$

the true index of real value added, which depends upon the selection of the reference prices (β_2^*, γ^*).[37]

In order to provide a nonparametric (statistical) approximation to (11.3), assume constant returns to scale. Also assume that V is translog and select (β_2^*, γ^*) to be the geometric means of those prices in periods t_0 and t_1. Diewert (1980a, p. 459) then has shown that (11.3) equals the discrete Divisia quantity index for aggregating over the primary inputs.

The need to select the reference prices (β_2^*, γ^*) becomes unnecessary if and only if g is separable, so that (11.1) can be written

$$M_t^b = G(\zeta(\alpha_{1t}), \alpha_{2t}).\tag{11.4}$$

In that case, V can be written[38]

$$V_t = V_1(\alpha_{1t})V_2(\beta_{2t}, \gamma_t).\tag{11.5}$$

---

[36] In some models all production by every firm is value added. In that case, all firms are completely vertically integrated, so no intermediate inputs exist. See Sato (1975, p. 280).

[37] Also see Diewert (1980a) and Bridge (1971, pp. 324–43). The variable profit function in real terms measures real income originating within the firm.

[38] See Lau (1978, sec. 2).

So clearly

$$V_{t_0, t_1} = V_1(\alpha_{1 t_0}) / V_1(\alpha_{1 t_1}), \tag{11.6}$$

which does not depend upon reference prices. The function V_1 has all of the properties of a conventional neoclassical production function. However in this case $\zeta(\alpha_{1t})$ is itself a category subproduction function, so we can more directly define the value added index to be[39]

$$V_{t_0, t_1}^* = \zeta(\alpha_{1 t_0}) / \zeta(\alpha_{1 t_1}). \tag{11.7}$$

If ζ is translog, then the discrete Divisia index is exact for either (11.7) or (11.6), so the discrete Divisia index provides a second-order approximation for V_{t_0, t_1}^* or V_{t_0, t_1} for any ζ. In continuous time, the Divisia index is always exact for $\zeta(\alpha_{1t})$, which is value added. Clearly high-powered money is all value added if and only if α_{1t} contains only high-powered money.

The source of the term "value added" can be found in the accounting conventions for measuring value added. The accounting convention, called "double deflation," requires the very restrictive assumption that (11.4) can be written in the form

$$M_t^b = \zeta_1(\alpha_{1t}) + \zeta_2(\alpha_{2t}). \tag{11.8}$$

Clearly $\zeta_1(\alpha_{1t})$ is value added, since it is added to $\zeta_2(\alpha_{2t})$ to get M_t^b. In that case, Sims (1969) has proved that value added is measured exactly by a Divisia index.

12   Macroeconomic and general equilibrium theory

In terms of its relationship with final targets of policy, the demand-side Divisia monetary aggregates are the most relevant. Those aggregates measure the economy's monetary service flow, as perceived by the users of monetary assets. As a result, it might seem that we would be interested only in the consumer and manufacturing firm, whose decisions are analogous and pose little difficulty. This convenient situation would arise, for example, if we were seeking monetary aggregates to be used as indicators. Frequently, however, money plays a more complex role in economics. For example, a money market appears in most macroeconomic models and in many recent general equilibrium models. Policy simulations with macroeconometric models usually require a modeled money market. In addition, targeting a monetary aggregate requires information about the supply function for the aggregate. All of these objectives would be facili-

---

[39] See Denny and May (1978).

tated if the supply-side Divisia monetary aggregates from the financial firm, along with the transmission mechanism from central bank instruments, were incorporated into a full model of the economy. Producing a cleared money market in a Divisia monetary aggregate along with a transmission mechanism operating through that market is an objective toward which the above research is tending. However, much research remains before such a closed model could be constructed.

If a model included only a demand-side Divisia monetary aggregate, then closing a complete model would require modeling the supply of every component in the Divisia monetary aggregate. Market clearing then would occur at the level of disaggregated component quantities, which then could be substituted into the Divisia demand monetary aggregate. While the resulting aggregate could be informative and useful, much of the potential simplification is lost by the need to produce completely disaggregated supply functions. However, incorporating both supply and demand aggregates in a model – which would be needed to produce a market for an aggregate – has been given very little consideration in aggregation theory. Many difficult issues arise. What do we do if the financial firm's technology is separable in different blockings of monetary assets from those that appear in the consumer's utility function or the manufacturing firm's technology? How do we deal with the fact that currency and primary monetary securities appear as components of the consumer's and manufacturing firm's monetary demand aggregate, but not as components of the financial firm's monetary output aggregate? What happens to the ability to close the money market if homotheticity applies on one side of the money market while nonhomotheticity requires use of a Malmquist index on the other side of the market?

One potential problem is immediately evident from the results in prior sections. The user-cost prices of monetary assets produced by the financial intermediary are different from those for the consumer (or manufacturing firm). The reason is the existence of reserve requirements, which produce an implicit tax on financial intermediaries. The tax does not affect the user cost of the same assets for consumers or financial firms. Income taxes produce similar "wedges" between user costs on the supply and demand sides of the money markets. As a result, even when the markets for every component are cleared, the Divisia demand and corresponding Divisia supply aggregate need not be equal because the different user costs can produce different weights, although all corresponding component quantities nevertheless may be equal.

Another potential problem results from the fact that in parts of some macroeconomic models, monetary wealth rather than the monetary service flow is relevant. This could be the case, for example, in producing an argument of a consumption function. Then it is necessary to compute the expected discounted present value of the service flow. The expected service flow in a future period is measured by its expected Divisia index. For a discussion of the appropria†e use of capital stocks and capital service flows, see Usher (1980, pp. 17–18).

We do not propose here to imbed our three economic agents (along with a government sector) into a closed model, since we view that objective as a subject for future research. However, we do present a few simple results relevant to the use of monetary aggregation theory within macroeconomics.

12.1   *The utility production function*

The supply of money function used in monetary theory often has not been a neoclassical supply function, in the traditional sense. Instead, the supply of money function often has been an equilibrium condition or reduced-form equation relating money to the monetary base through a multiplier.[40] As seen from our model of the financial intermediary, the relationship between such an equation and monetary production technology is not clear. In fact, although high-powered money is a factor of production for the financial intermediary, the total monetary base (which also includes currency held by the consumer and manufacturing firm) does not appear in the financial intermediary's decision. Problems produced by this fact have been discussed by Saving (1977, p. 294). In addition, as described above, the demand Divisia aggregate need not equal the corresponding supply Divisia aggregate.

Nevertheless, a straightforward interpretation can be given to the conventional multiplier-type "supply" function as a utility production function. As defined by Samuelson (1968), a utility production function is acquired by replacing the quantities in a utility function by their reduced-form equations. By applying that procedure to the consumer's monetary category subutility function and analogously to the manufacturing firm's monetary category subproduction function, equations can be produced

[40] Such equations often have been associated with Brunner and Meltzer (1964) and Johannes and Rasche (1979). In fact, a strong case can be made on econometric grounds for that sort of procedure with all durable goods. See Deaton and Muellbauer (1980, pp. 350–1), who advocate solving a two-equation durable demand and supply system to produce the single-equation specification to be estimated. In our case, we thereby would solve for the market-clearing value for the dual user-cost aggregate. That solution function then would be substituted back into either the demand or supply function for the quantity aggregate.

describing the equilibrium monetary service flows as functions of exogenous variables, including central bank instruments.[41] In continuous time, Sato (1975, p. 283) has shown that the left-hand side of a utility production function can be measured exactly by a Divisia index.[42]

12.2   Velocity function

The aggregation theory provided above can be used to derive the velocity function. The separability of the utility function in (2.2) can be used to produce a current period category utility function of the form $v(u(\mathbf{m}_t), v(\mathbf{x}_t), \bar{L}_t)$. Then a consistent current period conditional decision can be defined. That decision is to select $(\mathbf{m}_t, \mathbf{x}_t, \bar{L}_t)$ to

$$\text{maximize } v(u(\mathbf{m}_t), v(\mathbf{x}_t), \bar{L}_t) \quad \text{subject to } \pi_t' \mathbf{m}_t + \mathbf{p}_t' \mathbf{x}_t + w_t \bar{L}_t = Y_t, \tag{12.1}$$

where Y_t is total current period expenditure on goods, monetary services, and leisure. The variable Y_t is preallocated from a prior-stage intertemporal allocation decision.[43]

However, decision (12.1) can itself be solved in two stages. The first stage is to solve for $(M_t^c, X_t, \bar{L}_t)$ to

$$\text{maximize } v(M_t^c, X_t, \bar{L}_t) \quad \text{subject to } M_t^c \Pi_t^c + p_t^* X_t + w_t \bar{L}_t = Y_t, \tag{12.2}$$

where X_t is the goods quantity aggregate over $\mathbf{x}_t$. The solution function for M_t^c will be of the form

$$M_t^c = \Psi(Y_t, \Pi_t^c, p_t^*, w_t). \tag{12.3}$$

If v is linearly homogeneous, then (12.3) can be written in the form

$$M_t^c = Y_t \Phi(\Pi_t^c, p_t^*, w_t) \tag{12.4}$$

or

$$M_t^c (\Phi(\Pi_t^c, p_t^*, w_t))^{-1} = Y_t, \tag{12.5}$$

so that $(\Phi(\Pi_t^c, p_t^*, w_t))^{-1}$ is velocity relative to the "income" variable Y_t.

For some purposes it would be useful to solve (12.2) conditionally upon $\bar{L}_t$ with $w_t \bar{L}_t$ subtracted from both sides of the constraint in (12.2). Then the income variable would become $Y_t^* = Y_t - w_t \bar{L}_t$, and w_t would not appear as a variable in velocity. In addition, v could be the current period

---

[41] For related discussion see Saving (1977, pp. 300–1).

[42] Sato also recommends specifying the right-hand side as a linearly homogeneous production function, so that all variables can be measured in per capita terms.

[43] See Barnett (1980a, 1981a).

utility function for a representative consumer under the conditions for aggregation over consumers. Since the second-stage decision for the manufacturing firm is analgous to that for the consumer, (12.5) could be produced even after aggregation over consumers and manufacturing firms jointly.

It is particularly interesting to observe that the velocity function depends only on the tastes of consumers and the technology of manufacturing firms. The velocity function does not depend upon the technology of the financial firm, or upon Federal Reserve policy, or upon the money multiplier. As a result, the velocity function is not affected by structural change in the banking sector. In contrast, the velocity of the monetary base depends jointly upon money demand and money supply, and hence is affected by structural change in the banking industry.

When applying the aggregation and index number theory presented in this paper to produce macroeconomic results (such as the above results on velocity), it is critically important to assure that the behavioral theory upon which the index numbers are based is consistent with one's model. Many examples of such inconsistency exist in the literature on monetary aggregation.[44] For example, the official simple sum monetary aggregates are consistent with aggregation theory if and only if the components are indistinguishable perfect substitutes. Yet many models in which the official aggregates are used are structured in a manner inconsistent with that assumption.

A more recent example is the aggregate M_Q, proposed by Spindt, which uses the Fisher ideal index to produce a monetary aggregate and a velocity aggregate. However, turnover rates – rather than the user cost prices appearing in the usual Fisher ideal index – are treated as dual to quantities. The theory on which Spindt's aggregates are based is presented in Spindt (1985). Nevertheless, it is easily seen from the theory in Sections 5 and 6 above that his results are consistent with the relevant index number theory [including Diewert's (1976) theory, used by Spindt (1985)] *only if* economic agents solve one of the following two possible decision problems:

select $\mathbf{m}_t$ to maximize $M(\mathbf{m}_t)$ subject to $\mathbf{m}'_t \mathbf{v}_t = p_t^* X_t$ (12.6)

or

select $\mathbf{v}_t$ to maximize $V(\mathbf{v}_t)$ subject to $\mathbf{m}'_t \mathbf{v}_t = p_t^* X_t$,   (12.7)

where $\mathbf{v}_t$ is the vector of turnover rates corresponding to the vector of monetary asset quantities $\mathbf{m}_t$. The resulting monetary aggregate is $M(\mathbf{m}_t)$

---

[44] See Barnett (1986) for some examples.

and the resulting velocity aggregate is $V(\mathbf{v}_t)$. Either of the above two behavioral hypotheses would be consistent with Spindt's use of index number theory. In addition, if either of those two decision problems is applicable, and if M and V are linearly homogeneous, it follows from factor reversal that $M(\mathbf{m}_t)V(\mathbf{v}_t) = p_t^* X_t$, which is the "quantity equation."

However, it is not at all clear how either of those two decisions could be imbedded in a sensible way into a jointly rational decision over goods and monetary assets (for either a consumer or firm) under any kind of separability assumption. In addition, if (12.6) is solved, then $\mathbf{v}_t$ must be treated as exogenous to the decision maker. Alternatively, if (12.7) is solved, then $\mathbf{m}_t$ must be treated as exogenous to the decision maker. Neither possibility is reasonable, since both turnover rates $\mathbf{v}_t$ and monetary asset quantities demanded $\mathbf{m}_t$ are in actuality selected by monetary asset holders.

The source of this problem in Spindt's work is the fact that he used Diewert's (1976) result that the Fisher ideal index is exact for the square-root quadratic aggregator function; but Spindt overlooked the fact that Diewert's proof applies only for optimizing behavior. With the use of turnover rates rather than user costs, the optimizing behavior required for use of Diewert's theorem must be either (12.6) or (12.7).

Without rigorous internally consistent behavioral theory, a Fisher ideal index in monetary quantities and turnover rates (as opposed to the prices, which fall directly out of the existing aggregation and index number theory) is just an arbitrary combination of component quantities and turnover rates. An infinite number of such functions of monetary quantities and turnover rates exist, and they can produce any arbitrary growth rate for the aggregate from the same component data. As a result, Spindt's aggregate is entirely arbitrary. In short, rolling one's own index number, without access to the 100-year-old cumulative literature on quantity and price (not turnover rate) indexes, is a hazardous venture.

13   Conclusion

This paper has provided many aggregation-theoretic results relevant to producing rigorous microeconomic foundations for monetary economics and macroeconomics. A logical next step in this evolving research would be to imbed aggregation theory in a full macroeconomic model. However it is clear that this next step is a big one. Introducing the relevant aggregation theory throughout a full model of the economy is likely to be a formidable theoretical task. For example, producing comfortable aggregation on both sides of each market with market clearing in aggregates raises theoretical problems for which existing literature provides little guidance.

164   **William A. Barnett**

The literature on aggregation theory typically has taken the position that only one side of each market is relevant to each application of aggregation theory.[45] The literature then applies aggregation theory only to that relevant side of the market. However, when determining the transmission mechanism of monetary policy, no one side of any market is the sole correct side. Much work remains to be done before microeconomics and macroeconomics can be unified through the application of their logical link: aggregation theory.

REFERENCES

Allen, Robert C., and Erwin W. Diewert. 1981. "Direct Versus Implicit Superlative Index Number Formulae." *Review of Economics and Statistics* 63: 430–5.

Arrow, Kenneth J., and Frank H. Hahn. 1971. *General Competitive Analysis.* San Francisco: Holden-Day.

Attfield, C. L. F., and Martin J. Browning. 1985. "A Differentia Demand System, Rational Expectations, and the Life Cycle Hypothesis." *Econometrica* 53: 31–48.

Barnett, William A. 1978. "The User Cost of Money." *Economic Letters* 1: 145–9.

1980a. "Economic Monetary Aggregates: An Application of Index Number and Aggregation Theory." *Journal of Econometrics* 14: 11–48.

1980b. "Economic Monetary Aggregates: Reply." *Journal of Econometrics* 14: 57–9.

1981a. *Consumer Demand and Labor Supply: Goods, Monetary Assets, and Time.* Amsterdam: North-Holland.

1981b. "The New Monetary Aggregates: A Comment." *Journal of Money, Credit, and Banking* 13: 485–9.

1982a. "Divisia Indices." In Samuel Kotz and Norman L. Johnson (eds.), *Encyclopedia of Statistical Sciences,* vol. 2. New York: Wiley.

1982b. "The Optimal Level of Monetary Aggregation." *Journal of Money, Credit, and Banking* 14: 687–710.

1983a. "New Indices of Money Supply and the Flexible Laurent Demand System." *Journal of Business and Economic Statistics* 1: 7–23.

1983b. "Understanding the New Divisia Monetary Aggregates." *Review of Public Data Use* 11: 349–55.

1984. "Recent Monetary Policy and the Divisia Monetary Aggregates." *American Statistician* 38: 165–72.

1986. "Developments in Monetary Aggregation Theory." *Econometric Reviews,* to appear.

Barnett, William, Melvin Hinich, and Warren Weber. 1986. "The Regulatory Wedge between the Demand-Side and Supply-Side Aggregation-Theoretic Monetary Aggregates." *Journal of Econometrics* 33: 165–85.

Barnett, William A., Edward K. Offenbacher, and Paul A. Spindt. 1981. "New Concepts of Aggregated Money." *Journal of Finance* 36: 497–505.

1984. "The New Divisia Monetary Aggregates." *Journal of Political Economy* 92: 1049–85.

[45] See, e.g., Brown (1980, pp. 377–432).

Barnett, William A., and Paul A. Spindt. 1979. "The Velocity Behavior and Information Content of Divisia Monetary Aggregates." *Economic Letters* 4: 51-7.

  1982. "Divisia Monetary Aggregates: Their Compilation, Data, and Historical Behavior," Federal Reserve Board Staff Study no. 116, Washington: Publications Services, Federal Reserve Board.

Berndt, E., and L. Christensen. 1973. "The Internal Structure of Functional Relationships: Separability, Substitution, and Aggregation." *Review of Economic Studies* 40: 403-10.

Berndt, Ernst, and Mohammed S. Khaled. 1979. "Parametric Productivity Measurement and Choice among Flexible Functional Forms." *Journal of Political Economy* 87: 1220-45.

Blackorby, Charles, Daniel Primont, and Robert R. Russell. 1978. *Duality, Separability, and Functional Structure: Theory and Economic Applications.* New York: North-Holland.

Bliss, C. J. 1975. *Capital Theory and the Distribution of Income.* Amsterdam: North-Holland.

Bridge, J. L. 1971. *Applied Econometrics.* Amsterdam: North-Holland.

Brown, Murray. 1980. "The Measurement of Capital Aggregates: A Postreswitching Problem." In Dan Usher (ed.), *The Measurement of Capital,* pp. 377-432. Chicago: University of Chicago Press (for the N.B.E.R.).

Brown, Randall S., Douglas Caves, and Laurits Christensen. 1979. "Modelling the Structure of Cost and Production for Multiproduct Firms." *Southern Economic Journal* 46: 256-73.

Brunner, Karl, and Allen Meltzer. 1964. "Some Further Investigations of Demand and Supply Functions for Money." *Journal of Finance* 240-83.

Caves, Douglas W., Laurits R. Christensen, and Erwin W. Diewert. 1982a. "Multilateral Comparisons of Output, Input, and Productivity Using Superlative Index Numbers." *Economic Journal* 92: 73-86.

  1982b. "The Economic Theory of Index Numbers and the Measurement of Input, Output, and Productivity." *Econometrica* 50: 1393-1414.

Clements, Kenneth W., and H. Y. Izan. 1980. "A Note on Estimating Divisia Index Numbers." *International Economic Review,* to appear.

Cockerline, J. P., and J. D. Murray. 1981. "A Comparison of Alternative Methods of Monetary Aggregation: Some Preliminary Evidence." Technical Report No. 28, Bank of Canada, Ottawa.

Coen, Robert M., and Bert G. Hickman. 1970. "Constrained Joint Estimation of Factor Demand and Production Functions." *Review of Economics and Statistics* 287-300.

Deaton, Angus. 1979. "The Distance Function in Consumer Behaviour with Applications to Index Numbers and Optimal Taxation." *Review of Economic Studies* 46: 391-405.

Deaton, Angus, and John Muellbauer. 1980. *Economics and Consumer Behavior.* Cambridge: Cambridge University Press.

Debreu, Gerard. 1959. *Theory of Value.* New York: Wiley.

Denny, Michael, and J. Douglas May. 1978. "Homotheticity and Real Value-Added in Canadian Manufacturing." In Melvyn Fuss and Daniel McFadden, *Production Economics: A Dual Approach to Theory and Applications,* vol. 2, pp. 53-70. Amsterdam: North-Holland.

Denny, Michael, and Cheryl Pinto. 1978. "An Aggregate Model with Multi-Product Technologies." In Melvyn Fuss and Daniel McFadden, *Production Economics:*

A Dual Approach to Theory and Applications, vol. 2, pp. 249–68. Amsterdam: North-Holland.

Diewert, Erwin W. 1976. "Exact and Superlative Index Numbers." *Journal of Econometrics* 4: 115–45.

1978. "Superlative Index Numbers and Consistency in Aggregation." *Econometrica* 46: 883–900.

1980a. "Aggregation Problems in the Measurement of Capital." In Dan Usher (ed.), *The Measurement of Capital,* pp. 433–538. Chicago: University of Chicago Press (for the N.B.E.R.).

1980b. "Capital and the Theory of Productivity Measurement." *American Economic Review* 70: 260–7.

1980c. "Reply by Diewert." In Dan Usher (ed.), *The Measurement of Capital,* p. 538. Chicago: University of Chicago Press (for the N.B.E.R.).

1981. "The Economic Theory of Index Numbers: A Survey." In Angus Dean (ed.), *Essays in the Theory and Measurement of Consumer Behaviour in Honour of Sir Richard Stone,* pp. 163–208. Cambridge: Cambridge University Press.

Ewis, Nabil A., and Douglas Fisher. 1984. "The Translog Utility Function and the Demand for Money in the United States." *Journal of Money, Credit, and Banking* 16: 34–52.

1985. "Toward a Consistent Estimate of the Substitutability between Money and Near Monies: An Application of the Fourier Flexible Form." *Journal of Macroeconomics* 7: 151–74.

Fischer, Stanley. 1974. "Money and the Production Function." *Economic Inquiry* 12: 517–33.

Fisher, Franklin M., and Karl Shell. 1972. *The Economic Theory of Price Indices.* Academic Press: New York.

1979. "The Theory of Price Indices and Subindices for Output and Input Deflation: Progress Report." CARESS Working Paper #79-02, University of Pennsylvania.

1981. "Output Price Indices." CARESS Working Paper #81-05, University of Pennsylvania.

Fuss, Melvyn. 1977. "The Demand for Energy in Canadian Manufacturing." *Journal of Econometrics* 5: 89–116.

Gorman, W. M. 1970. "Tricks with Utility Functions." In M. Artis and R. Nobay, *Essays in Economic Analysis.*

Green, H. A. J. 1964. *Aggregation in Economic Analysis.* Princeton, New Jersey: Princeton University Press.

Hancock, Diana. 1985. "The Financial Firm: Production with Monetary and Nonmonetary Goods." *Journal of Political Economy* 93: 859–80.

1986. "A Model of the Financial Firm with Imperfect Asset and Deposit Elasticities." *Journal of Banking and Finance,* to appear.

Hall, Robert E. 1973. "The Specification of Technology with Several Kinds of Output." *Journal of Political Economy* 878–92.

Hulten, C. R. 1973. "Divisia Index Numbers." *Econometrica* 63: 1017–26.

Ishida, Kazuhiko. 1984. "Divisia Monetary Aggregates and Demand for Money: A Japanese Case." *Monetary and Economic Studies* 2: 49–80.

Johannes, James M., and Robert Rasche. 1979. "Predicting the Monetary Multiplier." *Journal of Monetary Economics* 5: 301–25.

Jorgensen, D. W., and L. J. Lau. 1975. "The Structure of Consumer Preferences." *Annals of Economic and Social Measurement* 4: 49–101.

Kloek, T. 1967. "On Quadratic Approximations of Cost of Living and Real Income Index Numbers." Report 6710, Econometric Institute, Netherlands School of Economics, Rotterdam.

Lau, Lawrence J. 1978. "Applications of Profit Functions." In Melvyn Fuss and Daniel McFadden, *Production Economics: A Dual Approach to Theory and Applications,* vol. 1, pp. 133–215. Amsterdam: North-Holland.

Malmquist, S. 1953. "Index Numbers and Indifference Surfaces." *Trabajos de Estadistica* 4: 209–41.

Marquez, Jaime. 1986. "Money in Open Economies: A Divisia Application to the U.S. Case." In W. Barnett and K. Singleton (eds.), *New Approaches to Monetary Economics,* New York: Cambridge University Press.

Moorsteen, R. H. 1961. "On Measuring Productive Potential and Relative Efficiency." *Quarterly Journal of Economics* 75: 451–67.

Ohta, Makoto. 1974. "A Note on the Duality between Production and Cost Functions: Rate of Returns to Scale and Rate of Technical Progress." *Economic Studies Quarterly* 25: 63–5.

Phlips, Louis, and Frans Spinnewyn. 1979. "Rationality versus Myopia in Dynamic Demand Systems." Discussion Paper 7918, Center for Operations Research & Econometrics, Universite Catholique de Louvain.

Samuelson, P. A. 1968. "Two Generalizations of the Elasticity of Substitution." In J. N. Wolfe, *Value, Capital, and Growth: Essays in Honour of Sir John Hicks,* pp. 467–80. Edinburgh: Edinburgh University Press.

Samuelson, P. A., and R. Sato. 1984. "Unattainability of Integrability and Definiteness Conditions in the General Case of Demand for Money and Goods." *American Economic Review* 74: 588–604.

Samuelson, P. A., and S. Swamy. 1974. "Invariant Economic Index Numbers and Canonical Duality: Survey and Synthesis." *American Economic Review* 64: 566–93.

Sato, Kazuo. 1975. *Production Functions and Aggregation.* Amsterdam: North-Holland.

Saving, Thomas R. 1977. "A Theory of the Money Supply with Competitive Banking." *Journal of Monetary Economics* 3: 289–303.

Serletis, Apostolos. 1984a. "The Substitutability and Separability of Monetary Assets." Ph.D. dissertation, McMaster University, Hamilton, Ontario.

1984b. "Monetary Asset Demand Functions: Theory and Estimates." Mimeograph, University of Calgary.

1986. "Monetary Asset Separability Tests." In W. Barnett and K. Singleton (eds.), *New Approaches to Monetary Economics.* New York: Cambridge University Press.

Serletis, A., and A. L. Robb. 1986. "Divisia Aggregation and Substitutability among Monetary Assets." *Journal of Money, Credit, and Banking* 18: 430–46.

Shephard, Ronald W. 1970. *Theory of Cost and Production Functions.* Princeton: Princeton University Press.

Sims, C. A. 1969. "Theoretical Basis for a Double Deflated Index of Real Value Added." *Review of Economics and Statistics* 51: 470–1.

Spindt, Paul A. 1985. "The Rates of Turnover of Money Goods under Efficient Monetary Trade: Implications for Monetary Aggregation." *Economic Letters* 17: 141–3.

Star, S., and R. E. Hall. 1976. "An Approximate Divisia Index of Total Factor Productivity." *Econometrica* 44: 257–64.

Swofford, James L., and Gerald A. Whitney. 1986. "Flexible Functional Forms and the Utility Approach to the Demand for Money: A Nonparametric Analysis." *Journal of Money, Credit, and Banking* 18: 383-9.

Theil, H. 1967. *Economics and Information Theory.* Amsterdam: North-Holland.

1968. "On the Geometry and the Numerical Approximation of Cost of Living and Real Income Indices." *De Economist* 116: 677-89.

Usher, Dan. 1980. "Introduction." In Dan Usher (ed.), *The Measurement of Capital,* pp. 1-21. Chicago: University of Chicago Press (for the N.B.E.R.).

Vartia, Y. O. 1976. "Ideal Log Change Index Numbers." *Scandanavian Journal of Statistics* 3: 121-6.

CHAPTER 7

Monetary asset separability tests

Apostolos Serletis

1   Introduction

A rapidly growing line of research has recently begun to appear on the rigorous use of microeconomic and aggregation-theoretic foundations in the construction of monetary aggregates. Much of the attention derives directly or indirectly from Barnett's (1980a) challenging paper, where he voiced objections to simple-sum aggregation procedures and derived the theoretical linkage between monetary theory and index number theory. He applied economic aggregation and index number theory to construct monetary aggregates based upon Diewert's (1976) class of "superlative" quantity index numbers. The new aggregates are Divisia quantity indexes, which are elements of the superlative class.

A number of recent works have provided a sharp quantitative assessment of the relative merits of summation versus Divisia monetary quantity indexes. Barnett, Offenbacher, and Spindt (1984), for example, compared the empirical performance of Divisia and simple-sum monetary aggregates in terms of various policy criteria such as causality, information content of an aggregate, and stability of money demand equations. Their main finding is the better performance of Divisia aggregates, especially at high levels of aggregation. Similarly, Serletis and Robb (1986) estimate the degree of substitutability between the services of money and checkable savings and time deposits (over institution types) in a quasi-homothetic translog utility framework. They investigate both summation and Divisia aggregation of the assets, and provide evidence further supporting the superiority of the Divisia aggregates.

A totally unresolved problem, however, is the method by which monetary assets are selected to be included in the monetary aggregate. Barnett

The author is grateful to W. A. Barnett, A. L. Robb, J. Leach, S. K. Fayyad, and two referees for comments that greatly improved this paper.

169

(1982a) argued that whenever monetary aggregates are used as economic variables (rather than as simple accounting identities), the aggregates should be computed in a rigorous and unique manner derived directly from the theory of economic quantity aggregation. In particular, an aggregate exists in aggregation theory if the aggregator function – defined over the items of the aggregate and other items as well – is weakly separable in the components of the aggregate.[1] If this weak separability condition [defined as the *existence condition*; see Barnett (1982a, p. 696)] is violated, stable preferences cannot exist over the aggregate in the sense that varying the relative quantities of the elements within the aggregate (while holding the aggregate level constant) will affect consumer preferences over other assets or goods.

But weak separability is not sufficient for aggregation in practical situations. For example, to actually measure the aggregate using only market data requires the additional assumption that the aggregator function be homothetically weakly separable.[2] Homothetic weak separability is necessary and sufficient for an aggregate to be a meaningful functional quantity index, in the sense that the growth rate of the aggregate would not differ from the growth rates of the components. Barnett (1982a, p. 696) calls this stronger condition the *consistency* condition.[3]

The main purpose of this paper is to provide evidence bearing on these issues. The analysis is conducted within a microtheoretical framework – utilizing the demand system approach – that views money as a durable good (or monetary assets as durable goods) yielding a flow of non-observable services (either transaction services or store-of-wealth services) that enter as arguments in aggregator functions. The existence of an aggregator function containing monetary assets (with or without other goods) as arguments is important, because substitutability is considered a property of an aggregator function. Moreover, this aggregator function would itself, once estimated, imply the appropriate aggregation procedure.

Our major contribution is the systematic testing for the appropriateness of the weak separability conditions using a flexible functional form interpretation of the quasihomothetic translog functional form. As Denny

---

[1] According to the original definition of separability by Sono (1961) and Leontief (1947), an aggregator function $f(\cdot)$ is said to be weakly separable in (i, j) from k if and only if

$$\partial[(\partial f/\partial x_i)/(\partial f/\partial x_j)]/\partial x_k = 0 \quad i \neq j \neq k,$$

where the expression in brackets refers to the marginal rate of substitution. This implies the possibility of writing the aggregator function $f(\cdot)$ as $f(x) = f[g(x_i, x_j), x_k]$ with $g(x_i, x_j)$ as a subaggregator function.

[2] An aggregator function $f(\cdot)$ is homothetically weakly separable if it is weakly separable with homothetic subaggregator functions.

[3] Note that consistency implies existence, but the converse is not true.

and Fuss (1977) have shown (and as we will discuss later), the approximate translog model permits a less restrictive test of separability than the Berndt–Christensen exact translog framework. Moreover, approximate demand systems impose theoretical restrictions through explicit side constraints on the parameters, thus permitting statistical tests of their validity.

The paper proceeds as follows. Section 2 presents a general model of individual utility maximization that recognizes the interdependence between the real and financial decisions (of the economic unit). A functional form for the utility function is chosen that allows for nonseparability, in contrast to traditional forms (such as Cobb–Douglas and C.E.S.) which are strongly separable and, in addition, require all partial elasticities of substitution to be equal. Section 3 spells out the stochastic specification and the method of estimation. Section 4 outlines the approximate weak separability hypotheses to be tested and discusses some further econometric problems. Section 5 presents and interprets the empirical results, and Section 6 concludes with a discussion of the merits of the estimates and some comments and directions for future research.

2   Specification of the model

We postulate an economy with identical individuals whose direct utility function is homothetically weakly separable (a direct tree) of the form

$$u = u(c, \ell, f(m)),\tag{2.1}$$

where c is a vector of the services of consumption goods, ℓ is leisure time, and m is a vector of the services of monetary assets.[4]

Implicit in a utility-tree structure is a two-stage model of consumer behavior. In the first stage the consumer allocates his expenditure among broad categories (relying on price indexes for these categories) and then in the second stage he allocates expenditures within each category.[5] The particular two-level structure we wish to utilize can be expressed by the following classical consumer problem:

$$\max_{m} f(m) \quad \text{subject to } p'm = y,\tag{2.2}$$

---

[4] The utility-tree structure (2.1) is treated as a maintained (untested) hypothesis in this paper. However, it implies the assumption that the demand for monetary services is independent of relative prices outside the monetary group. This is an unlikely and therefore unattractive assumption, but appears necessary for the type of empirical demand analysis with which we are concerned.

[5] The notion of two-stage optimization was investigated in the context of consumer theory by Strotz (1957, 1959) and Gorman (1959).

where $f(m)$, the monetary services aggregator function (quantity index), is assumed to satisfy the usual regularity conditions. The expenditure on the services of monetary assets is denoted by y, and p is a vector of monetary asset user costs with the ith component given by[6]

$$p_i = (R - r_i)/(1 + R),\tag{2.3}$$

which denotes the discounted interest forgone by holding a dollar's worth of that asset. Here, R is the "benchmark" rate of interest and r_i is the market yield on the ith asset.

One important point has yet to be considered: the specification of the monetary services aggregator function $f(m)$. Although much recent work on the specification of utility-tree structures rests on the assumption of homothetically separable preferences, we replace homotheticity with the far more reasonable assumption of quasihomotheticity – that is, homotheticity with respect to a point which is not necessarily the origin.[7] The specification of quasihomothetic preferences makes the Engel curves (income-consumption paths for fixed prices) linear, but does not require them to pass through the origin. In addition, quasihomothetic separability, like homothetic separability, is a sufficient condition for two-stage optimization.

The indirect quasihomothetic translog function has the form

$$\ln V = a_0 + \sum_i a_i \ln\left[p_i \bigg/ \left(y - \sum_k p_k \gamma_k\right)\right]$$
$$+ \frac{1}{2} \sum_i \sum_j \beta_{ij} \ln\left[p_i \bigg/ \left(y - \sum_k p_k \gamma_k\right)\right] \ln\left[p_j \bigg/ \left(y - \sum_k p_k \gamma_k\right)\right]\tag{2.4}$$

with the restrictions imposed that $\beta_{ij} = \beta_{ji}$ and $\sum_i \beta_{ij} = 0$ for all j. Applying Roy's identity, the following quasihomothetic translog expenditure system is obtained:

$$s_i = p_i \gamma_i / y + \left[1 - \left(\sum_k p_k \gamma_k\right)\bigg/ y\right]\left(a_i + \sum_j \beta_{ij} \ln p_j\right) \quad i = 1, 2, \ldots,\tag{2.5}$$

where the normalization $\sum_i a_i = 1$ has been imposed.

3   Stochastic specification and the method of estimation

The first step in implementing the model is to assume that errors in the process of utility maximization give rise to additive stochastic errors with

[6] The theoretical derivation of the user-cost formula is by Barnett (1978).

[7] For a discussion of quasihomotheticity see Gorman (1961, 1976), Deaton and Muellbauer (1980), and Barnett (1983b).

the budget-share equations. These equations can be described generally as

$$S_t = f_t(x_t, \Theta) + u_t. \tag{3.1}$$

Here S_t is the vector of observed budget shares at time t, x_t is the vector of exogenous variables (total expenditure and prices), Θ represents the vector of unknown parameters, and u_t is a "classical" disturbance term with the following properties:

$$E(u_t) = 0,$$

$$E(u_t, u_s') = \begin{cases} \Sigma & \text{for } s = t \\ 0 & \text{for } s \neq t \end{cases} \quad \text{all } s, t,$$

where Σ is a symmetric and positive semidefinite covariance matrix and 0 is a null matrix.

Since the sum of the budget shares equals one, it follows that the covariance matrix is singular. If autocorrelation in the disturbance is absent, Barten (1969) has shown that full-information maximum-likelihood estimates of the parameters can be obtained by arbitrarily deleting an equation in such a system, and that the resulting estimates are invariant with respect to the equation deleted. However, if autocorrelation is present (as assumed here) – that is,

$$u_t = Ru_{t-1} + v_t, \tag{3.2}$$

where $R = [R_{ij}]$ is a matrix of unknown parameters and v_t is a non-auto-correlated vector disturbance term with constant variance matrix – then a result developed by Berndt and Savin (1975) can be used. They have shown that the adding-up property of a singular system with autocorrelation imposes additional restrictions on the parameters of the autoregressive process. In particular, if one assumes no autocorrelation across equations (i.e., if R is diagonal) then the autocorrelation coefficients for each equation must be identical (i.e., $R_{11} = R_{22} = \cdots = R$). Consequently, this is what we have assumed.

Writing equation (3.1) for period $t - 1$, multiplying by R, and subtracting from (3.1), we obtain the final model

$$S_t = f_t(x_t, \Theta) - Rf_{t-1}(x_{t-1}, \Theta) + RS_{t-1} + v_t, \tag{3.3}$$

which was estimated using the same procedure as described above.

The data consists of quarterly Canadian observations for the period 1968I–1982IV on four types of monetary assets. The four (henceforth referred to as monetary subaggregates) are: money (currency and demand deposits) C, checkable deposits D, savings deposits S, and time deposits T. The four subaggregates mentioned are formed by aggregating 19 more basic assets such as checkable deposits at banks, checkable deposits at trust companies, and so forth.[8] Data sources and adjustment methods are explained in detail in Serletis and Robb (1986).

For purposes of providing a quantitative assessment of the relative merits of simple-sum versus Divisia monetary aggregation, we use both a simple-sum and a Divisia aggregation procedure. Simple-sum and Divisia monetary subaggregates are then used as data in estimating the demand system specified in equation (3.3). Corresponding to each of the two quantity aggregation methods we construct price indexes for the monetary subaggregates. Following Barnett (1983a), when those monetary subaggregates are computed as Divisia indexes we make use of Fisher's (1922) weak factor reversal test to compute the corresponding price indexes.[9] On the other hand, when the monetary subaggregates are computed as simple-sum indexes, the price indexes we use are Laspeyres indexes.[10]

Prior to estimation, the price indexes were all scaled to equal 1.0 in 1968II. To ensure that the products of price and quantity indexes remained unchanged by the rescaling, the quantity series were adjusted accordingly by multiplying each one by the original base-period value of the corresponding price series. All the estimations were carried out with the TSP (version 4.0) econometric package on a Honeywell DPS 7/80 Multics system at the University of Calgary.

4   Hypotheses concerning the structure of preferences

Once the model is estimated, the structure of preferences could be discovered by testing for weak separability. The tests we carry out for the

---

[8] This a priori subaggregation of the assets can be thought of as being based on either a separability assumption or on Hick's price aggregation condition (relative prices remain in fixed proportions). We are forced to appeal to such maintained hypotheses because the estimation of a highly disaggregated demand system encompassing the full range of assets is not possible in practice, since the number of parameters to be estimated would be extremely large. For example, with 19 assets the quasi-homothetic translog would have 208 free parameters.

[9] The test states that the product of the values of the price and quantity indexes should be equal to the ratio of total expenditures in the two periods.

[10] Barnett instead used the Leontief indexes (the smallest element of the vector of component user costs), arguing that "simple sum quantity aggregation implies perfect substitutability of components and hence consumption only of the least expensive good" [Barnett, (1983a, p. 18)]. While we agree with this argument, we note that the Leontief index leads to zero values when the benchmark rate is determined in each period as the maximum among all own rates (as is the case here, because it was extremely difficult to find a single rate that exceeds all rates for all time periods). Zero values, however, are inadmissible in the translog formulation, and our choice seemed to be a reasonable compromise.

Table 1. *Parametric restrictions for approximate weak separability*

Separability pattern	Parametric restrictions
$F[G(\ln q_i, \ln q_j), \ln q_k, \ln q_l]$	$a_i/a_j = \beta_{ik}/\beta_{jk} = \beta_{il}/\beta_{jl}$
$F[G(\ln q_i, \ln q_j), H(\ln q_k, \ln q_l)]$	$a_i/a_j = \beta_{ik}/\beta_{jk} = \beta_{il}/\beta_{jl}$
	$a_k/a_l = \beta_{ik}/\beta_{il} = \beta_{jk}/\beta_{jl}$
$F[G(\ln q_i, \ln q_j, \ln q_k), \ln q_l]$	$a_i/a_j = \beta_{il}/\beta_{jl}, a_i/a_k = \beta_{il}/\beta_{kl},$
	$a_j/a_k = \beta_{jl}/\beta_{kl}$

separability conditions are based on the assumption that the translog functional form is a second-order approximation to an arbitrary utility function. This approach has been suggested by Denny and Fuss (1977) and provides a less restrictive test for separability than the Berndt–Christensen (1973a, b) framework, which is based on the maintained hypothesis that the translog specification is exact.

At an intuitive level, the Berndt–Christensen exact test is a test for global separability (separability at all points of the utility surface), while the Denny–Fuss approximate test is a test for local separability (exact separability only at the point of expansion and approximate separability elsewhere). Denny and Fuss also pointed out that the Berndt–Christensen exact test is a joint test of weak separability and a linear logarithmic aggregator function, and that this test is nested in the approximate test.

To derive our approximate tests for weak separability, we consider the separability restrictions associated with restrictions on the functional form. With four variables, three separability patterns exist: the separability of two variables from the other two variables; the symmetric separability of two variables from the other two variables; and the separability of three variables from the fourth. These possibilities and the corresponding parametric restrictions[11] are shown in Table 1.

Since we have four variables, with the first weak separability pattern $(f[G(\ln q_i, \ln q_j), \ln q_k, \ln q_l])$, there are six ways of choosing a group of two variables to be separable from the other variables. Corresponding to each possibility there are two parametric restrictions analogous to those in Table 1. Under the second type of weak separability $(f[G(\ln q_i, \ln q_j), H(\ln q_k, \ln q_l)])$, there are three ways of placing two

---

[11] The derivation of these restrictions is based on the apparatus developed by Denny and Fuss (1977). The parameters are those in the share equations (2.5). These restrictions hold under the maintained hypothesis of quasihomotheticity ($\sum_i \beta_{ij} = 0$ for all j).

variables in each group. Corresponding to each possibility there are four parametric restrictions. However, only three of these restrictions are independent, for if we add any three we can obtain the fourth. Finally, under the third type of weak separability ($f[G(\ln q_i, \ln q_j, \ln q_k), \ln q_l]$), we can distinguish among four possible ways with three variables in one group. Corresponding to each possibility there are three restrictions, though only two are independent.

For each null hypothesis, we express the approximate weak separability conditions in terms of the free parameters of the model,[12] and calculate the Wald test statistic which is distributed asymptotically as a chi-square with degrees of freedom equal to the number of independent parametric restrictions.[13] The Wald test statistic is asymptotically equivalent to the likelihood-ratio test statistic but the Wald test (unlike the likelihood-ratio test) does not require the numerical minimization of both constrained and unconstrained models. The Wald test is most convenient when the unrestricted model is easier to estimate than the restricted one because (say) restricted optimization is extremely difficult (as it is here) due to the nonlinear parametric restrictions.[14]

---

[12] Consider, for example, the approximate separability restrictions for
$$f[G(\ln q_1, \ln q_2), \ln q_3, \ln q_4]$$
weak separability, in terms of the parameters of the translog function
$$a_1/a_2 = \beta_{13}/\beta_{23} = \beta_{14}/\beta_{24}.$$
Deleting (say) the first equation, we express these conditions in terms of the thirteen free parameters (i.e., parameters that are estimated directly): a_2, a_3, a_4, β_{22}, β_{23}, β_{24}, β_{33}, β_{34}, β_{44} and the four γ's. If we substitute into the above conditions the quasihomotheticity restriction $\sum_i \beta_{ij} = 0$ for all j, and the normalization $\sum_i a_i = 1$, then by rearranging we obtain
$$(1 - a_2 - a_3 - a_4)\beta_{23} = -a_2(\beta_{23} + \beta_{33} + \beta_{34}) \quad \text{and}$$
$$(1 - a_2 - a_3 - a_4)\beta_{24} = -a_2(\beta_{24} + \beta_{34} + \beta_{44}).$$

[13] Given a set of estimates of a parameter vector b, the associated covariance estimate $V(b)$, and a set of nonlinear constraints on b, $g(b) = 0$, we compute the constraints $g(b)$ and their covariance matrix
$$V[g(b)] = (\partial g/\partial b)' V(b)(\partial g/\partial b)$$
and consequently the Wald test statistic
$$\eta g(b)' V[g(b)]^{-1} g(b).$$
This was carried out in a somewhat automatic fashion by using the ANALYZ command in TSP.

[14] However, we must note that – as argued by Burguete, Gallant, and Souza (1982) and by Gregory and Veall (1985) – the Wald test has a drawback in finite samples: Wald tests of different but algebraically equivalent nonlinear restrictions give different results. Gregory and Veall also argue, based on Monte Carlo evidence, that there is some statistical advantage in testing the restrictions in the multiplicative form. (This is what was done here; see note 12.)

Table 2. *Separability hypotheses tests under the quasihomothetic translog*

	Hypothesis	D.F.	Divisia aggregation		Simple-sum aggregation	
			χ^2	*p*-value	χ^2	*p*-value
1.	$[(C, D), S, T]$	2	4.653	(0.097)	3.495	(0.174)
2.	$[(C, S), D, T]$	2	11.410	(0.003)	21.810	(0.000)
3.	$[(C, T), D, S]$	2	16.720	(0.000)	9.401	(0.009)
4.	$[(D, S), C, T]$	2	10.565	(0.005)	38.379	(0.000)
5.	$[(D, T), C, S]$	2	7.343	(0.025)	9.795	(0.007)
6.	$[(S, T), C, D]$	2	3.707	(0.156)	3.736	(0.154)
7.	$[(C, D), (S, T)]$	3	4.726	(0.192)	5.461	(0.140)
8.	$[(C, S), (D, T)]$	3	43.281	(0.000)	22.158	(0.000)
9.	$[(C, T), (D, S)]$	3	18.570	(0.000)	24.757	(0.000)
10.	$[(C, D, S), T]$	2	16.088	(0.000)	0.402	(0.817)
11.	$[(D, S, T), C]$	2	8.427	(0.014)	16.759	(0.000)
12.	$[(C, D, T), S]$	2	10.192	(0.006)	4.633	(0.098)
13.	$[(C, S, T), D]$	2	10.097	(0.006)	17.714	(0.000)

5 Empirical results and their interpretation

In what follows we will be pursuing a dual objective. On the one hand, we wish to discover the structure of preferences over monetary assets by empirically testing for the appropriateness of the weak separability assumptions; on the other hand, we wish to elaborate the results of the empirical tests and their implications for monetary theory. Table 2 gives the results for formal tests of the separability restrictions imposed on the quasihomothetic translog model. This is done twice for each separability type: first using Divisia data and second using simple-sum data. The first column of Table 2 describes the maintained hypothesis. The model estimates that appear in Serletis and Robb (1986) are presented as Appendix Table A1.

With the first approximate weak separability pattern

$$(f[G(\ln q_i, \ln q_j), \ln q_k, \ln q_l]),$$

there are six null hypotheses (the first six entries of Table 2). We find that the $[(C, D), S, T]$, $[(D, T), C, S]$ and $[(S, T), C, D]$ types of weak separability are consistent with our Divisia data for an α (risk level) of .01, while only the first two are consistent with our simple-sum data. The *p*-values decisively reject all the other possible separability types (rows 2,

3, 4, and 5 in the case of simple-sum data), with the margins of rejection generally being smaller under Divisia monetary subaggregation.

With regard to the second approximate weak separability pattern $(f[G(\ln q_i, \ln q_j), H(\ln q_k, \ln q_l)])$, the only separability condition that our data (either Divisia or simple-sum) cannot reject is the $[(C, D), (S, T)]$ weak separability restriction. (The p-value of 0.192 with Divisia data and 0.140 with simple-sum data is greater than .01; hence we conclude H_0.[15]) This implies that we cannot reject the conditions for the further aggregation of C and D and of S and T. Thus we can establish two inter-mediate quantity aggregator functions, $f_1(C, D)$ and $f_2(S, T)$,[16] and deal independently with the C–D and S–T substitutions inherent within these functions.

Finally, with regard to the last approximate weak separability pattern $(f[G(\ln q_i, \ln q_j, \ln q_k), \ln q_l])$, there are four null hypotheses (the last four entries of Table 2). The p-values for these four hypotheses indi-cate that the $[(C, D, S), T]$ and $[(C, D, T), S]$ types of weak separabil-ity are consistent with the simple-sum data but not with the Divisia data. On the basis of these results we argue that, when money is measured using a simple-sum aggregation procedure, the independent estimation of the three-argument quantity aggregator functions $f_1(C, D, S)$ and $f_2(C, D, T)$ is possible. Alternatively, the values of these functions could be candidates for a definition of a monetary aggregate suggested by this approach.

We now turn to examine the implications for monetary theory of these results. The question is whether the results provide a rationale for the choice of assets to be included in a monetary aggregate. The conventional wisdom regarding this question suggests that the means of payment–type assets (money and checkable deposits) are the most likely candidates for inclusion, followed by the next best substitute.

Looking at the test results of Table 2, it would appear that a narrow definition of money can be employed in empirical studies because the $[(C, D), S, T]$ weak separability type cannot be rejected throughout. This is certainly a separability type which would have been selected a priori without having to exploit the sample to find other more suitable grouping patterns.

---

[15] In fact, separability of the type tested in row 7 is implied by the separability types of rows 1 and 6. Similarly, the separability types in rows 8 and 9 are implied by the separa-bility types in rows 2 and 5 and 3 and 4, respectively. Therefore, the separability tests in rows 7 through 9 are unnecessary, but we report on them for purposes of completeness.

[16] These functions measure the total service flow produced by different categories of mone-tary assets. For example, $f_1(C, D)$ represents an index of monetary assets closely asso-ciated with the transactions or liquidity function, while $f_2(S, T)$ represents an index of monetary assets associated with the store-of-wealth function.

A surprising result is that other admissible groupings exist with the simple-sum data (see rows 10 and 12), and that these groupings are in line with the conventional wisdom: Broad-based monetary aggregates should be nested about monetary components that can normally be used to make payments (money and checkable deposits in our case). On the other hand, the only type of weak separability that our Divisia data cannot reject (for an α of .01) is the $[(D, S, T), C]$ type in row 11. Nonrejection of this separability type strongly suggests that the inclusion of money in a broad-based Divisia monetary aggregate can be questioned.[17] This result is also consistent with the low substitutability between C and D reported in Serletis and Robb (1986).

6 Conclusions

To briefly sum up, the results of the separability hypotheses tests suggest that a narrow definition of money could be employed, but there is no conclusive evidence regarding the assumption that broader-based monetary aggregates should be nested about the means of payment-type assets. Of course, adoption of a narrow definition of money should not preclude the introduction into a monetary model of other monetary assets. The question is whether these assets should be introduced by means of defining money more broadly, as the simple-sum data suggest, or by other means, as the Divisia data seem to suggest.

Moreover, the separability tests carried out here cannot be conclusive, but rather should be viewed as a first step toward shedding some light on the problem of choosing one aggregate as the appropriate definition of money. Further research is clearly needed in this area. While we have investigated the quasihomothetic translog, other flexible functional forms such as the basic translog or the generalized translog could be used. However, since the translog flexible functional form family provides only a local approximation, a particularly constructive approach would be based on the use of flexible functional forms that possess global properties. Three such forms are the Fourier flexible functional form [see Gallant (1981)] and the minflex Laurent generalized Leontief and minflex Laurent translog flexible functional forms [see Barnett (1985), Barnett and Lee (1985), and Barnett, Lee, and Wolfe (1985, 1986)]. In addition, as these authors argue, the regular region of the last two models is often larger than that of the translog.[18]

---

[17] Cagan (1982, p. 673) raised a similar objection: "The traditional inclusion of currency in monetary aggregates can be questioned. Currency is used primarily to service retail trade and is issued in the short run largely on the demand of the public."

[18] Here, as Serletis and Robb (1986) report, the quasihomothetic translog violates the theoretical regularity conditions at many points of the data set.

Appendix Table A1. *Model estimates (1968:1–1982:4) for money C, checkable deposits D, savings deposits S, and time deposits T*[a]

Asset i	γ_i	β_{i1}	β_{i2}	β_{i3}	β_{i4}	R
(a) Divisia aggregation						
C	.200 (.105)	.522 (.061)	.237 (.017)	-.105 (.027)	.003 (.011)	.952 (.013)
D	.007 (.048)	.139 (.028)	-.135 (.027)	-.035 (.030)	-.014 (.006)	
S	.033 (.056)	.301 (.063)	-.105 (.017)	.123 (.023)	.017 (.006)	
T	.164 (.011)	.036 (.030)	.003 (.011)	.017 (.006)	-.005 (.013)	
Log of likelihood function = 643.107						
(b) Simple-sum aggregation						
C	11.209 (.300)	.039 (.061)	.057 (.020)	-.031 (.012)	-.010 (.016)	.943 (.009)
D	5.644 (.222)	.129 (.036)	-.054 (.025)	-.010 (.012)	.007 (.007)	
S	17.882 (2.160)	.314 (.063)	-.010 (.012)	.259 (.026)	-.217 (.021)	
T	25.019 (1.456)	.517 (.056)	.007 (.007)	-.217 (.021)	.220 (.016)	
Log of likelihood function = 642.214						

[a] Symmetry imposed; standard errors in parentheses.

REFERENCES

Barnett, W. A. 1978. "The User Cost of Money." *Economics Letters* 1: 145–9.
  1980a. "Economic Monetary Aggregates: An Application of Aggregation and Index Number Theory." *Journal of Econometrics* 14: 11–48.
  1980b. "Economic Monetary Aggregates: Reply." *Journal of Econometrics* 14: 57–9.
  1981a. *Consumer Demand and Labor Supply: Goods, Monetary Assets, and Time.* Amsterdam: North-Holland.
  1981b. "The New Monetary Aggregates: A Comment." *Journal of Money, Credit, and Banking* 13: 485–9.
  1982a. "The Optimal Level of Monetary Aggregation." *Journal of Money, Credit, and Banking* 14: 687–710.
  1982b. "Divisia Indices." In Norman Johnson and Samuel Katz (eds.), *Encyclopedia of Statistical Sciences,* pp. 412–5. New York: John Wiley.
  1983a. "New Indices of Money Supply and the Flexible Laurent Demand System." *Journal of Business and Economic Statistics* 1: 7–23.
  1983b. "The Recent Reappearance of the Homotheticity Restriction on Preferences." *Journal of Business and Economic Statistics* 1: 215–18.
  1985. "The Minflex-Laurent Translog Flexible Functional Form." *Journal of Econometrics* 30: 33–4.
Barnett, W. A., and Y. W. Lee. 1985. "The Global Properties of Minflex Laurent Generalized Leontief, and Translog Flexible Functional Forms." *Econometrica* 53: 1421–37.
Barnett, W. A., Y. W. Lee, and M. Wolfe. 1985. "The Three-Dimensional Global Properties of the Minflex Laurent, Generalized Leontief, and Translog Flexible Functional Forms." *Journal of Econometrics* 30: 3–31.
  1986. "The Three-Dimensional Global Properties of the ML Translog and ML Generalized Leontief Flexible Functional Forms." *Journal of Business and Economic Statistics,* forthcoming.
Barnett, W. A., E. K. Offenbacher, and P. A. Spindt. 1981. "New Concepts of Aggregated Money." *Journal of Finance* 36: 497–505.
  1984. "The New Divisia Monetary Aggregates." *Journal of Political Economy* 92: 1049–85.
Barten, A. P. 1969. "Maximum Likelihood Estimation of a Complete System of Demand Equations." *European Economic Review* 1: 7–73.
Berndt, E. R., and L. R. Christensen. 1973a. "The Specification of Technology in U.S. Manufacturing." Working Paper No. 18, Bureau of Labor Statistics, Washington.
  1973b. "The Internal Structure of Functional Relationships: Separability, Substitution and Aggregation." *Review of Economic Studies* 60: 403–10.
Berndt, E. R., and N. E. Savin. 1975. "Estimation and Hypothesis Testing in Singular Equation Systems with Autoregressive Disturbances." *Econometrica* 43: 937–57.
Burguete, J. F., A. R. Gallant, and G. Souza. 1982. "On Unification of the Asymptotic Theory of Nonlinear Econometric Models." *Econometric Review* 1: 151–90.
Cagan, P. 1982. "The Choice among Monetary Aggregates as Targets and Indicators for Monetary Policy." *Journal of Money, Credit, and Banking* 14: 661–86.

Deaton, A. S., and J. Muellbauer. 1980. *Economics and Consumer Behavior.* Cambridge: Cambridge University Press.

Denny, M., and M. Fuss. 1977. "The Use of Approximation Analysis to Test for Separability and the Existence of Consistent Aggregates." *American Economic Review* 67: 404-18.

Diewert, W. E. 1976. "Exact and Superlative Index Numbers." *Journal of Econometrics* 4: 115-46.

Fisher, I. 1922. *The Making of Index Numbers.* Boston: Houghton Mifflin.

Gallant, R. A. 1981. "On the Bias in Flexible Functional Forms and an Essentially Unbiased Form: The Fourier Functional Form." *Journal of Econometrics* 15: 211-45.

Gorman, W. M. 1959. "Separable Utility and Aggregation." *Econometrica* 27: 469-81.

   1961. "On a Class of Preference Fields." *Metroeconomica* 13: 53-6.

   1976. "Tricks with Utility Functions." In M. Artis and R. Nobay (eds.), *Essays in Economic Analysis.* Cambridge: Cambridge University Press.

Gregory, A. W., and M. R. Veall. 1985. "Formulating Wald Tests of Nonlinear Restrictions." *Econometrica* 53: 1465-7.

Leontief, W. W. 1947. "Introduction to a Theory of the Internal Structure of Functional Relationships." *Econometrica* 15: 361-73.

Serletis, A., and A. L. Robb. 1986. "Divisia Aggregation and Substitutability among Monetary Assets." *Journal of Money, Credit, and Banking* 18: 430-46.

Sono, M. 1961. "The Effect of Price Changes on the Demand and Supply of Separable Goods." *International Economic Review* 2: 239-71.

Strotz, R. H. 1957. "The Empirical Implications of a Utility Tree." *Econometrica* 75: 511-12.

   1959. "The Utility Tree - A Correction and Further Appraisal." *Econometrica* 78: 482-8.

Wales, T. J. 1979. "On the Flexibility of Functional Forms - An Empirical Approach." *Journal of Econometrics* 5: 183-93.

CHAPTER 8

Money demand in open economies:
a Divisia application to the U.S. case

Jaime Marquez

Abstract: Knowledge of the extent to which monies of different countries can substitute for each other is important for the design and implementation of monetary policy. However, existing empirical analyses of money demand in open economies rest on official estimates of money holdings that imply an infinite elasticity of substitution among different monetary assets. Existing analyses of Divisia monetary aggregates do not impose such an assumption, but do not allow foreign exchange considerations. This paper combines both approaches into a unified explanation of domestic money holdings. The empirical analysis suggests that U.S. Divisia money holdings are influenced by foreign exchange considerations. Foreign monetary policies, through their effects on both foreign interest and exchange rates, might influence domestic monetary policy directly via currency substitution.

1 Introduction

The purpose of this paper is to determine whether domestic money holdings are influenced by foreign exchange considerations, an influence generally known as currency substitution. Intuitively, one would expect such considerations to influence holdings of domestic money, given the increased integration of international markets and the interdependency of asset holdings. As a result, changes in either foreign interest rates or

An earlier version of this paper was presented at the conference on New Approaches to Monetary Economics, The University of Texas at Austin, May 23–24, 1985; at the Financial Analysis Committee meetings of the Federal Reserve System, November 22, 1985; and at the International Macro Workshop of the Federal Reserve Board. I have benefited from comments by William Barnett, Benjamin Friedman, Ronald McKinnon, Steve Meyer, Neil Ericsson, Peter Tinsley, Neil Wallace, Paul Spindt, Karen Johnson, Lois Stekler, Peter Isard, Sean Craig, and Janice Shack-Marquez. Finally, I am thankful to two anonymous referees who made a number of important suggestions and comments. I retain sole responsibility for remaining errors. This paper represents the views of the author and should not be interpreted as reflecting the views of the Board of Governors of the Federal Reserve System or other members of its staff.

183

exchange rates should induce changes in the optimal portfolio mix with a corresponding impact on domestic money holdings.

Knowledge of whether currency substitution exists is important for the design and implementation of monetary policy for several reasons. First, the intended effect of an open-market operation will not materialize if offsetting portfolio changes take place through currency substitution. Second, the argument that a flexible exchange rate system insulates domestic monetary policy from foreign monetary policy focuses on the inability of the latter to affect the stock of domestic money supply. This argument rests, however, on the belief that domestic money holdings are not influenced directly by foreign exchange variables. If money demand were influenced by such variables, then foreign monetary policy could impinge on domestic monetary policy through currency substitution. Thus whether the latter exists is an important empirical question.[1]

Given its implications for monetary policy, it is not surprising that the possibility of currency substitution has been the subject of an increasing amount of attention. Specifically, some investigators have argued that failure to recognize the influence of foreign exchange considerations might result in a misspecification of the demand for money, which could bias its parameter estimates and be responsible for the large errors in forecasting money demand. For example, Brittain (1981) finds that foreign interest rates explain a considerable amount of the observed instability of velocity in both the United States and Germany; Hamburger (1977) and Arango and Nadiri (1981) find strong empirical support for the inclusion of foreign interest rates and exchange rates in the specification of money demand in several industrialized countries. Relying on Chetty's work, Miles (1978) applies a production-of-monetary-services model to Canada and finds that Canadians treat U.S. dollars as a good substitute for Canadian dollars.[2]

Despite their contribution to the literature, these analyses rely on official estimates of money holdings, which assume that the elasticity of substitution among different monetary assets is infinite. The restrictive nature of official estimates of money holdings has been recognized by Barnett

---

[1] McKinnon (1982) and Miles (1978) are among the first to argue that a flexible exchange rate system does not insulate domestic monetary policy from foreign monetary policy in the presence of currency substitution. Willms (1971) is one of the first to model empirically the influence of foreign exchange considerations on the behavior of domestic money demand.

[2] Cuddington (1983) examines whether currency substitution exists for a number of industrialized countries, without finding empirical support for its existence in the U.S. case. Ewis and Fisher (1984) estimate a money-demand system that allows for currency substitution, and find strong currency substitution effects for the United States.

(1981), who develops a monetary aggregation framework in which rational individuals determine their money holdings by trading off the different attributes of monetary assets against their associated opportunity costs. Barnett finds that Divisia monetary aggregation provides an aggregate of money holdings that is consistent with individuals' optimizing behavior.

Based on this result, Barnett, Offenbacher, and Spindt (1984) use the Divisia monetary aggregate to investigate the behavior of money demand, focusing on a number of issues including the direction of causality between money and income, the stability of structural parameters, and the behavior of velocity. They find that the Divisia aggregate outperforms official aggregates in terms of forecasting results and parameter stability, among other criteria. However, their analysis makes no allowance for foreign exchange considerations.

As the preceding discussion suggests, studies of both Divisia monetary aggregation and currency substitution have proceeded independently of each other. On the one hand, proponents of Divisia monetary aggregates give little or no consideration to the influence of foreign variables in modeling money demand. On the other hand, the literature on currency substitution treats domestic monetary aggregates as if individuals' elasticities of substitution among these assets were infinite. Our purpose here is to integrate these two strands of literature into a unified explanation of domestic money holdings.

Section 2 applies the framework of monetary aggregation to develop a money demand function relevant for open economies. Section 3 implements empirically the framework of Section 2, and Section 4 presents estimates of the effects of foreign exchange considerations on U.S. money demand behavior. The main conclusion to be drawn from this study is that foreign exchange considerations are important determinants of U.S. Divisia money holdings. As a result, monetary policies abroad – by influencing foreign interest rates and exchange rates – affect domestic money holdings directly, and thus might influence the extent to which domestic monetary policy can accomplish domestic objectives. Section 5 summarizes the paper and indicates directions for further research.

2 Monetary aggregation and currency substitution

2.1 *Optimizing behavior*

The point of departure of this analysis is the empirical observation that the public maintains monetary balances denominated in both domestic and foreign currency.[3] Specifically, multinationals and investment corporations carry out productive activities at home and abroad, the financing of which requires maintenance of monetary balances denominated in more than one currency. By doing so, they can arbitrage interest rate differentials and fluctuations in currency rates and thus reduce the financing cost associated with a given scale of operations worldwide.

In this context, the problem is how to determine the optimal mix of domestic and foreign monetary holdings while recognizing that these assets are not necessarily perfect substitutes for each other in the provision of an aggregate level of monetary services. The ease with which different monetary assets can substitute for each other depends on the degree of integration of international financial and goods markets (King et al. 1978) and these characteristics are captured by a transactions technology, or utility aggregator, $T(M^d, M^f)$.

To determine the aggregate levels of both domestic and foreign money holdings, it is assumed that individuals find the minimum cost portfolio capable of supporting a given level of aggregate monetary services M^*:[4]

$$\min \pi_d M^d + \pi_f M^f \quad \text{subject to} \quad T(M^d, M^f) \geq M^*, \qquad (2.1)$$

where

$\pi_d =$ opportunity cost of domestic money,
$\pi_f =$ opportunity cost of foreign money,
$M^d =$ aggregate domestic holdings of domestic money, and
$M^f =$ aggregate domestic holdings of foreign money.

According to (2.1), individuals require an aggregate level of monetary services M^* in order to support a given level of transactions. Because some of these transactions are international in nature, individuals have incentives to hold domestic and foreign balances, the mix of which depends on their associated opportunity costs and on the extent to which these balances can substitute for each other in the provision of monetary services.[5]

---

[3] For example, the *Federal Reserve Bulletin,* the *Balance of Payments Statistics* of the Deutsche Bundesbank, and the *Bank of Canada Review* publish residents' monetary claims on foreigners.

[4] Using a multistage budgeting decision process, Barnett (1981, chap. 7, and 1982, p. 696) formally proves the existence of both M^* and $T(\cdot)$ for a closed economy. This paper applies Barnett's framework in the context of an open economy. Note that the transactions technology assumes weak separability between domestic and foreign assets, which permits aggregation of all domestic monetary assets into one domestic monetary aggregate without having to include foreign assets in such an aggregate. [Ewis and Fisher (1984) make a similar assumption.] The validity of this separability assumption should be the subject of future empirical work.

[5] As Miles (1978) has indicated, even if productive activities were aimed at the domestic market, firms may reduce their domestic operating costs by holding monetary assets denominated in several currencies.

The solution to problem (2.1) yields the optimal aggregate level of both domestic and foreign asset holdings, M^{d*} and M^{f*} respectively:[6]

$$M^{d*} = M^d(\pi_d, \pi_f, M^*),\tag{2.2}$$

$$M^{f*} = M^f(\pi_d, \pi_f, M^*).\tag{2.3}$$

The determinants of óptimal holdings of domestic money are given by equation (2.2). Because this equation stems from the solution to optimizing problem (2.1), it internalizes the transactions technology and thus contains all the relevant information regarding the degree to which foreign exchange considerations influence domestic money holdings. In other words, whether currency substitution exists can be established from equation (2.2) without having to examine the behavior of M^{f*}. Central to this result is the separability assumption made for the transactions technology.

2.2   Observability, optimality, and Divisia aggregation

Although equation (2.2) provides a justification for the inclusion of open-economy variables in the explanation of optimal holdings of domestic money, the latter are not observable directly and need to be constructed. From an empirical standpoint, the chief problem is how to construct this aggregate while ensuring that it is consistent with optimizing behavior. Official estimates of aggregate money eliminate the observability problem by assuming that individuals are perfectly indifferent among all monetary assets. As a result, rational behavior implies that M^{d*} can be constructed as the sum of observable elementary monetary assets, M^{di}: $M^{d*} = \sum_i M^{di}$.

However, the existing empirical evidence found in Barnett (1981) indicates that different domestic monetary assets are not perfect substitutes for each other. Recognition of this imperfect substitutability implies the existence of a general aggregator function relating M^d to holdings of its elementary monetary components M^{di}:

$$M^d = \delta(M^{d1}, ..., M^{dn}),$$

---

[6] The solution also yields the user cost of M^*: $\pi_m = \pi(\pi_d, \pi_f)$. Note that (2.1) represents a constrained minimization problem, which implies that equations (2.2) and (2.3) are Hicksian demand functions. The analyses of Barnett (1981, 1985a) rely on constrained maximization problems which permit the estimation (as Barnett does) of demand systems with all of the theoretical restrictions introduced in a consistent way. I am grateful to William Barnett for pointing out the differences in the two approaches. Ewis and Fisher (1984) pursue the system approach with a translog utility function and find support for the hypothesis of currency substitution for the United States. Barnett (1983, 1985b) and Barnett and Lee (1985) eliminate the restrictive assumptions associated with the translog formulation.

188   **Jaime Marquez**

where $\delta =$ functional aggregator of elementary domestic monetary assets. Although each M^{di} is observable, the aggregate M^d is not because the aggregator δ is not generally known. Furthermore, simply knowing δ does not guarantee consistency between optimal holdings of M^d and optimal holdings of M^{di}. To ensure this consistency, it is assumed that individuals determine optimal holdings of M^{di} by finding the minimum cost portfolio subject to the constraint that the aggregate of optimal M^{di}'s is at least as high as M^{d*} (Barnett 1981). Defining π_{di} as the opportunity cost of M^{di}, the solution to the above optimization problem yields a set of domestic money demand equations, $M^{di*} = M^{di}(\pi_{d1}, ..., \pi_{dn}, M^{d*})$, which when substituted into the aggregator δ give $M^{d*} = \delta(M^{d1*}, ..., M^{dn*})$, ensuring consistency between the optimal aggregate M^{d*} and the optimal holdings of its components.

Having obtained consistency, an estimate of M^{d*} could be constructed if knowledge of δ were available. However, such knowledge rarely exists, and even if δ were econometrically estimated, the properties displayed by the resulting monetary aggregate would be conditional on the choice of the functional form for δ. The (discrete time) Divisia aggregator, by virtue of being a second-order approximation to *any* functional aggregator, can be used to approximate the aggregate of optimal holdings of elementary monetary assets. Specifically, the (discrete time) Divisia aggregate of optimal holdings of monetary balances, DM^{d*}, is constructed as

$$\Delta \ln DM^{d*} = \sum_s \left(\frac{\pi_{ds} M^{ds*}}{\sum_k \pi_{dk} M^{dk*}} \right) \Delta \ln M^{ds*}$$

$$\cong \Delta \ln \delta(M^{d1*}, ..., M^{dn*}) = \Delta \ln M^{d*}. \quad (2.4)$$

According to equation (2.4), the growth rate of the Divisia monetary aggregate is a weighted average of the growth rates of its elementary monetary components, which are observable.[7] The weights change over time and are equal to the expenditure share of the sth component in total expenditures on monetary services.[8]

As the preceding analysis suggests, the framework of monetary aggregation has several advantages for the present analysis. First, it treats cur-

[7] Time subscripts have been omitted for convenience. Note that $\delta(M^{d1*}, ..., M^{dn*})$ depends only on quantities of monetary assets, whereas DM^{d*} depends on both prices and quantities. However, it can be shown that DM^{d*} changes only when the quantities of monetary assets change. See Barnett (1981).

[8] The π_{dk}'s are also observable; see Barnett (1981). Note that M^{f*} could be computed using a Divisia aggregate as in (2.4), but it would require data on U.S. bilateral holdings of foreign monetary assets which are not generally available. This analysis does not require an estimate of M^{f*} because of the separability assumption made for the transactions technology.

rency substitution within the general framework of optimal portfolio determination. As a result, it formalizes the dependence of domestic money holdings on foreign exchange considerations. Second, because the solution to the optimizing problem internalizes the extent of money substitutability, it is possible to focus exclusively on the behavior of aggregate domestic money without having to compute domestic holdings of foreign assets. Third, it provides an observable measure of M^{d*} that is consistent with optimizing behavior and that does not rely on the assumption of perfect substitutability among monetary assets.

3   Empirical analysis

3.1   *Money demand in open economies: narrow and broad views of money*

With the increased interdependency of the world economy and the advent of a flexible exchange rate system, individuals have developed incentives to include foreign monetary assets in their portfolios in order to minimize the cost of carrying out a given level of transactions. As a result, fluctuations in either foreign interest rates or exchange rates (and their expectations) change the optimal portfolio mix with a corresponding impact on holdings of domestic money. To model these influences, it is assumed that real Divisia holdings respond to changes in domestic and foreign interest rates, to expected depreciation of the domestic currency, and to real income:

$$DM^{d*}/P = f(r, i^*, x, Y),$$ (3.1)

where

DM^{d*} = Divisia aggregate of domestic monetary assets,
P = price level,
r = domestic interest rate,
i^* = foreign interest rate,
x = expected depreciation of domestic currency, and
Y = scale variable, generally real income.

Although there is little disagreement in the theoretical literature about the choice of arguments in (3.1), there is considerably less agreement about the exact specification of their influences, a disagreement that stems from the interpretation of what constitutes money. According to one view, advanced by Cuddington (1983), money is narrowly defined as cash – that is, the riskless asset that receives no *explicit* interest. In this context, currency substitution can only take place between domestic and foreign cash, even if highly liquid and interest-bearing foreign monetary assets are available. For example, an increase in the interest rate of a checking account in a British Building Society would not induce currency substitution but rather capital mobility, because such an account would be treated as a foreign bond even if it renders the same monetary services that cash does. In the absence of interest-rate effects, currency substitution will only take place if there is an expected depreciation of the domestic currency – that is, a purely speculative motive.

Under this narrow interpretation, (3.1) is specified as

$$DM^{d*}/P = f(r, i^*+x, x, Y). \tag{3.2}$$

An expected depreciation of the domestic currency lowers domestic money holdings for two reasons. First, it raises the return to holding foreign "bonds," i^*+x, which is denoted capital mobility; second, it raises the return to holding foreign cash, which is denoted currency substitution. Thus the latter is said to exist only if the coefficient associated with exchange rate expectations is significantly below zero.

In contrast to the narrow interpretation of money, there is a broader view in which individuals substitute among a whole class of interest-bearing monetary assets that perform services similar to that of cash. In this context, currency substitution only requires that individuals maintain a diversified portfolio (including foreign monetary assets) and to be indifferent at the margin between holding domestic and foreign money. Note that this is the view underlying the analysis of Section 2.

Under this broader concept, (3.1) is specified as

$$DM^{d*}/P = f(r, \max(i^*+x, x), Y) = f(r, i^*+x, Y). \tag{3.3}$$

As expected, depreciation of the domestic currency reduces domestic money holdings by raising the return to holding foreign balances. Moreover, equation (3.3) states that individuals, when confronted with a choice between holding foreign cash and an interest-bearing checking account, will choose to hold the latter. This seems a reasonable implication given that the exchange rate risk is the same for both foreign cash and the checking account, but the latter return dominates cash. Thus currency substitution is said to exist if the influence of the foreign return on domestic money holdings is significantly below zero.

3.2   Econometric specification: reduced-form coefficients

The empirical implementation of our analysis takes Goldfeld's (1973) specification of aggregate money demand behavior, and extends it to include foreign exchange considerations:

$$\ln(DM^{d*}/P)_t = a_0 + a_1 \ln Y_t + a_2 r_t + a_3 r_t^*$$

$$+ a_4(E(e_{t+1})/e_t - 1) + a_5 \Delta \ln P_t + u_t, \qquad (3.4)$$

with

$$a_1 > 0, \quad a_2 < 0, \quad a_3 < 0, \quad a_4 < 0, \quad a_5 < 0$$

and where

DM^{d*} = Divisia aggregate of domestic monetary assets,
P = price deflator for Gross National Product,
Y = Gross National Product in real terms,
r = nominal 90-day U.S. interest rate,
r^* = nominal 90-day foreign return,
$\quad = ((1 + i^*)[E_t(e_{t+1})/e_t]) - 1$,
i^* = foreign interest rate index,
e_t = exchange rate index (U.S.\$/foreign currency),
$E_t(e_{t+1})$ = one-period-ahead expected exchange rate, and

$$u_t = u_{t-1} + v_t, \quad u_t \sim N(0, \sigma^2(u)), \quad v_t \sim N(0, \sigma^2(v)), \quad E(v_t v_{t-1}) = 0.$$

According to (3.4), holdings of domestic money respond to changes in real income and domestic interest rates as the traditional formulation suggests; these holdings also respond to changes in both the foreign interest rate and the expected exchange rate.[9] The inclusion of the inflation rate in (3.4) is less traditional but not less important. Marquez (1985) shows that the aggregate of individuals' money holdings depends on the distribution of nominal income, which in turn depends on the inflation rate.

Three difficulties arise in estimating the parameters associated with equation (3.4). First, the estimation requires information on exchange-rate expectations, which are not observable directly. Second, the spurious correlations characteristic of most time-series data might affect the usual interpretation of significance tests. Finally, the intercorrelation among the three rates of return creates multicollinearity problems, which prevent isolation of the estimated ceteris paribus effects.

To address the first of these difficulties, the present analysis considers two expectation mechanisms. The first expectation mechanism treats the forward exchange rate as the best one-period-ahead predictor of future exchange rates. Forward market expectations have been criticized on the basis that they do not recognize the existence of a risk premium, among other reasons (see Tryon 1983, Hansen and Hodrick 1981), but they are considered here because of their widespread use in the literature.[10]

[9] Expectations are generated using the logarithm of the exchange rate. Meese and Rogoff (1983, p. 11) explain the reason for this choice.
[10] See Cuddington (1983), Arango and Nadiri (1981), and Daniel and Fried (1983).

The second mechanism rests on the rational expectations hypothesis where expectations, conditional on today's information, are unbiased predictors of future exchange rates. In this paper, exchange rate expectations are assumed to follow an AR(2) process, which is among the more successful forecasting models within the class of models examined by Meese and Rogoff (1983).[11] Note that, because of the need to assume an exchange rate expectation model, testing for currency substitution involves a joint test of the hypothesis of currency substitution and of the hypothesized validity of the exchange-rate expectations model.

Time series are known for possessing a relatively high degree of serial correlation which, if not taken into account in estimation, could result in invalid statistical inferences. For simplicity, it is assumed that the error term $u(t)$ in (3.4) has a correlation coefficient of one. With this assumption, it is possible to use first differences of the variables involved in the specification, as recommended by Granger and Newbold (1974).[12] The problem of collinearity among rates of return is avoided by following Daniel and Fried (1983), who impose covered interest arbitrage to eliminate one rate of return.

The specification of money demand behavior under the assumption that currency substitution can only take place between domestic and foreign cash (narrow interpretation of money) is

$$\Delta \ln(DM^{d*}/P)_t = \alpha_0 + \alpha_1 \Delta \ln Y_t + \alpha_2 \Delta r_t$$
$$+ \alpha_4 \Delta(E_t(e_{t+1})/e_t) + \alpha_5 \Delta^2 \ln P_t + v_t, \qquad (3.5)$$

where $\alpha_4 < 0$ indicates the existence of currency substitution.

Holdings of domestic money, under the broad interpretation of currency substitution, are specified as

$$\Delta \ln(DM^{d*}/P)_t = \beta_0 + \beta_1 \Delta \ln Y_t + \beta_2 \Delta r_t$$
$$+ \beta_3 \Delta \max\{(1+i^*)(E_t(e_{t+1})/e_t), (E_t(e_{t+1})/e_t)\}$$
$$+ \beta_4 \Delta^2 \ln P_t + v_t, \qquad (3.6)$$

[11] Meese and Rogoff (1983) find that the random-walk model, $E(e_{t+1}) = e_t$, has the largest predicting power relative to more sophisticated models. Unfortunately, this model is observationally equivalent to one where the coefficient for expectations of the exchange rate is zero. Alternatives to an AR(2) include structural models or a vector autoregressive process. However, the results presented by Meese and Rogoff indicate that these two alternatives have very little predictive power relative to either a univariate model or the random-walk hypothesis.

[12] Differencing the equation is potentially troublesome because the characterization of long-run money demand depends on the initial condition for the solution of the differential equation. I have benefited from discussions with Neil Ericsson on this point.

and currency substitution is said to exist if β_3 is significantly less than zero.[13]

3.3   Testing error properties and parameter stability

Nearly all econometric analyses of money demand behavior rest on the notion that the classical properties for the error term do indeed hold. While the hypothesis of serially independent errors is usually tested, the hypotheses of homoskedasticity and normality are generally taken for granted. Here we test the hypotheses of normality, serial independence, and homoskedasticity for the residual $v(t)$ in equations (3.5) and (3.6). In addition, we test the hypothesis of parameter stability.[14]

Testing for the hypothesis that the errors behave according to the normal distribution relies on the Jarque–Bera (JB) statistic (Jarque and Bera 1980). This statistic compares the extent to which the skewness and kurtosis of the distribution of estimated residuals, $\hat{v}$, depart from the skewness and kurtosis associated with the normal distribution. In particular, the JB statistic is computed as

$$JB = T[\mu_3^2/(6\mu_2^3) + (1/24)(\mu_4/\mu_2^2 - 3)^2] \sim \chi^2(2),$$

where T = sample size and μ_j is the jth moment of the empirical distribution of the residuals. The first term of the JB statistic represents the skewness of the distribution of $\hat{v}(t)$; the second measures departures of the estimated kurtosis from the kurtosis associated with the normal distribution.

The test for homoskedasticity rests on the work of Engle (1982) on disturbances with autoregressive conditional heteroskedasticity (ARCH). Based on the following model,

$$E(\hat{v}_t^2 \mid \hat{v}_{t-1}) = \gamma_0 + \gamma_1 \hat{v}_{t-1}^2,$$

the null hypothesis for homoskedasticity cannot be rejected if $\gamma_1 = 0$, which is tested with a t-statistic. Finally, serial independence in the residuals is tested with an F-statistic for the null hypothesis that all the coefficients, in an AR(4) for the residuals, are equal to zero.

Accuracy in forecasting the consequences of regime shifts or changes in the exogenous variables requires stability of the parameter estimates.

[13] Marquez (1985) shows that the intercept in both equations (3.5) and (3.6) is a function of the growth rate of population. Note that Goldfeld's specification includes a lagged dependent variable, whereas equations (3.5) and (3.6) do not. Results not shown here indicate that when such a variable is included, it is not significant in any of the specifications considered here.

[14] These four tests are obtained using the GIVE computer software developed by David Hendry.

In the present context, one may question the assumed parameter constancy in view of the unprecedented 95 percent increase in the value of the dollar that began at the end of 1980. To test for this hypothesis, equations (3.5) and (3.6) are estimated using data through 1980 and then used to forecast money holdings for the remaining eight quarters. Under the null hypothesis of parameter stability, the expected forecast error is zero. The statistic associated with this hypothesis is (Chow 1960, p. 590):

$$
\frac{\left(\sum_{t=1}^{T} \hat{v}(t)^2 - \sum_{t=1}^{T_1} \hat{v}(t)^2\right)\Big/ T_2}{\left(\sum_{t=1}^{T_1} \hat{v}(t)^2 \Big/ (T_1 - K)\right)} \sim F(T_2, T_1 - K),
$$

where

   T_1 = number of observations in the estimation period,
   T_2 = number of observations in the forecast period, and
   T = total number of observations = $T_1 + T_2$.

Note that this test applies to the forecast errors of the *growth* rate of money holdings, and not to the forecast errors in their *levels*. Small forecast errors in levels do not imply small forecast errors in growth rates.

4   Empirical results

The parameters associated with equations (3.5) and (3.6) are estimated using quarterly data for the U.S. from 1974.1 to 1982.4. The analysis considers two exchange rate expectation models and three Divisia monetary aggregates. The latter are computed using the same classification of assets found in the official estimates of M1, M2, and M3.[15] Parameters are estimated with ordinary least squares if the exchange rate expectations rely on the forward market. We use an instrumental variable estimator if these expectations are formed rationally.[16] Tables 1 and 2 display the estimated coefficients, the tests of the statistical properties associated with the error term, and the Chow test for the hypothesis of parameter stability.

[15] The data for Divisia monetary aggregates are available from the Federal Reserve Board on request. Data for nominal GNP, its deflator, and the 90-day U.S. and foreign interest rates come from the data files of the Multi-Country Model of the Federal Reserve Board. Further details are found in Marquez (1985).

[16] The AR(2) for the exchange rates is

   $\ln e(t) = 0.0054 + 1.0265 \ln e(t-1) - 0.1866 \ln e(t-2),$
       (1.0)   (6.6)   (1.2)

   $R^2 = 0.70, \quad DW = 1.97, \quad SER = 0.026, \quad 1972.1–82.4.$

The coefficient on $e(t-1)$ is positive and less than 2; the sum of coefficients is less than one and positive; finally, $(1.0265)^2 > -4(-0.187)$. Thus this AR(2) process is stable.

Table 1. *Divisia monetary aggregation of U.S. money demand: narrow interpretation of currency substitution[a] (1974.1–1982.4)*

	Forward market expectations			Rational expectations		
	DM1	DM2	DM3	DM1	DM2	DM3
Constant	0.021	0.029	0.027	0.017	0.029	0.027
	(4.2)	(5.0)	(5.2)	(3.5)	(4.8)	(5.1)
Income	0.093	0.274	0.273	0.140	0.290	0.280
	(0.7)	(1.7)	(2.0)	(1.1)	(1.8)	(2.1)
Domestic return	−0.001	−0.004	−0.003	−0.0012	−0.0042	−0.0035
	(−1.0)	(−2.8)	(−2.6)	(−1.1)	(−3.2)	(−3.1)
Foreign return[b]	−0.002	0.002	0.002	0.041	0.094	0.085
	(−0.4)	(0.3)	(0.4)	(0.8)	(1.6)	(1.6)
Inflation	−1.145	−1.762	−1.615	−1.01	−1.74	−1.61
	(−4.6)	(−6.0)	(−6.2)	(−4.0)	(−5.7)	(−6.0)
$\bar{R}^2$	0.41	0.60	0.62	0.37	0.62	0.64
Normality[c]	0.93	0.42	0.61	0.91	0.03	0.55
Autocorrelation[d]	0.11	0.76	0.49	0.46	0.46	0.09
Homoskedasticity[e]	0.59	0.34	0.34	0.78	0.64	0.58
Chow[f]	0.52	0.63	0.38	0.26	0.58	0.20

[a] Equation (3.5) in the text. t-statistics in parentheses.
[b] Foreign return equals the expected depreciation of the dollar.
[c] Significance level for the normality hypothesis, $\chi^2(2)$.
[d] Significance level for the no autocorrelation hypothesis, $F(4, 28)$.
[e] t-statistic for the homoskedasticity hypothesis.
[f] Significance level for the parameter stability hypothesis, $F(8, 23)$.

The results of Table 1 reveal that the narrow view – that foreign currency is held for speculative purposes only – is not supported by the data. Specifically, the coefficient on exchange-rate expectations is not significant for any of the Divisia aggregates or for any of the exchange-rate expectation models considered here. Moreover, it has the wrong sign in five of the six cases. This lack of support for the currency substitution hypothesis is broadly consistent with Cuddington's (1983) findings, which reject this hypothesis for both the United States and the United Kingdom while accepting it for Germany.[17]

[17] Cuddington's analysis uses forward market exchange-rate expectations. Using a perfect foresight model for these expectations, Marquez (1985) finds that the narrow view of currency substitution receives empirical support.

Table 2. *Divisia monetary aggregation of U.S. money demand: broad interpretation of currency substitution[a] (1974.1–1982.4)*

	Forward market expectations			Rational expectations		
	DM1	DM2	DM3	DM1	DM2	DM3
Constant	0.019	0.026	0.024	0.016	0.027	0.026
	(4.0)	(5.3)	(5.4)	(3.5)	(5.5)	(5.8)
Income	0.09	0.25	0.25	0.12	0.26	0.25
	(0.7)	(2.0)	(2.2)	(1.0)	(2.0)	(2.2)
Domestic return	−0.0040	−0.0020	−0.0020	−0.0005	−0.0024	−0.0019
	(−0.4)	(−2.0)	(−1.8)	(−0.5)	(−2.1)	(−2.0)
Foreign return[b]	−0.004	−0.007	−0.006	−0.0028	−0.0073	−0.0062
	(−2.1)	(−4.0)	(−3.7)	(−1.7)	(−4.3)	(−4.1)
Inflation	−1.06	−1.60	−1.48	−0.99	−1.68	−1.56
	(−4.5)	(−6.5)	(−6.7)	(−4.1)	(−6.8)	(−7.1)
$\bar{R}^2$	0.48	0.73	0.73	0.41	0.75	0.75
Normality[c]	0.89	0.05	0.01	0.91	0.20	0.19
Autocorrelation[d]	0.46	0.75	0.41	0.40	0.81	0.64
Homoskedasticity[e]	0.19	−0.30	−0.70	0.06	−0.19	−0.75
Chow[f]	0.33	0.98	0.77	0.22	0.94	0.45

[a] Equation (3.6) in the text. t-statistics in parentheses.
[b] Foreign return is defined as the foreign interest rate plus the expected depreciation of the dollar.
For other notes, see Table 1.

These results suggest that, following an expected depreciation of the dollar, U.S. residents will not shift from a domestic monetary asset to foreign cash if interest-bearing (and highly liquid) foreign monetary assets are available. In other words, given that the exchange-rate risk associated with holding cash is the same as the risk associated with maintaining an interest-bearing checking account, individuals will hold the checking account. Note that the lack of support for the narrow view of currency substitution is not due to a violation of error properties or to parameter instability. The various statistical diagnostics suggest that the maintained hypotheses about the error term cannot be rejected by the data; also, the Chow test reveals that the specifications possess stable parameters for the period under consideration.

The results shown in Table 2 tend to support the broad interpretation of currency substitution. The coefficient for the foreign return variable is negative and highly significant for most of the Divisia monetary aggregates under both exchange rate expectation models considered here. These empirical results, which are fairly robust, suggest that the behavior of U.S. money holdings is influenced by foreign exchange considerations. As a result, monetary policy developments abroad might influence domestic monetary policy through currency substitution.

The income-elasticity estimates, which range from 0.09 to 0.26, are similar to the short-run estimates presented by Judd and Scadding (1982, p. 1016), but lower than their long-run estimates. The parameter estimates associated with domestic interest rates are smaller than those available in the survey of Judd and Scadding (1982). Note that they are also smaller than the coefficient estimates on foreign returns. This might be a plausible result because, as explicitly indicated by Barnett (1982, pp. 690-1), the construction of Divisia monetary aggregates internalizes the substitution effects associated with changes in domestic interest rates.

The empirical results obtained here tend to confirm one of the findings of Barnett et al. (1984); namely, the higher the Divisia aggregate the better is its statistical performance. For example, the significance levels associated with the normality test are lower for the Divisia aggregate DM3 than for DM1. Finally, it is not possible to reject the hypothesis that the residuals behave according to the maintained assumptions of classical least squares, which strengthens the validity of the statistical inferences made here. The results also indicate that in five out of six cases, the hypothesis of structural stability cannot be rejected.

5   Conclusions

This paper has been motivated by the need to determine whether aggregate holdings of domestic money are influenced systematically by foreign interest rates and exchange rates - that is, whether currency substitution exists.

Although this issue has been examined previously, the existing analyses rest on official estimates of domestic money holdings which assume perfect substitutability among domestic monetary assets. The present analysis removes this assumption and therefore extends the existing literature on currency substitution by using the Divisia monetary aggregates developed by Barnett.

Extending the traditional formulation of money demand holdings to an open-economy setting, our empirical analysis suggests that money demand behavior in the U.S. for the period 1974-82 is significantly influenced by foreign interest rates and expected movements in the value of the dollar. As a result, it seems that basing the conduct of monetary policy on the assumption of a closed-economy money demand specification might not be appropriate for the U.S. case. Foreign monetary policies, through their influences on both foreign interest rates and exchange rates, might influence domestic monetary policy directly via currency substitution.

This conclusion, provocative as it may be, is preliminary because some of the assumptions made need not hold in practice. Specifically, the assumed weak separability between domestic and foreign assets should be tested following the minflex Laurent model developed by Barnett (1983, 1985b). In a similar context, the construction of the Divisia aggregates using an official classification of monetary assets is very convenient from the point of view of relating this analysis to existing papers. However, it might be of interest to continue the work of Barnett (1982) on determining the aggregate of monetary assets most relevant from the standpoint of money demand modeling. Finally, the behavior of money demand of firms might be more responsive to foreign exchange considerations than households' money demand. Recent data-collection efforts could very well make a test of this hypothesis possible in the near future. Research effort in each of these areas will, no doubt, enhance our understanding of the influences of foreign exchange considerations on money holdings.

REFERENCES

Arango, S., and M. Nadiri. 1981. "Demand for Money in Open Economies." *Journal of Monetary Economics* 7: 69–83.

Barnett, W. 1981. *Consumer Demand and Labor Supply: Goods, Monetary Assets, and Time.* Amsterdam: North-Holland.

1982. "The Optimal Level of Monetary Aggregation." *Journal of Money, Credit, and Banking* 14: 687–710.

1983. "New Indices of Money Supply and the Flexible Laurent Demand System." *Journal of Business and Statistics* 1: 7–23.

1985a. "The Microeconomic Theory of Monetary Aggregation." In W. Barnett and K. Singleton (eds.), *New Approaches to Monetary Economics.* Cambridge: Cambridge University Press.

1985b. "The Minflex-Laurent Translog Flexible Functional Form." *Journal of Econometrics* 30: 33–44.

Barnett, W., and Y. Lee. 1985. "The Global Properties of the Minflex Laurent, Generalized Leontieff, and Translog Flexible Functional Forms." *Econometrica* 53: 1421–38.

Barnett, W., E. Offenbacher, and P. Spindt. 1984. "The New Divisia Monetary Aggregates." *Journal of Political Economy* 92: 1049–85.

Brittain, B. 1981. "International Currency Substitution and the Apparent Instability of Velocity in Some Western European Economies and in the United States." *Journal of Money, Credit, and Banking* 13: 135–55.

Chow, G. 1960. "Tests of Equality Between Sets of Coefficients in Two Linear Regressions." *Econometrica* 28: 591–605.

Cuddington, J. 1983. "Currency Substitution, Capital Mobility, and Money Demand." *Journal of International Money and Finance* 2: 111-33.

Daniel, B., and H. Fried. 1983. "Currency Substitution, Postal Strikes, and Canadian Money Demand." *Canadian Journal of Economics* 16: 612-24.

Engle, R. 1982. "Autoregressive Conditional Heteroskedasticity with Estimates of the Variance of the United Kingdom Inflation." *Econometrica* 50: 997-1008.

Ewis, N., and D. Fisher. 1984. "The Translog Utility Function and the Demand for Money in the United States." *Journal of Money, Credit, and Banking* 16: 34-52.

Goldfeld, S. 1973. "The Demand for Money Revisited." *Brookings Papers on Economic Activity* 3: 577-638.

Granger, C., and P. Newbold. 1974. "Spurious Regressions in Econometrics." *Journal of Econometrics* 2: 111-20.

Hamburger, M. 1977. "The Demand for Money in an Open Economy: Germany and the U.K." *Journal of Monetary Economics* 3: 25-40.

Hansen, L., and R. Hodrick. 1981. "Forward Exchange Rates as Optimal Predictors of Future Spot Rates: An Econometric Analysis." *Journal of Political Economy* 88: 829-53.

Jarque, C. E., and A. Bera. 1980. "Efficient Tests for Normality, Homoscedasticity, and Serial Independence of Regression Residuals." *Economics Letters* 6: 255-9.

Judd, J., and J. Scadding. 1982. "The Search for a Stable Money Demand Function." *Journal of Economic Literature* 20: 993-1023.

King, D., B. Putnam, and D. Wilford. 1978. "A Currency Portfolio Approach to Exchange Rate Determination: Exchange Rate Stability and Independence of Monetary Policy." In B. Putnam and D. Wilford (eds.), *The Monetary Approach to International Adjustment*. New York: Praeger.

Marquez, J. 1985. "Currency Substitution and the New Divisia Monetary Aggregates: The U.S. Case." International Finance Discussion Paper No. 257, Federal Reserve Board.

McKinnon, R. 1982. "Currency Substitution and Instability in the World Dollar Standard." *American Economic Review* 72: 320-33.

Meese, R., and K. Rogoff. 1983. "Empirical Exchange Rate Models of the Seventies: Do They Fit Out of Sample?" *Journal of International Economics* 14: 3-24.

Miles, M. 1978. "Currency Substitution, Flexible Exchange Rates and Monetary Policy." *American Economic Review* 68: 428-36.

Tryon, R. 1983. "Small Empirical Models of Exchange Market Intervention: A Review of the Literature." Staff Studies No. 134, Federal Reserve Board.

Willms, M. 1971. "Controlling Money in an Open Economy: The German Case." *Federal Reserve Bank of St. Louis Economic Review* 4: 10-27.

CHAPTER 9

Aggregation of monetary goods:
a production model

Diana Hancock

1   Introduction

The objective of this paper is to examine the impact of money on production for the individual financial firm, and to determine whether the monetary goods used can be aggregated on the supply side. Monetary goods are liquid financial assets and liabilities. They include cash as well as demand and time deposits. The financial firm is a profit-maximizing intermediary between borrowers and lenders. The technology of the financial firm includes quantities of monetary goods, other financial goods, and physical goods such as labor and materials. Financial firms are able to set interest rates on monetary goods, and so are not necessarily price takers in such markets.

A test procedure is developed to determine whether monetary goods are separable from nonmonetary goods in production.[1] The test is general. It imposes no functional form restriction on money, and no restriction on which goods can be contained in money. Although the application is to firm data, the test can be applied at the aggregate level. Linear homogeneity of the money index is not required, although it may be imposed by data restrictions.

The financial firm operates to maximize variable profit – revenue less variable cost. The resulting profit function depends on the prices of nonmonetary goods and the quantities of monetary goods. If a monetary index exists at the level of the firm, then marginal rates of substitution or transformation between nonmonetary goods do not depend on quantities

I am grateful to William Barnett, Sudipto Bhattacharya, Peter Chinloy, Erwin Diewert, Jerome Stein, and a referee for their comments and suggestions. Data have been obtained from the Federal Reserve Bank of New York, with the assistance of Carl Allen and Ken Behrens.
[1] In the context of monetary subaggregation and financial production, the relevant separability conditions are developed in Barnett (1986, Section 3.2). "Subaggregation" refers to an index containing fewer than all the prices or quantities used in production.

of monetary goods. An increase in the quantity of money affects variable profit, but it affects neither the productivity of money nor the efficiency of the financial firm.

The separability test for the existence of money is derived in Section 2.1. The variable profit function permits any functional form to be used for the monetary index. The application of a separability test to the cost or production function imposes stringent restrictions on the form of the monetary index. As a specific case, a translog cost or production function for the financial firm implies (under separability) a Cobb–Douglas form for money. The test structure is applied to a longitudinal sample of eighteen commercial banks in New York and New Jersey for 1973–1978.

Two issues in selecting a monetary index are examined. The first issue is which components are to be included in the index of money. The second issue is whether the simple sum, where money is defined as the sum of real balances, is to be preferred over other functional forms. The simple sum requires perfect one-for-one substitutability between monetary components.[2] To examine other forms requires user returns to holding money. The user return is the increase in variable profit from holding one dollar for one period. It depends on liquidity, service charges, and required reserves. These user returns are derived in Section 2.2.

Two alternative monetary indexes – including cash and demand deposits versus cash, demand deposits, and time deposits – are considered in Section 3. Simple sum, Cobb–Douglas, and translog specifications for money are compared. These are embedded in the optimal behavior of financial firms. The tests have general applicability in order to determine whether monetary goods ought to be included explicitly in the production process of any firm.

Estimated results permit the examination of the effect of changes in the quantities of money on markets for nonmonetary goods such as loans, labor, capital, and materials. Financial firms can be compared in efficiency of converting real money balances to output. The degree of response to changes in relative quantities of money at the firm level is also obtainable.

2   Money and production in the financial firm

2.1   *Monetary subaggregation*

The conventional test for separability, implying the existence of subaggregator functions, requires the monetary index to be at most a first-

---

[2] The relative prices of monetary goods must be constant, and equal. Barnett (1981) and Barnett, Offenbacher, and Spindt (1984) have shown that differences arise between monetary indexes involving the simple sum and other functional forms, using consumer demand-based user costs for money.

order approximation to the underlying form.[3] This imposes strong restrictions on the monetary index. Specifically, if the underlying form for the aggregate cost or production function is translog then the test requires unit elasticities of substitution between monetary goods.[4] The implied index of monetary goods involves constant rather than variable shares in monetary compensation. By using a variable profit function, testing is permitted for any form of monetary index.

The problem of restricted functional forms is particularly acute, since empirical evidence supports, at least for the consumer demand for money, second-order Törnqvist functional forms.[5] It is not clear ex ante whether monetary or other financial goods are inputs or outputs in production. This problem arises with demand and time deposits. Since the financial firm provides services based on deposits, these can be argued as being outputs. Alternatively, the provision of loans requires a base of deposits, so the latter can be considered inputs.[6] A classification rule is developed to determine whether monetary goods are inputs or outputs.

For the financial firm, production occurs with both monetary and nonmonetary goods. Quantities of nonmonetary goods are $x = (x_I, ..., x_J)$. Quantities of monetary goods are $m = (m_0, ..., m_{I-1})$, ordered by liquidity. If m_0 denotes cash and m_1 demand deposits, the simple sum index of narrowly defined money is $m_0 + m_1$. A potential monetary index can include all goods up to m_{I-1}. Quantities of monetary goods are given to the firm, which sets interest rates. The financial firm is not a price taker for monetary goods, and may have monopsonistic power. Competitive

[3] Humphrey (1981) has employed this test to examine weak separability of bank liabilities from bank capital.

[4] Berndt and Christensen (1974) develop a test of weak separability on the parameters of a translog function. Blackorby, Primont, and Russell (1978) show that the parameter restrictions require that the aggregator function be Cobb–Douglas. A similar issue arises for all functions that are second-order approximations. If the variable profit function depends on prices of variable inputs and quantities of goods to be aggregated, Woodland (1978) shows that the parameter restrictions can be imposed without implying a Cobb–Douglas technology. This approach is followed here, relaxing the assumption of linear homogeneity within the goods subaggregate. An alternative procedure, following Denny and Fuss (1977), is to impose the required separability on an arbitrary underlying function. Then a second-order approximation can be taken to the restricted function.

[5] For aggregate indexes of money, Barnett, Offenbacher, and Spindt (1984) and Cagan (1982) find – for (respectively) generalized liquidity L and narrowly defined money M1-B – a Törnqvist index to be best fitting. The monetary index is imposed directly, and not tested as separable from consumer labor supply and demand for physical and nonmonetary financial goods. A Törnqvist index is based on a weighted average of growth rates of components. Weights are two-period moving averages of compensation shares.

[6] Whether deposits are inputs or outputs affects estimates of technological substitution and transformation, the measurement of economies of scale, and the productivity of financial operations.

markets for deposits are not necessarily imposed.[7] The financial firm determines other components of the return per dollar, such as service charges. The firm is a price taker for labor and materials, and in other nonmonetary markets.

For nonmonetary goods, prices are $p = (p_I, \ldots, p_J)$. With p_i positive, by the Debreu (1959, p. 38) convention, x_i is positive for outputs and negative for inputs, $i = I, \ldots, J$. For monetary quantities, m_i is positive for $i = 0, \ldots, I-1$. The transformation function, defined on the convex set of production possibilities S, is $T(x, m) = 0$. The variable profit function is

$$\pi(p, m) = \max_x \left\{ \sum_{i=I}^{J} p_i x_i, \; x, m \in S, \; p > 0 \right\}, \qquad (2.1)$$

linearly homogeneous in prices, increasing in output prices and decreasing in input prices. The variable profit function is normalized, given linear homogeneity in prices, by setting the Jth price at unity.

If there exists a money index, let this be $M(m_0, \ldots, m_{I-1})$. Then the transformation function is $T(x, M) = 0$, where M is a scalar. The transformation function is continuous from above, nonincreasing in x and nondecreasing in M, because outputs are positive, inputs are negative, and monetary quantities are positive. The transformation function can be expressed as

$$M(m) = h(x) \qquad (2.2)$$

or $M(m) - h(x) = T(x, M) = 0$. This implies that $M(m)/h(x) = 1$. Since the variable profit function is linearly homogeneous in prices p, by duality the transformation function T and its subfunction h exhibit the same property in x. Using the linear homogeneity of $h(x)$, (2.1) becomes

$$\pi(p, m) = \max_x \left\{ \sum_{i=I}^{J} p_i x_i : M(m) = h(x) \right\}$$

$$= e(p, M(m)) = e(p, 1)M(m) = g(p)M(m). \qquad (2.3)$$

Linear homogeneity of $M(m)$ is not required to obtain the decomposition of π.

If a money index exists, $g(p) = \pi(p, m)/M(m) = \partial\pi/\partial M$ is a variable profit function, dependent only on the prices of nonmonetary goods and not on the quantities of monetary goods. Also, $g(p)$ is the variable profit

---

[7] An imperfectly competitive model of the financial firm is developed in Hancock (1986). If there is homothetic loan-deposit separability from nondeposit liabilities and physical goods, there is corresponding homothetic separability of the price of loans and deposits. Let loans and deposits be further subaggregated into separate indexes. In general, these separability restrictions must be tested. Then, under the failure of price taking, the prices of loans and deposits are related.

per unit of money, and can be compared between financial firms and time as a measure of productivity and efficiency. A financial firm more efficient in converting money to profit has a higher level of $g(p)$.

Where a money index exists, a conventional profit function $g(p)$ summarizes the technology of the financial firm. Only under these conditions can the components of money be excluded from the production technology. Where a money index does not exist, the variable profit function $\pi(p, m)$ cannot be decomposed into the product of two functions representing nonmonetary prices and monetary quantities. The quantities of monetary goods affect marginal rates of substitution and transformation between nonmonetary goods, and cannot be regarded as constituting a veil. In (2.3), there is no restriction on the number of monetary goods in m. No prior restriction on the functional form is imposed. If the money index is expressible as a simple sum then $M = \sum_{i=0}^{I-1} m_i$. The components of M can be either inputs or outputs.

There are two potentially important special cases. First, if all monetary goods are inputs and $M(m)$ exists, then g is the marginal and average user return to money and is positive. Second, suppose all money goods are outputs. Multiplying (2.3) by negative unity produces a cost function $c = -\pi$. The marginal cost of producing monetary goods for a money index M is $\partial c/\partial M$ and is positive, while $\partial \pi/\partial M$ is negative. The elasticity of cost with respect to money is $\partial \ln c/\partial \ln M$. If this elasticity is less than unity, economies of scale arise in the production of the services from monetary goods.

The supplies of outputs and demands for inputs are

$$x_i = \partial \pi/\partial p_i \quad i = I, ..., J-1. \tag{2.4}$$

In elasticity form, $e_i = p_i x_i/\pi = \partial \ln \pi/\partial \ln p_i$, $i = I, ..., J-1$, where e_i is positive for outputs and negative for inputs, regardless of whether a cost or variable profit function is used.[8] For the quantities of monetary goods, $\partial \pi/\partial m_i = r_i$ for $i = 0, ..., I-1$, where r_i is the user return per dollar held. The user return to holding a monetary input is positive. For a monetary output, r_i is negative because the marginal cost of producing an output is positive. In elasticity form, $r_i m_i/\pi = \partial \ln \pi/\partial \ln m_i$ for $i = 0, ..., I-1$.

The variable profit function has only nonnegative arguments. Because $\pi = \sum_{i=I}^{J} p_i x_i$ and total net income from monetary goods is also $\pi = \sum_{i=0}^{I-1} r_i m_i$, income from monetary goods is equal to income from nonmonetary goods. There is a linear dependence among each of the two sets

[8] For a cost function, net revenues from nonmonetary goods are negative and $c = -\pi$. Input demands are $x_i = \partial c/\partial p_i$ and are positive. So $e_i = p_i x_i/c = -p_i x_i/\pi$ and is negative. A similar argument obtains for output supplies.

of goods, and one of each can be used as a numeraire. Once a specification for the variable profit function is made, together with the demands and supplies for nonmonetary goods and the user returns for monetary goods, the parameters can be estimated.

2.2 User costs and returns for monetary and other financial goods

It is necessary to obtain prices for monetary and other financial goods.[9] The current period user cost of liability i is, for L liability categories,

$$U_i = P(h_i - R)/(1 + R) \quad i = 1, ..., L, \tag{2.5}$$

where P is a general price index, h_i the own current period holding yield on liability i, and R the common discounting rate. Let q_i be the interest rate payable on liability i, d_i the deposit insurance premium rate, s_i the service charge rate per dollar, and b_i the reserve requirement on liability i. For each dollar deposited, $(1 - b_i)$ is available for use by the firm.

The holding period yield h_i is the net cost of paying for the services of one dollar per period. This is the sum of the interest rate paid to the depositor, deposit insurance premium, and effective tax Rb_i imposed by the reserve requirement, less service charge revenue s_i. Then

$$h_i = q_i + d_i + Rb_i - s_i$$
$$= q_i + d_i - s_i + R - R(1 - b_i). \tag{2.6}$$

The differential between the holding cost and discounting rate is

$$h_i - R = q_i + d_i - s_i - R(1 - b_i)$$
$$= (1 - b_i + q_i + d_i - s_i) - (1 - b_i)(1 + R). \tag{2.7}$$

The real discounted user cost of the services of liability i is

$$u_i \equiv U_i/P = (h_i - R)/(1 + R)$$
$$= -(1 - b_i) + (1 - b_i + q_i + d_i - s_i)/(1 + R)$$
$$= -1 + (1 + q_i + Rb_i + d_i - s_i)/(1 + R) \quad i = 1, ..., L. \tag{2.8}$$

On the asset side of the balance sheet, with A categories, q_i is the interest rate earned per dollar per period; service charges, including late loan payments and stand-by charges, are at rate s_i; and capital gains are at rate z_i. Provisions for loan losses and insurance premia are at rate

---

[9] Details on this user-cost derivation are in Hancock (1985). The user costs are derived in the context of an intertemporal model of financial production.

d_i. The holding revenue per period for an asset is the sum of interest earned, service charge income, capital gains, and insurance premia, or $h_i = q_i + z_i + s_i - d_i$. The differential between the discounting rate and holding revenue is $R - h_i = R - q_i - z_i - s_i + d_i$. The real discounted user cost of asset i is

$$u_i = U_i/P = (R - h_i)/(1 + R)$$
$$= 1 - (1 + q_i + z_i + s_i - d_i)/(1 + R), \quad i = L+1, \ldots, L+A. \quad (2.9)$$

Because variable profit is reduced if u_i is nonnegative and increased if u_i is negative, the former condition classifies good i as an input and the latter as an output.

For monetary goods where m_i is positive, the firm equates the marginal user return with the marginal user cost of purchasing the services of one dollar per period: $r_i = u_i$ $(i = 0, \ldots, I-1)$. For nonmonetary goods, $p_i = |u_i|$, $i = I, \ldots, J$, where $|u_i|$ is the absolute value of u_i, and x_i is positive if u_i is negative while x_i is negative if u_i is positive.

2.3   *Data: monetary and other financial goods*

The principal data source is the *Functional Cost Analysis* (FCA), an annual survey conducted by the Federal Reserve. The data are 1973–1978 longitudinal observations on the balance sheet, profit and loss statement, and employment for eighteen New York and New Jersey banks, members of Federal Reserve District Number 2.

The discounting rate R_t $(t = 1973, \ldots, 1978)$ satisfies the feasibility condition that variable profit be nonnegative each year; the highest feasible interest rate is used. The set of interest rates tested for feasibility is those either paid on deposits or received on loans by a sample bank in a given year. Discounting rates high enough to affect the classification of inputs versus outputs are infeasible, with variable profit negative for at least one sample bank in the given year. Lower discounting rates than those used do not alter the classification.

For calculation of the holding costs h_i, data are available on q_i, s_i, and d_i for five types of loans receivable: investments and securities; real estate mortgages; installment loans; credit card loans; and commercial, agricultural and other loans. Capital gains and losses z_i are included for investments and securities on a realized basis. The implicit price deflator for finance and insurance in the national accounts issues of the *Survey of Current Business* is used for the price index P. This permits data on financial quantities to be constructed as real balances, and user costs of monetary and nonmonetary goods to be expressed in nominal terms. Financial goods quantities are measured in real terms, analogous to those for physical goods.

Among assets, all loan categories have negative real user costs u_i for the sample. The real user cost of cash is $u_0 = R/(1+R)$, since q, z, s, and d are zero. The corresponding real balance for cash, m_0, is the amount of real excess reserves held above required reserves.

Demand and time deposits are monetary goods 1 and 2. The interest rate, service charges, and deposit insurance premium rates paid to the Federal Deposit Insurance Corporation (FDIC) are from the FCA. Reserve requirements are obtained from the *Federal Reserve Bulletin* for demand deposits, and from the FCA for time deposits. For all observations, u_1 is negative and u_2 positive, so demand deposit services are an output and time deposit services an input. Quantities m_1 and m_2 are dollar amounts on the balance sheet deflated by the price index. Since $r_i = u_i$ ($i = 0, ..., 2$), r_0 is positive, r_1 negative, and r_2 positive, with the corresponding quantities m_0, m_1, and m_2 strictly positive.

This produces user returns to holding unit real balances. Monetary goods differ in characteristics such as liquidity, risk, and return. If there is no difference in these characteristics, user returns are identical.

For the simple sum $m_0 + m_1$ containing the real balances of cash and demand deposits, the rate of return is $(r_0 m_0 + r_1 m_1)/(m_0 + m_1)$. The numerator is the value of services produced by the monetary goods in M1. For the simple sum $m_0 + m_1 + m_2$, which includes time deposits, the return is $\sum_{i=0}^{2} r_i m_i / \sum_{i=0}^{2} m_i$. Likelihood ratio tests can be used to determine whether the simple sum is acceptable as a restriction from a form with a larger number of parameters.

There are two other liability categories, for borrowed and purchased funds and nondeposit funds, and user costs are constructed for these. A Törnqvist index of net loans, with price, is constructed from the five types of loan assets and two nondeposit liabilities. This index of loans is x_3 with user cost u_3.

2.4   Data: labor, materials, and capital

For labor input, the FCA distinguish managerial and nonmanagerial employees. A Törnqvist quantity index of labor input is constructed. The price of labor services is the ratio of the total labor compensation to the labor quantity index.

Material services include stationery, printing and supplies, telephone and telegraph, and postage, freight, and delivery.[10] The quantity of materials is the ratio of total expenditures to a Törnqvist materials price

---

[10] The prices of the various services are from the wholesale and producer price indexes of the U.S. Departments of Commerce and Labor, from the *Survey of Current Business*. Total expenditures are as reported in the financial statements.

index. The price and quantity of labor and materials are (p_4, x_4) and (p_5, x_5), respectively, with x_4 and x_5 negative, being inputs.

Real physical capital is an index of structures, computers, and other equipment. Stocks are constructed by the perpetual inventory method. Each year, constant dollar investment is added to the previous stock and depreciation subtracted. Depreciation rates are obtained from the U.S. Treasury Department *Bulletin F* series on asset lives. Financial capital is the difference between real financial assets and liabilities. The sum of financial and real physical capital is total real capital x_6, equal to economic shareholders' equity.

The value of capital services is the difference between payments to other nonmonetary goods and the value of monetary returns. This is $\sum_{i=1}^{J} p_i x_i - \sum_{i=1}^{I-1} r_i m_i$, where i excludes capital in the first summand. The user cost of capital u_6 is the value of capital services divided by the capital stock x_6, and the price its absolute value. Prices for nonmonetary goods p_i are the absolute values of the user costs, or $|u_i|$.

3   Money index forms: specification and empirical results

The prices and quantities of the goods used in estimation are:

(r_0, m_0) nominal user return and real balance of cash,
(r_1, m_1) nominal user return and real balance of demand deposits,
(r_2, m_2) nominal user return and real balance of time deposits,
(p_3, x_3) price and real balance of loans,
(p_4, x_4) price per efficiency unit and efficiency index of labor services,
(p_5, x_5) rental price and real balance of capital, and
(p_6, x_6) price per efficiency unit and efficiency index of materials.

The variable profit function is $\pi(p, m)$, where m denotes the quantities of monetary goods and p the prices of nonmonetary goods. Separability between the two is equivalent to the existence of a monetary index, implying the multiplicative form $\pi(p, m) = g(p)M(m)$. The $g(p)$ is a conventional variable profit function that can be used to derive demands for labor and other inputs, and supplies of output independent of the quantities of money.

Two groupings into m are considered. In the first, m includes cash and demand deposits. Nonmonetary goods are time deposits, loans, labor, capital, and materials. The data (r_2, m_2) are converted to a nonmonetary pair (p_2, x_2) by $r_2 = u_2$ and $p_2 = |u_2|$. The quantity of time deposits is

$x_2 = -m_2$, measured negatively as an input. Variable profit is $\sum_{i=2}^{6} p_i x_i$. In the second grouping, m contains cash, demand, and time deposits. Nonmonetary goods are loans, labor, capital, and materials. Variable profit is $\sum_{i=3}^{6} p_i x_i$.

In both cases, relative expenditures on nonmonetary goods are obtained as $p_i x_i / \pi$, where π is the relevant variable profit. A translog form is specified for the unrestricted variable profit function $\pi(p, m)$. Since the variable profit function is linearly homogeneous in prices, the price of materials is normalized at unity. The demand for materials is not estimated, since it is linearly dependent on the remaining input demands and output supplies.

Demands for inputs and supplies for outputs among nonmonetary goods are obtained by equating relative expenditures with the logarithmic derivatives of the variable profit function. For each case,

$$e_i = p_i x_i / \pi = \partial \ln \pi / \partial \ln p_i$$

$$= \alpha_i + \sum_{j=k}^{5} \beta_{ij} \ln p_j + \sum_{j=1}^{k-1} \beta_{ij} \ln m_j \quad i = k, \dots, 5, \tag{3.1}$$

where $k = 2$ if time deposits are excluded from money and $k = 3$ if time deposits are included in the potential money index. The α and β elements denote parameters. For loans, x_3 is positive; for labor and capital, x_4 and x_5 are negative. For time deposits, x_2 is negative. These signs are the same for relative expenditures e_i. The quantities of money are expressed relative to the quantity of excess reserves, or cash, with linear homogeneity of money imposed. For this reason, the second summand in (3.1) starts at unity rather than zero.

The user return to cash is not estimated, as it can be obtained from the remaining monetary equations. In logarithmic form, the user returns to holding real balances are, for each of the two monetary forms,

$$r_i m_i / \pi = \partial \ln \pi / \partial \ln m_i$$

$$= \alpha_i + \sum_{j=k}^{5} \beta_{ij} \ln p_j + \sum_{j=1}^{k-1} \beta_{ij} \ln m_j, \tag{3.2}$$

where $i = 1, \dots, k-1$. The $5-k$ equations of the form (3.1), and the $k-1$ for (3.2) with additive errors having contemporaneous covariances not necessarily zero, constitute the estimating system.[11]

Prior to examining the technology of production of monetary services, some regularity conditions must be satisfied. First, monotonicity is tested at each data point, as opposed to the sample mean. This requires $p_3 x_3 > 0$

---

[11] The prices of nonmonetary goods and the quantities of monetary goods are exogenous, and the shares on the left-hand sides of (3.1) and (3.2) are endogenous.

for loans, and $p_i x_i < 0$ for labor, capital, materials, and time deposits in the first case. Also $r_1 m_1 < 0$ for demand deposits, and $r_0 m_0 > 0$ for cash and time deposits in the second case. Nonparametric inspection of the data points for all observations indicates that this condition is satisfied. Second, the variable profit function should satisfy convexity in prices. Convexity requires that the matrix of π be positive semidefinite. For arbitrary π, this has typical element

$$\pi_{ij} = [e_i e_j + p_j \, \partial e_i / \partial p_j - p_j x_i (\partial p_i / \partial p_j) / \pi] \pi / p_i p_j,[12]$$

where $i, j = k, ..., 5$. For the translog specification $\partial e_i / \partial p_j = \beta_{ij} / p_j$, so

$$\pi_{ij} = [e_i e_j + \beta_{ij} - v e_i] \pi / p_i p_j, \tag{3.3}$$

where v is an indicator variable equal to unity if $i = j$ and zero otherwise. If the principal minors of this matrix are nonnegative then π is convex. The matrices of the π_{ij} with the sample considered satisfy the convexity property at each observation.

The test for a monetary index imposes zero restrictions on the monetary parameters β_{ij} $(j = 1, ..., k-1)$ in the demands and supplies for nonmonetary goods (3.1). Zero restrictions also apply to the β_{ij} $(j = k, ..., 5)$ in (3.2). If these are not rejected statistically, the resulting monetary index has a translog form, and exponentiating

$$M = m_0 \exp\left(\sum_{i=1}^{k-1} \alpha_i \ln m_i + \frac{1}{2} \sum_{i=1}^{k-1} \sum_{j=1}^{k-1} \beta_{ij} \ln m_i \ln m_j \right). \tag{3.4}$$

If the second-order terms β_{ij} $(i, j = 1, ..., k-1)$ are zero, then the monetary index has a Cobb–Douglas form.

Tests for a monetary index are performed for the two groupings into m, with the level of significance assigned at .01 for each index. Likelihood ratio test statistics, asymptotically distributed as chi-squared divided by the number of degrees of freedom, are calculated for the various monetary forms.[13] None of the monetary indexes is accepted for the first grouping m, including cash and demand deposits. If a translog form is imposed for a money index containing cash and demand deposits, the logarithm of the likelihood function is 404.72. The unrestricted logarithm of the likelihood function is 419.75. The test statistic for the translog form, with four degrees of freedom, is 7.50 (3.32). (The critical value of chi-squared

[12] Forms such as the Generalized Barnett functional form of Diewert and Wales (1984) do not require the testing of curvature conditions.
[13] The model is estimated as a pooled time series and cross section. Structural stability tests are performed that permit the reduction of the number of bank categories to five, for which dummy variables are introduced.

is in parentheses for this and other tests.) The Cobb–Douglas form is not accepted, with a test statistic of 25.37 (3.02) with 5 degrees of freedom. Monetary goods are not separable from nonmonetary goods in this case.

Tests for a monetary index containing cash, demand, and time deposits are performed. The translog form is not rejected statistically, with a test statistic of 2.41 (2.80) with six degrees of freedom. The Cobb–Douglas form is not rejected, with a likelihood ratio test statistic of 1.52 (2.32) with 10 degrees of freedom, as compared with the unrestricted case. Conditional on the translog form, the Cobb–Douglas structure is not rejected, with a likelihood ratio test statistic of 0.20 (3.32).

In Table 1 are parameter estimates for the translog monetary index containing cash and demand deposits. Indicated are the estimates when a Cobb–Douglas form is imposed. The constant terms represent the expenditures relative to variable profit. For time deposits, labor and capital, this is negative, confirming that these are inputs. The constant terms are the same in all estimates: 2.93 for loans and -0.44, -1.14, and -2.13 (respectively) for time deposits, labor, and capital. The signs on these confirm monotonicity in nonmonetary markets at the geometric sample mean. Variable profit is increasing in the price of loans, and decreasing in the prices of time deposits, labor, and capital. For demand deposits, the constant term is -1.15. The user return to demand deposits is negative if these are outputs.

The empirical results for the estimated system – for the monetary index containing cash, demand, and time deposits – are in Table 2. The first column contains the parameter estimates with no restriction other than the regularity conditions that the second-order terms be symmetric. The logarithm of the likelihood function is in the last row. In the second column are the estimates for the translog monetary index form, and in the third column are the parameter estimates when a Cobb–Douglas aggregator function is imposed. For nonmonetary goods, the constant terms (in the last two columns) for loans, labor, and capital are 13.51, -4.57, and -8.89, respectively. These confirm the monotonicity conditions. Among monetary goods, demand deposits are an output with a constant term of -3.85, and time deposits an input.

4   Substitution and transformation

Between any two nonmonetary goods in p, inputs or outputs, the partial elasticity of transformation is

$$\sigma_{ij} = \pi \pi_{ij}/\pi_i \pi_j \quad i, j = k, \ldots, 6, \tag{4.1}$$

Table 1. *Parameter estimates, monetary index, cash, and demand deposits (asymptotic standard errors in parentheses)*

		Unrestricted	Translog	Cobb–Douglas
Nonmonetary goods				
Time deposits	Constant	−0.44 (0.04)	−0.44 (0.04)	−0.44 (0.04)
$p_2 x_2 / \pi_1 < 0$	$\ln m_1$	−0.02 (0.01)	0	0
	$\ln p_2$	−0.21 (0.03)	−0.20 (0.03)	−0.21 (0.03)
	$\ln p_3$	0.11 (0.05)	0.09 (0.05)	0.11 (0.05)
	$\ln p_4$	0.01 (0.02)	0.02 (0.02)	0.01 (0.02)
	$\ln p_5$	0.10 (0.02)	0.11 (0.02)	0.10 (0.02)
Loans	Constant	2.93 (0.14)	2.93 (0.15)	2.93 (0.15)
$p_3 x_3 / \pi_1 > 0$	$\ln m_1$	−0.01 (0.01)	0	0
	$\ln p_2$	0.11 (0.05)	0.09 (0.05)	0.11 (0.05)
	$\ln p_3$	0.76 (0.15)	0.82 (0.15)	0.73 (0.15)
	$\ln p_4$	−0.28 (0.06)	−0.29 (0.06)	−0.25 (0.06)
	$\ln p_5$	−0.57 (0.09)	−0.60 (0.09)	−0.58 (0.09)
Labor	Constant	−1.14 (0.04)	−1.14 (0.04)	−1.14 (0.04)
$p_4 x_4 / \pi_1 < 0$	$\ln m_1$	0.02 (0.01)	0	0
	$\ln p_2$	0.01 (0.02)	0.02 (0.02)	0.01 (0.02)
	$\ln p_3$	−0.28 (0.06)	−0.29 (0.06)	−0.25 (0.06)
	$\ln p_4$	−0.13 (0.04)	0.13 (0.04)	0.11 (0.04)
	$\ln p_5$	0.10 (0.03)	0.11 (0.03)	0.11 (0.03)
Capital	Constant	−2.13 (0.11)	−2.13 (0.11)	−2.13 (0.11)
$p_5 x_5 / \pi_1 < 0$	$\ln m_1$	−0.01 (0.01)	0	0
	$\ln p_2$	0.10 (0.05)	0.11 (0.02)	0.10 (0.02)
	$\ln p_3$	−0.57 (0.09)	−0.60 (0.09)	−0.58 (0.09)
	$\ln p_4$	0.10 (0.03)	0.11 (0.03)	0.11 (0.03)
	$\ln p_5$	0.34 (0.07)	0.35 (0.07)	0.34 (0.07)
Monetary goods				
Demand deposits	Constant	−1.15 (0.01)	−1.15 (0.01)	−1.15 (0.01)
$r_1 m_1 / \pi_1 < 0$	$\ln m_1$	0.14 (0.01)	0.15 (0.01)	0
	$\ln p_2$	−0.02 (0.01)	0	0
	$\ln p_3$	−0.01 (0.01)	0	0
	$\ln p_4$	0.02 (0.01)	0	0
	$\ln p_5$	−0.01 (0.01)	0	0
$\ln L$		419.75	404.72	356.33

Notes: Goods are: 0 cash, 1 demand deposits, 2 time deposits, 3 loans, 4 labor, 5 capital, 6 materials. Variable profit is $\sum_{i=2}^{6} p_i x_i$. Prices and variable profit are normalized by the price of materials. The real balance of demand deposits is measured relative to the real balance of cash. All estimates are with symmetry and equality across second-order parameters imposed.

Table 2. *Parameter estimates, monetary index, cash, demand deposits, and time deposits (asymptotic standard errors in parentheses)*

		Unrestricted	Translog	Cobb–Douglas
Nonmonetary goods				
Loans	Constant	13.15 (4.94)	13.51 (4.93)	13.51 (5.67)
$p_3 x_3/\pi_2 > 0$	$\ln m_1$	−3.12 (1.05)	0	0
	$\ln m_2$	3.05 (0.94)	0	0
	$\ln p_3$	14.80 (4.35)	0.94 (0.28)	0.93 (0.28)
	$\ln p_4$	−4.42 (1.40)	−0.27 (0.13)	−0.29 (0.13)
	$\ln p_5$	−9.13 (2.60)	−0.73 (0.27)	−0.70 (0.28)
Labor	Constant	−4.48 (1.56)	−4.57 (1.56)	−4.57 (1.77)
$p_4 x_4/\pi_2 < 0$	$\ln m_1$	0.97 (0.38)	0	0
	$\ln m_2$	−0.85 (0.32)	0	0
	$\ln p_3$	−4.42 (1.40)	−0.27 (0.13)	−0.29 (0.13)
	$\ln p_4$	1.40 (0.53)	0.11 (0.11)	0.11 (0.11)
	$\ln p_5$	2.58 (0.83)	0.08 (0.08)	0.09 (0.08)
Capital	Constant	−8.68 (2.97)	−8.89 (2.97)	−8.89 (3.43)
$p_5 x_5/\pi_2 < 0$	$\ln m_1$	1.87 (0.62)	0	0
	$\ln m_2$	−1.83 (0.56)	0	0
	$\ln p_3$	−9.13 (2.60)	−0.73 (0.27)	−0.70 (0.28)
	$\ln p_4$	2.58 (0.83)	0.08 (0.08)	0.09 (0.08)
	$\ln p_5$	5.70 (1.57)	0.58 (0.34)	0.53 (0.35)
Monetary goods				
Demand deposits	Constant	−3.79 (1.17)	−3.86 (1.17)	−3.85 (1.33)
$r_1 m_1/\pi_2 < 0$	$\ln m_1$	0.72 (0.31)	−0.02 (0.15)	0
	$\ln m_2$	−0.58 (0.25)	0.05 (0.10)	0
	$\ln p_3$	−3.12 (1.05)	0	0
	$\ln p_4$	0.97 (0.38)	0	0
	$\ln p_5$	1.87 (0.62)	0	0
Time deposits	Constant	2.42 (1.06)	2.50 (1.06)	2.51 (1.21)
$r_2 m_2/\pi_2 > 0$	$\ln m_1$	−0.58 (0.25)	0.05 (0.10)	0
	$\ln m_2$	0.70 (0.23)	0.01 (0.09)	0
	$\ln p_3$	3.05 (0.94)	0	0
	$\ln p_4$	−0.85 (0.32)	0	0
	$\ln p_5$	−1.82 (0.56)	0	0
$\ln L$		−535.80	−543.04	−543.44

Notes: Goods are: 0 cash, 1 demand deposits, 2 time deposits, 3 loans, 4 labor, 5 capital, 6 materials. Variable profit is $\sum_{i=4}^{6} p_i x_i$. Prices of nonmonetary goods are normalized by price of materials. Real balances of demand deposits and time deposits m_1 and m_2 are measured relative to that for cash. Estimates are with symmetry and equality imposed.

where one and two subscripts respectively denote first and second derivatives. This is the elasticity of relative quantities with respect to relative prices, nonmonetary goods. The partial elasticity of transformation with a translog variable profit function is

$$\sigma_{ij} = 1 + \beta_{ij}/e_i e_j - v/e_j \quad i, j = k, \ldots, 6. \tag{4.2}$$

At the geometric sample mean, $e_i = \alpha_i$. The compensated price elasticity of supply for an output or demand for an input is

$$\eta_{ij} = \sigma_{ij} \alpha_j. \tag{4.3}$$

These elasticities permit estimation of the degree of response in the markets for loans, labor, capital, and materials when their prices change.

5   Elasticities of transformation, supply, and demand

5.1   *Response to price changes*

In Table 3 are the elasticities of transformation between nonmonetary goods, evaluated at the geometric sample mean. In the upper panel are the estimates where time deposits are nonmonetary. In the lower panel, time deposits are considered monetary.

In Table 4 are the compensated price elasticities of supply and demand for nonmonetary goods, with asymptotic standard errors in parentheses. For both sets of estimates, the own-price elasticities of supply and demand for loans, labor, and capital (on the principal diagonal) are greater than unity in absolute value. The own-price elasticity of supply for loans is positive as an output, and those for labor and capital negative. There is a relatively flexible response in these markets to the own price. The estimates are larger in absolute value when the monetary index contains time deposits.

The demand for time deposits is relatively inelastic. The first column reports the elasticity of the quantity of each nonmonetary good when the price of time deposits changes. The major component of the price of time deposits is the interest rate paid to depositors. Interest rates on time deposits have an inelastic impact on employment, as measured by the cross-elasticity of demand for labor in the price of time deposits, at -0.45 and not significantly different from zero. All estimates of the own- and cross-price elaticities between time deposits and other goods are less than unity in absolute value. Between loans, labor, and capital there is a relatively flexible technology. All cross-price elasticities between these three exceed unity in absolute value.

Table 3. *Elasticities of transformation, nonmonetary goods*

	Time deposits, nonmonetary			
	Time deposits	Loans	Labor	Capital
Time deposits	2.19	0.91	1.02	1.11
Loans	0.91	0.75	1.08	1.09
Labor	1.02	1.08	1.77	1.04
Capital	1.11	1.09	1.04	1.54

	Time deposits, monetary		
	Loans	Labor	Capital
Loans	0.93	1.01	1.01
Labor	1.01	1.23	1.00
Capital	1.01	1.00	1.12

Notes: Elasticities of transformation are $\pi\pi_{ij}/\pi_i\pi_j$, where $i, j = k, ..., 5$ for nonmonetary goods. Elasticities are evaluated at the geometric sample mean.

5.2 *Response to monetary quantity changes*

Monetary quantities are predetermined, and the financial firm seeks to maximize the user return from holding one dollar per period. In the lower panel of Table 4 are estimates, where time deposits are nonmonetary, of the elasticity of the return to holding demand deposits when various prices change. When time deposits are monetary, separability between monetary and nonmonetary goods obtains. The return to holding demand deposits is not affected by prices of loans, labor, and capital.

An increase of 1% in the return to loans (an output) increases the return per dollar of demand deposits by 2.94%. A similar increase in the price of time deposits reduces the user return per dollar of demand deposits by 0.42%. A general rise in interest rates, across loans and deposits, increases the return to holding money for the financial firm.

The elasticity of the return to holding demand deposits with respect to the price of capital is greater than unity in absolute value. The corresponding estimate for labor is not significantly different from zero at the 1% level. Increases in labor costs do not substantially reduce the return to holding money.

Table 4. *Nonmonetary goods: own- and cross-price elasticities (compensated) of supply and demand (at geometric sample mean, with asymptotic standard errors in parentheses)*

| | Time deposits, nonmonetary | | | |
	Time deposits	Loans	Labor	Capital
Time deposits	−0.96 (0.21)	2.68 (1.39)	−1.16 (0.54)	−2.36 (0.61)
Loans	−0.40 (0.39)	2.19 (0.21)	−1.24 (0.46)	−2.32 (0.75)
Labor	−0.45 (0.54)	3.18 (1.64)	−2.02 (0.04)	−2.22 (0.86)
Capital	−0.48 (0.22)	3.20 (0.96)	−1.19 (0.31)	−3.29 (0.25)

| | Time deposits, monetary | | |
	Loans	Labor	Capital
Loans	12.22 (0.94)	−4.50 (0.20)	−8.73 (0.06)
Labor	13.21 (0.80)	−5.50 (0.93)	−8.70 (0.52)
Capital	13.23 (0.82)	−4.49 (1.69)	−9.74 (1.12)

	Elasticity of return to demand deposits with respect to price of good	Elasticity of demand/supply for good with respect to demand deposit quantity
Time deposits	−0.42 (1.04)	−1.10 (0.26)
Loans	2.94 (1.14)	1.15 (0.01)
Labor	−1.15 (1.04)	−1.17 (0.26)
Capital	−2.12 (1.11)	−1.15 (0.10)

Notes: Based on the parameter estimates where time deposits are nonmonetary. The unrestricted estimates of Table 1 are used, since money indices involving only cash and demand deposits are not accepted.

The second column reports the elasticity of supply or demand for nonmonetary goods with respect to the quantity of demand deposits. A 1% increase in the quantity of demand deposits reduces the demand for time deposits, labor, and capital by greater than 1%, although unity is contained in a 95% confidence interval in each case. The quantity of loans can be increased by 1.15% with a 1% increase in demand deposits. The financial firm is relatively responsive to changes in the quantity of money, as measured by demand deposits.

6   Concluding remarks

At the base of the demand for money is the behavior of consumers and firms, and their preferences and technology. While the central bank may nominally determine the quantity of money, the supply of such services is delivered by financial firms. Examined is a subsample subject to reserve requirements, but any depository financial intermediary is engaged in the production of monetary services.

There is uncertainty in some variables potentially entering user costs. For example, there is a nonzero probability of withdrawal, or of a bank run. This uncertainty affects the decision to hold cash, or excess reserves, even where deposit insurance obtains. An extension of the user costs would include uncertainty explicitly.

The financial firm responds to the prices of nonmonetary goods and the quantities of monetary goods. The marginal user return per dollar of real balance is equated with the marginal user cost. This user return depends on some components not controlled by the firm, such as deposit insurance premia and reserve requirements, and others which are controllable, such as interest rates and service charges. Since this return is an endogenous variable, interest rates are endogenous, responding to changes in the quantity of money. Adjustments in other regulations, such as on capital adequacy, are included through the price of capital. The endogeneity of interest rates and service charges – with respect to monetary quantities and the prices of labor and other goods – attempts to capture the reality facing financial firms. An extension is to test for the exogeneity of monetary quantities in the specification.

Profit maximization has been assumed in the derivation of the variable profit function. Financial firms may satisfice, or not be operating on the boundary of the production possibility set. Regulatory policy can create some monopoly profit in the financial sector. Extensions are to apply these modifications to monetary aggregation, and to apply the model empirically to other data sets and potentially to data at the economy level.

REFERENCES

Barnett, W. A. 1981. *Consumer Demand and Labor Supply: Goods, Monetary Assets, and Time.* Amsterdam: North-Holland.
    1982. "The Optimal Level of Monetary Aggregation." *Journal of Money, Credit and Banking* 14: 687–710.
    1986. "The Microeconomic Theory of Monetary Aggregation." In W. A. Barnett and K. Singleton (eds.), *New Approaches to Monetary Economics.* New York: Cambridge University Press.
Barnett, W. A., E. Offenbacher, and P. Spindt. 1984. "The New Divisia Monetary Aggregates." *Journal of Political Economy* 92: 1049–85.
Berndt, E. R., and L. R. Christensen. 1974. "Testing for the Existence of a Consistent Aggregate Index of Labor Inputs." *American Economic Review* 64: 391–404.
Blackorby, C., D. Primont, and R. R. Russell. 1978. *Duality, Separability and Functional Structure.* New York: North-Holland.

Cagan, P. B. 1982. "The Choice among Monetary Aggregates as Targets and Guides for Monetary Policy." *Journal of Money, Credit and Banking* 14: 661–86.

Debreu, G. 1959. *The Theory of Value – An Axiomatic Analysis of Economic Equilibrium.* New York: John Wiley.

Denny, M., and M. Fuss. 1977. "The Use of Approximation Analysis to Test for Separability and the Existence of Consistent Aggregates." *American Economic Review* 67: 404–18.

Diewert, W. E. 1982. "Duality Approaches to Microeconomic Theory." In K. J. Arrow and M. Intriligator (eds.), *Handbook of Mathematical Economics,* vol. II. New York: North-Holland.

Diewert, W. E., and T. J. Wales. 1984. "Flexible Functional Forms and Global Curvature Conditions." Discussion Paper No. 40, National Bureau of Economic Research, Cambridge, Mass.

Federal Reserve Bank Board. *Federal Reserve Bulletin.* Washington, D.C., various issues.

Federal Reserve Bank Board. *Functional Cost Analysis.* Washington, D.C., various issues.

Hancock, D. 1985. "The Financial Firm: Production with Monetary and Non-Monetary Goods." *Journal of Political Economy* 93: 859–80.

      1986. "A Model of the Financial Firm with Imperfect Asset and Deposit Elasticities." *Journal of Banking and Finance,* to appear.

Humphrey, D. B. 1981. "Intermediation and Cost Determinants of Large Bank Liability Composition." *Journal of Banking and Finance* 5: 167–85.

United States Department of Commerce, Bureau of Economic Analysis. 1979. *Survey of Current Business: Revised Estimates of the National Income and Product Accounts.* Washington, D.C.: U.S. Government Printing Office.

United States Department of the Treasury, Bureau of Internal Revenue. 1942. *Bulletin F – Income Tax, Depreciation and Obsolescence. Estimated Useful Lives and Depreciation Rates.* Washington, D.C.: U.S. Government Printing Office.

Woodland, A. D. 1978. "On Testing Weak Separability." *Journal of Econometrics* 8: 383–98.

CHAPTER 10

Money in the utility function: an empirical implementation

James M. Poterba and Julio J. Rotemberg

Abstract: This paper studies household asset demands by allowing certain assets to contribute directly to utility. It estimates the parameters of an aggregate utility function that includes both consumption and liquidity services. These liquidity services depend on the level of various asset stocks. We apply these estimates to investigate the long- and short-run interest elasticities of demand for money, time deposits, and Treasury bills. We also examine the impact of open market operations on interest rates, and present new estimates of the welfare cost of inflation.

This paper studies households' demand for different assets by allowing certain assets to contribute directly to household utility.[1] We permit the utility function to capture the "liquidity" services of money, certain time deposits, and even some government securities. Our approach yields estimates of the utility function parameters which can be used to study the effects of a variety of changes in asset returns. We investigate how asset holdings and consumption react to both temporary and permanent changes in returns, and study the effects of government financial policy.

Our approach provides an integrated system of asset demands of the form that Tobin and Brainard (1968) advocate for studying the effects of government interventions in financial markets. It provides a tractable alternative to the atheoretical equations that are commonly used to study the demand for money and other assets. Those equations, which cannot

This paper was prepared for the 1985 Austin Symposium in Economics. We thank Sunny Kim for research assistance and William Barnett, Olivier Blanchard, Stan Fischer, Lars Hansen, a referee, the participants at an NBER Financial Markets Conference, and especially Lawrence Summers for comments on an earlier draft. This research was supported by the National Science Foundation, and is part of the NBER Programs in Economic Fluctuations and Financial Markets. Any views are those of the authors and do not reflect upon the NBER or NSF.

[1] Theoretical work in monetary economics often uses this approach. The Sidrauski (1967) model is part of most economists' standard toolkit; it has been extended by Fischer (1979), Calvo (1979), and Obstfeld (1984, 1985).

be interpreted as the rational response of any economic agent to changes in the economic environment, are unlikely to remain stable when the supply of various nonmonetary assets changes.

Our approach to studying asset demands is somewhat controversial. Its opponents argue that assets do not yield utility directly. They explain that rate-of-return–dominated assets such as money are held because they reduce transactions costs, which should be modeled explicitly. Unfortunately, explicit models with transactions costs are too restrictive to be useful in analyzing aggregate data. Baumol (1952) and Tobin (1956) assume that the individual receives a constant income stream and faces a constant interest rate. By assuming that the individual consumes at a constant rate, they derive the optimal timing of financial transactions. If individuals are uniformly distributed over the time of their last visit to their financial intermediary, then aggregate money holdings are a function of the representative individual's average holdings, which are given by the famous square-root formula.

This approach suffers from a number of drawbacks. Even assuming that consumption is constant, the optimal timing of individual transactions is extremely hard to compute when interest rates and income vary stochastically. Such a computation is well beyond the modern transactions-based models of Jovanovic (1982), Grossman and Weiss (1983), Romer (1986), and Rotemberg (1984).[2] Moreover, the assumption of constant consumption cannot be justified if the individual is maximizing utility from consumption, unless the real rate of return on money is equal to the discount rate. Thus, while Goldfeld (1973) appeals to transactions-based models to justify his money demand regressions, these models provide an unacceptable basis for empirical work.

On the other hand, the objections to estimating the utility flow of liquidity services seem to apply equally well to the estimation of the demand for many durable goods. Like many durables, money is not utilized constantly, but in bursts. Just like some durables, even unused money provides some utility in the form of security. Whether or not money's services provide utility in the same fashion as other goods is a moot point. Various consumer goods provide different types of utility, and to single out money services as a particular variety unworthy of inclusion in a consumer's utility function seems arbitrary at best.

A number of researchers – including Barnett (1980, 1983), Chetty (1969), Ewis and Fisher (1984), and Husted and Rush (1984) – have attempted to

---

[2] An alternative, much less explicit, set of transactions cost models is quite similar to the assets-in-the-utility function approach. These models assume that liquid asset stocks reduce the amount of leisure spent transacting [see Saving (1971)]. Models of this type do not fully capture the structure of financial transactions costs because they neglect the discrete character of these transactions.

estimate a utility function for assets. Feige and Pierce (1977) survey the earlier literature. These attempts have encountered a number of difficulties. First, Chetty (1969) fails to recognize that when a consumer chooses to hold an asset with a relatively low rate of return, he will have to reduce his consumption at some point. To evaluate this loss in consumption, it is necessary to specify and measure the consumer's marginal utility of consumption. A second problem, which affects all previous work, arises from the inherent uncertainty of the opportunity cost of money. The alternative to holding money or other assets that yield liquidity services is to hold assets with uncertain returns. Therefore, the opportunity cost of these assets is a random variable at the time when the consumer allocates his portfolio. This makes it inappropriate to model the consumer's portfolio allocation problem as one of choosing expenditures (opportunity cost times quantity held) on different assets.[3] To avoid these problems we follow Hansen and Singleton (1982) and estimate the parameters of a representative individual's utility function from the first-order conditions of the individual's maximization problem.

The paper is organized into five sections. The first outlines the representative consumer model and explains the factors motivating our choice of a parametric utility function. Section 2 describes our data and estimation procedure. Estimation results are presented in the third section, and the estimated parameters are used for comparative statics calculations in Section 4. A brief conclusion evaluates our findings on the usefulness of the assets-in-the-utility-function model, and suggests several directions for future work.

1   Theoretical background

We maintain the convenient fiction that movements in per capita consumption, as well as real asset holdings, can be attributed to the optimizing behavior of a rational representative consumer. He is infinite-lived, has constant preferences, and derives utility by consuming and by holding assets. In principle, it would be possible to allow a wide variety of different assets to yield utility. We focus only on those that constitute a substantial fraction of household wealth and have easily measured market values and rates of return. This limits us to four asset classes: money, time deposits, short-term marketable government debt, and corporate

---

[3] This problem has also arisen in previous attempts to construct Divisia monetary aggregates [see Barnett (1980, 1981, 1982, 1983)]. With standard nondurable goods, the rate of growth of a Divisia quantity aggregate equals the inner product of current expenditure shares and quantity growth rates. The expenditure on liquidity services (and other durables), however, is unknown at the time the services are purchased. This raises difficulties for Divisia aggregation that should be addressed in future work.

equity. Long-term debt holdings are excluded because of difficulties in measuring their market value.

We begin with a specification of preferences that is additively separable across time, and then examine a case in which costs of adjusting asset stocks violate this restriction. In the additively separable case, the consumer's expected discounted utility at time t may be written

$$V_t = E_t \sum_{\tau=t}^{\infty} \rho^{\tau-t} U\left(C_\tau, \frac{M_\tau}{P_\tau}, \frac{S_\tau}{P_\tau}, \frac{G_\tau}{P_\tau}\right). \tag{1.1}$$

The expectations operator E_t is conditional on information available at t; ρ is a discount factor, assumed constant through time. The four arguments of the period-by-period utility function are real consumption C_τ, real money holdings M_τ/P_τ, real savings and time deposits S_τ/P_τ, and real holdings of short-term government debt G_τ/P_τ. Equity holdings, represented as Q_τ, provide the numeraire asset in defining preferences.[4] They are not a direct source of utility. The utility function $U(\cdot)$ is concave and increasing in consumption and all three asset stocks.

The evolution of equity holdings is given by

$$Q_\tau = Q_{\tau-1}(1+r_{E\tau-1}) + G_{\tau-1}(1+r_{G\tau-1}) + S_{\tau-1}(1+r_{S\tau-1}) + M_{\tau-1}$$
$$- P_\tau C_\tau - G_\tau - S_\tau - M_\tau + P_\tau Y_\tau \quad \tau = t, t+1, ..., \tag{1.2}$$

where P_τ is the price of consumption at τ, Y_τ is real income, $r_{E\tau}$ is the nominal return on equity between τ and $\tau+1$, and $r_{G\tau}$ and $r_{S\tau}$ are the nominal one-period holding returns on government debt and time deposits, respectively. Solving (1.2) for C_τ, substituting the result into (1.1), and differentiating with respect to Q_t, G_t, S_t, and M_t yields necessary first-order conditions which (upon rearrangement) are

(EC): $\quad E_t\left[\dfrac{\partial U}{\partial C_t} - \rho\,\dfrac{P_t(1+r_{Et})}{P_{t+1}}\,\dfrac{\partial U}{\partial C_{t+1}}\right] = 0,$ \hfill (1.3)

(M): $\quad E_t\left[\dfrac{\partial U}{\partial (M/P)_t} - \rho\,\dfrac{P_t\,r_{Et}}{P_{t+1}}\,\dfrac{\partial U}{\partial C_{t+1}}\right] = 0,$ \hfill (1.4)

(S): $\quad E_t\left[\dfrac{\partial U}{\partial (S/P)_t} - \rho\,\dfrac{P_t(r_{Et}-r_{St})}{P_{t+1}}\,\dfrac{\partial U}{\partial C_{t+1}}\right] = 0,$ \hfill (1.5)

(G): $\quad E_t\left[\dfrac{\partial U}{\partial (G/P)_t} - \rho\,\dfrac{P_t(r_{Et}-r_{Gt})}{P_{t+1}}\,\dfrac{\partial U}{\partial C_{t+1}}\right] = 0.$ \hfill (1.6)

The Euler equation for consumption (EC) states that along an optimal path the representative individual cannot raise his expected utility by

---

[4] If all assets give utility directly, one could redefine preferences to exclude the asset which gives the least utility and attribute its utility to future consumption.

forgoing one unit of consumption in period t, investing its value in equities, and consuming the proceeds in period $t+1$. The utility cost of giving up a unit of consumption in period t is $\partial U/\partial C_t$. The expected utility gain from reducing C_t is given by $E_t[\rho(\partial U/\partial C_{t+1})/(P_t(1+r_{Et})/P_{t+1})]$. Equating the cost and gain from this perturbation yields the first-order condition (EC). If several assets that yield no utility are traded by the representative consumer then (EC) should also hold with r_{Et} replaced by the return on any of these assets.

Euler equation (M) specifies that utility cannot be increased by holding one dollar less of money at time t, investing it in equities, and consuming the proceeds at time $t+1$. The forgone utility associated with a one-dollar reduction in money holding is $[(\partial U/\partial(M/P)_t)\cdot 1/P_t]$. Switching a dollar from money to equities at t increases real wealth at $t+1$ by r_{Et}, because money yields no nominal return while equity does. The expected gain in utility if these higher proceeds are consumed in period $t+1$ is $E_t[\rho\cdot\partial U/\partial C_{t+1}\cdot r_{Et}/P_{t+1}]$. Equating this to the forgone utility yields (M). Similarly, Euler equations (S) and (G) equate the costs and benefits of transferring one dollar from Treasury bills or savings deposits into equities for one period at time t.

Given a specification of preferences, the budget constraint (i.e., the condition that net worth does not become infinitely negative), and the conditional distributions of all future prices and rates of return, we could find the representative consumer's consumption and asset holdings at time t. However, solving the consumer's problem analytically is almost impossible in all but a few restrictive cases. We therefore follow previous authors in estimating the parameters of U from equations (1.3)–(1.6).

If expectational errors are the only source of error in our equations, then our system of first-order conditions can, by suitable linear combination, be transformed into two stochastic and two nonstochastic equations.[5] This implies that the error covariance matrix for the system of

---

[5] If r_{Gt} and r_{St} are known at t and there are no other errors, then (EC), (M), (S), and (G) may be combined to obtain two nonstochastic equations:

$$\frac{\partial U}{\partial S_t^*} - (1+r_{St})\frac{\partial U}{\partial M_t^*} = r_{St}\frac{\partial U}{\partial C_t} \quad \text{and} \quad \frac{\partial U}{\partial G_t^*} - (1+r_{Gt})\frac{\partial U}{\partial M_t^*} = r_{Gt}\frac{\partial U}{\partial C_t},$$

which can be combined to yield

$$\left[\frac{\partial U}{\partial S_t^*} - \frac{\partial U}{\partial M_t^*}\right]r_{Gt} = \left[\frac{\partial U}{\partial G_t^*} - \frac{\partial U}{\partial M_t^*}\right]r_{St},$$

where $G^* = G/P$, $M^* = M/P$, and $S^* = S/P$. The first of these equations requires that a consumer cannot raise his utility by reducing his holdings of money by $(1+r_{Gt})$ dollars in period t, raising his holdings of Treasury bills by one dollar to ensure that the original plan is still feasible, and consuming the difference (r_{Gt}) today. The second equation requires that a similar set of asset swaps (performed with time deposits and money) cannot raise utility. In practice, only r_{St} is known over short periods of time.

equations which we estimate could be singular. This problem does not arise if errors also result from random shocks to preferences. For example, if the consumer's utility function includes terms such as $v_{Mt}M_t$ and $v_{St}S_t$, where the v_{Mt} and v_{St} are stochastic, then the covariance matrix would be nonsingular.

We assume that the representative consumer's preferences are given by:

$$U\left(C_t, \frac{M_t}{P_t}, \frac{S_t}{P_t}, \frac{G_t}{P_t}\right) = \frac{1}{\sigma}\left\{C_t^\beta \cdot L_t\left(\frac{M_t}{P_t}, \frac{S_t}{P_t}, \frac{G_t}{P_t}\right)^{1-\beta}\right\}^\sigma, \qquad (1.7)$$

where L_t is a liquidity aggregate given by

$$L_t = \left[\delta_M\left(\frac{M_t}{P_t}\right)^\gamma + \delta_S\left(\frac{S_t}{P_t}\right)^\gamma + (1-\delta_S-\delta_M)\left(\frac{G_t}{P_t}\right)^\gamma\right]^{1/\gamma}. \qquad (1.8)$$

This utility function exhibits constant relative risk aversion in an aggregate of consumption and liquidity services.[6] This aggregate is Cobb–Douglas in consumption and liquidity, ensuring that more consumption raises the marginal utility of liquidity and vice versa. Our liquidity measure is a CES function of our three assets. Such functions have been pioneered by Chetty (1969) and used by Husted and Rush (1984), among others.[7] It must be pointed out that these preferences are quite restrictive. In particular, they impose homogeneity and require separability between leisure and other sources of utility. These restrictions will hopefully be relaxed in future work.[8]

With these preferences, equations (1.3)–(1.6) become:

$$\text{(EC):}\quad E_t\left[\rho\,\frac{P_t(1+r_{Et})}{P_{t+1}}\left(\frac{C_{t+1}}{C_t}\right)^{\sigma\beta-1}\left(\frac{L_{t+1}}{L_t}\right)^{\sigma(1-\beta)}\right] = 1 \qquad (1.3')$$

$$\text{(M):}\quad E_t\left[C_t^{\sigma\beta}L_t^{\sigma(1-\beta)-\gamma}\delta_M\left(\frac{M_t}{P_t}\right)^{\gamma-1}\right.$$

$$\left. -\frac{\beta\rho}{1-\beta}\,\frac{P_t r_{Et}}{P_{t+1}}C_{t+1}^{\sigma\beta-1}L_{t+1}^{\sigma(1-\beta)}\right] = 0, \qquad (1.4')$$

[6] Assuming that the theoretical concept of money corresponds to our measure of liquidity, our utility function is identical to the one used in Fischer (1979), Calvo (1979), and Obstfeld (1984, 1985).

[7] Chetty (1969) uses a more general functional form in which each asset is allowed its own γ. Since he focuses only on the instantaneous utility function, he cannot identify the exponent of this CES aggregate.

[8] Barnett (1980, 1981) has relaxed these homogeneity restrictions at the cost of neglecting the uncertainty of asset returns.

(S): $\quad E_t\left[C_t^{\sigma\beta}L_t^{\sigma(1-\beta)-\gamma}\delta_S\left(\dfrac{S_t}{P_t}\right)^{\gamma-1}\right.$

$$\left.-\frac{\beta\rho}{1-\beta}\frac{P_t(r_{Et}-r_{St})}{P_{t+1}}C_{t+1}^{\sigma\beta-1}L_{t+1}^{\sigma(1-\beta)}\right]=0, \tag{1.5'}$$

(G): $\quad E_t\left[C_t^{\sigma\beta}L_t^{\sigma(1-\beta)-\gamma}(1-\delta_M-\delta_S)\left(\dfrac{G_t}{P_t}\right)^{\gamma-1}\right.$

$$\left.-\frac{\beta\rho}{1-\beta}\frac{P_t(r_{Et}-r_{Gt})}{P_{t+1}}C_{t+1}^{\sigma\beta-1}L_{t+1}^{\sigma(1-\beta)}\right]=0. \tag{1.6'}$$

We report estimates of the parameters $\{\sigma, \rho, \gamma, \beta, \delta_M, \delta_S\}$ from these equations in Section 3.

The second set of preferences that we consider allows for costs of portfolio adjustment.[9] We assume that individuals face utility costs proportional to the square of the percentage change in their nominal asset holdings.[10] Their expected discounted utility is therefore

$$V_t' = E_t \sum_{\tau=t}^{\infty} \rho^{\tau-t}\left[U\left(C_\tau, \frac{M_\tau}{P_\tau}, \frac{S_\tau}{P_\tau}, \frac{G_\tau}{P_\tau}\right) - \frac{\Theta_M}{2}\left(\frac{M_\tau-M_{\tau-1}}{M_{\tau-1}}\right)^2\right.$$

$$\left.-\frac{\Theta_S}{2}\left(\frac{S_\tau-S_{\tau-1}}{S_{\tau-1}}\right)^2 - \frac{\Theta_M}{2}\left(\frac{G_\tau-G_{\tau-1}}{G_{\tau-1}}\right)^2\right]. \tag{1.9}$$

The first-order conditions that must be satisfied by the optimal consumption-portfolio plan corresponding to these preferences are:

(EC'): $\quad E_t\left[\dfrac{\partial U}{\partial C_t} - \rho\dfrac{P_t(1+r_{Et})}{P_{t+1}}\dfrac{\partial U}{\partial C_{t+1}}\right]=0, \tag{1.10}$

(M'): $\quad E_t\left[\dfrac{\partial U}{\partial(M/P)_t} - \rho\dfrac{P_t r_{Et}}{P_{t+1}}\dfrac{\partial U}{\partial C_{t+1}}\right.$

$$\left.-\Theta_M\left(\frac{M_t-M_{t-1}}{M_{t-1}}\right)\frac{1}{M_{t-1}} + \rho\Theta_M\frac{M_{t+1}}{M_t^2}\cdot\left(\frac{M_{t+1}-M_t}{M_t}\right)\right]=0, \tag{1.11}$$

---

[9] Utility functions that incorporate costs of adjustment are similar in many respects to models with habit formation, such as that in Barnett (1980, 1981). In Barnett's work, the quasi-first-difference of asset holdings appears in the representative consumer's one-period utility function. Allowing adjustment costs to enter the utility function explicitly strikes us as preferable to the common approach of deriving asset demands without adjustment costs and then imposing partial adjustment schemes, as in Goldfeld (1973) and Barnett (1980, 1981).

[10] If it is a matter of physically adjusting one's asset stock, the nominal and not the real magnitude is relevant. However, a better specification would recognize the automatic changes in money caused by consumption expenditures.

(S'): $E_t\left[\dfrac{\partial U}{\partial (S/P)_t} - \dfrac{\rho P_t(r_{Et}-r_{St})}{P_{t+1}} \dfrac{\partial U}{\partial C_{t+1}}\right.$

$$\left. -\Theta_S\left(\frac{S_t-S_{t-1}}{S_{t-1}}\right)\frac{1}{S_{t-1}} +\rho\Theta_S\frac{S_{t+1}}{S_t^2}\left(\frac{S_{t+1}-S_t}{S_t}\right)\right]=0, \quad (1.12)$$

(G'): $E_t\left[\dfrac{\partial U}{\partial (G/P)_t} - \dfrac{\rho P_t(r_{Et}-r_{Gt})}{P_{t+1}} \dfrac{\partial U}{\partial C_{t+1}}\right.$

$$\left. -\Theta_G\left(\frac{G_t-G_{t-1}}{G_{t-1}}\right)\frac{1}{G_{t-1}} +\rho\Theta_G\frac{G_{t+1}}{G_t^2}\left(\frac{G_{t+1}-G_t}{G_t}\right)\right]=0.$$

$$(1.13)$$

In this case, there is no transformation of the first-order conditions which holds nonstochastically.[11] Section 3 reports estimates of this system of equations assuming the functional form of $U(\cdot)$ is given by (1.9) and (1.10).

2   Data and estimation

We employ aggregate time series data on asset holdings by the household sector. These data, computed each quarter by the Federal Reserve Board and published in the Flow of Funds sector balance sheets, are available since the first quarter of 1952. Our money variable M_t is the sum of demand deposits and currency; S_t is the total holding of time and savings deposits, and G_t is the holding of short-term marketable government debt.[12]

There are several problems with our data series on asset holdings. First, household currency holdings are computed as a residual after subtracting corporate currency holdings from the outstanding currency stock. Errors can arise if currency has flowed abroad, since it will be allocated

[11] Any plausible model of adjustment costs, including ours, allows the marginal rate of substitution between various assets and consumption in period $t+1$ to depend upon the asset stocks in period t. This is because higher asset holdings in period t raise the future marginal utility of this asset relative to consumption. The utility function will therefore fail to exhibit intertemporal weak separability. This precludes using two-stage budgeting, as (for example) in Barnett (1980, 1981). His use of "habit formation," making the utility function in period t dependent upon asset holdings at $t-1$, leads to the same problem because rational consumers at t will notice that their choice of asset holdings affects tomorrow's marginal rate of substitution.

[12] The data for G are drawn from unpublished Federal Reserve Board tabulations which are not available after 1982:2. We experimented with another measure of short-term debt – computed as the sum of Treasury bill holdings, open market paper, and money market mutual fund accounts – and found results similar to those reported below.

mistakenly to the U.S. household sector. Despite this difficulty, these data have been used in almost all previous investigations of money demand.

A second problem which is less significant for money than for other assets is that the household sector includes households as well as personal trusts and nonprofit institutions. These institutions probably hold little cash and a small quantity of demand deposits, but their holdings of short-term Treasury bills could be substantial. Personal trusts may be aggregated with the households who are their beneficial owners. This argument is inappropriate for nonprofit groups, however, and the resulting biases are unclear.

Our measure of consumption, C_t, is seasonally adjusted real personal expenditures on nondurables from the National Income and Product Accounts. Our choice of nondurable consumption raises further aggregation issues. Nondurables are only a part of total consumption, excluding both the service flow from durables and services which are purchased directly. We implicitly restrict the utility function to be additively separable between nondurable and other consumption. We deflate each of our asset stocks, as well as consumption expenditure, by the personal nondurable consumption deflator and convert to a per capita basis by dividing by the total population over age sixteen.

We calculate quarterly equity returns (r_{Et}) using data on both the dividend yield and the level of the Standard and Poors' 500-Stock Composite Index. The total pretax return is $r_{Et} = g_t + d_t$, where d_t is the dividend yield and g_t the ex post rate of capital gains. The after-tax rate of return is $r_{Et} = (1 - \tau_d)d_t + (1 - \tau_g)g_t$, where τ_d is the dividend tax rate and τ_g is the effective capital gains tax rate from Feldstein, Dicks-Mireaux, and Poterba (1983).[13]

One-period returns on T-bills and savings deposits are computed in a similar fashion. The annual interest rates on these securities are reported each quarter in the *Federal Reserve Bulletin*. We convert each to a quarterly return and then multiply by $(1 - \tau_d)$ to obtain the after-tax return.[14] Yields on savings deposits are available beginning in the first quarter of 1955; this determines the beginning of our estimation period.

One difficulty with our return measures is that each asset aggregate includes a variety of assets with different rates of return. Demand deposits

---

[13] We assume perfect loss-offset in the taxation of capital gains. Assuming that the losses on equity could not have been offset against other taxable income would induce only minor changes in our rate of return series.

[14] Previous calculations of weighted-average marginal tax rates yield different tax rates on dividends and interest income. In the spirit of the representative consumer model, we recognize that for any taxpayer the two tax rates must be equal. We therefore apply the dividend tax rate to all interest and dividend income.

and currency includes some interest-bearing NOW accounts, while time deposits include both large time deposits (which may pay market-rate interest) at commercial banks, as well as those at savings and loan institutions.[15]

We estimate the parameters $\{\sigma, \gamma, \rho, \beta, \delta_M, \delta_S\}$ by fitting the implied first-order conditions (EC), (M), (G), and (S) to the time series data using three-stage least squares. The residuals in our equations are, at least partially, forecast errors uncorrelated with information available at t.[16] The other component of our residuals, the ν's, are assumed to be i.i.d. and thus uncorrelated with our instruments. We employ two different sets of instruments. The first includes a constant term, two lagged values of the real returns on equity, time deposits, and T-bills, as well as the growth rates in money, consumption, time deposits, and T-bills. The second includes a constant term, two lagged values of equity, savings deposit, and time deposit returns, as well as two lagged values of consumption, money, time deposits, and T-bill holdings. The second instrument set is unattractive because some of the instruments may be nonstationary, but its advantage is that these instruments are probably more correlated with the variables appearing in our equations. For each system of equations, we report the minimized value of the objective function J, which Hansen and Singleton (1982) show to be a test statistic for the validity of the overidentifying restrictions.

We constrain our estimates of the utility function parameters in two ways. First, we require that δ_M, δ_S, and $(1 - \delta_M - \delta_S)$ be positive by estimating α_0 and α_1, where $\delta_M = \cos^2(\alpha_0)$ and $\delta_S = [1 - \cos^2(\alpha_0)] \cdot [1 - \cos^2(\alpha_1)]$. Second, we require β to be positive and between zero and one by defining $\beta = \cos^2(\alpha_2)$ and estimating α_2. Standard errors for the parameter transformations that define δ_M, δ_S, and β are obtained by standard asymptotic methods.

3   Estimation results

Table 1 shows the results of estimating our systems of Euler equations for the case of time-additive preferences. We report four sets of estimates,

---

[15] We use the commercial bank savings deposit rate to measure the rate of return on time deposits.

[16] Equations (EC), (M), (S), and (G) only hold in *expectation* as of period t. Eliminating the expectations operator and using ex post realizations of returns, prices, future consumption, and future asset holdings (as we do in estimating these equations) adds an error term to each equation. These residuals are interpreted as forecast errors. When the return on equity is small relative to that on other assets, the forecast errors in (M), (S), and (G) are positive. Yet this does not pose a problem for either our theory or our empirical work, because equity offers a higher expected rate of return than the other assets.

Table 1. *Estimates of utility function parameters*

	Returns without tax adjustment		Tax-adjusted returns	
Instrument set:	I	II	I	II
Parameter				
σ	−6.091	−6.247	−6.099	−5.570
	(0.653)	(0.666)	(0.733)	(0.569)
ρ	1.007	1.006	1.016	1.014
	(0.006)	(0.006)	(0.005)	(0.005)
γ	0.269	0.990	0.187	0.534
	(1.169)	(0.305)	(1.381)	(0.468)
β	0.965	0.961	0.979	0.969
	(0.019)	(0.015)	(0.197)	(0.012)
δ_M	0.316	0.458	0.349	0.320
	(0.184)	(0.262)	(0.252)	(0.073)
δ_S	0.515	0.311	0.587	0.430
	(0.273)	(0.256)	(0.348)	(0.124)
δ_G	0.168	0.231	0.064	0.250
	(0.138)	(0.122)	(0.281)	(0.068)
J	41.005	47.432	39.380	55.501

Notes: Estimates correspond to the utility function $V_t = \sum_{\tau=0}^{\infty} \rho^{\tau} U_{t+\tau}$ where $U_{t+\tau}$ is defined by (1.7) and (1.8) in the text. The estimation period is 1955:1 to 1982:1 (109 observations) in each case. Standard errors are shown in parentheses. The .95 critical value of the J-statistic, which is distributed as $\chi^2(54)$ under the null hypothesis, is 72.4.

corresponding to each of the two instrument sets using both pre-tax and post-tax returns. The estimates are remarkably stable across specifications. All J-statistics are well within the 95 percent confidence bounds, so we can never reject the validity of our overidentifying restrictions.

The results provide strong support for the view that liquidity is a direct source of utility. We estimate β, the share of expenditure which is devoted to consumption, to be between .961 and .979. In three of the four equations we reject the hypothesis that $\beta = 1$ at the .05 confidence level. This null hypothesis corresponds to our included assets yielding no utility.

Our estimate of γ, the exponent in our CES liquidity aggregator function, is .27 when we use our preferred instrument set and pre-tax returns, and .19 with post-tax returns. These estimates imply an elasticity of substitution between assets, $1/(\gamma-1)$, larger than that in Husted and Rush (1984) but smaller than that in Chetty (1969). These point estimates argue against linear aggregation of our three assets. However, $\gamma = 1$ (the case where linear aggregation is appropriate) cannot be rejected. When we use Instrument Set II, the estimates of γ increase and make the $\gamma = 1$ case more plausible.

Within our monetary aggregator, the coefficients on the various assets are estimated with relatively large asymptotic standard errors.[17] The general pattern which emerges from the point estimates is $\delta_S > \delta_M > 1 - \delta_S - \delta_M$. If all real asset stocks were of equal size, this would imply that the marginal utility associated with another dollar of time deposits would exceed that from another dollar of demand deposits or currency. However, it is essential to recognize that at current asset levels, with time deposits five times larger than demand deposits and currency, rather different conclusions emerge. In 1981:4 our estimates from column 1 imply that the marginal utility of money is twice that of savings accounts and four times that of government securities. The estimates in column 3 imply even larger differences.

Although we have allowed government securities to provide liquidity services, our estimates do not suggest a major liquidity role for these assets. When we reestimate our system imposing the constraint that $\delta_S = 1 - \delta_M$, the value of our objective function deteriorates very little. Thus we cannot reject the hypothesis that Treasury bills are not a direct source of utility. Yet, Mehra and Prescott (1985) show that the riskiness of equities is not sufficient to explain their high expected rate of return relative to T-bills. They use a utility function like (1.7), imposing $\beta = 1$ so liquidity services play no role. There are two ways of reconciling Mehra and Prescott's findings with ours. First, it may be impossible to capture the rate of return dominance of equities over T-bills in our utility-based framework. For example, the correct model of the utility services from T-bills may be different from (1.7). Second, the rate-of-return dominance puzzle may only have arisen because they misspecified the aggregate utility function by excluding liquidity services.

Our results also provide estimates of the intertemporal elasticity of substitution σ, which has been the focus of many previous studies in the representative consumer framework. Earlier estimates range between $-.8$ and -6.0. Our estimates are at the edge of this range; they vary between -6.2 and -5.6. Moreover, they are estimated quite precisely with standard errors of about .60.[18] Our estimates of the discount factor, ρ, all

---

[17] These standard errors overstate the imprecision of our estimates because they do not recognize that the δ's must lie between 0 and 1.

[18] In Obstfeld (1985), $\sigma < 0$ implies that anticipated disinflation leads to the kind of capital inflows that have been experienced in the Southern cone, rather than to capital outflows. In Obstfeld (1984), uniqueness of the economy's rational expectations equilibrium requires that $(1 - \sigma) < \beta/(1 - \beta)$. This condition is always satisfied by our estimates.

Table 2. *Estimates of cost-of-asset-adjustment models*

	Returns without tax adjustment		Tax-adjusted returns	
Instrument set:	I	II	I	II
Parameter				
σ	−6.109	−6.469	−6.066	−5.617
	(0.583)	(0.659)	(0.710)	(0.584)
ρ	1.007	1.007	1.016	1.014
	(0.006)	(0.006)	(0.006)	(0.005)
γ	0.604	0.050	0.253	0.470
	(0.802)	(1.429)	(0.857)	(0.509)
β	0.962	0.961	0.977	0.969
	(0.016)	(0.014)	(0.017)	(0.127)
δ_M	0.366	0.309	0.383	0.307
	(0.138)	(0.252)	(0.188)	(0.079)
δ_S	0.408	0.509	0.546	0.451
	(0.184)	(0.321)	(0.225)	(0.136)
δ_G	0.225	0.182	0.071	0.241
	(0.985)	(0.127)	(0.199)	(0.074)
Θ_M	−0.011	−0.032	−0.003	−0.010
	(0.017)	(0.057)	(0.011)	(0.013)
Θ_S	0.513	0.649	0.070	0.231
	(0.472)	(0.296)	(0.192)	(0.450)
Θ_G	−0.001	−0.002	−0.005	−0.001
	(0.005)	(0.006)	(0.007)	(0.003)
J	39.768	42.560	39.106	54.722
J (Table 1) −J (Table 2)	1.237	4.872	0.274	0.779

Notes: Estimates correspond to the lifetime utility function defined in (1.9), with U given by (1.7) and (1.8). Standard errors are shown in parentheses. All equations are estimated for 1955:1–1982:1 (109 observations). The J-statistic on the penultimate line is distributed as $\chi^2(51)$ under the null hypothesis, with .95 critical value of 69.0. The statistic on the final line is distributed as $\chi^2(3)$, with a .95 critical value of 7.8.

exceed unity. This is a feature common to many empirical papers of this type.[19]

Table 2 reports four sets of estimates corresponding to preferences that incorporate costs of adjusting asset stocks. To allow us to perform

---

[19] The paper by Mankiw, Rotemberg, and Summers (1985) is one example.

hypothesis tests these estimates are obtained using the same estimates of the residual covariance matrix as in Table 1. The differences between the J-statistics reported here and in Table 1 are distributed $\chi^2(3)$ under the null hypothesis that adjustment costs are unimportant. The pattern of coefficients $\{\sigma, \rho, \gamma, \beta, \delta_M, \delta_S\}$ does not change significantly when adjustment costs are introduced. More importantly, however, we can never reject at the 95 percent level the joint null hypothesis that all of the adjustment cost parameters are zero.

More generally, our results show a very small role for dynamics because lagged variables appear uncorrelated with our residuals.[20] This lack of dynamics is puzzling in light of the pervasive differencing and quasi-differencing which is typical in other studies of asset demand. It is possible that these lags in others' studies capture expectations of returns and future consumption which enter independently in our formulation.

4   Comparative statics

Our parameter estimates can be used to study the effects of changes in interest rates and inflation on consumption and asset holdings. To fully characterize the consumer's responses to random shocks, we would need to find a closed form solution to the stochastic control problem posed in Section 1. Because such solutions remain intractable, we concentrate on the effects of various changes in deterministic environments, asking how the representative consumer would respond to these changes if he maximized (2.1).

We consider both short-run and long-run comparative statics. The short-run responses are the responses of asset demands at t to changes in interest rates from t to $t+1$. We analyze them by neglecting the effect of these changes on choices after $t+1$. We also study how the vector of returns is affected by changes in the supply of assets. Although these are equivalent exercises, the latter is more useful for policy analysis. Our short-run effects are similar in spirit to those analyzed by Mankiw, Rotemberg, and Summers (1985). Their neglect of the effect of changes in interest rates at t on decisions at $t+1$ is necessarily incorrect. However, it is likely to be a good approximation because the changes in subsequent periods are mediated through changes in future wealth. For consumers with long horizons, future wealth is essentially unaffected by changes in current decision variables. The long-run responses are derived by considering steady states with different interest rates. Across different steady

---

[20] Durbin–Watson statistics calculated from our residuals ranged between 1.15 and 1.9. Their statistical properties in our estimation procedure are unknown, but they may provide some evidence of dynamic misspecification.

states, consumption and asset holdings for a given level of wealth are different. We study these differences holding lifetime wealth constant.

A   Short-run responses

We compute two types of short-run responses. The first fixes consumption at t, as well as all future choices. This is very much in the spirit of money demand studies which hold the transactions variable fixed when computing interest elasticities. The second short-run calculation allows consumption at t to vary optimally, while fixing all choices in future periods. The implied consumption responses are similar to those studied by Hansen and Singleton (1982). However, intertemporal consumption decisions now depend on nominal as well as real rates since nominal rates affect asset choices that affect the marginal utility of consumption.

For a given path of consumption, the demand for the three assets we consider depends on the three differences between the return on equities and the return on the utility-bearing assets. These return differentials are denoted

$$u_M = r_{Et} P_t / P_{t+1}, \qquad u_S = (r_{Et} - r_{St}) P_t / P_{t+1}, \quad \text{and}$$

$$u_G = (r_{Et} - r_{Gt}) P_t / P_{t+1}.$$

In the short run we allow M, S, and G to change in response to the u's; we calculate the effects by differentiating (M), (S), and (G).

Table 3 (Part A) presents the results of this differentiation for our estimates obtained in the specification without costs of adjustment, using our first set of instruments. We report the percent change in the assets held in the fourth quarter of 1981 when the u's increase by 100 basis points, holding constant asset stocks and consumption for the first quarter of 1982.[21] The first column can be interpreted as the effect of inflation in a world in which the Fisher effect describes the behavior of all interest rates. Thus $(1 + r_{Et}) P_t / P_{t+1}$, $(1 + r_{St}) P_t / P_{t+1}$, and $(1 + r_{Gt}) P_t / P_{t+1}$ are unaffected by inflation, while $r_{Et} P_t / P_{t+1}$ increases by approximately the increase in the inflation rate. Such an increase in inflation reduces money holdings and promotes the use of other liquid assets. Nonetheless, total liquidity falls substantially.

The response of money to u_M is the closest analogue in our model to "the" interest elasticity of money demand because, if all nominal interest

---

[21] To actually differentiate these equations we must first modify them to make them hold without error. To do this we compute the value of the u's which make (M), (G), and (S) hold exactly. These can be interpreted as the expected returns which rationalize actual subsequent consumption and asset holdings. Then we use these u's instead of the actual u's.

Table 3. *Short-run linkages between returns and asset stocks*

A. Semielasticities of asset demand

| | Yield spread | | |
	Equity–money	Equity–time deposits	Equity–Treasury bills
Change in asset demand			
Demand deposits and currency			
Pre-tax returns	−.587	.335	.167
Post-tax returns	−.732	.307	.246
T-bills			
Pre-tax returns	.048	.226	−2.545
Post-tax returns	.070	.341	−12.995
Time deposits			
Pre-tax returns	.071	−.981	.168
Post-tax returns	.065	−1.404	.253

B. Yield effects of changing asset supply

| | Asset stock | | |
	Demand deposits and currency	Time deposits	T-bills
Change in yield spread			
Equity–money			
Pre-tax	−2.256	−.174	−.058
Post-tax	−1.752	−.083	−.012
Equity–time deposits			
Pre-tax	−.174	−.289	−.029
Post-tax	−.083	−.195	−.006
Equity–T-bills			
Pre-tax	−.058	−.029	−.145
Post-tax	−.011	−.006	−.028

Notes: Each entry in Part A shows the percentage change in asset demand which results from a one hundred basis point change in the yield spread. The calculations in Part B show the change in the yield spread which results from a thousand- (1972) dollar increase in per capita asset stocks. Calculations are based on parameter estimates using instrument set I, pre-tax and post-tax returns, as reported in Table 1. The calculations are described in the text.

rates rise by the same amount, only u_M is affected. Indeed, we find that our semielasticities are between .6 and .8. Mankiw and Summers (1986) find similar values, using consumption as the transactions variable in an aggregate money demand equation. The second and third columns of

Table 3 (Part A) give the responses to changes in the return premia of time deposits and T-bills. As we move from money to time deposits to T-bills (i.e., toward assets that yield less marginal liquidity services), the own semielasticity with respect to the return premium increases. In some sense, these assets are increasingly good substitutes for equity.

Table 3 (Part B) shows the effect of changes in assets supplied to the household sector on yield spreads. An increase in liquid asset supplies raises their yields relative to that on equity. The biggest effect is on the own-yield spread; for example, an increase in money has the biggest depressing effect on u_M. As a result, increases in household money which the government finances by buying back government bonds tend to depress u_M and therefore nominal rates, even if money is exchanged for bonds on a one-to-one basis. In practice the money multiplier exceeds one so the effect is even larger.

Alternative measures of households' short-run responses to rate of return movements can be obtained by letting consumption at t vary as well. These can be obtained by differentiating all four first-order conditions with respect to decisions at t and returns from t to $t+1$. The results of this differentiation are given in Table 4. The liquid assets respond to the nominal yield spreads in much the same way they do when consumption is held constant. A 100-basis-point increase in the real rate has only a mild depressing effect on consumption, due to our high estimate for the coefficient of relative risk aversion. In turn, precisely because this coefficient is so large, the reduction in consumption depresses instantaneous utility and raises substantially the marginal utility provided by the Cobb–Douglas consumption-liquidity aggregator. This, in turn, raises the marginal utility of liquidity and thus promotes a slight increase in liquid assets. Similarly, reductions in liquid assets which are prompted by increases in the yield spreads lower instantaneous utility, increasing the marginal utility of consumption. Savings therefore rise when nominal yield spreads shrink or when inflation falls. This finding suggests that anti-inflationary policies promote savings.

B   Long-run effects

We can also use our estimated utility function parameters to examine changes in steady-state asset holdings and consumption. Long-run elasticities are computed by holding steady-state real financial wealth, W_t/P_t, constant. We ignore all assets and liabilities other than money, savings deposits, government securities, and equities. Wealth is therefore defined as $W_t = Q_t + S_t + G_t + M_t$. Dividing by P_{t+1} in equation (1.2), we obtain

Table 4. *Short-run return semielasticities of consumption and asset holdings*

	Equity–money yield spread	Equity–time deposits yield spread	Equity–T bill yield spread	Equity return
Percent change in:				
Demand deposits and currency				
Pre-tax	−.602	.256	.110	.008
Post-tax	−.751	.218	.165	.009
Time deposits				
Pre-tax	.055	−1.067	.106	.009
Post-tax	.047	−1.496	.170	.009
T-bills				
Pre-tax	.032	.146	−2.60	.009
Post-tax	.045	.241	−13.087	.010
Consumption				
Pre-tax	.325	1.680	1.215	−.179
Post-tax	.342	1.682	1.536	−.169

Notes: Calculations based on parameter estimates using instrument set I, pre-tax and post-tax returns, reported in Table 1. The calculations are described in the text.

$$\frac{W_{t+1}}{P_{t+1}} = \frac{W_t}{P_t}\frac{P_t(1+r_{Et+1})}{P_{t+1}} + \frac{(r_{St}-r_{Et})P_t}{P_{t+1}}\frac{S_t}{P_t}$$

$$+ \frac{(r_{Gt}-r_{Et})P_t}{P_{t+1}}\frac{G_t}{P_t} - \frac{r_{Et}P_t}{P_{t+1}}\frac{M_t}{P_t} - C_{t+1} + Y_{t+1}. \qquad (4.1)$$

To find the long-run elasticities we differentiate (M), (G), (S), and (4.1).

Table 5 reports the results of this differentiation for our data. We assume that the consumption and asset holdings of the fourth quarter of 1981 are steady-state values, and that $(1+r_{Et})P_t/P_{t+1}$ remains at $1/\rho$ forever. However, we let the u's jump to new steady-state values and consider the percentage change in C, M, S, and G as a result of a change in u of 100 basis points. The calculations show that consumption itself is relatively unaffected by changes in yield spreads. The results also show that the responses of asset holdings are basically the same as those in Table 3. Because consumption is relatively unaffected by changes in yield spreads, there is little difference between the marginal utility of asset holdings in Tables 3 and 5. Moreover, the future variation in consumption and asset holdings is of relatively minor consequence. These changes affect the current holdings only to the extent that they affect the product

Table 5. *Steady-state return semielasticities of asset demand*

	Yield spreads		
	Equity–money	Equity–time deposits	Equity–treasury bills
Percentage change in			
Demand deposits and currency			
Pre-tax returns	−.635	.275	.104
Post-tax returns	−.761	.232	.144
Time deposits			
Pre-tax returns	.596	−1.098	.101
Post-tax returns	.049	−1.523	.283
T-bills			
Pre-tax returns	.030	.135	−2.708
Post-tax returns	.041	.380	−113.125
Consumption			
Pre-tax returns	−.011	−.173	−.071
Post-tax returns	−.012	−.106	−.045

Notes: All estimates are based on parameters estimated using instrument set I, reported in Table 1. See text for further discussion of the elasticity calculations.

of the yield spread and the future marginal utility of consumption. Since the yield spreads are small, even relatively large changes in the future marginal utility of consumption have only small current effects.

We can use the first column of Table 5 to compute a measure of the welfare costs of inflation. This column gives the response of C, S, T, and G to permanent inflation. By multiplying these changes by the marginal utilities of these variables, we obtain an estimate of the instantaneous loss in utility. We then translate this loss in utility into the fall in consumption which would have produced the same loss. A 100-basis-point increase in inflation would lower utility by the same amount as a 0.4 percent fall in consumption. This estimate is insensitive to our choice of pre- or post-tax data.

5   Conclusions

We have presented a method of estimating consistent systems of asset demand equations which permits analysis of a variety of government interventions in asset markets. Although reduced-form evidence suggests that these interventions change aggregate output, it does not clarify the mechanism by which they work. The need for empirical measures of the effects of open market operations was the original motivation for the estimation of structural money demand functions, which were supposed to capture the aggregate LM curve. However, in the presence of many assets which are imperfect substitutes, more complete modeling of the financial sector is needed. This paper takes a step in that direction.

Our analysis suffers from several shortcomings. These are primarily limitations of our particular implementation of the assets-in-the-utility function approach, and not difficulties with the approach in general. First, it is difficult to maintain that the marginal utility of one liquidity-producing asset is independent of the holdings of other such assets. Yet, if many assets yield these services in substitutable forms, the exclusion of some assets from the analysis may bias conclusions about the importance of other assets. Eventually, our approach should therefore be extended to incorporate a broader range of assets. This will present measurement problems with respect to both asset stocks and rates of return, especially for long-term nominal assets such as corporate bonds with various maturities and risk characteristics.

A second, and related, issue is that the menu of important assets changes over time. Financial innovations, like the recent improvements in money-market mutual funds, allow assets to be repackaged to yield different liquidity services. Although our approach can in principle address these issues, this has been left for future research. An important policy issue which our pre-1982 data probably cannot address is the extent to which the new popularity of money market mutual funds has changed the power of open market operations.

A third direction for future work concerns the utility flows which assets provide. We have modeled assets' utility flows as a simple function of the asset level. Although this is similar to the traditional approach to modeling the demand for consumer durables, recent studies have focused attention on the actual service flows yielded by these durables. For example, air-conditioners provide two services: They cool one's house, and they also yield the pleasure of knowing one's house need never be hot. The former, at least, is subject to measurement (Hausman, 1979). Similarly, the service flow from a liquid asset depends on the transactions it simplifies, as well as the help it might have provided had more transactions taken place. The former might be measurable. This line of inquiry could potentially reconcile the view that these assets are held because they give utility with transactions-based models.

REFERENCES

Barnett, William A. 1980. "Economic Monetary Aggregates: An Application of Index Number and Aggregation Theory." *Journal of Econometrics* 14: 11–48.

1981. *Consumer Demand and Labor Supply: Goods, Monetary Assets, and Time.* New York: North-Holland.

1982. "The Optimal Level of Monetary Aggregation." *Journal of Money, Credit, and Banking* 14: 687–710.

1983. "New Indices of Money Supply and the Flexible Laurent Demand System." *Journal of Business and Economic Statistics* 1: 7–23.

Baumol, William J. 1952. "The Transactions Demand for Cash: An Inventory Theoretic Approach." *Quarterly Journal of Economics* 65: 545–56.

Calvo, G. A. 1979. "On Models of Money and Perfect Foresight." *International Economic Review* 20: 83–103.

Chetty, V. Karuppan. 1969. "On Measuring the Nearness of Near-Moneys." *American Economic Review* 59: 270–81.

Ewis, Nabil, and Douglas Fisher. 1984. "The Translog Utility Function and the Demand for Money in the United States." *Journal of Money, Credit, and Banking* 16: 34–53.

Feige, E., and D. Pierce. 1977. "The Substitutability of Money and Near Monies: A Survey of the Time Series Evidence." *Journal of Economic Literature* 15: 439–69.

Feldstein, Martin S., Louis Dicks-Mireaux, and James M. Poterba. 1983. "The Effective Tax Rate and the Pretax Rate of Return." *Journal of Public Economics* 21: 129–58.

Fischer, Stanley. 1979. "Capital Accumulation on the Transition Path in a Monetary Optimizing Economy." *Econometrica* 47: 1433–9.

Goldfeld, Stephen M. 1973. "The Demand for Money Revisited." *Brookings Papers on Economic Activity* 3: 577–638.

Grossman, Sanford J., and Laurence Weiss. 1983. "A Transactions Based Model of the Monetary Transmission Mechanism." *American Economic Review* 73: 871–80.

Hansen, Lars Peter, and Kenneth Singleton. 1982. "Generalized Instrumental Variables Estimation of Nonlinear Rational Expectations Models." *Econometrica* 50: 1269–86.

Hausman, Jerry A. 1979. "Individual Discount Rates and the Purchase and Utilization of Energy-Using Durables." *Bell Journal of Economics* 10: 33–54.

Husted, Steven, and Mark Rush. 1984. "On Measuring the Nearness of Near Monies: Revisited." *Journal of Monetary Economics* 14: 171–82.

Jovanovic, Boyan. 1982. "Inflation and Welfare in the Steady State." *Journal of Political Economy* 90: 561–77.

Mankiw, N. Gregory, Julio J. Rotemberg, and Lawrence H. Summers. 1985. "Intertemporal Substitution in Macroeconomics." *Quarterly Journal of Economics* 100: 225–51.

Mankiw, N. Gregory, and Lawrence H. Summers. 1986. "Money Demand and the Effects of Fiscal Policies." *Journal of Money, Credit, and Banking* 18: 415–29.

Mehra, Rajnish, and Edward C. Prescott. 1985. "The Equity Premium: A Puzzle." *Journal of Monetary Economics* 15: 145–62.

Obstfeld, Maurice. 1984. "Multiple Stable Equilibria in an Optimizing Perfect-Foresight Model." *Econometrica* 52: 223–8.

1985. "The Capital Inflows Problem Revisited: A Stylized Model of Southern Cone Disinflation." *Review of Economic Studies* 52: 605–24.

Romer, David. 1986. "A Simple General Equilibrium Version of the Baumol-Tobin Model." *Quarterly Journal of Economics* 101: 663–86.

Rotemberg, Julio J. 1984. "A Monetary Equilibrium Model with Transaction Costs." *Journal of Political Economy* 92: 40–58.

Saving, Thomas R. 1971. "Transactions Costs and the Demand for Money." *American Economic Review* 61: 407–20.

Sidrauski, Miguel. 1967. "Inflation and Economic Growth." *Journal of Political Economy* 75: 796–810.

Tobin, James. 1956. "The Interest-Elasticity of Transactions Demand for Cash." *Review of Economics and Statistics* 38: 241–7.

Tobin, James, and William Brainard. 1968. "Pitfalls in Financial Model Building." *American Economic Review* 58: 99–122.

CHAPTER 11

Comment on papers in Part III

William A. Barnett

1   Barnett's paper

In Part III of this volume, Barnett's paper (Chapter 6) brings together all of the currently available aggregation and index number theory relevant to monetary aggregation under perfect certainty. That theory includes demand side aggregation theory – which deals with aggregation over monetary assets when the aggregator functions are weakly separable input blocks in production functions or in utility functions – and supply side aggregation theory, which deals with aggregation over monetary assets when the aggregator functions are weakly separable output blocks in the transformation functions of multiproduct financial intermediaries. The theory also deals with aggregation over firms and consumers, technical change, and value added in financial intermediation. However, when uncertainty exists, the theory presented in Barnett's paper assumes risk neutrality. In that case all economic agents can be viewed as solving decision problems in a perfect-certainty form, with all random variables replaced by their expectations. In other words, a form of certainty equivalence is assumed.

2   Poterba and Rotemberg's paper

The risk neutrality assumption produces tremendous simplification and provides access to all of the existing literature on aggregation and index number theory. Nevertheless, if firms and consumers are very risk-averse, a more general approach to modeling uncertainty could be preferable. The Poterba and Rotemberg paper (Chapter 10) seeks to tackle that difficult problem through the use of the expected utility approach to modeling decisions under uncertainty. In principle, that approach could be used to produce a generalization of the results in Barnett's paper, because expected utility maximization contains risk-neutral "certainty equivalence"

241

as a special case. However, Poterba and Rotemberg, while making an important first step in that ambitious direction, do not produce a generalization of my results.

There are two reasons. First, their paper uses a more restrictive utility function specification than I have used in any of my work.[1] Particularly troublesome is their assumption of linear homogeneity of the utility function. As a result, all income elasticities are unitary.[2] However the restrictiveness of their utility function specification could, in principle, be weakened without necessitating fundamental change in their approach. Hence, the extension of their work to more general specifications of preferences under uncertainty seems possible and worthwhile.

However, their approach contains a more fundamental limitation that renders their approach noncomparable with mine. In my work I demonstrate that the Divisia (Törnqvist) index provides a nonparametric and easily computed second-order approximation to any arbitrary aggregator function produced by my aggregation theory. Poterba and Rotemberg provide no nonparametric approximation to the aggregator functions that they estimate. Although their approach is correctly based upon relevant aggregation theory, estimated aggregator functions are useful only in research – not in the production of usable data. No governmental agency supplies data produced from estimated aggregator functions, because such econometrically estimated aggregates are specification- and estimator-dependent. In fact, the purpose of statistical index number theory is to provide the needed nonparametric approximations to the exact aggregates of aggregation theory. Poterba and Rotemberg provide no such statistical index numbers or other nonparametric approximations to their theoretical aggregator functions. Hence their paper provides only a research tool and not a practical approach to producing monetary aggregate data.

Nevertheless, I see no reason to believe that nonparametric approximations are impossible in the risk-averse case; but unfortunately the large literature presently available on statistical index number theory is not relevant to the risk-averse case, and hence an entirely new literature on nonparametric approximations would have to be developed to permit practical application of the Poterba and Rotemberg approach to monetary

---

[1] In contrast, see Barnett (1983), who uses a sophisticated utility function specification based upon the Laurent series expansion.

[2] The well-known very restrictive implications of linearly homogeneous utility apply under expected utility maximization as well as in the more familiar perfect-certainty case, since the perfect-certainty case is a nested special case and hence remains relevant to determining the restrictiveness of the utility specification under expected utility maximization. For example, Engel's law is violated and low price elasticities are impossible.

aggregation. This is not to suggest that the work should not be done, but rather to suggest that successful extension of statistical index number theory to the risk-averse case is probably a long way off.[3] The Poterba and Rotemberg paper is an important first step in that difficult direction.

In the meantime, it is worth observing that the problem of risk-averse consumer behavior in monetary aggregation theory is no greater than that in capital or consumer durables aggregation theory, and the consensus of opinion in that literature is well known. The currently preferred approach to capital and consumer durables aggregation is use of the Divisia index with user cost prices, as is discussed in the many papers on the subject by Diewert.[4] It is also worth observing that risk-averse behavior by economic agents cannot weaken the assumptions needed for simple-sum aggregation, and hence would make the Federal Reserve's official simple-sum monetary aggregates even less satisfactory. This conclusion follows from the fact that the perfect certainty case, in principle, is a nested special case of the risk-averse uncertainty case.

3   Serletis's paper

In my empirical work on Divisia monetary aggregation, I usually have used Divisia aggregation over monetary assets that are grouped in accordance with the Federal Reserve's official monetary assets groups (M1, M2, etc.). However, I have observed in Barnett (1982) that the criteria used by the Federal Reserve to cluster monetary assets into groups did not include the aggregation-theoretic criterion. The aggregation-theoretic approach to selecting admissible component groupings is to test for blockwise separability, as has been done in many other areas of applied econometrics. Serletis (Chaper 7) carefully ran those tests in accordance with the best-known available econometric methods, using the very popular translog model. The only other such attempt that I have seen to cluster monetary assets into blockwise weakly separable groups is that of Fayyad (1986),

---

[3] An easy solution to this problem can be produced only in the simplest case considered by Poterba and Rotemberg. In particular, in the case considered in note 5 of Poterba and Rotemberg's paper, it can be shown that my Divisia monetary index would exactly track their monetary aggregator function, L_t, in continuous time. The demonstration is as follows. Substitute Barnett's (1986) first-order conditions (2.11) into the combined first-order condition in Poterba and Rotemberg's note 5. Poterba and Rotemberg's first-order condition is found to be satisfied. But the Divisia index is just an algebraic transformation of those first-order conditions [see, e.g., Theorem 1 in Barnett (1986) for an analogous demonstration], and hence must also be derivable from Poterba and Rotemberg's first-order conditions. Therefore, the Divisia index must exactly track L_t.

[4] Diewert's relevant papers on capital aggregation are cited in the references to Chapter 6 of this volume. Especially see Diewert (1980).

who used the currently less popular Rotterdam model and also Varian's new nonparametric approach.

The work by Serletis and Fayyad pretty much exhaust the well-known methods of econometrically implementing the aggregation-theoretic test, and hence provide the best currently available results on monetary asset component grouping. Nevertheless, recent work by Barnett and Choi (1986) has cast doubt on all of the available methods for testing blockwise separability when the utilized specification is generated from a local approximation. The translog and Rotterdam models are examples of such local approximations. Barnett and Choi have shown in Monte Carlo simulations that local tests of blockwise weak separability at a point produce very unreliable inferences when the specified model is the translog, generalized Leontief, or Rotterdam model.

Although the results produced by Serletis and Fayyad are the best currently available, better methods of testing for blockwise weak separability seem to be needed.

4   Hancock's results

In Chapter 6 of this volume I present the aggregation theory relevant to constructing output aggregates for financial intermediaries. That theory is relevant to producing supply-side monetary service aggregates; and comparisons between the dynamical behavior of the demand- and supply-side Divisia monetary aggregates have been provided by Barnett, Hinich, and Weber (1986). Hancock empirically implements the supply-side structural theory in a very systematic fashion in her paper (Chapter 9). Unlike most earlier studies in this area, she uses all of the relevant neoclassical economic theory in her econometric research; and her work is therefore pathbreaking in this field. While her work currently applies to commercial banks, it could advantageously be extended to include studies of output aggregation for many other categories of financial intermediaries, such as savings and loan associations, mutual savings banks, and securities brokers. It would also be useful to incorporate directly the supply of non-intermediated primary securities by the government. It is true that some primary securities are supplied by financial intermediaries. For example, banks supply cash, although the role of banks in that case is not one of financial intermediation. Nevertheless, many primary securities are acquired directly from the government or from brokers. For example, Treasury bills can be acquired directly from Federal Reserve Banks or from securities brokers. In short, complete aggregation-theoretic supply-side monetary aggregation requires consideration of the complexity of the institutional structure of the financial sector of the economy. Hancock's research could advantageously be extended further in that direction.

There is also the unpleasantly complicating matter of the regulatory wedge between the demand and supply side of the aggregated money markets. That wedge is produced by the existence of an implicit tax on banks as a result of the existence of required reserves paying no interest. The theoretical issues are discussed in Barnett's Chapter 6, and empirical assessment of the magnitude of the problem is presented in Barnett, Hinich, and Weber (1986). In brief, it is possible in principle for all component monetary asset markets to be cleared, while the aggregate market in monetary services may not be cleared. Although the magnitude of the problem empirically appears to be small [according to Barnett, Hinich, and Weber (1986)], the theoretical issue seems to be potentially very troublesome.

5   Marquez's paper

In my empirical work with Divisia monetary aggregation, I have included no foreign denominated monetary assets as components in the aggregates; and in the demand systems that I have estimated with that data, I have not considered foreign currency substitution. Marquez has extended much of that empirical research to include foreign currency substitution. This extension is important because closed-economy models are becoming decreasingly relevant to the U.S. economy. In his paper (Chapter 8), Marquez uses specifications of the sort that are common in macroeconometric modeling. Those models usually are not directly derivable from microeconomic theory and cannot be shown to be consistent with utility maximization by consumers and profit maximization by firms. I have myself used such models (without foreign currency substitution) in some of my empirical research, and it is natural to extend that work in the direction initiated by Marquez, especially as a result of the policy relevance of that conventional macroeconometric modeling approach.

Nevertheless, it also would be useful to explore foreign currency substitution within an integrable system of demand functions of the sort used in Barnett (1983). In that case, the theory that produced the Divisia monetary aggregates would also consistently generate the specified model used to test for foreign currency substitution.

REFERENCES

Barnett, William A. 1982. "The Optimal Level of Monetary Aggregation." *Journal of Money, Credit, and Banking* 14: 687–710.

1983. "New Indices of Money Supply and the Flexible Laurent Demand System." *Journal of Business and Economic Statistics* 1: 7–23.

1986. "The Microeconomic Theory of Monetary Aggregation." Chapter 6, this volume.

Barnett, William A., and Seungmook Choi. 1986. "A Monte Carlo Study of Tests of Blockwise Weak Separability." University of Texas.

Barnett, William A., Melvin J. Hinich, and Warren E. Weber. 1986. "The Regulatory Wedge between the Demand-Side and Supply-Side Aggregation Theoretic Monetary Aggregates." *Journal of Econometrics* 33: 165–85.

Diewert, Erwin W. 1980. "Aggregation Problems in the Measurement of Capital." In Dan Usher (ed.), *The Measurement of Capital*, pp. 433–538. Chicago: University of Chicago Press (for the National Bureau of Economic Research).

Fayyad, Salam. 1986. "Monetary Asset Component Grouping and Aggregation: An Inquiry into the Definition of Money." Ph.D. dissertation, University of Texas.

Issues on aggregate fluctuations

CHAPTER 12

Asset prices in a time-series model with disparately informed, competitive traders

Kenneth J. Singleton

1   Introduction

Surveys of the participants in organized securities markets indicate that traders hold widely different beliefs about the future course of economic activity. Expectations not only differ, but they evidently respond significantly to unexpected movements in such variables as real economic growth and the weekly changes in the money stock [see Cornell (1983) for a review of some of this literature]. Furthermore, French and Roll (1984) have found that the variance of stock prices is greater over periods when the stock market is open than when it is closed. Together, these observations suggest that disparate beliefs and the sharing of information through the trading process may be important ingredients in modeling asset-price determination. The purpose of this paper is to explore the implications of disparate expectations for the time-series properties of asset prices in the context of a simple model with competitive traders facing serially correlated shocks.

While the models examined are partial equilibrium in nature, this exploration is motivated in part by the apparent inconsistency of representative agent, dynamic equilibrium models with the behavior of asset prices. The variances and autocorrelation functions of asset returns seem to be inconsistent with the implications of both linear expectations models [see, e.g., Shiller (1979, 1981), Singleton (1980, 1985), Scott (1985)] and the nonlinear models studied by Hansen and Singleton (1982), Ferson (1983), Dunn and Singleton (1985), and Eichenbaum and Hansen (1985),

I have benefited from discussions with Anat Admati, Rick Green, Pete Kyle, Ben McCallum, Paul Pfleiderer, Charles Plosser, Chester Spatt, and members of the finance workshops at Northwestern and Stanford Universities and the University of Chicago. Research assistance was provided by Ravi B. Financial support from the National Science Foundation is gratefully acknowledged.

249

among others. Now all of these models assume that agents have a common information set. In light of the evidence to the contrary, it seems worthwhile to explore the consequences – for the time-series properties of asset returns – of introducing heterogeneity in the form of disparate information sets. This paper compares the implied variances and autocorrelations of prices for alternative specifications of agents' information sets in the context of a simple, partial equilibrium asset-pricing model.

There is an extensive literature on asset pricing in the presence of disparately informed traders. The role of equilibrium security prices as aggregators of individual traders' information has been investigated by Grossman (1976), Grossman and Stiglitz (1980), Hellwig (1980), Diamond and Verrecchia (1981), Kyle (1984), Admati (1985), and Altug (1984), among others. Attention is restricted to one-period models in these studies, and the focus is primarily on the extent to which prices reveal private information to all traders.[1] None of these studies have considered the implications of disparate expectations for the time-series properties of security prices. Indeed, the models investigated to date have typically not been designed to address this issue.

Hellwig (1982) considers a time-series model for stock prices in which agents condition their expectations on past rather than current prices. He shows that as the length of the trading interval decreases, the equilibrium price process obtained from conditioning on past prices approximates the fully revealing equilibrium price that emerges in his model when agents condition on current prices. Hellwig does not examine the time-series properties of his model. More recently, Shiller (1984) has studied a simple dynamic model of stock prices in which there are two groups of traders: One group responds to expected returns optimally forecasted and the other responds myopically. Agents do not explicitly have different

---

[1] Williams (1977) and Jarrow (1980) have taken a different approach to modeling with heterogeneous beliefs in their extensions of the capital asset pricing model. At least some of the agents in their models do not know all of the parameters of the price process, and must therefore learn about the parameters over time. Unlike the studies of aggregation of information in securities markets, these studies of capital asset–pricing models are not concerned with solving for an endogenous price on which agents condition when forming expectations about future prices.

A third and closely related literature is represented by the work of Feldman (1983), Detemple (1983), and Gennotte (1984). These studies investigate the implications for asset-pricing models of partial information about the underlying state variables. It is shown that, in continuous time and under normality, the unobserved state variables can simply be replaced by agents' best forecast of these variables in deducing equilibrium price representations. These studies also do not address the properties of prices in models where equilibrium prices imperfectly convey the private information to other traders.

information sets in this model. Furthermore, neither Hellwig (1982) nor Shiller (1984) examine equilibria where agents condition on current prices and prices are not fully revealing.

This paper takes a first step toward filling this void by examining a model (with a continuum of traders) in which the underlying sources of uncertainty in the economy exhibit serial dependence over time. An economy with a single risky asset, in which traders have a one-period investment horizon, is studied. By restricting attention to a one-period investment horizon, I am able to isolate the consequences for equilibrium asset prices of serially dependent shocks in a model with disparate expectations. Although I do not attempt to model formally the price of an existing risky security, the specifications of both the objective functions and information sets of the traders are motivated partially by the structure of U.S. government bond markets.

In Section 2, I describe the model as well as the equilibrium time-series representation for the price of the risky security in the presence of disparate information and serially correlated shocks. The equilibrium price depends on the average forecast (across disparately informed traders) of the next period's price. This dependence gives rise to an infinite regress problem in expectations that is similar to the problem discussed by Townsend (1983a, b). Following Townsend (1983b), a technique of undetermined coefficients is used to solve this infinite regress problem and obtain an expression for the equilibrium price. Details of this derivation are presented as an appendix, which is available from the author upon request.

In Section 3 the price relation is compared to the corresponding relations obtained from several related models. First, I consider a model in which agents have complete current information. It is shown that the disturbances have a more persistent effect on prices in the model with disparate expectations than in the model with complete information. To help interpret this finding, these models are also compared briefly with a model in which agents are imperfectly, but homogeneously, informed. Additionally, I examine the consequences for prices of setting the variances of some of the disturbances to zero under disparate expectations.

In Section 4, two models are solved numerically to obtain the time-series representations of the equilibrium price of the risky security, for various sets of hypothetical values of the parameters characterizing preferences, uncertainty, and the supply of the security. First, the general model set forth in Section 2 is solved. Then the solutions of a model in which traders are imperfectly, but homogeneously, informed are calculated. Using these price representations, I investigate the consequences of subsets of agents having better information than others or different levels of risk aversion. In addition, I examine the implications for prices of different specifications of the stochastic process for the underlying uncertainty in the model.

Concluding comments are presented in Section 5.

2   A model with a continuum of traders with one-period investment horizons

Suppose there is a continuum of investors indexed by $i \in [0,1]$. Each investor has the opportunity to invest in a single risky security with price p_t and stochastic coupon payment c_t at date t. Purchases of these securities may be financed by borrowing at the constant rate $\bar{r}$. Then the wealth of the ith investor evolves according to the relation

$$w_{it+1} = z_{it}(p_{t+1} + c_{t+1}) - (z_{it}p_t - w_{it})(1+\bar{r}), \tag{2.1}$$

where w_{it} is the level of wealth and z_{it} denotes the holdings of the risky security at date t. Relation (2.1) does not constrain the net worth of each trader to exceed some minimum level, nor are short sales limited. Incorporating minimum capital requirements, constraints on short sales, and other limitations on trading that are present in U.S. stock and bond markets is of interest, but is beyond the scope of this analysis.

The ith investor is assumed to have a one-period investment horizon and to rank alternative investment strategies using the exponential utility function

$$E_t^i - \exp[-\gamma_i w_{it+1}], \tag{2.2}$$

where E_t^i denotes the expectation of investor i conditioned on his information set (sigma-algebra) Φ_t^i at date t and γ_i is the constant coefficient of absolute risk aversion. The assumption that investors have a one-period investment horizon simplifies the analysis by removing the intertemporal dependence between investment decisions at dates t and $t+j$, $j \geq 1$, that would be induced by multiperiod horizons [see Pfleiderer (1984)]. In this manner I am able to focus on the implications of disparate expectations for the time-series properties of p_t in models where the persistence of shocks is the primary source of dynamics in the model.

The coupon stream $\{c_t\}$ is assumed to be normally distributed and to follow a first-order autoregressive process

$$c_t = \bar{c} + \psi c_{t-1} + u_t, \quad Eu_t = 0, \quad \text{Var } u_t = \sigma_u^2; \quad |\psi| \leq 1.$$

The disturbance $\{u_t\}$ is assumed to be independent of other sources of uncertainty in the model. If the risky security is a bond (stock), then $\{c_t\}$

represents a stochastic coupon (dividend). Some implications for prices of altering the stochastic process for coupons are discussed in Section 3.

In order to deduce an equilibrium expression for p_t under disparate expectations, the underlying sources of uncertainty facing investors are assumed to be normally distributed. This assumption implies that the distribution of the price of the risky security at date $t+1$, conditional on Φ_t^i, is normal with mean $E_t^i p_{t+1}$ and variance $\mathrm{Var}_t^i p_{t+1}$, and the conditional variance $\delta_i = \mathrm{Var}_t^i(p_{t+1}+c_{t+1})$ is a constant. Furthermore, the first-order conditions for the maximization of (2.2), subject to the wealth equation (2.1), are

$$-\gamma_i E_t^i(p_{t+1}-\alpha p_t) - \gamma_i \psi c_t + \gamma_i^2 z_{it}\delta_i - \gamma_i \bar{c} = 0, \tag{2.3}$$

where $\alpha \equiv [1+\bar{r}] > 1$. Solving for z_{it} gives the demand for the risky security by the ith trader:

$$z_{it} = \{E_t^i p_{t+1} - \alpha p_t\}/(\gamma_i \delta_i) + (\bar{c}+\psi c_t)/(\gamma_i \delta_i) \quad i \in [0,1]. \tag{2.4}$$

A negative value of z_{it} indicates short selling by the ith investor.

In addition to the continuum of risk-averse traders with demand functions (2.4), I assume that there is a class of traders whose net supply of securities at date t has the linear form (an interpretation of this class is provided subsequently)

$$z_t^a = \theta_t + \epsilon_t + \xi p_t. \tag{2.5}$$

The disturbance θ_t is serially correlated and is assumed to follow either an autoregressive process of order one or a moving average process of order two:

$$\theta_t = \rho\theta_{t-1} + \nu_t \quad \text{or} \quad \theta_t = \nu_t + \phi_1\nu_{t-1} + \phi_2\nu_{t-2}. \tag{2.6}$$

In both representations ν_t is distributed as a normal random variate with mean zero and variance σ_ν^2, and in the AR representation $|\rho| < 1$. The choices of AR(1) and MA(2) processes allow for a variety of serial correlation patterns in θ_t; modification of the following analysis for more general processes is conceptually straightforward. The disturbance ϵ_t is serially independent and normally distributed with mean zero and variance σ_ϵ^2.

It remains to specify the information set for agent $i \in [0,1]$. Speculative traders observe current and past prices and coupon payments. Furthermore, there is no private information about future coupon payments. In this respect the model differs from previous models of information aggregation in security markets, which assumed that there is private information about the future dividend. Imperfect and private information is introduced into the model here as follows. The speculative traders are assumed to observe ν and ϵ with a two-period lag. The only information they have at date t about ϵ_t and ϵ_{t-1} is the information that can be extracted from p_t and p_{t-1}, so traders are (equally) imperfectly informed about the process $\{\epsilon_t\}$. In contrast, the ith trader is assumed to receive a private signal $s_{it} = \theta_t + \eta_{it}$ about θ_t. The $\{\eta_{it}\}$ are mutually and serially independent processes that are independent of the other disturbances in the model and have mean zero and variances $\sigma_{\eta i}^2$, $i \in [0, 1]$.[2] Thus, at date t, traders are disparately informed about the disturbance θ_t underlying z_t^a and will accordingly have disparate expectations about future security prices. Combining these assumptions leads to the following information set for the ith investor:

$$\Phi_t^i = \sigma a\{s_{it-j}, p_{t-j}, c_{t-j}: j \ge 0; \nu_{t-j}, \epsilon_{t-j}: j \ge 2\}, \qquad (2.7)$$

where $\sigma a\{\cdot\}$ denotes the sigma-algebra generated by the variables in brackets.[3] The two-period lag in acquiring information about ν and ϵ was chosen arbitrarily; any informational lag of at least one period for θ leaves traders disparately informed.

While this partial equilibrium model is intended primarily to be illustrative of the consequences of disparate expectations for the temporal behavior of security prices, the specification adopted is motivated by the structure of trading in U.S. government bonds. The number of active traders in bonds is large, so the assumption of competitive traders seems like a useful starting point. Furthermore, many traders finance their trading activity through repurchase agreements or short-term borrowing, which is consistent with the presence of the term $(z_{it} p_t - w_{it})(1 + \bar{r})$ in the wealth equation (2.1).

The net supply z_t^a in (2.5) can be interpreted as the trading activity of agents who do not seek primarily to maximize wealth through speculative trading, but rather who trade for nonspeculative purposes. Candidates for such traders in the U.S. bond markets are the U.S. Treasury, the Federal Reserve, (to a lesser extent) financial intermediaries, and those who are classified as "liquidity" traders in several previous models of trading under heterogeneous information. Pursuing this interpretation of the model, suppose that collectively the nonspeculative agents trade both to satisfy certain macroeconomic objectives related to movements

---

[2] These independence assumptions could easily be relaxed, although the computations in Section 4 would be somewhat more complicated.

[3] Subsequent examples could be modified to incorporate a larger common information set. In particular, the price of the risky security need not be the only commonly observed variable at date t. For illustrative purposes, I shall work with Φ_t^i in (2.7).

in output or unemployment, and for technical reasons related to the intermediation process or to changes in the monetary base due to activities of foreign official institutions. If these traders have more information than the speculative traders, of if there are systematic random components to their objective functions, then a component like θ_t, which is unobserved by the speculative traders, will appear in the trading rule z_t^a. At the same time, additional shocks that are unobserved by speculative traders and that relate to the intermediation process will affect the trading rules of intermediaries and the Federal Reserve. A second disturbance like ϵ_t might capture the effects on trading of such shocks.

Finally, the specification of a trader's information set Φ_t^i also captures some features of the actual information sets of bond traders. There is typically little uncertainty about the value of the coupon payment one period in the future, so there is not private information about $\{c_t\}$ in this model. On the other hand, there is substantial uncertainty about the current motives for the trading activity of the Federal Reserve and financial intermediaries. After some time has elapsed, both information about the trading rule of the central bank and the balance sheets of intermediaries are released (open market committee minutes are published, for example).[4] The introduction of the signal s_{it} and the two-period information lag are motivated by these observations.[5]

The idiosyncratic shocks η_{it} are the formal manifestation of the assumption that traders are differentially informed. One interpretation of the η_{it} is as follows. No trader can infer the Federal Reserve's operating procedures perfectly from available information, yet some information is available. Furthermore, traders differ in their innate ability to perceive the truth. Endowing agents with different measurement errors is one way of representing these different forecasting abilities. In particular, having the η_{it} drawn from distributions with different variances induces different forecast error variances across traders. The ability of trader i to extract the truth from the available data depends on the relative magnitudes of $\sigma_{\eta i}^2$ and σ_θ^2, where σ_θ^2 is the variance of θ_t. Traders are assumed not to

---

[4] A similar structure of uncertainty could be rationalized using the analysis in Siegel (1985). Specifically, measures of real economic growth are published with a lag, but there are economic indicators published before the announcement of the growth figures that are correlated with real growth. Siegel (1985) discusses a signaling interpretation of the effects of money stock announcements on interest rates that is based on such a correlation between money and real income.

[5] In practice, some information about the trading activity of the Federal Reserve is available to traders. Given the structure of uncertainty considered here, current knowledge of z_t^a would fully reveal θ_t and ϵ_t to traders. Full revelation would not be present if there were additional sources of uncertainty, however.

share their assessment (s_{it}) of the value of θ_t with other traders. Also, this analysis abstracts completely from the possibility that high quality information (signals) may be available at a price; there are no costs to acquiring the signal s_{it}.[6]

The remainder of this section is devoted to describing a procedure for solving the model for the equilibrium time-series representation of the price of the risky security in the presence of disparate information (p_t^D). Henceforth constant terms will be suppressed, so the price process derived will be in deviation from mean form. Suppose initially that all investors have the same coefficient of absolute risk aversion (γ) and the variance of the η_{it} are the same (σ_η^2), for all $i \in [0, 1]$. Then the net aggregate demand of the speculative traders is[7]

$$z_t^d = \int_0^1 z_{it}\, d\mu(i) = \left[\int_0^1 E_t^i p_{t+1}^D\, d\mu(i) - \alpha p_t^D + \psi c_t \right] \bigg/ (\gamma \delta^D), \quad (2.8)$$

where μ denotes Lebesgue measure on the interval $[0, 1]$ and δ^D denotes the (common) conditional variance of ($p_{t+1}^D + c_{t+1}$). Equating supply and demand and solving for the price gives

$$p_t^D = \lambda^D \left\{ \int_0^1 E_t^i p_{t+1}^D\, d\mu(i) \right\} + \lambda^D \psi c_t - \delta^D \gamma \lambda^D \{\theta_t + \epsilon_t\}, \quad \lambda^D \equiv 1/[\xi\gamma\delta^D + \alpha].$$

$$(2.9)$$

Notice that the equilibrium price depends on the average forecast across traders of p_{t+1}^D. Thus, each trader's forecast of p_{t+1}^D depends on his forecast of the marketwide average forecast of p_{t+2}^D, so the marketwide average forecast of p_{t+1}^D depends on the marketwide average forecast of the marketwide average forecast of p_{t+2}^D. Pursuing this logic, it is apparent that there is an infinite regress problem in expectations of the type discussed by Townsend (1983a, b). Following Townsend (1983b), this section uses a technique of undetermined coefficients to solve this problem and obtain an expression for the equilibrium price. This approach restricts attention to equilibrium price processes that are linear functions of the underlying disturbances in the economy.

---

[6] The model is not, however, inconsistent with a desire on the part of traders to acquire information, because prices are not fully revealing of θ_t and ϵ_t.

[7] Formally, the integrals in (2.8) may not be well-defined, since realizations of the process $\{E_t^i p_{t+1}^D\}_{i \in [0,1]}$ need not be measurable [but see Judd (1985)]. Throughout this analysis I shall assume that the integrals are well-defined and that a version of the strong law of large numbers holds. Specifically, the integral $\int_0^1 \eta_{it}\, d\mu(i) = 0$ because the η_{it} ($i \in [0,1]$) are independent.

The procedure for obtaining a solution is as follows. First, I conjecture a value for δ^D (which determines λ^D) and a solution for p_t^D of the form

$$p_t^D = A(L)\nu_t + B(L)\epsilon_t + \frac{\psi\lambda^D}{1 - \psi\lambda^D} c_t, \tag{2.10}$$

where $A(L) = \sum_{j=0}^{\infty} A_j L^j$ and $B(L) = \sum_{j=0}^{\infty} B_j L^j$ are polynomials in the lag operator L. Then, leading (2.10) one period and substituting this expression into (2.9) gives

$$p_t^D = \lambda^D \Bigg\{ \int_0^1 [A_1 E_t^i \nu_t + A_2 E_t^i \nu_{t-1} + A^*(L)\nu_{t-2}] \, d\mu(i)$$

$$+ \int_0^1 [B_1 E_t^i \epsilon_t + B_2 E_t^i \epsilon_{t-1} + B^*(L)\epsilon_{t-2}] \, d\mu(i) \Bigg\}$$

$$+ \frac{\psi\lambda^D}{1 - \psi\lambda^D} c_t - \lambda^D \delta^D \gamma(\theta_t + \epsilon_t), \tag{2.11}$$

where $A^*(L) = \sum_{j=0}^{\infty} A_{j+3} L^j$ and $B^*(L) = \sum_{j=0}^{\infty} B_{j+3} L^j$. In arriving at (2.11), I have used the fact that the optimal forecasts of ν_{t+1} and ϵ_{t+1} at date t are their unconditional means (zero), since $\{\nu_t\}$ and $\{\epsilon_t\}$ are serially independent. Also, the coefficient on c_t in (2.10) and (2.11) comes from solving the recursion (2.9) forward to obtain p_t^D as a function of c_t with coefficient $\psi\lambda^D/(1 - \psi\lambda^D)$.[8]

Inspection of (2.11) reveals that calculating the equilibrium price requires a solution for the optimal forecasts of ν_t, ν_{t-1}, ϵ_t, and ϵ_{t-1}, as well as the conditional variance of p_{t+1}^D. Only forecasts of the current and first lagged value of these disturbances are required, because ν_{t-s} and ϵ_{t-s} $(s \geq 2)$ are Φ_t^i measurable by assumption. Without this simplifying assumption, each trader would have to forecast the disturbances ν_{t-j} infinitely far into the past.

To determine the optimal forecasts of the unknown ν and ϵ, consider the variables

$$p_t^* = A_0 \nu_t + A_1 \nu_{t-1} + B_0 \epsilon_t + B_1 \epsilon_{t-1},$$

$$s_{it}^* = \nu_t + \phi_1 \nu_{t-1} + \eta_{it},$$

which are observed by trader i at date t and embody information about the unobserved shocks. These variables, together with ϵ_{t-2} and ν_{t-2}, comprise the observer equation

---

[8] This simple expression for the coefficient on c_t obtains because c_t is common information at date t and is independent of θ_t and ϵ_t.

$$\begin{bmatrix} \epsilon_{t-2} \\ \nu_{t-2} \\ s_{it}^* \\ p_t^* \end{bmatrix} = \begin{bmatrix} 0 & 0 & L^2 \\ L^2 & 0 & 0 \\ (1+\phi_1 L) & 1 & 0 \\ (A_0+A_1 L) & 0 & (B_0+B_1 L) \end{bmatrix} \begin{bmatrix} \nu_t \\ \eta_{it} \\ \epsilon_t \end{bmatrix}, \qquad (2.12)$$

or, more concisely, $y_t = M(L)\omega_t$, where $y_t' \equiv [\epsilon_{t-2}, \nu_{t-2}, s_{it}^*, p_t^*]$, and so on. Equation (2.12) cannot be used directly to determine the optimal forecast at date t of the unobserved shocks, because it is not a fundamental moving average representation. That is, the matrix $M(z)$ viewed as a matrix of polynomials in the complex variable z is not of full rank for all z with $|z| \le 1$. [In the appendix, a fundamental moving average representation for y_t is derived using the approach suggested by Townsend (1983a, b), suitably modified to apply to the model in this paper.]

Having deduced the fundamental moving average representation, the forecasts of the unobserved shocks that appear in price equation (2.11) can be derived using the Weiner-Kolmogorov optimal prediction formulas (Whittle 1963). Specifically, it follows that $E_t^i \epsilon_t$, $E_t^i \epsilon_{t-1}$, $E_t^i \nu_t$, and $E_t^i \nu_{t-1}$ can be expressed as

$$E_t^i \nu_t = f_{\nu 0}(\nu_t, \nu_{t-1}, \epsilon_t, \epsilon_{t-1}, \eta_{it}, \eta_{it-1})$$

$$E_t^i \nu_{t-1} = f_{\nu 1}(\nu_t, \nu_{t-1}, \epsilon_t, \epsilon_{t-1}, \eta_{it}, \eta_{it-1})$$

$$E_t^i \epsilon_t = f_{\epsilon 0}(\nu_t, \nu_{t-1}, \epsilon_t, \epsilon_{t-1}, \eta_{it}, \eta_{it-1}) \qquad (2.13)$$

$$E_t^i \epsilon_{t-1} = f_{\epsilon 1}(\nu_t, \nu_{t-1}, \nu_{t-2}, \epsilon_t, \epsilon_{t-1}, \epsilon_{t-2}, \eta_{it}, \eta_{it-1}, \eta_{it-2}),$$

where the f functions are linear under normality. In all cases, the coefficients are functions of the parameters characterizing s_{it}, z_t^a, and (A_0, A_1, B_0, B_1). Because the variance σ_η^2 is common to all traders, the functions in (2.13) are not indexed by i.

Returning to the equilibrium price relation (23.11), the marketwide average forecasts are obtained by integrating the optimal forecasts in (2.13) across all traders. For any fixed j, ν_{t-j}, ϵ_{t-j}, and c_t are constant functions of i. Furthermore, the η_{it} are independent across i and therefore $\int_0^1 \eta_{it-j} \, d\mu(i) \equiv 0$ (see note 7). Thus, the marketwide average forecasts will depend only on current and past values of ν_t, ϵ_t, and u_t [which confirms the conjecture in (2.10) that p_t^D is a function only of these variables]. Next, the conditional variance of p_{t+1}^D is calculated as

$$\text{Var}_t^i p_{t+1}^D = A_0^2 \sigma_\nu^2 + A_1^2 \, \text{Var}_t^i \nu_t + A_2^2 \, \text{Var}_t^i \nu_{t-1}$$

$$+ B_0^2 \sigma_\epsilon^2 + B_1^2 \, \text{Var}_t^i \epsilon_t + B_2^2 \, \text{Var}_t^i \epsilon_{t-1} + [\psi \lambda^D / (1 - \psi \lambda^D)]^2 \sigma_u^2,$$

$$(2.14)$$

where the conditional variances of the disturbances are also functions of the A_j, B_j and of the parameters characterizing the processes in (2.6) and $\{\eta_{it}\}$. The conditional variance of c_{t+1} is σ_u^2, so $\delta^D = \text{Var}_t^i(p_{t+1}^D + c_{t+1})$ equals the expression in (2.14) plus $[1 + 2\lambda^D\psi/(1 - \lambda^D\psi)]\sigma_u^2$. The resulting value of δ^D is used to calculate a new value for λ^D.

Finally, the coefficients on the ν_{t-j} and ϵ_{t-j} in $\lambda^D \int_0^1 E_t^i p_{t+1}^D \, d\mu(i)$ and $-\lambda^D\delta^D\gamma(\theta_t + \epsilon_t)$ are combined to obtain a new set of moving average parameters (the coefficients for the latter term will depend on whether the AR or MA representation of θ_t is adopted). Equating these coefficients to the corresponding coefficients in (2.9) and substituting (2.14) for $\text{Var}_t^i p_{t+1}^D$ yields a set of (nonlinear) relations that can be solved for the undetermined coefficients A_j and B_j. This is accomplished by repeating the process just described until the conjectured values of the coefficients equal the values in the derived representation (2.11). When this occurs, a fixed point in the space of moving average representations for p_t^D has been reached. Numerical examples of such equilibrium price representations are presented in Section 4.

3   Properties of the equilibrium price representation

It is instructive to compare the time-series representations for prices from the model with disparate expectations to the representations implied by related models in which agents have partial or full information. Suppose that $\gamma_i = \gamma$ and $\text{Var}(\eta_{it}) = \sigma_\eta^2$, for all $i \in [0, 1]$. Also, suppose all agents have full current information, so their information set is $\Phi_t^F = \sigma a\{\nu_{t-j}, \epsilon_{t-j}, c_{t-j} : j \geq 0\}$. Then, when $\{\theta_t\}$ follows an AR(1) process, the equilibrium price is given by

$$p_t^F = \frac{-\lambda^F\delta^F\gamma}{(1-\lambda^F\rho)}\theta_t - \lambda^F\delta^F\gamma\epsilon_t + \frac{\lambda^F\psi}{(1-\lambda^F\psi)}c_t, \qquad (3.1)$$

where $\delta^F \equiv \text{var}[p_t^F + c_t \mid \Phi_{t-1}^F]$ and $\lambda^F = 1/[\xi\delta^F\gamma + \alpha]$. The price p_t^F is a function only of the current value of ϵ, since only ϵ_t affects the aggregate holdings of securities by nonspeculative traders (z_t^a). In contrast, the price p_t^D is affected by ϵ_t and ϵ_{t-1} (i.e., $B_0 \neq 0$, $B_1 \neq 0$), because $E_t^i\epsilon_{t-j}$ and $E_t^i\nu_{t-j}$ $(j = 0, 1)$ depend on ϵ_{t-1}, for all $i \in [0, 1]$.[9] Longer lags of ϵ_t do not affect p_t^D, because $B_2 = 0$ in (2.11) for all values of the primitive parameters and, therefore, $E_t^i\epsilon_{t-1}$ does not enter (2.11). Similarly, $B_j = 0$ for $j \geq 3$, so $B^*(L) = 0$. The number (here, one) of additional MA terms in the representation for p_t^D is linked directly to the informational lag

[9] Of course, if $\{\epsilon_t\}$ were serially correlated than longer lags of ϵ_t would appear in (3.1).

(two periods). An informational lag of k periods adds $k-1$ to the order of the MA component of p_t involving $\{\epsilon_t\}$. This feature of time-series models with disparately informed agents was stressed previously by Townsend (1983b).

Notice, however, that the more persistent effect of ϵ_t on p_t^D is due to the assumption that all agents have *incomplete* information about v_t and ϵ_t for two periods, and not to the presence of *disparate* expectations per se. For suppose all agents are partially, but homogeneously, informed and receive a common signal s_t about θ_t. Then the equilibrium price in this economy (p_t^H) will be given by a version of (2.11), with the expectations in (2.13) augmented to include the η_{t-j} (since they are now common shocks). Furthermore, calculating the optimal forecasts in this case proceeds exactly as in the model with disparate expectations.

Digressing briefly, these observations imply that an observational equivalence property across alternative information structures is satisfied by an important class of linear models. Specifically, suppose aggregate demand is a linear function of prices and an exogenous disturbance and that the decision rules of firms depend linearly on expected future prices, but not on higher order moments of prices. Then, in the decision rules of firms, the coefficients on the aggregate shocks in a model with disparately informed firms will be identical to those on the same shocks in the corresponding model with homogeneously and imperfectly informed firms. In particular, the response of the equilibrium price to shocks in Townsend's (1983a, b) linear-quadratic, symmetric information models of firm behavior are identical to the responses that would be obtained from the corresponding model with homogeneous information. An analogous observational equivalence obtains for models of consumers facing linear supply functions.

The asset-pricing model described in Section 2 is not a member of the class of models for which this observational equivalence obtains. The reason for this is that the time-series representation of the equilibrium price depends on the conditional second moment of next period's price, which is not invariant to the information structure. More precisely, p_t^H is a function of the common measurement error η_t, while p_t^D is not a function of the idiosyncratic errors η_{it}. Consequently, $\text{Var}_t^i p_t^D \neq \text{Var}_t^i p_t^H$ and, hence, $\delta^D \neq \delta^H$. The moving average coefficients of p_t^D and p_t^H depend on δ^D and δ^H, respectively, as follows. When θ_t follows an MA(2) process, then the coefficients on the v's in the expression for p_t^D are $A_j = 0$ for $j \geq 3$ and $A_2 = -\lambda^D \gamma \delta^D \phi_2$. On the other hand, when θ_t follows an AR(1) process then $A_j = -\lambda^D \delta^D \gamma \rho^j/(1-\lambda^D \rho)$ for $j \geq 3$ and $A_2 = \lambda^D A_3 - \lambda^D \delta^D \gamma \rho^2$. The corresponding coefficients for p_t^H have the same form, with λ^H and δ^H in place of λ^D and δ^D, respectively. In sum, the shocks ϵ_t and v_t may have very different effects on prices in the full, partial, and disparate information economies. For comparison, the coefficients of the time-series representation of p_t^H are also calculated in Section 4.

There are two related partial information economies that are also of interest. First, suppose that $\sigma_\epsilon^2 = 0$, so that only ν_t affects aggregate non-speculative supply z_t^a. (As in the original model, agents receive different signals s_{it}.) For this case, ϵ_t can be removed from (2.12) and p_t^* can be replaced by $\nu_t + \phi_1 \nu_{t-1}$. Then, in solving for the undetermined coefficients in (2.10), we can set $B_j = 0$ for $j \ge 0$. Furthermore, given the entire past history of p_t, it is now possible to infer ν_t. In other words, $\{p_{t-j}^D : j \ge 0\}$ and $\{\nu_{t-j} : j \ge 0\}$ span the same linear space, and all agents are fully informed (the signals s_{it} are redundant). Consequently, p_t^D is given by a special case of the full information solution (3.1) with $\epsilon_t = 0$ for all t. Evidently, a nondegenerate distribute for ϵ_t prevents prices from being fully revealing of the unobserved disturbances.

Second, it is instructive to examine the role of uncertain coupon payments in the context of the model (2.9). If $\sigma_u^2 = 0$ and $c_t = \bar{c}$, for all t, then the traded security is no longer risky. That is, a constant price $\bar{p} = (\bar{c}/\bar{r})$ solves the first-order condition (2.3) and, hence, is an equilibrium price in this setting. The traded security is a riskless consol that is a perfect substitute for the riskless security with return $\bar{r}$, and therefore in equilibrium $\bar{r} = (\bar{c}/\bar{p})$, the one-period return on the consol. It follows that, with $\sigma_u^2 = 0$ and $\bar{p} = (\bar{c}/\bar{r})$, the fact that agents are disparately informed has no effect on the equilibrium price $\bar{p}$.

The constant-price equilibrium is not the only rational-expectations equilibrium solution to this model, however. If all agents believe that past prices convey information about current and past shocks, and hence future prices, then prices will in fact have a nontrivial moving average representation in terms of current and past shocks ν and ϵ. Thus, there are multiple rational-expectations equilibria for this model. Note that the equilibrium in which p_t^D has a nonzero variance is not a "bubble" equilibrium of the type discussed by Taylor (1977) and McCallum (1984). Agents are not conditioning on nonfundamental information. The presence of multiple equilibria is a "knife-edge" phenomenon in the context of (2.9). If $\sigma_u^2 > 0$ (c_{t+1} is not perfectly forecastable), then $\delta^D = \text{Var}_t^j(p_{t+1}^D + c_{t+1}) > 0$. Consequently, a constant price is not an equilibrium price. Indeed, even if σ_u^2 is small, the variance of p_t^D may be relatively large because θ_t and ϵ_t may dominate the behavior of prices. The price p_t^D has a nontrivial time-series representation because, with $\sigma_u^2 > 0$, p_t^D is a function of θ_t and ϵ_t and because past prices convey information about future prices. Of course, even if $\sigma_u^2 > 0$, there are bubble equilibria for this model, since traders are "myopically rational" with a one-period investment horizon (see Tirole 1982). In Section 4, attention is restricted to the nonbubble solutions for p_t^D.

4   Time-series implications of the model

A minor modification of the model with disparately informed agents will be useful for presenting numerical examples. Suppose that there are two distinct subsets of traders, each with positive measure, that have different risk characteristics or qualities of information (as measured by $\sigma_{\eta_i}^2$). Then the equilibrium price is obtained by integrating over the subspaces of agents:

$$p_t^D = \lambda^* \left[\int_0^\Lambda E_t^i p_{t+1}^D \, d\mu(i)/(\gamma_i \delta_1) + \int_\Lambda^1 E_t^i p_{t+1}^D \, d\mu(i)/(\gamma_2 \delta_2) \right]$$
$$- \lambda^*(\theta_t + \epsilon_t) + \lambda^* \psi c_t, \tag{4.1}$$

where $0 \le \Lambda \le 1$; traders indexed by $i \in [0, \Lambda]$ have parameters γ_1, δ_1, and $\sigma_{\eta_1}^2$; traders indexed by $i \in (\Lambda, 1]$ have parameters γ_2, δ_2, and $\sigma_{\eta_2}^2$; and

$$\lambda^* = \left\{ \xi + \alpha \left[\frac{\Lambda}{\gamma_1 \delta_1} + \frac{(1-\lambda)}{\gamma_2 \delta_2} \right] \right\}^{-1}.$$

To shed more light on the quantitative properties of the price process under disparate expectations, the equilibrium moving average representations and several population moments were calculated using hypothetical parameter values. These calculations differ in several important respects from the comparative static analysis in Hellwig (1980). Perhaps the most important difference is that δ^D and δ^H represent the conditional variances of endogenous variables (p_t^D and p_t^H), whereas the payoff from the security in Hellwig's model is drawn from an exogenous distribution. For the model of this paper, a change in any parameter that alters the time-series representation for price will also change the conditional variance. Thus, unlike in many previous studies, the conditional variance cannot be held fixed when comparing models.

Table 1 displays the parameters for the various models considered. For all the models with θ_t following an MA process (Models 1–11), $\sigma_\nu = 1.$, $\alpha = 1.02$, and c_t follows an AR(1) process with autoregressive parameter $\psi = .7$ and innovation variance $\sigma_u^2 = .1$. For the first four models, the parameter σ_ϵ was set at unity and θ_t was assumed to follow a moving-average process with parameters $\phi_1 = .8$ and $\phi_2 = .64$. This MA process is a truncated version of an AR(1) process with decay parameter $\rho = .8$. The implied variance of θ_t is 2.05, since $\sigma_\nu^2 = 1$. The quality of an individual trader's signal depends on the relative values of σ_η^2 and 2.05; the smaller is

Table 1. *Description of the models solved for equilibrium prices*

Model	Λ	γ_1	γ_2	$\sigma_{\eta 1}$	$\sigma_{\eta 2}$	ξ	ρ	ϕ_1	ϕ_2
1	1	2	*	2	*	1.5	*	.8	.64
2	1	1	*	2	*	1.5	*	.8	.64
3	1	1	*	0.75	*	1.5	*	.8	.64
4	0.9	2	1	2	.75	1.5	*	.8	.64
5	1	2	*	2	*	1.5	*	−.8	.64
6	1	1	*	2	*	1.5	*	−.8	.64
7	0.9	2	1	2	.75	1.5	*	−.8	.64
8	1	2	*	2	*	1.5	.8	*	*
9	1	1	*	2	*	1.5	.8	*	*
10	0.9	2	1	2	.75	1.5	.8	*	*
11	1	2	*	2	*	1.5	−.8	*	*
12	1	1	*	2	*	1.5	−.8	*	*

$\sigma_\eta^2/\sigma_\theta^2$, the better informed is the trader. The variation in the coupon payment is made small relative to the variation in $\{\theta_t\}$ and $\{\epsilon_t\}$ in order to focus on the implications for price movements of disparate beliefs about the actions of nonspeculative traders. This is consistent with the fact that the profits of bond traders are determined largely by the movements in prices and not by variation in coupon income (McCurdy 1978).

The parameter ξ was set at 1.5. With $\xi > 0$, upward pressure on prices induces an increase in nonspeculative supply. This supply, in turn, attenuates the upward pressure on prices. I would expect ξ to be positive if z_t^a represents a trading rule of the Federal Reserve and the Open Market Committee gives positive weight in their objective function to low variation in interest rates. On the other hand, the sign of ξ might be changed by the presence of other types of nonspeculative suppliers. In the absence of a more detailed model of z_t^a, I shall proceed under the assumption that $\xi > 0$.

The nonlinear equations that must be solved for the undetermined coefficients (A_0, A_1, B_0, B_1) are cubic equations. Accordingly, there may be multiple equilibria for some configurations of the parameters. The possibility of multiple equilibria in rational-expectation models in which conditional variances enter demand equations was illustrated by McCafferty and Driskill (1980) in the context of a speculative model of inventory holdings. I have been unable to demonstrate that there are unique solutions for the models displayed in Table 1. However, for these models, the successive-approximations method always converged rapidly to a moving-average representation with coefficients that are insensitive to their initial values over a broad range of initial values. Furthermore, for some other combinations of parameters, the successive-approximations method did not converge, which suggests both that some models will have either no or multiple linear equilibria and that for these models the solution method fails. Finally, when $\sigma_u^2 = 0$ and there are (at least) two equilibria, the successive approximations method found two different linear equilibria, depending on which initial values were used. These observations provide some assurance that I have found unique linear equilibria for the models displayed in Table 1.

The parameters of the equilibrium price and several descriptive statistics for models 1–11 are displayed in Table 2. For the ℓth model, the row ℓ.D in Table 2 displays the moving average coefficients for p_t^D; Var p_t^D and (δ_1^D, δ_2^D); the first two autocorrelation coefficients of p_t^D; and the variances of the stochastic "inputs" into the price process [see, e.g., (2.11)]. The row ℓ.H displays the corresponding statistics for p_t^H. The objective here is to compare the quantitative features of alternative specifications of the model, and therefore the parameters were chosen simply to provide benchmark sets of results for the purpose of comparisons.

For model 1, Λ is set at unity so there is only one type of trader (i.e., traders have common values of γ and σ_η^2), $\gamma = 2.$, and $\sigma_\eta = 2$. Model 2 is identical to model 1 except for the value of the risk-aversion parameter. A lower value of γ leads to a smaller variance for p_t^D. Providing an interpretation of this finding is complicated by the dependence of net speculative demand and nonspeculative supply on p_t^D. Intuitively, an increase in nonspeculative supply due to (say) an increase in ν_t puts downward pressure on prices. With $\xi > 0$, the price pressure induces a reduction in supply which partially offsets the supply shock ν_t. Now a reduction in γ makes demand more sensitive to price changes [see (2.4)]. Thus, as γ falls, prices must respond less to a given supply shock in order to clear the market, and therefore price is less variable. Lower risk aversion also leads to smaller autocorrelations for p_t^D.

Next, consider the consequences of reducing σ_η^2. In model 3, σ_η is set at .75 (with $\gamma = 1$), which implies that $\sigma_\eta^2/\sigma_s^2 = .215$ ($\sigma_s^2 \equiv$ Var s_{it}) and Var $p_t^D = .463$. The noise-to-signal ratio for the comparable model 2 is $\sigma_\eta^2/\sigma_s^2 = .66$, and Var p_t^D is .481 for this model. Thus, a uniform increase in the quality of each trader's signal leads to a decrease in the variance of the equilibrium price. This result is explained by the decline in δ_1^D with a reduction in σ_η. A smaller conditional variance also leads to relatively more sensitive demands for a given expected price change and, hence, to lower volatility in prices. The roles of γ and δ are not entirely symmetric, however. A smaller value of σ_η also increases the autocorrelations in p_t^D. Put differently, for this θ_t process, a uniform increase in the quality of

Table 2. *Time-series representations of equilibrium prices: moving average θ processes*

Model	A_0	A_1	A_2	B_0	B_1	C_0	F_0	F_1	Var(p_t)	Var$_i\, p_{t+1}$	Corr (p_t, p_{t-1})	Corr (p_t, p_{t-2})	Var(INP)^a	Var p_t^F
1.D	−.572	−.470	−.322	−.558	−.097	.544	*	*	1.02	.839	.456	.208	.796	.867
1.H	−.574	−.470	−.322	−.558	−.010	.545	−.019	−.026	1.03	.842	.460	.208	.798	*
2.D	−.410	−.337	−.192	−.385	−.067	.266	*	*	.481	.403	.447	.178	.284	.570
2.H	−.420	−.338	−.195	−.382	−.093	.271	−.038	−.037	.500	.419	.455	.178	.292	*
3.D	−.431	−.336	−.185	−.342	.003	.254	*	*	.463	.371	.465	.186	.263	.570
3.H	−.439	−.339	−.188	−.333	.011	.258	−.106	−.063	.475	.382	.473	.187	.271	*
4.D	−.564	−.463	−.310	−.540	.083	.513	*	*	.971	.796/.765	.458	.206	.738	.876
4.H	−.566	−.462	−.310	−.536	−.091	.514	−.030	−.032	.971	.803/.766	.460	.207	.740	*
5.D	−.327	.232	−.247	−.340	−.025	.370	*	*	.365	.292	−.291	.257	.467	.351
5.H	−.327	.227	−.244	−.330	−.025	.364	.004	−.027	.357	.282	−.291	.259	.458	*
6.D	−.090	.051	−.073	−.097	−.018	.086	*	*	.027	.022	−.203	.205	.040	.244
6.H	−.093	.050	−.072	−.091	−.018	.086	−.002	−.014	.027	.021	−.200	.273	.040	*
7.D	−.264	.183	−.209	−.289	−.025	.297	*	*	.252	.203	−.273	.258	.336	.351
7.H	−.277	.176	−.205	−.275	−.024	.289	.007	−.033	.238	.190	−.275	.264	.323	*

^{a} Var(INP) = Var$(\lambda^*[\theta_t + \epsilon_t + \psi c_t])$.

traders' information leads to a less choppy price process, while decreasing risk aversion leads to a more choppy process.

In model 4 there are two types of investors. Ninety percent of the investors have preferences with $\gamma_1 = 2$ and $\sigma_{\eta 1} = 2$, while the remaining 10 percent have $\gamma_2 = 1$ and $\sigma_{\eta 2} = .75$. Consistent with previous results, the price is less volatile relative to the comparable model 1 where all investors have $\gamma = .2$ and $\sigma_\eta = 2$. The decline in the variance of p_t^D (from 1.02 to .971) is quite small, however. Solving the comparable model with ($\gamma_1 = 1$, $\sigma_{\eta 1} = 2$) and ($\gamma_1 = .5$, $\sigma_{\eta 2} = .75$) gives Var $p_t^D = .348$. Comparing this to Var $p_t^D = .481$ from model 2, it follows that halving the coefficient of absolute risk aversion for 10 percent of the traders leads to a larger percentage decline in Var p_t^D at low levels of risk aversion. In both cases, the effects on the autocorrelations are small.

In sum, the presence of a small group of relatively well-informed and more risk-tolerant traders reduces the volatility of the price of the risky asset. A similar result is obtained in the "large market" models of Hellwig (1980) and Admati (1985). This finding is interesting in light of the recent analyses of Kyle (1984) and Altug (1984) of one-period models where a finite number of agents behave strategically. They found that a trader with inside information may act to conceal this information and in doing so reduce the variance of the price. Here it has been shown that a model with competitive traders leads to a qualitatively similar result, but for different reasons. Furthermore, in the competitive model, the primary source of reduced volatility is lower risk aversion, not better information.[10]

In models 5–7, $\{\theta_t\}$ follows an MA(2) process with coefficients $\theta_1 = -.8$ and $\theta_2 = .64$ (and $\sigma_\epsilon = 1$). This MA process is a truncated version of an AR(1) process with autoregressive parameter $\rho = -.8$. The two MA representations considered lead to θ processes with the same variances but different autocorrelations. The relatively choppy MA process ($\phi_1 = -.8$, $\phi_2 = .64$) leads to a smaller variance for p_t^D (compare models 1.D and 5.D). Another difference across the two MA processes is that the first autocorrelation coefficient is negative when $\phi_1 = -.8$. Qualitatively, the effects on the variances of prices of changing γ or σ_η are the same as in the first four models.

Consider next the properties of p_t^H, obtained when agents are homogeneously but imperfectly informed. The equilibrium time-series representations for p_t^H involve both the coefficients (A_0, A_1, B_0, B_1) and the coefficients F_0 and F_1 on η_t and η_{t-1}, respectively. For models 1–4, the variance of p_t^H is greater than or equal to the variance of p_t^D. However, a

---

[10] If $\xi < 0$, then the variances of p_t^D are much larger than in the corresponding models with $\xi > 0$. Furthermore, Var p_t^D is inversely related to the values of γ and σ_η when $\xi < 0$.

notable feature of the results is that in all cases the differences between these variances are small. This similarity is a consequence of the similarity in the corresponding MA coefficients and the relatively small values of F_0 and F_1. Note also that the autocorrelations for p_t^D and p_t^H are also very similar. Thus, for the models examined, the time-series properties of p_t^D are induced largely by the incompleteness of information rather than the disparate nature of information.

In models 5–7, the variance of p_t^D is greater than the variance of p_t^H, but again the differences are small. Evidently, when nonspeculative supply is choppy, differential information leads to a more volatile price process than homogeneous, partial information, in this economic environment.

There is another interesting feature of the variances. The column of Table 2 labeled Var(INP) displays the variances of the stochastic inputs into the difference equation for p_t^D and p_t^H [see (4.1)]. A question that is often asked in the context of linear rational-expectations models is whether the variance of the output variable (here, price) exceeds the variance of the input variable (here, $\lambda^*(\theta_t + \epsilon_t) - \lambda^* \psi c_t$). In some contexts it can be shown that, as long as the inputs are not explosive processes, the variance of the output must be less than the variance of the input. This observation underlies the volatility tests of (for instance) expectations theories of the term structure of interest rates (Shiller 1979, Singleton 1980) and the monetary model of exchange rate determination (Meese and Singleton 1983). Interestingly, Var p_t^D is not always less than the sum of the variances of the inputs in the security model being investigated here. For the MA process ($\phi_1 = -.8$, $\phi_2 = .64$) the sum of Var($\lambda^* \theta_t$), Var($\lambda^* \epsilon_t$), and Var($\lambda^* \psi c_t$) is greater than Var(p_t^D). However, for the MA process ($\phi_1 = .8$, $\phi_2 = .64$) the variances of p_t^D and p_t^H exceed the sum of the variances of the inputs. Thus, under disparate expectations, a smooth trading rule by nonspeculative traders leads to a price process that is more volatile than the input process, while the variability of the price process is attenuated for a choppy trading rule.

That Var p_t^D may exceed Var$[\lambda^*(\theta_t + \epsilon_t - \psi c_t)]$ is attributable to the risk-aversion of traders. Shiller (1981) showed that the variance of the price of a security is less than or equal to the variance of the dividend, under the implicit assumption of risk neutrality. In the context of a model with logarithmic utility, Michener (1982) demonstrated that Shiller's bound may be violated if agents are risk-averse. The results in Table 2 provide another example of this fact in the context of a model with exponential utility and differential or partial information. Notice that for this model the ratio of Var p_t^D to Var$[\lambda^*(\Theta_t + \epsilon_t - \psi c_t)]$ increases as γ decreases (compare models 1 and 2).

Table 3. *Time-series representations of equilibrium prices: autoregressive θ processes*

Model	A_0	A_1	A_2	B_0	B_1	C_0	F_0	F_1	Var(p_t)	Var$_i\,p_{t+1}$	Corr (p_t, p_{t-1})	Corr (p_t, p_{t-2})	Var(INP)^a	Var p_t^F
8.D	-.648	-.570	-.931	-.641	-.045	.873	*	*	5.59	1.80	.633	.463	2.17	2.24
8.H	-.649	-.569	-.932	-.638	-.047	.874	-.011	-.038	5.60	1.81	.633	.463	2.18	*
9.D	-.627	-.569	-.746	-.612	-.057	.666	*	*	3.99	1.57	.647	.436	1.60	2.10
9.H	-.629	-.566	-.748	-.601	-.667	.668	-.028	-.068	4.02	1.58	.646	.435	1.61	*
10.D	-.647	-.573	-.908	-.634	-.044	.846	*	*	5.37	1.77/1.66	.636	.460	2.10	2.24
10.H	-.648	-.572	-.910	-.630	-.047	.848	-.018	-.048	5.38	1.79/1.66	.636	.461	2.10	*
11.D	-.465	.389	-.148	-.471	.015	.732	*	*	1.39	.803	-.290	.329	1.79	.847
11.H	-.467	.388	-.148	-.467	-.017	.732	-.0006	-.039	1.40	.805	-.290	.328	1.79	*
12.D	-.177	.166	-.055	-.183	.023	.259	*	*	.244	.122	-.419	.351	.422	.666
12.H	-.190	.168	-.057	-.168	-.033	.266	-.022	-.054	.271	.135	-.385	.334	.442	*

^{a} Var(INP) = Var($\lambda^*[\theta_t + \epsilon_t + \psi c_t]$).

The time-series representations of prices for several models with $\{\theta_t\}$ following autoregressive processes are displayed in Table 3. The parameters for these models are different from those for models 1–7. Specifically, $\sigma_v^2 = 2$ and $\sigma_\epsilon^2 = .5$, which gives $\sigma_\Theta^2 = 4$. Also, $\sigma_u^2 = .2$ and $\psi = .8$. These parameters were chosen to induce larger autocorrelations in prices and to assure that a majority of the variation in prices is attributable to variation in θ.

Models 8, 9, and 10 correspond to models 1, 2, and 4 of Table 2, and models 11 and 12 correspond to models 5 and 6. Qualitatively, the implications for prices of lowering risk aversion or increasing the quality of traders' signals are the same. One difference across the two sets of results is that $(\text{Var}_t^i \, p_{t+1}^D / \text{Var} \, p_{t+1}^D)$ is much smaller for the AR models than for the MA models. Evidently, the conclusions drawn from models 1–4 are insensitive to this ratio.

Finally, a comparison of the variances of the full-information price p_t^F to the corresponding variances of p_t^D is interesting. For the MA representation ($\phi_1 = .8$, $\phi_2 = .64$), $\text{Var} \, p_t^D$ is larger than $\text{Var} \, p_t^F$ for $\gamma = 2$, but $\text{Var} \, p_t^D < \text{Var} \, p_t^F$ for $\gamma = 1$.[11] Thus, for low levels of risk aversion, disparate expectations does not lead to a more volatile price in this model. On the other hand, $\text{Var} \, p_t^D > \text{Var} \, p_t^F$ for $\gamma \geq 1$ when θ follows the AR(1) model with $\rho = .8$. Thus, if much of the variation in nonspeculative supply is due to persistent shocks about which there is partial information, the price may be much more volatile than what would be obvserved in a full-information economy even if speculative traders do not exhibit much risk aversion.

5 Discussion and extensions

In the context of a simple model of security prices, it has been shown that both the variance and autocorrelations of prices are affected by the presence of disparately informed traders. Precisely how prices are affected depends critically on whether the trading rule of the nonspeculative traders is smooth or choppy. When the persistent shock to the positions of nonspeculative traders is "smooth" and these positions are positively related to the current price, security prices may be much more volatile than the variables which determine equilibrium prices. Moreover, the price has a larger variance and is more choppy than the price in the corresponding model with full current information. Finally, introducing traders with

---

[11] What makes this possible, of course, is the fact that the equilibrium prices are functions of their respective conditional variances. Consequently, arguments based on the law of iterated expectations cannot be applied to order the variances for all possible representation of $\{\theta_t\}$ and $\{\epsilon_t\}$.

relatively low levels of absolute risk aversion and high quality information leads to a decline in price variability. These orderings among second moments are typically reversed in the case of "choppy" forcing variables. Many of the aggregate economic variables that affect trading over the business cycle (e.g., output, unemployment, inflation) are in fact quite smooth. If the time-series characteristics of these variables are inherited by the trading rules of the nonspeculative traders, then the case of smooth forcing variables may be relevant for modeling security markets in the United States. However, in light of the sensitivity of the results to the specification of nonspeculative traders, a more systematic analysis of their objective functions is an important topic for future research.

Another interesting finding is that the equilibrium prices for models with disparate information and partial, homogeneous information follow very similar time-series processes. It remains to be seen whether this similarity carries over to alternative parameterizations and information structures. Based on the findings to date, however, it appears that disparate information per se in a competitive market does not significantly affect the equilibrium price process. That is, imperfect information is the primary source of the difference between models with complete current information and imperfect and disparate information.

There are many extensions of the simple model considered here that warrant investigation. The assumption that traders have a one-period investment horizon is certainly restrictive. Traders are concerned about their inventory holdings over time. Furthermore, they surely are trying to anticipate economic developments several periods ahead when making their investment decisions in the current period. As noted above, another important extension is the development of a more complete model of the trading activity of nonspeculative traders. This would lead to more readily interpretable disturbances and possibly allow for a more direct link of the model's quantitative properties to the properties of the data for U.S. securities markets.

REFERENCES

Admati, A. R. 1985. "A Noisy Rational Expectations Equilibrium for Multi-Asset Securities Markets." *Econometrica* 53: 629–57.

Altug, S. 1984. "The Effect of Insider Trading by a Dominant Trade in a Simple Securities Model." Unpublished manuscript, University of Minnesota.

Cornell, B. 1983. "The Money Supply Announcements Puzzle: Review and Interpretation." *American Economic Review* 73: 644–57.

Detemple, J. 1983. "A General Equilibrium Model of Asset Pricing with Partial or Heterogeneous Information." Unpublished manuscript.

Diamond, D. W., and R. E. Verrecchia. 1981. "Information Aggregation in a Noisy Rational Expectations Economy." *Journal of Financial Economics* 9: 221–35.

Dunn, K. B., and K. J. Singleton. 1985. "Modeling the Term Structure of Interest Rates under Nonseparable Utility and Durability of Goods." *Journal of Financial Economics,* to appear.

Eichenbaum, M., and L. P. Hansen. 1985. "Estimating Models with Intertemporal Substitution Using Aggregate Time Series Data." Unpublished manuscript, Carnegie-Mellon University.

Feldman, D. 1983. "The Term Structure of Interest Rates in a Partially Observable Economy." Unpublished manuscript, Vanderbilt University.

French, K., and R. Roll. 1984. "Is Trading Self-Generating?" Unpublished manuscript, University of California–Los Angeles.

Gennotte, G. 1984. "Continuous Time Production Economies Under Incomplete Information I: A Separation Theorem." Unpublished manuscript, Massachusetts Institute of Technology.

Grossman, S. 1976. "On the Efficiency of Competitive Stock Markets When Traders have Diverse Information." *Journal of Finance* 31: 573–85.

Grossman, S., and J. Stiglitz. 1980. "On the Impossibility of Informationally Efficient Markets." *American Economic Review* 70: 393–408.

Hansen, L. P., and K. J. Singleton. 1982. "Generalized Instrumental Variables Estimation of Nonlinear Rational Expectation Models." *Econometrica* 50: 1269–86.

Hellwig, M. F. 1980. "On the Aggregation of Information in Competitive Stock Markets." *Journal of Economic Theory* 22: 477–98.

1982. "Rational Expectations Equilibrium with Conditioning on Past Prices: A Mean-Variance Example." *Journal of Economic Theory* 26: 279–312.

Jarrow, R. 1980. "Heterogeneous Expectations, Restrictions on Short-Sales, and Equilibrium Asset Prices." *Journal of Finance* 35: 1105–13.

Judd, K. 1985. "The Law of Large Numbers with a Continuum of IID Random Variables." *Journal of Economic Theory* 35: 19–25.

Kyle, P. 1984. "Equilibrium in a Speculator Market with Strategically Informed Trading." Unpublished manuscript, Princeton University.

LeRoy, S., and R. Porter. 1980. "The Present-Value Relation: Tests Based on Implied Variance Bounds." *Econometrica* 49: 555–74.

McCafferty, S., and R. Driskill. 1980. "Problems of Existence and Uniqueness in Nonlinear Rational Expectations Models." *Econometrica* 48: 1313–18.

McCallum, B. T. 1984. "Macroeconomics and Finance: The Role of the Stock Market." *Carnegie-Rochester Conference Series on Public Policy* 21: 109–16.

McCurdy, C. 1978. "The Dealer Market for United States Government Securities." Federal Reserve Bank of New York *Quarterly Review* 2: 35–47.

Meese, R., and K. J. Singleton. 1983. "Rational Expectations and the Volatility of Floating Exchange Rates." *International Economic Review* 24: 721–33.

Michener, R. 1982. "Variance Bounds in a Simple Model of Asset Pricing." *Journal of Political Economy* 90: 166–75.

Pfleiderer, P. 1984. "The Volume of Trade and the Variability of Prices." Unpublished manuscript, Stanford University.

Scott, L. O. 1985. "The Present-Value Model of Stock Prices: Empirical Tests Based on Instrumental Variables Estimation." *Review of Economics and Statistics,* to appear.

Shiller, R. J. 1979. "The Volatility of Long-Term Interest Rates and Expectations Models of the Term Structure." *Journal of Political Economy* 87: 1190–1219.

1981. "Do Stock Prices Move Too Much to Be Justified by Subsequent Changes in Dividends?" *American Economic Review* 71: 421–36.

272   Kenneth J. Singleton

1984. "Stock Prices and Social Dynamics." Discussion Paper No. 719, Cowles Foundation.

Siegel, J. 1985. "Money Supply Announcements and Interest Rates: Does Monetary Policy Matter?" *Journal of Monetary Economics* 15.

Singleton, K. J. 1980. "Expectations Models of the Term Structure and Implied Variance Bounds." *Journal of Political Economy* 88: 1159–76.

1985. "Specification and Estimation of Intertemporal Asset Pricing Models." In B. Friedman and F. Hahn (eds.), *Handbook in Monetary Economics.*

Taylor, J. B. 1977. "Conditions for Unique Solutions in Stochastic Macroeconomic Models with Rational Expectations." *Econometrica* 45: 1377–85.

Tirole, J. 1982. "On the Possibility of Speculation under Rational Expectations." *Econometrica* 50: 1163–81.

Townsend, R. 1983a. "Equilibrium Theory with Learning and Disparate Expectations: Some Issues and Methods." In R. Frydman and E. Phelps (eds.), *Industrial Forecasting and Aggregate Outcomes,* Chapter 9. Cambridge: Cambridge University Press.

1983b. "Forecasting the Forecasts of Others." *Journal of Political Economy* 91: 546–88.

Whittle, P. 1963. *Prediction and Regulation.* Princeton: Van Nostrand.

Williams, J. 1977. "Capital Asset Prices with Heterogeneous Beliefs." *Journal of Financial Economics* 5: 219–39.

CHAPTER 13

Nominal surprises, real factors, and propagation mechanisms

Robert G. King and Charles I. Plosser

1   Introduction

A predominant focus of macroeconomic research in the last ten years
has been on the origins of the business cycle. In particular, it has been
popular to view the business cycle as arising from surprise movements in
aggregate demand and to argue that these impulses are transmitted to
real activity through movements in the price level.[1] In order to generate
empirically relevant fluctuations, however, such models must incorporate
mechanisms to propagate price surprises over time. That is, to replicate
economic fluctuations, it is necessary to transform serially uncorrelated
price surprises into serially correlated macroeconomic time series. Unfortunately, despite the large amount of effort devoted in recent years
to this type of equilibrium business cycle modeling, relatively little attention has been focused on isolating the empirically important propagation
mechanisms.

More recently, we have pursued a line of research that we call "real
business cycle theory," in which disturbances are propagated over time as
a result both of economic agents' desire to smooth commodity profiles
and capitalistic production with rich intertemporal substitution opportunities.[2] To date, however, these models incorporate only real supply-
side or technological disturbances, abstracting from real demand-side influences (such as government spending) or nominal shocks. Nevertheless,

We thank Ching-Sheng Mao for research assistance. This research has been supported by
the National Science Foundation.

[1] For example, both the standard version of Lucas' (1972, 1973) incomplete information
theory and the single-period contact version of Fischer's (1977) sticky wage model have
this implication. By standard version, we mean the version of Lucas' theory that constrains agents to base current perceptions on local prices and not aggregate endogenous
variables such as the interest rate [Barro (1980)] or exogenous variables such as the money
stock [King (1981)].

[2] See Long and Plosser (1983) and King and Plosser (1984a, b).

273

the results on propagation mechanisms appear to be relevant for more fully developing the monetary theories of business fluctuation discussed above.

Of course, interest in propagation mechanisms is not new. Indeed, it was the major focus of many of the interwar business cycle theorists. As discussed briefly in King and Plosser (1984b), these theorists [e.g., Hayek (1931)] stressed that the intertemporal character of production was central to understanding economic fluctuations. Keynesian economists were also forced to come to grips with propagation, but because of their narrow focus on demand, propagation was introduced through "partial adjustment" models or "accelerator" mechanisms that determined the dynamic character of aggregate demand. As illustrated by Long and Plosser (1983) and Kydland and Prescott (1982), an equilibrium theory of the business cycle must involve, as a key element, the earlier focus on capitalistic production.

This paper is an exploratory empirical study that attempts to evaluate the relative contribution of three factors – price surprises, real factors, and propagation mechanisms – to the overall variance of real economic activity in the postwar United States. Our investigation is divided into two main parts. First, in Section 2, we lay out a basic real output equation that depends on nominal surprises, real shocks, and propagation mechanisms. We develop a statistic called the propagation ratio for evaluating the contribution of propagation mechanisms to the variance of economic time series. The empirical investigation in Section 3 treats monetary surprises as the pertinent nominal disturbances and is largely supportive of the proposition that propagation mechanisms are the central first-order aspect of business cycles, suggesting an important redirection of macroeconomic research.

In Section 3, we attempt to isolate the relative importance of price surprises in output and unemployment fluctuations. We employ an instrumental variables procedure to estimate the Lucas slope coefficient. There are two important results of this empirical investigation. Perhaps surprisingly, it is difficult to pin down the relative importance of price surprises. Fundamentally, we believe, this difficulty reflects the fact that it is difficult to explain price surprises with variables typically thought to drive aggregate demand (money, government expenditures, etc.). This is an important finding in its own right, for it calls into question aspects of the mechanisms discussed by Lucas (1972, 1973) and Fischer (1977). Section 4 discusses potential extensions of our research as well as our conclusions from the evidence so far.

2   Neoclassical propagation mechanisms

The real business cycle theories of Kydland and Prescott (1982) and Long and Plosser (1983) provide important examples of how rich possibilities for intertemporal substitution in production lead the effects of economic disturbances to be propagated over time. In each of these models, the existence of many capital goods leads to the rich intertemporal production possibilities. In this paper, we focus on how these mechanisms lead nominal shocks to be propagated across time, working by analogy to the more completely spelled-out general equilibrium models and adopting a linear specification throughout.

We start by considering a $N \times 1$ vector of current activities y_t, which are "flow" economic decisions such as output, work effort, consumption, and investments of various sorts – that is, the principal endogenous quantity variables of most macroeconomic models. In real business cycle models, the equilibrium levels of these variables depend on the $M \times 1$ vector of previously accumulated capital stocks k_{t-1} and the current values of a $P \times 1$ vector of exogenous real state variables s_t. We assume that the vector s_t is Markov (i.e., $s_t = \Lambda s_{t-1} + \epsilon_t$), so that the influence of s_t on y_t incorporates both current and expectational factors. Thus, under a linear real business cycle model, the decision rules that govern the evolution of the vector y_t can be expressed as

$$y_t = \theta k_{t-1} + \beta s_t, \tag{2.1}$$

where θ is an $N \times M$ matrix and β is an $N \times P$ matrix. Next, technological considerations dictate that the vector of capital stocks evolves according to actions taken at date t (y_t) and prior capital stocks:

$$k_t = Ay_t + \Delta k_{t-1}, \tag{2.2}$$

where A is an $M \times N$ matrix and Δ is an $N \times N$ matrix.

Combining equations (2.1) and (2.2), it follows that

$$k_t = (I - (A\theta + \Delta)L)^{-1} A\beta s_t; \tag{2.3}$$

that is, the capital stock vector is a function of current and past real factors s_t. Consequently, the current flow variables can be expressed as

$$y_t = \beta s_t + \theta (I - (A\theta + \Delta)L)^{-1} A\beta s_{t-1}. \tag{2.4}$$

For example, even if real factors s_t are serially uncorrelated ($\Lambda = 0$), the capitalistic structure of production permits commodity flows y_t to exhibit rich patterns of serial correlation.[3] More generally, though, the dynamics of real fluctuations arise from the interaction of internal propagation mechanisms (governed by $A\theta + \Delta$) and the dynamics of the exogenous, real forcing variables (governed by the matrix Λ).[4] This makes it difficult

---

[3] As noted by Long and Plosser (1983) this result holds even if there is no long-lived capital, i.e., if the depreciation rate is 100% ($\Delta = 0$).

[4] There is a deeper sense in which this is even more important. If A and Δ are technological, but β and θ are at least partly determined by behavior, then the optimal values of

to distinguish exogenous and endogenous sources of serial correlation if macroeconomic time series are generated by unobservable real disturbances.[5]

Nominal shocks and the propagation ratio

Lucas (1972, 1977, 1980) argues that an empirically relevant theory of business fluctuations arises principally from invoking information frictions that allow nominal shocks to exert temporary real effects on real macroeconomic flows. Given the internal propagation mechanisms, these nominal impulses are transmitted over time, even though they do not themselves have direct long-lived effects. Letting $(x_t - E_{t-1}x_t)$ be a vector of nominal shocks, we then modify (2.1) as follows:

$$y_t = \tau(x_t - E_{t-1}x_t) + \theta(k_{t-1}) + \beta s_t, \tag{2.5}$$

where τ is an $N \times G$ matrix and x_t is a $G \times 1$ vector. Thus, we can write the vector of commodity flows as

$$y_t = (I - (A\theta + \Delta)L)^{-1}A\tau(x_t - E_{t-1}x_t) + y_t^*, \tag{2.6}$$

where y_t^* represents the influence of real factors s_t given by (2.4).

The maintained assumption that only unanticipated nominal disturbances have real effects implies that such shocks are especially useful for studying the statistical importance of the economy's internal propagation mechanisms. If we consider a single nominal shock and a particular element of the real commodity flow vector y_j, (2.6) implies that

$$y_{jt} = \sum_{h=0}^{H} \alpha_{jh}(x_{t-h} - E_{t-h-1}x_{t-h}) + y_{jt}^*, \tag{2.7}$$

where H is (in principle) infinite but we assume that the lag structure is well approximated by a finite lag length H. The α coefficients are functions only of the internal propagation mechanism - that is, of $I - (A\theta + \Delta)L^{-1}$ and the value of τ. Since nominal surprises are serially uncorrelated, the only way that such a surprise can affect real commodity flows with a lag is through the internal propagation mechanism.[6]

β and θ depend (in principle) on Λ. For example, the degree of permanence of s_t influences an optimizing agent's response to this factor, i.e., values of β. For a more detailed discussion of such linear business cycle models, see King (1983).

[5] For example, in Kydland and Prescott (1982) it is unclear whether the bulk of serial correlation arises from internal propagation mechanisms or exogenous productivity disturbances.

[6] It is interesting to note that if one assumes the real shocks to be serially uncorrelated then the distributed lag weights for the nominal surprise and the real shocks are proportional for lags greater than one. Alternatively, this fact could be used to uncover the serial correlation properties of the underlying real disturbances.

The variance of y_{jt} attributable to the *impulse* effect of nominal shocks is $(\alpha_{j0})^2 \sigma_{\tilde{x}}^2$, where $\sigma_{\tilde{x}}^2$ is the variance of the nominal surprise $\tilde{x}_t = x_t - E_{t-1} x_t$. The variance of y_{jt} attributable to the *propagation* effects – that is, the effects of past values of $\tilde{x}_t$ – is $\sum_{h=1}^{H} (\alpha_{jh})^2 \sigma_{\tilde{x}}^2$. As our measure of the relative importance of propagation and impulse effects, we consider the *propagation ratio* for y_j:

$$\Phi_j = \frac{\sum_{h=1}^{H} (\alpha_{jh})^2}{(\alpha_{j0})^2 + \sum_{h=1}^{H} (\alpha_{jh})^2}. \tag{2.8}$$

This ratio will vary between zero and one. Values close to one are associated with nominal disturbances that are principally important due to propagation. For example, if $\alpha_{j0} = \alpha_{j1} = \cdots = \alpha_{jH}$ then it follows that $\Phi_j = H/(H+1)$; that is, propagation effects explain $H/(H+1) \cdot 100$ percent of the variance in y_j due to the nominal disturbance. As another example, assume a geometric lag structure such that $\alpha_{jh} = \alpha_j^{h+1}$ for $h = 0, \ldots, H$ and $|\alpha| < 1$. In this case $\Phi_j = 1 - [(1 - \alpha_j^2)/(1 - \alpha_j^{2(H+1)})]$, which of course approaches α_j^2 as $H \to \infty$.

3 Evidence on propagation mechanisms

In the empirical analysis that follows, we consider two alternative nominal shock hypotheses. First, we treat the case of unanticipated money growth as developed by Robert Barro in a series of studies (1977, 1978). The key identifying restriction in these studies is, of course, that money is exogenous. However, as argued by King and Plosser (1984a), there are important theoretical reasons for believing that the usual measure of money employed in empirical studies is endogenous. Furthermore, on postwar data King and Plosser (1984a) show that inside and outside money behave differently with respect to real variables. Consequently, we also investigate the effects of unanticipated money using the monetary base, instead of using currency plus demand deposits as employed by Barro and other researchers.

Second, we analyze the effects of unanticipated price movements as previously considered by Lucas (1973) and Sargent (1976). Different statistical techniques are necessary in this case because – in the theoretical analyses of Lucas (1973) and Fischer (1977) – unanticipated price level movements are clearly not exogenous with respect to current quantities. In other words, unanticipated price level movements are correlated with the error term y_{jt}^* in (2.7) through effects of output on money demand.

The data used in the empirical work are summarized in Table 1 (sources are given in the appendix). These data exhibit the patterns familiar to students of postwar business cycles. The unemployment rate is highly serially correlated while the growth rates of other real variables are less

Table 1. *Summary statistics*

Variable	Period	Standard mean (%)	Deviation (%)	r_1	r_2	r_3	r_4	r_5	r_6
U_t	1948:1–1983:3	5.52	1.73	.94	.84	.72	.60	.50	.44
Δy_t	1948:1–1983:3	3.31	4.47	.39	.20	−.01	−.16	−.13	−.09
Δp_t	1948:1–1983:3	4.03	3.13	.70	.62	.55	.41	.37	.32
Δb_t	1948:1–1981:3	4.06	3.70	.53	.53	.49	.50	.41	.32
Δm_t	1948:1–1983:3	4.30	3.53	.48	.47	.32	.27	.32	.27
Δg_t	1948:1–1983:3	3.43	16.64	.60	.36	.21	.07	.02	.00
l_t	1948:1–1982:4	−.53	.03	.96	.94	.91	.89	.86	.84
Δw_t	1948:1–1983:3	5.46	3.48	.37	.26	.26	.41	.11	.05
Δn_t	1948:1–1982:4	1.50	.47	.52	.51	.52	.49	.48	.45
R_t	1948:1–1983:3	4.71	3.27	.92	.87	.86	.81	.77	.73

Sample autocorrelations span the r_1–r_6 columns.

Notes: U_t is the unemployment rate for the last month of the quarter; Δy_t, Δp_t, and Δg_t are the annualized percentage growth rates of real GNP, the GNP deflator, and real federal government purchases, respectively; Δb_t, Δm_t, Δw_t, and Δn_t are the annualized growth rates in quarter t of the monetary base, the money supply (M_1), the nominal wage rate, and the population. The nominal 3 month T-bill rate is R_t, and l_t is the log of the labor force participation rate. The large sample standard error of the sample autocorrelations $(r_1,...,r_6)$ is approximately .08.

so. Nominal variables, however, display much more serial dependence than real variables, with the exception of the unemployment rate.

Propagation and unanticipated money

In order to demonstrate the relative importance of propagation mechanisms and impulses, we begin by estimating the relation between unanticipated money and real variables, specifically the unemployment rate and real output. The results are summarized in Table 2. Unanticipated money is estimated as the residual from a regression that predicts monetary growth using four quarterly lags of money growth, real output growth, inflation, three-month treasury bills, labor force participation rate, population growth, wage inflation, and the growth rate of real federal purchases of goods and services. The real quantity variables are then regressed on the current and eight lags of unanticipated money, using a generalized least squares procedure to correct for serial correlation in the errors.[7]

[7] We use this procedure because it corresponds most closely to what previous authors have done. However, Marty Eichenbaum has pointed out to us that, alternatively, we could

Table 2. *Unanticipated money regressions*, $Y_t = \text{const.} + \sum_{j=0}^{8} a_j(x_{t-j} - E_{t-1-j}x_{t-j}) + bt + e_t$

| Dependent variable | Period | Const. | Coefficients | | | | | | | | | b | r_1 | r_2 | r_3 | r_4 | $s(e)$ | Φ |
			a_0	a_1	a_2	a_3	a_4	a_5	a_6	a_7	a_8							
A. Money stock – M_1																		
U_t	1948:1–1982:4	5.60 (.37)	−.04 (.02)	−.09 (.03)	−.14 (.04)	−.16 (.04)	−.15 (.04)	−.12 (.04)	−.09 (.04)	−.04 (.03)	−.01 (.02)		1.19 (.09)	−.22 (.14)	−.13 (.09)	.06 (.09)	.42	.981 (.013)
y_t	1948:1–1982:4	6.22 (.01)	.52 (.17)	.82 (.26)	1.52 (.32)	1.60 (.36)	1.33 (.37)	1.03 (.36)	.65 (.32)	.41 (.26)	.01 (.18)	3.31 (.06)	1.07 (.09)	−.15 (.13)	.02 (.13)	.09 (.09)	3.86	.971 (.012)
Δy_t	1948:1–1982:4	3.12 (.41)	.46 (.16)	.70 (.26)	1.34 (.34)	1.38 (.39)	1.14 (.41)	.86 (.39)	.52 (.34)	.30 (.27)	−.05 (.16)		.38 (.09)	−.06 (.09)	.01 (.09)	−.13 (.09)	3.64	.973 (.020)
B. Money stock – base																		
U_t	1948:1–1981:3	5.31 (.38)	−.01 (.02)	−.01 (.02)	−.02 (.03)	−.02 (.03)	−.05 (.03)	−.03 (.03)	.00 (.03)	.00 (.02)	.01 (.02)		1.24 (.09)	−.26 (.14)	−.10 (.14)	.03 (.09)	.41	.984 (.047)
y_t	1948:1–1981:3	6.21 (.01)	.15 (.16)	.22 (.22)	.14 (.28)	.26 (.28)	.29 (.29)	.22 (.29)	.06 (.27)	.16 (.23)	.09 (.16)	3.40 (.06)	1.10 (.09)	−.19 (.13)	.01 (.13)	−.09 (.09)	4.05	.925 (.122)
Δy_t	1948:1–1981:3	3.77 (.46)	.07 (.14)	.09 (.22)	.01 (.27)	.09 (.30)	.10 (.31)	.02 (.31)	−.11 (.28)	.00 (.23)	.00 (.14)		.37 (.09)	.04 (.10)	−.06 (.10)	−.13 (.09)	3.95	.973 (.116)

Notes: U_t is the unemployment rate, y_t is the log of real GNP, and Δy_t is the annual percentage growth rate of real GNP. The coefficients a_j are the estimated coefficients on current ($j=0$) and lagged ($j=1,...,8$) money surprises and b is the estimated coefficient for a time trend. The coefficients are estimated using a generalized least squares procedure where $r_1,...,r_4$ describes the autocorrelation structure of the errors; $s(e)$ is the standard error of the regression. Φ is the propagation ratio. Large sample standard errors are in parentheses.

The results in the first equation in Table 2 indicate a significantly negative impact of unanticipated money on the unemployment rate that reaches a peak with a lag of about three or four quarters.[8] However, the error term in this equation contains substantial serial correlation, which should come as no surprise given our discussion of equations (2.4) and (2.6). This serial correlation arises from a mixture of the same internal propagation mechanism that transmits the nominal shock over time as well as potential serial correlation in exogenous real factors.

The unemployment propagation ratio Φ is estimated to be .98, with a large sample standard error of .013. Thus, in the context of the model outlined in the previous section, 98 percent of the explanatory power of unanticipated money is attributable to the internal propagation mechanism. Without such a mechanism the effects of unanticipated money on unemployment would be largely uninteresting. Thus, if one maintains the view that monetary disturbances are a central business cycle impulse, then understanding the nature and character of business cycles requires an understanding of propagation mechanisms.

We have also estimated equation (2.7) using the log of real GNP (y_t) as the dependent variable and a differenced version where the growth rate of real GNP is the dependent variable. The results are similar and are reported in Table 2 as well.[9] There is a significantly positive relation between unanticipated money and output that reaches a peak at lag 3. The propagation ratio for both equations exceeds .97, supporting once again the proposition that propagation plays the dominant role in shaping the business cycle, at least in the context of Barro's implementation of the equilibrium monetary theory of the cycle.

Results using the monetary base

In some prior research [King and Plosser (1984a)] we have constructed model economies in which inside money shocks, rather than being exogenous, are driven by real factors. Consequently, we re-estimate the reduced form using the monetary base as the exogenous monetary aggregate. The results are presented in part B of Table 2. Unanticipated base

---

have estimated a vector autoregression and that the coefficients on our unanticipated money variable isolate one portion of the moving average response function of that system. Our identifying restriction would appear through the choice of an orthogonalization of the variance–covariance matrix of the innovations. This perspective makes clear that other orthogonalizations could be chosen and would lead to different impulse response functions and thus different propagation ratios.

[8] These results are similar to those obtained by Barro and Rush (1980), despite the fact that we employ a different money prediction equation.

[9] Once again, these results are similar to those reported by Barro and Rush (1980).

growth is generated in a manner analogous to unexpected money growth above. The results are not supportive of the view that exogenous surprise movements in base growth have significant real effects. They suggest that the predominate source of correlation between money surprises and real variables is with the inside money component of M_1. Although the propagation ratios are almost as large as those obtained using M_1, they probably cannot be relied on given the insignificant results. That is, we suspect that the large sample standard errors of Φ are not very good in this instance.

Price surprises and real activity

Some theoretical analyses [e.g., Lucas (1973) and Fischer (1977)] highlight the role of surprise movements in the price level. In these analyses, the nominal impulse is $\tilde{p}_t = p_t - E_{t-1}p_t$. Consequently, we estimate real quantity specifications of the form

$$y_{jt} = \sum_{h=0}^{H} \alpha_{jh}\tilde{p}_{t-h} + y_{jt}^*, \tag{3.1}$$

where

$$\tilde{p}_{t-h} = p_{t-h} - E_{t-h-1}p_{t-h}.$$

The estimation of the price surprise coefficients $\{\alpha_{jh}\}_{h=0}^{H}$ involves some econometric issues discussed by Sargent (1976). The "error term" in this equation represents omitted real factors influencing the economy y_{jt}^* and is serially correlated for reasons discussed earlier. Further, with the price level determined by monetary equilibrium, surprise movements in the price level will be correlated with surprise movements in real determinants of economic activity $(y_{jt}^* - E_{t-1}y_{jt}^*)$. That is, as Sargent (1976) notes, it is not possible to consistently estimate the impact of price surprises by least squares; some form of instrumental variables procedure is required.

For purposes of discussion, we focus on the relation [previously considered by Sargent (1976)] between unemployment and price surprises. We start by estimating an eight-variable, fourth-order vector autoregression with a large set of macroeconomic variables: inflation, unemployment, money growth, the Treasury-bill rate, labor force participation rate, population growth rate, growth rate of nominal wages, and the growth rate of real federal expenditures.

Correlation of innovations

The correlation matrix of one-step-ahead prediction errors from the multivariate time-series model is shown in Table 3. Of principal interest for

Table 3. *Correlation matrix of innovations*

Variable	Abbre-viation	Δp_t	U_t	Δm_t	R_t	l_t	Δn_t	Δw_t
Inflation rate	Δp_t							
Unemployment rate	U_t	−.20 (.02)						
Money growth rate	Δm_t	.19 (.02)	−.29 (.00)					
Treasury bill rate	R_t	−.15 (.08)	−.35 (.00)	−.02 (.79)				
Labor force participation rate	l_t	.19 (.03)	−.01 (.94)	−.01 (.92)	.03 (.76)			
Population growth rate	Δn_t	.12 (.16)	−.03 (.71)	.07 (.45)	−.12 (.16)	.09 (.27)		
Growth rate of wages	Δw_t	.41 (.00)	−.06 (.52)	.03 (.69)	−.17 (.05)	−.06 (.49)	.03 (.72)	
Growth rate of real federal purchases	Δg_t	−.03 (.77)	.02 (.82)	−.05 (.57)	−.19 (.03)	−.09 (.28)	.12 (.16)	.06 (.51)

Notes: Innovations are obtained from a vector autoregression using all the variables in the table. *P*-values associated with the hypothesis that the correlation is zero are in parentheses.

current purposes is the fact that the correlation between money growth and price surprises is small but significant, while the correlation between price surprise and another aggregate demand variable (real federal expenditure) is insignificant. This reflects a more general difficulty we encountered in constructing an instrumental variable for price surprises: It is difficult to find variables that are significantly correlated with price surprises and whose innovations are plausibly econometrically exogenous – that is, uncorrelated with current or future y_j^*. (For example, nominal wage innovations satisfy the former but not the latter condition.)

Estimates of Price Surprise Effects

Table 4 presents some alternative estimates of the effects of price surprises on unemployment. Part A estimates the price surprise coefficients using a variety of different estimation techniques. The unemployment rate is expressed as a percentage while inflation (and its surprises) is an annual percentage rate. Thus, if $a_0 = .5$, then this implies that a one percentage-

Table 4. *Price surprises and unemployment*

A. Distributed lag effects of price surprises, $U_t = \text{const.} + \sum_{j=0}^{8} a_j \tilde{p}_{t-j} + e_t$

Estimation method	a_0	a_1	a_2	a_3	a_4	a_5	a_6	a_7	a_8	r_1	r_2	r_3	r_4	Φ
OLS	-.02	.00	-.04	-.05	-.02	.01	-.02	.01	.09					
Autoregressive errors	-.01 (.03)	-.02 (.04)	-.05 (.05)	-.06 (.06)	-.06 (.06)	-.07 (.06)	-.05 (.05)	-.05 (.04)	-.00 (.02)	1.16	-.20	-.04	-.02	.996 (.019)
IV (all lags)	-.24 (.04)	-.43 (.06)	-.71 (.09)	-.79 (.12)	-.72 (.13)	-.56 (.12)	-.43 (.09)	-.16 (.06)	.03 (.04)	1.39	-.07	-.54	.15	.977 (.006)
IV (first lag only)	-.08 (.02)	-.05 (.05)	-.08 (.07)	-.12 (.08)	-.14 (.09)	-.14 (.08)	-.12 (.07)	-.09 (.07)	-.01 (.05)	1.47	-.23	-.44	.13	.921 (.073)

B. Sargent's autoregressive model, $U_t = \text{const.} + a_0(\tilde{p}_t) + \sum_{j=1}^{4} \lambda_j U_{t-j} + e_t$

Estimation method	a_0	λ_1	λ_2	λ_3	λ_4	Φ^*
OLS	-.04 (.02)	1.44 (.09)	-.35 (.15)	-.28 (.15)	.15 (.09)	.95*
IV	-.33 (.16)	1.47 (.08)	-.36 (.15)	-.30 (.15)	.15 (.09)	.95*

point shock to the annual inflation rate is associated with a one-half percentage-point effect on unemployment in the initial quarter. The first two rows are estimates using the raw price surprises, with and without a correction for serial correlation. In both cases, the coefficients are numerically small and insignificant according to conventional statistical standards.

The final two rows of part A provide estimates using current money growth as an instrumental variable for price surprises.[10] In the first instrumental-variables estimate, we use instruments for current and lagged price shocks. Thus, the results amount to a rescaling of the earlier Table 2 estimates of effects of unanticipated money. The estimation routine is two-stage and involves a correction for a fourth-order autoregressive error term. (Although this procedure is not efficient, it is consistent under the assumption that unanticipated money growth is a valid instrument.) These instrumental-variables estimators are numerically larger than the OLS estimates, and are significant by conventional statistical standards. The implied value of the propagation ratio is .977, with an asymptotic standard error of .006. Thus the bulk of nominal shock effects is again due to propagation mechanisms.

It is appropriate to be cautious, however, about interpreting this instrumental-variables estimate. First, as discussed earlier, monetary shocks may not be exogenous and hence may not be a legitimate instrument. Second, even if monetary shocks are exogenous, the R^2 of the first-stage regression is very small (.04) and thus money shocks are not a particularly good predictor of $\tilde{p}_t$. Third, there is evidence that the fourth-order autogressive model of the error term is inappropriate, so that the standard errors calculated under that assumption are presumably inaccurate. Specifically, in the fourth row of Table 4, we employ an instrument only for the current price surprise in the second stage of our estimation routine, following a procedure proposed by Hatanaka (1976). If a fourth-order autoregression is appropriate, the estimates should be close to those in the third row. But in fact they are substantially attenuated, which indicates either misspecification of the error term [e.g., see Hausman (1978) or Plosser, Schwert, and White (1982)] and/or an illegitimate instrument.

Autoregressive estimates

For purposes of comparison, we also estimate the specification due to Sargent (1976), in which unemployment depends on price surprises $\tilde{p}_t$, a serially uncorrelated supply shock ϵ_t, and past values of unemployment.

---

[10] That is, the instrument for the price surprise was formed by regressing price surprises against the current value of money growth and four lags of all variables in Table 3. The estimated coefficient of prices on current money was .16, statistically significant at the usual levels.

$$U_t = \alpha_0(\tilde{p}_t) + \sum_{h=1}^{H} \lambda_h U_{t-h} + \epsilon_t. \tag{3.2}$$

In terms of our earlier discussion, this sort of specification is appropriate if the real forcing variables s_t are serially uncorrelated and the effects of propagation mechanisms are captured by an Hth order polynomial distributed lag.[11]

It is straightforward to demonstrate that the propagation ratio for the Sargent specification is simply the R^2 of an Hth order autoregression (absent the price surprise term), which is .94. That is, because it is assumed that real disturbances are strictly temporary, all of the serial correlation in the time series is due to internal propagation mechanisms.

As with our earlier estimates in part A of Table 4, in part B the impact effect of price surprises in the Sargent-style autoregressions is much higher with the instrumental-variables estimator (with money surprises as the instrument) than with the ordinary least square estimate. The Table 4 estimate implies that a 3 percent surprise inflation causes a 1 percent decline in unemployment on impact, with this being subsequently magnified as it is transmitted over time.

Price surprises vs. real factors

It is of some interest to examine the decomposition of unemployment into effects of price surprises and real factors, using estimates reported in part A of Table 4. That is, in terms of our earlier discussion, we examine estimated decomposition of y_{jt} into

$$\sum_{h=0}^{H} \alpha_{jh} \tilde{p}_{t-h} \quad \text{and} \quad y_{jt}^*.$$

We focus on two versions of this decomposition. The first is the ordinary least-square decomposition which, by construction, limits the role for real factors (in the sense that the distributed lag on price surprises is selected so as to have the largest contribution to variance of unemployment while maintaining orthogonality with the error term). From the Table 4 estimates, however, the estimated coefficients are small and switch sign frequently. Thus, the price surprise component $\sum_{h=0}^{H} \alpha_{jh} \tilde{p}_{t-h}$ (see Table 4) does not exhibit much serial correlation and appears as a choppy series (see Figure 1), exhibiting few business cycle characteristics. Consequently, real factors assume the more familiar pattern, with a high degree of serial correlation (see Table 4) with protracted ups and downs (see Figure 2). In this case, there is (by construction) no correlation between price surprise and real business cycle components.

---

[11] As discussed previously, part A estimates do not appear to be consistent with a simple autoregressive model for real factors.

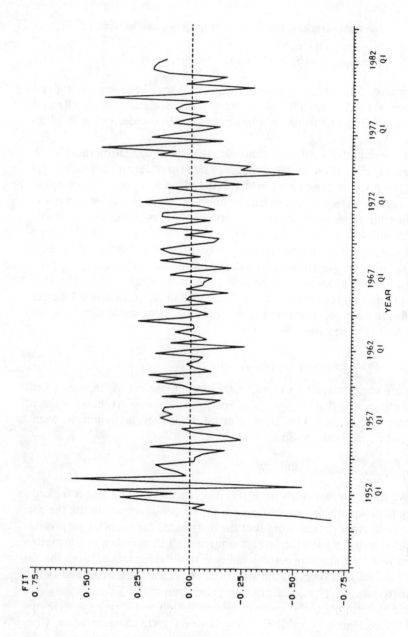

Figure 1. Price surprise component of unemployment (OLS coefficient estimates).

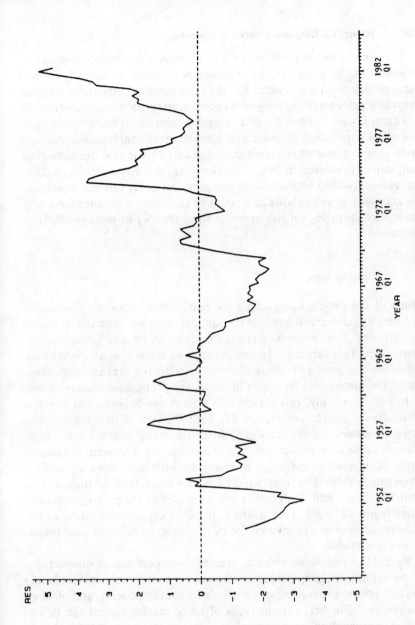

Figure 2. Real component of unemployment (OLS coefficient estimates).

The second decomposition we study involves instrumental-variables estimates of the price surprise parameters reported in Table 4, formed using money as an instrument. But the price surprise component employs the whole price surprise, not just its projection on monetary surprises. In this case, Figure 3 shows the price surprise component has a strong positive serial correlation estimate and a much more characteristic business cycle shape. These characteristics are shared by the real business cycle component presented in Figure 4. However, there is a strong negative correlation ($-.93$) between these components; under this interpretation, the economy is less volatile as a result of real factors because these produce price surprises (of the opposite sign) that set in motion offsetting variations.

4   Conclusions

Much of the debate surrounding the equilibrium monetary theories of business has concerned whether (i) nominal surprises are a major source of economic fluctuations and (ii) the mechanism by which nominal surprises affect real variables. In this paper,[12] we argue that an understanding of the character and nature of business cycles requires an understanding of the mechanism by which impulses are propagated through time.

In fact, ironically, this is especially true if one believes that business cycles are induced by surprises in M_1, for the effects of Barro-style unanticipated money shocks are distributed over many quarters (far longer than plausible information lags). In this paper, we document the importance of internal propagation mechanisms with a measure we call the propagation ratio. For unanticipated money regressions of the sort presented by Barro and Rush (1980), our estimates of the propagation ratio range from .92 to .98. That is, the bulk of the explanatory power of unanticipated money is accounted for by the presence of an internal propagation mechanism.

Recent theoretical research has stressed the importance of various types of capital in producing persistent effects of temporary shocks, including finished goods inventories, inventories of goods in process, and plant or equipment.[13] Further, various types of labor market capital can be important propagation mechanisms [see Lucas and Sargent (1979) and King

---

[12] See also King and Plosser (1984b).

[13] Blinder and Fischer (1981) study finished good inventories. Long and Plosser's (1983) one-period intertemporal production structure can be interpreted as a type of goods-in-process inventory. Kydland and Prescott (1982) stress multiperiod gestation of investment and effects of plant/equipment accumulation.

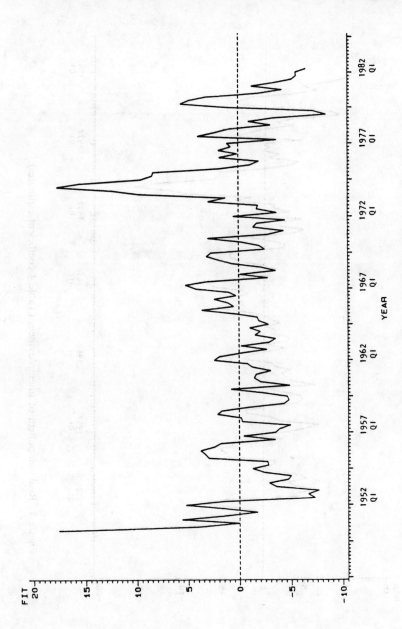

Figure 3. Price surprise component of unemployment (Table 4 coefficient estimates).

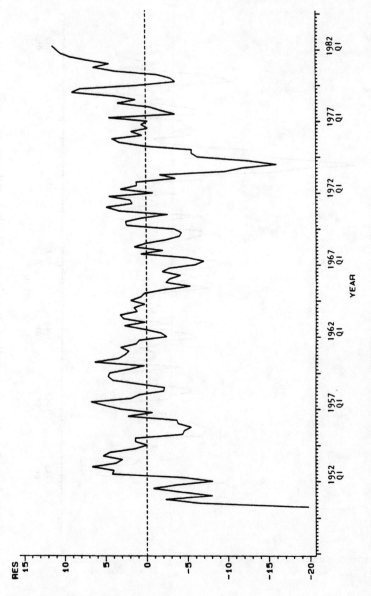

Figure 4. Real component of unemployment (Table 4 coefficient estimates).

and Plosser (1984b)]. These theoretical investigations provide foundations for future, detailed empirical inquiries into the structure of propagation mechanisms in business cycles. In future empirical research based on these foundations, we envision a valuable interplay – between multivariate time-series modeling and structural model building – in determining the empirically relevant mechanisms that generate business cycles.

Data appendix

The Citibase data tape was the basic source for all series. The series were obtained in monthly, non–seasonally adjusted form or in quarterly seasonally adjusted form. For monthly series, quarterly values were selected as the last month of each quarter.

The following series (summarized in Table 1) were employed and are listed below along with variable name, description, and Citibase identifier:

U: Unemployment, all workers 16 years and older (LHUR), monthly, NSA.

y: Gross National Product, 1972 dollars (GNP), quarterly, SA.

P: GNP Implicit price deflator, (GD), quarterly SA.

B: Monetary base, produced by splicing several Citibase series, monthly NSA:

    after 1958, monetary base (FMFB),

    before 1959, sum of member bank reserve (FCMB) and currency held by the public (FMSCU).

Series prior to 1959 was multiplied by a ratio of annual averages for 1959 to scale appropriately.

M: Narrow money stock, produced by splicing two Citibase series, monthly NSA:

    after 1958 (FMI),

    before 1959 (FMF).

Same splicing techniques as used for the monetary base.

g: Federal government purchases, 1972 dollars (GGE72), quarterly, SA.

l: Labor force participation rate, defined as the ratio of civilian labor force (LHC) to population (POPT16), monthly, NSA.

W: Average hourly earnings for production workers, excluding overtime, in manufacturing, monthly, NSA.

n: Population over age of 16 (POPT16) monthly, NSA.

R: Three-month Treasury bill rate, percent per annum, (FYGM3), monthly, NSA.

REFERENCES

Barro, R. J. 1977. "Unanticipated Money Growth and Unemployment in the United States." *American Economic Review* 67: 101–15.

1978. "Unanticipated Money, Output, and the Price Level in the United States." *Journal of Political Economy* 86: 549–80.

1980. "A Capital Market in an Equilibrium Business Cycle Model." *Econometrica* 48: 1393–1417.

Barro, R. J., and M. Rush. 1980. "Unanticipated Money and Economic Activity." In S. Fischer (ed.), *Rational Expectations and Economic Policy.* Chicago: University of Chicago Press (for the National Bureau of Economic Research).

Blinder, A. S., and S. Fischer. 1981. "Inventories, Rational Expectations and the Business Cycle." *Journal of Monetary Economics* 8: 277–304.

Fischer, Stanley. 1977. "Long-Term Contracts Rational Expectations and the Optimal Money Supply Rule." *Journal of Political Economy* 85: 191–205.

Hatanaka, M. 1976. "Several Efficient Two-Step Estimators for the Dynamic Simultaneous Equations Model with Autoregressive Disturbances." *Journal of Econometrics* 4: 189–204.

Hausman, J. A. 1978. "Specification Tests in Econometrics." *Econometrica* 46: 1251–72.

Hayek, F. A. 1931. *Prices and Production.* London: George Routledge & Sons.

King, R. G. 1981. "Monetary Information and Monetary Neutrality." *Journal of Monetary Economics* 7: 195–206.

1983. "Notes on Linear Business Cycle Models." Unpublished manuscript.

King, R. G., and C. I. Plosser. 1984a. "Money, Credit and Prices in a Real Business Cycle." *American Economic Review* 74: 363–80.

1984b. "Production, Growth and Business Cycles." Unpublished manuscript.

Kydland, F., and E. C. Prescott. 1982. "Time to Build and Aggregate Fluctuations." *Econometrica* 50: 1345–70.

Long, J. B., and C. I. Plosser. 1983. "Real Business Cycles." *Journal of Political Economy* 91: 39–69.

Lucas, R. E., Jr. 1972. "Expectations and the Neutrality of Money." *Journal of Economic Theory* 103–24.

1973. "Some International Evidence or Output Inflation Tradeoffs." *American Economic Review* 63: 326–34.

1977. "Understanding Business Cycles." In K. Brunner and A. Meltzer (eds.), *Stabilization of the Domestic and International Economy,* Carnegie-Rochester Conference Series, Vol. 4, pp. 1–29. Amsterdam: North-Holland.

1980. "Methods and Problems in Business Cycle Theory." *Journal of Money, Credit and Banking* 12: 696–715.

Lucas, R. E., and T. J. Sargent. 1979. "After Keynesian Macroeconomics." *Federal Reserve Bank of Minnesota Quarterly Review* 23: 1–16.

Plosser, C. I., G. W. Schwert, and H. White. 1982. "Differencing as a Test of Specification." *International Economic Review* 23: 535–52.

Sargent, T. J. 1976. "A Classical Macroeconometric Model for the United States." *Journal of Political Economy* 84: 207–37.

CHAPTER 14

A rational expectations framework for short-run policy analysis

Christopher A. Sims

1   Introduction

There is increasing recognition that Lucas's (1976) critique of econometric policy evaluation, at least under its usual interpretation, is logically
flawed. The point has been forcefully made recently by Sargent (1984) and
by Cooley, Leroy, and Rahman (1984) (henceforth referred to as CLR), as
well as in my own paper (1982). The problem is that if the parameters of
the policy "rule" are subject to change, as they must be if it makes sense
to evaluate changes in them, then the public must recognize this fact and
have a probability distribution over the parameters of the rule. But then
these parameters are themselves policy variables, taking on a time series
of values drawn from some probability law. Predicting how the economy
will behave if we set the parameters of the rule at some value and keep
them there is logically equivalent to predicting the behavior of the economy conditional on a certain path of a policy variable. Yet this is just the
kind of exercise that Lucas claimed to be meaningless.

It is also evident that the methods of policy evaluation that Lucas criticized are still in wide use nine years after the appearance of his paper.
During discussions of monetary and fiscal policy, statistical models prepared by the Congressional Budget Office, the Federal Reserve Board,
numerous other agencies, and by private entities are used to prepare predictions of the likely future path of the economy, conditional on various
possible paths for policy variables. These conditional projections influence policy makers' views of the likely consequences of the choices they
must make. Though Lucas suggested an alternative paradigm for policy
analysis, it is still little used.

This paper is a revision of one prepared for presentation at the "New Approaches to Monetary Economics" conference, May 23-24, 1985, at the IC² Institute of the University of Texas at Austin. The research for the paper was supported in part by NSF grant SES 8309329.

294 Christopher A. Sims

Nonetheless, we are not quite to the point where well-trained young macroeconomists can collaborate – without feeling queasy – in preparing and interpreting conditional projections of the effects of alternative paths for policy variables. Sargent, while clearly explaining the problems with the rational-expectations paradigm for policy analysis and finding no way around them, claims we must ignore them if we are to avoid the conclusion that policy recommendations of any kind are meaningless. CLR show that projections of the future path of the economy conditional on paths of policy variables are not meaningless, even in the presence of shifts in policy rule. But they never explicitly address the central question of whether such conditional projections could ever be used in the process of policy choice without invalidating them. My own paper (1982) asserts that policy choice based on conditional projection from models that do not identify the parameters of tastes and technology can be logically coherent, but it does not support the assertion with formal modeling and many remain unconvinced.

The remainder of this paper attempts to make that assertion more convincing by analyzing more closely how properly constructed and interpreted conditional projections sidestep the Lucas critique, and by presenting examples of model economies in which policy makers steadily make good use of conditional projections from loosely identified statistical models.

2 Finding a coherent interpretation of the Lucas critique

Lucas formulates his critique most baldly and succinctly at the beginning of Section 6 of his paper, where he writes ". . . there are compelling empirical and theoretical reasons for believing that a structure of the form

$$y_{t+1} = F(y_t, x_t, \theta, \epsilon_t) \tag{2.1}$$

(F known, θ fixed, x_t 'arbitrary') will not be of use for forecasting and policy evaluation in actual economies." He goes on to observe that for short-term forecasting the problem can be avoided – indeed, has been avoided in practice – by allowing the parameters to drift in time. But for policy evaluation he argues that a completely different approach is required, in which models are given the form

$$x_t = G(y_t, \gamma, \eta_t), \tag{2.2}$$

$$y_{t+1} = F(y_t, x_t, \theta(\gamma), \epsilon_t), \tag{2.3}$$

where G and F are known, γ is a fixed parameter vector, and η_t and ϵ_t are vectors of disturbances. The econometric problem is now that of estimating the function $\theta(\gamma)$, not a fixed vector of real numbers θ, and policy evaluation is performed by considering the effects of alternative settings for γ, not by comparing choices of paths for x.

These assertions make no sense if taken at face value. The most widely used method for allowing for parameter drift in forecasting models takes those parameters to be a time series evolving according to

$$\theta(t) = H(\theta(t-1), \alpha, v(t)), \tag{2.4}$$

where v is a vector of random disturbances, H is a known function, and α is a fixed vector of parameters. By recursively substituting lagged versions of (2.4) into itself, we can obtain

$$\theta(t) = H_1(\alpha, V(t), \theta(0)), \tag{2.5}$$

where $V(t) = \{v(1), \ldots, v(t)\}$. If the influence of $\theta(0)$ on H_1 is nonnegligible, we can merge it with the parameter vector α to form the new parameter vector $\alpha^* = (\alpha, \theta(0))$, so that

$$\theta(t) = H^*(\alpha^*, V(t)). \tag{2.6}$$

Substituting (2.6) into (2.1) produces

$$y_{t+1} = F(y_t, x_t, H^*(\alpha^*, V(t)), \epsilon_t) = F^*(y_t, x_t, \alpha^*, \epsilon^*(t)), \tag{2.7}$$

where $\epsilon^*(t) = (V(t), \epsilon(t))$. Now obviously F^* in (2.7) has exactly the same form as F in (2.1). If a "time-varying parameter" model such as that described by F^* can in fact provide good forecasts, which Lucas claims it can, then it would seem he cannot consistently claim also that a structure of the form (2.1) "will not be of use for forecasting . . . in actual economies." Of course, if F in (2.1) is linear, or in some other sense "simple," F^* in (2.7) will generally not be. But Lucas says only that F is known, not that it is linear, and he undoubtedly meant to be saying something stronger than that we need nonlinear models.

There is a similar problem with the claim that evaluating policy by using (2.2) and (2.3) to gauge the consequences of changing γ is different from using (2.1) to gauge the consequences of various choices of time path for x. The fixed parameter γ is itself necessarily a time series with at least two possible values (the value before we change policy and the value after). Putting the appropriate subscript on γ and substituting (2.2) into (2.3) gives us

$$y_{t+1} = F(y_t, G(y_t, \gamma_t, \mathfrak{M}_t), \theta(\gamma_t), \epsilon_t) = F^{**}(y_t, \gamma_t, \epsilon_t^{**}), \tag{2.8}$$

where $\epsilon_t^{**} = (\epsilon_t, \eta_t)$. Now we have transformed (2.2) and (2.3) into (2.8), wherein F^{**} has exactly the functional form of F, with γ playing the role of x. There are no unknown parameters in (2.8) at all, but of course in practice there would be unknown parameters in the functional form of the $\theta(\gamma_t)$ function, to take the place of the original fixed θ parameters.

Again, if F were linear then F^{**} would probably not be, but surely most economists interpret Lucas's argument as asserting more than that we need nonlinear models to do good policy analysis.

It is also true that Lucas wants us to take γ as fixed. Of course if we contemplate changing γ it cannot really be fixed, but the spirit of the argument is that we ought to consider once-and-for-all changes in γ – that is, paths of γ_t that are constant up to some date T and constant thereafter, with a discontinuity at T. Furthermore, according to this interpretation we ought to concentrate on predicting the long-run effects of the change after γ has been at its new level long enough for behavior to have completely adjusted. From the point of view of equation (2.8), this is the suggestion that we should limit ourselves to comparative statics based on the long-run properties of the model. But this recommendation, if we admit that F^{**} is the same form as displayed by standard econometric models, is not at all revolutionary. And it is a dubious recommendation – in practice, econometric models are probably less reliable in their long-run properties than in their short-run properties.

Some readers undoubtedly have given Lucas's critique the interpretation outlined above. Sargent's paper is one example. Under this interpretation, equation (2.1) is considered general enough to correspond to any statistical model relating endogenous variables y to lagged endogenous variables, policy variables x, some parameters θ, and random disturbances ϵ. The claim is that any use of such a model to make policy will have to change the model, making the model invalid. This leads to skepticism toward all use of data in forming policy, since there is no way to do so without using a model in the general form (2.1). Concentration on the choice of parameters of a policy rule is of no help, since there is no logical distinction between such parameters and policy variables. Thus on this interpretation, if one takes seriously the rational-expectations critique of standard econometric policy evaluation, it applies with equal force to the rational-expectations program for correct econometric evaluation of policy.

As we will see through an example in Section 3, the argument in this form is simply incorrect. It is possible for an optimizing, benevolent, immortal policy maker to make policy every period forever, by choosing among conditional projections from a statistical model while the model remains accurate. However, this version of the argument distorts the original. When Lucas writes (2.1) in Section 6 of his paper, he introduces it as a "structure" of the form (2.1). By this he probably means to imply that F is not some general statistical model, but rather the kind of entity he described in more detail when using (2.1) earlier in the paper. There he requires that "the function F and the parameter vector θ are derived from decision rules (demand and supply functions) of agents in the economy, and these decisions are, theoretically, optimal given the situation in which agent is placed." Furthermore, in the examples Lucas considers there is in every case one or more functions contained in the model that represent or are directly affected by agents' expectation-formation rules.

The lesson of rational expectations is that, when we use a model in whose functional form is embedded agents' expectational rules, we are likely to make errors even in forecasting if we insist that those expectational rules are fixed through time, and that we will make even more serious errors in policy evaluation if we pretend that those rules will remain fixed despite changes in policy that make them clearly suboptimal. The difference between (2.1) and the system (2.2)–(2.3) as frameworks for policy analysis is not the superficial one that in the latter we think of ourselves as choosing a fixed parameter while in the former we are choosing arbitrary values of policy variables x. The difference is that in (2.1) the parameters in fact depend on the hidden policy variable γ. If we try to use (2.1) to guess the effects of various x paths that are in fact accompanied by changes in γ, we will make errors. The advantage of (2.2)–(2.3), or the equivalent model (2.8), is that either of them takes proper account of the effect of γ on θ.

Thus we should not necessarily expect a different mathematical form or a different probabilistic treatment of policy variables for models that take proper account of rational expectations. It is even in principle possible for such models to have F^{**} functions that turn out to be a set of linear stochastic difference equations, with the corresponding mistaken F function being of complicated nonlinear form.

Most important, the problems of identification for rational-expectations models are not fundamentally different from those for what used to be standard models. In the happy circumstance where the historically observed data contain exogenous variation in policy along the lines we are currently contemplating, we can estimate the effects of our policy choices by reduced-form modeling. We can estimate regressions of current data on current and past policy variables and correctly use the results to project the likely effects of our policy choices. To do this we need not separate the effects of policy occurring directly from those occurring indirectly through modifications in expectation-formation rules of the public. It is exactly this point that is so neatly laid out by CLR.

This is not to deny that identification is a hard problem. Identification for purposes of policy evaluation is roughly the same hard problem whether or not we take account of rational expectations. Historical data on policy variables will usually reflect some systematic pattern of response of policy to disturbances originating elsewhere in the economy. Therefore conditional distributions of other variables given policy variables do not necessarily correspond to conditional distributions of those variables given autonomously induced changes in policy variables.

3   Optimal policy using conditional projections

If policy is made optimally, it is always reacting correctly to all available information about the state of the economy. Presumably it does not then display capricious or arbitrary variation. This suggests that it should contain no autonomous randomness, so that policy variables should be exact functions of past data. In this case, there would be no way to separate the effects of policy variables from the effects of variables that policy depends on, except by use of strong auxiliary assumptions. On the other hand, if policy is made suboptimally it might contain a lot of capricious variation; we might then easily obtain estimates of the effect of this variation. Yet if policy makers use our estimates to improve policy, the amount of autonomous variation in policy will shrink, the probability structure of the economy is likely to change, and our estimates may quickly become obsolete.

Is there any way that policy could both be chosen optimally, on the basis of a correct model, and at the same time contain enough autonomous variation to allow accurate estimation of the effects of deliberately induced variations in policy?

It is not hard to see that the answer must be yes. All that is required is the existence of some source of variation in policy choice which, as far as the public is concerned, is indistinguishable from an error or a capricious shift in policy choice. One obvious possibility arises when we recognize that macroeconomic policy is in fact set through a political process, in which groups with varying knowledge and objectives contest to influence policy. The public does not know with certainty the identity, the objectives, or the relative political strength of these groups. Hence actual policy always contains an unpredictable element from this source. The public has no way of distinguishing an error by one of the political groups in choosing its target policy from a random disturbance in policy from the political process. Hence members of such a group can accurately project the effects of various policy settings they might aim for by using historically observed reactions to random shifts in policy induced by the political process. The group will itself, if it behaves optimally according to its own objective function, make its target policy a deterministic function of data it observes. But it can implement that function correctly by using, at each date, a statistical model to make conditional projections of the effects of alternative policy variable paths, and choosing the projected path it likes best.

CLR include regime switches in their model, but provide no explanation for why policy differs under the two regimes. It should be apparent, though, that something at least very much like their model could emerge if their two regimes were generated by two optimizing political coalitions.[1]

Although policy randomness due to political struggles is probably the most realistic and important source of identifying variation in policy, it leads to analytically challenging models. A simpler way to approach the question of how to design good policy posits a unitary policy authority. In such a framework, the most plausible source of identifying variation in policy is noisy information available to the policy authority, information that is visible to the econometrician (if at all) only with a delay. The optimizing policy maker will use the noisy information, but because it is noisy his use of it will introduce into policy a random error. The reaction of the economy to this random error will provide a statistical basis for determining the reaction of the economy to hypothetical optimization errors. To some it may be apparent immediately that this set-up will work. But since I am not aware of a closely similar construction in the literature, we work out an explicit model here.

The typical agent in this economy chooses the vector C_t (consumption) at t. The government chooses G_t at t, government activity per capita. Utility of the agent is

$$E\left[\sum_{t=1}^{\infty} R^t \cdot 5(C_t'AC_t + G_t'BG_t + K_t'FK_t)\right]. \tag{3.1}$$

The technology imposes the constraint

$$K_t = HC_t + MG_t + NK_{t-1} + X_t, \tag{3.2}$$

[1] Recently Roberds (1985) has produced an explicit model that goes some way toward capturing optimal behavior of stochastically alternating regimes of policy makers. Like CLR, he holds the regime switch to be a purely exogenous random process; but instead of arbitrarily changing policy rules, regime switches in Roberds's model change policy makers' objective functions. His model is not ready to be tacked onto CLR's, however, because it does not follow CLR in giving the public an inference problem of trying to determine the current regime. This also means that, unlike CLR, Roberds does not make the stochastic regime switches a source of identifying variation in policy; the public sees regime switches directly in Roberds's model, so they are an extra observable policy variable rather than an underlying source of variation in observable policy variables. Roberds also ignores the interesting problem of strategic interaction between the two regimes. Each regime takes account of the fact that the public is modeling its behavior, but neither attempts to model the behavior of the other regime or considers the possibility that its own behavior could affect the behavior of the other regime. It would be interesting to see work (along the lines Roberds has begun) that ties more directly to the setting dealt with by CLR.

where the stochastic process X is exogenous to both private agents and the government. Although this framework is very general and looks like the canonical quadratic-linear control problem, it is unconventional in that it does not assert that X_t is i.i.d., only that its evolution is unaffected by choices of G, C, or K.

The government and the agents both try to maximize the same objective function (3.1). There is an "information process" containing three subvectors: Q_t, W_t, and Z_t. When private agents choose C_t, they do so with knowledge of all values of Q_s, W_s, and Z_s for $s \leq t$. The government must choose G_t based on knowledge only of these variables for $s \leq t-1$, plus an observation on Z_t.

We assume special relationships among Q, W, X, and Z to generate our example: Q and W are Granger causally prior to Z, X is a linear function of current and past Q and W alone, and Z_t has the form of a noisy measurement of W_t. That is, assuming Q, W, and Z form a linear process with an autoregressive representation,

$$E_t\begin{bmatrix} Q_{t+1} \\ W_{t+1} \end{bmatrix} = a * \begin{bmatrix} Q_t \\ W_t \end{bmatrix}, \tag{3.3}$$

$$E[Z_t \mid W_s, Q_s, Z_{s-1}, \text{ all } s \leq t] = W_t, \tag{3.4}$$

$$X_t = b * \begin{bmatrix} Q_t \\ W_t \end{bmatrix}, \tag{3.5}$$

where $a(s) = b(s) = 0$ for $s < 0$ (a and b are one-sided) and $E_t[\cdot]$ stands for $E[\cdot \mid Q_s, W_s, Z_s, \text{ all } s \leq t]$.

The Granger causal priority assumption means that the information the government obtains at t is strictly redundant from the point of view of agents at t. This means in turn that the solution to this problem can be found as if there were a single optimizing agent who must choose G_t at a stage where his information set is smaller than at the next stage (when he chooses C_t). This would be impossible if (say) private agents also observed only noisy information on X_t at t, but with a noise different from that facing the government.

Because K_{t-1} enters the constraint (3.2), the public cares about future values of G, leaving a role for the rational expectations hypothesis. Because the model is quadratic-linear, we can solve it using dynamic certainty-equivalence.

The main point of the example does not depend on the explicit solution of the model. Consider the government's problem at t, which is to choose G_t. Dynamic certainty equivalence tells us that a correct approach to this problem can begin by forming forecasts of the paths X using the data available to the government at this point: that is, values of Q_s, W_s

for $s < t$ together with the current observation on Z_t. The objective function (3.1) can then be maximized with respect to the future paths of C, G, and K, subject to the constraint (3.2), replacing future X's by their expectations. The G_t that emerges from this computation will be the correct period-t decision for the government.

However, suppose historical data on C, G, K, and W are publicly available, the government has access to an econometrician capable of estimating a vector autoregression (VAR) for these variables, and current and past values of these variables constitute an information set equivalent to current and past Q, W, and Z. In this case the government can simplify its problem by having the econometrician estimate the vector autoregression and generate predictions with it conditional on various possible paths for G.

In particular, the government should use its observation on Z_t to form an estimate of W_t. It should ask the econometrician to put his vector autoregression in triangular form, in the order W, G, then K and C. (That is, the regression equations for C, G, and K should all contain contemporaneous W.) Then the conditional projections should be formed with all disturbances in the VAR set to zero, except for those in the G equation (which are varied to generate various paths for G) and for the contemporaneous disturbance in the W equation (which is determined by the government's estimate of W_t). If the government evaluates the paths generated this way using the utility function (3.1), ignoring uncertainty, and chooses the value of G_t associated with the projected path maximizing utility, it will make exactly the optimal choice of G_t. In proceeding this way the government avoids any need to know the structure of the constraints (3.2), trusting that the private sector has systematically taken care of optimizing relative to these constraints and will continue to do so.

The reason this procedure works is that over any class of paths for C, G, and K, within which only the part of the innovation in G orthogonal to W varies, the path of X remains fixed. This is true because the only contemporaneous innovation on which G_t depends is that of Z_t, which in turn depends only on the W_t innovation and e_t, the error in Z_t as a measure of W_t. So the part of G_t orthogonal to the W_t innovation is a function of e_t alone, which is independent of X_t. But if in this class of paths X is being fixed at its projected value given Z_t, while G varies, the paths all satisfy (3.2) with this fixed X. Thus the paths being considered are a subset of those considered in the full certainty-equivalent solution when C, K, and G are all varied while (3.2) is imposed and the path of X held fixed at its predicted value. The only question remaining is whether we can be sure that this subset of the feasible paths actually contains the optimum. But it does, because another way to characterize the certainty-equivalent solution is that at t it sets the paths of G, C, K, and W equal to their conditional expectations given information available to the government (i.e., data up to $t-1$ together with Z_t). But this is just what is obtained from the VAR when the innovations in X_t and G_t are set at their conditional expectations given Z_t and past data, while all other innovations in the triangularized system at t and later are set to zero.

The foregoing verbal argument is complete except for the absence of any proof that it is possible for current and past G, C, K, and W to be an information set equivalent to current and past Q, W, and Z. Because the foregoing argument is intricate and possibly hard to follow, and because the general conditions for equivalence of the information sets appear difficult to set down, we will work out a specific example in some detail below. First, though, we display the general form of the first-order conditions:

$$C: \ AC_t = -H\lambda_t, \tag{3.6}$$

$$G: \ BG_t = -ME_{zt}[\lambda_t], \tag{3.7}$$

$$K: \ FK_t = \lambda_t - RNE_t[\lambda_{t+1}], \tag{3.8}$$

where λ_t is a stochastic Lagrange multiplier vector and $E_{zt}[\cdot]$ stands for $E[\cdot \mid Z_s, Q_{s-1}, W_{s-1}, \text{all } s \le t]$.

Because this is a quadratic-linear problem, we could solve it in closed form by assuming some simple form for the autoregressive representation of the Q, W, Z process, then deriving the decision rules. Even for simple cases, however, the parameters of the decision rules and therefore of the AR representation of the system are fairly complicated nonlinear functions of the problem's original parameterization. To keep the algebra simpler, we will derive a solution "backward" [see Sims (1984)]. We proceed by not using (3.5), instead assuming directly

$$t = f * \begin{bmatrix} Q_t \\ W_t \\ Z_t \end{bmatrix}, \tag{3.9}$$

and treating (3.2) now as defining X_t after (3.6)–(3.8) have been used to determine C, G, and K from Q, W, and Z. We cannot use the most straightforward backward solution method, because we cannot choose f arbitrarily and still guarantee that the constraint in (3.5) - that X_t not depend on current Z_t - be satisfied. Nonetheless, it proves to be easy to adjust our choice of f to impose this constraint.

To make the example really simple, we assume that C, K, and G all have dimension one. W and Z must then be scalar also. (Because Z's innovation affects only G, we will not be able to recover Z from data on

C, K, G, and W unless G's dimension at least matches Z's and W and Z are assumed to be of the same dimension.) If C, K, G, and W are not to be jointly singular, we must have the dimension of C and K jointly no greater than the dimension of Q, and if we are to recover the history of Q, W, and Z from that of C, K, G, and W, we must have C and K jointly no smaller in dimension than Q. So Q is 2×1.

We assume $A = B = F = H = M = N = 1$. We take a in (3.3) to be such that

$$E_t \begin{bmatrix} Q_{t+1} \\ W_{t+1} \end{bmatrix} = \text{diag}(\delta) \begin{bmatrix} Q_t \\ W_t \end{bmatrix}, \tag{3.10}$$

where δ is a vector with distinct elements all less than one in absolute value. We use lowercase letters to refer to the innovations in the corresponding uppercase stochastic processes. We define π as the vector of coefficients projecting the innovations in Q and W onto the innovation in Z, that is,

$$E_t \begin{bmatrix} q_t \\ w_t \end{bmatrix} = \pi z_t. \tag{3.11}$$

Obviously π is determined by the covariance matrix of the innovations in the information process Q, W, Z. We choose f in (3.9) so that

$$-\lambda_t = 1'Q_t + W_t + \{\varphi/(1-\gamma L)\}Z_t. \tag{3.12}$$

It will turn out that we can keep Z from affecting X [maintain the validity of (3.5)] by setting φ and γ properly.

Now we can use our simplifying assumptions to rewrite the first-order conditions (3.6)–(3.8) as

$$C_t = 1'Q_t + W_t\{\varphi/(1-\gamma L)\}Z_t, \tag{3.13}$$

$$G_t = 1' \text{diag}(\delta) \begin{bmatrix} Q_{t-1} \\ W_{t-1} \end{bmatrix} + \{\varphi/(1-\gamma L)\}Z_t + 1'\pi(Z_t - \delta_3 W_{t-1}), \tag{3.14}$$

$$K_t = -1'Q_t - W_t - \{\varphi/(1-\gamma L)\}Z_t$$
$$+ RN\left\{ 1' \text{diag}(\delta) \begin{bmatrix} Q_t \\ W_t \end{bmatrix} + \delta_3 W_t \right\}. \tag{3.15}$$

The simplified version of (3.2), written as solved for X, is

$$X_t = K_t - NK_{t-1} - C_t - G_t. \tag{3.16}$$

It is easy to see that the terms in Z that result when (3.13)–(3.15) are substituted into (3.16) are given by

$$[-\{3\varphi/(1-\gamma L)\} - 1'\pi - NL\{\varphi/(1-\gamma L)\}]Z_t. \tag{3.17}$$

This term vanishes if and only if

$$(3 + NL) - 1'\pi(1 - \gamma L), \qquad (3.18)$$

which will be true if $\gamma = -N/3$ and $\varphi = -1'\pi/3$. We can choose γ and φ to satisfy these relations so long as $|N| < 3$.

To verify that the relation – between C, K, G on the one hand and Q, Z on the other – is invertible, we must check the characteristic roots of the matrix polynomial in the lag operator that makes up the right-hand side of (3.13)–(3.15); that is, of

$$\begin{bmatrix} 1 & 1 & \{\varphi/(1-\gamma L)\} \\ \delta_1 L & \delta_2 L & \{\varphi/(1-\gamma L)\} + 1'\pi \\ -1 + RN\delta_1 & -1 + RN\delta_2 & -\{\varphi/(1-\gamma L)\} \end{bmatrix}. \qquad (3.19)$$

Some algebra leads to the conclusion that there is just one root to the determinant of this matrix, and it is less than one in absolute value so long as $|N| < 4$.

Denoting the matrix polynomial in the lag operator in (3.19) by (L), the full relation between C, G, K, W and Q, Z, W is

$$\begin{bmatrix} C \\ G \\ K \\ W \end{bmatrix} = \begin{bmatrix} \Gamma(L) & 1 \\ & \delta_3(1 - 1'\pi)L \\ & -1 + RN\delta_3(1+\varphi) \\ 0 & 1 \end{bmatrix} \begin{bmatrix} Q \\ Z \\ W \end{bmatrix}, \qquad (3.20)$$

where the partition of the columns of the matrix on the right-hand side corresponds to a partition of the Q-Z-W vector between (Q, Z) and W. This means that the relation between innovations in the two processes is

$$\begin{bmatrix} c \\ g \\ k \\ w \end{bmatrix} = \begin{bmatrix} 1 & 1 & \varphi & 1 \\ 0 & 0 & \varphi + 1'\pi & 0 \\ -1 + RN\delta_1 & -1 + RN\delta_2 & -\varphi & -1 + RN\delta_3(1+\varphi) \\ 0 & 0 & 0 & 1 \end{bmatrix} \begin{bmatrix} q_1 \\ q_2 \\ z \\ w \end{bmatrix}. $$

$$(3.21)$$

From (3.21) we see confirmation of what we have already argued for the general case: The innovation in G is a function of the innovation in Z alone. From (3.10) we can observe that in this example, as in the general case, Q and W can be expressed entirely in terms of current and lagged values of their own innovations (a consequence of their not being Granger-caused by Z). Thus a class of projections of future values of G, C, and K generated by varying only the part of g orthogonal to w will leave the corresponding [via the inverse of (3.20)] class of projections of future

Q, W, and Z unchanged in Q and W, with only Z varying. Optimal choice of G_t is described by the second row of (3.20) or (3.21), and the jointly optimal certainty-equivalent path for all variables conditional on the government's information at t is obtained by setting z_t to its actual value and q_t, w_t according to (3.11), generating future values for Q, W, Z by solving the equations of their VAR with these initial conditions, and translating these to future values for $C, G, K,$ and W via (3.20). But as we can now see explicitly, this whole process can be described equivalently as setting w_t and g_t, then generating future values for $C, G, K,$ and W according to the VAR for these variables themselves.

4   Remarks

The example of Section 3 is set in a canonical quadratic-linear form, with no constants or linear terms in the objective function and all stochastic terms in the constraints. Models with stochastic terms in the objective function, or cross-product and linear terms there, can be transformed into the canonical form. Thus even if the government could deduce the form of some or all of the constraints on the canonical form from the VAR (which it can't in this example), it would not necessarily have found the economy's "technology."

If Z_t were an observable variable, there would be an exact linear relation connecting Z_t and past data to current G_t which could be quickly deduced from the data. Our example depends on thinking of policy makers as agents who can collect unpublished, informal data and use it to make a guess at W_t, but who cannot characterize their data as a number and (say) plot it against their previous choices of G_t. This is of course not very realistic, but neither is the idea of a unitary, optimizing macroeconomic policy maker. If policy makers were truly rational agents, of course, they could fit and solve econometric models in their heads and would have no need for econometricians.

The example is rigged so that identification does not even require estimation by instrumental-variables techniques – it uses a Wold causal chain style of identification. It could have been rigged so that the identification problem was a little more interesting.

The Lucas critique raises no problems for the example of Section 3, not because expectation-formation does not enter the model (it is an important part of the model's dynamics), but because the model is one in which policy is already optimal and persists in being so. Thus the process of policy choice does not change the expectations formation behavior implicit in the model's structure. The point of the example is that it is one for which the Lucas statement (quoted in Section 2) about the uselessness of models in the general form of (2.1) is completely incorrect if taken at face value.

The only coherent interpretation of the Lucas critique is that it states that if one uses a model that incorrectly describes the reaction of expectations formation to policy choice, it will produce incorrect evaluations of policy. The implication is not that econometric evaluation of policy using models fitted to history is impossible, but that it requires correct specification of the reaction of the economy to policy. And the notion strongly associated with the rational expectations literature – that the only correct way to model such reactions is to ignore the probabilistic character of policy choice – is spurious baggage.

Some readers might be convinced by the example, but suppose that it only shows a minor qualification to the Lucas critique: that when there are no changes in the policy rule, policy choice using econometric conditional projections is at least possibly logically coherent. When we contemplate truly important changes in policy, or changes that may approach permanence, then we are in the realm of changes in policy rule, and it may be thought that Lucas is still right that econometric conditional projections cannot be used for analyzing changes in rule.

But this brings us back to the argument in the first part of the paper. Changes in rule are changes in policy variables, just as is any other kind of change in policy. Very persistent or very large changes in policy are likely to generate nonlinear effects in the reaction of the economy to policy. These nonlinearities (e.g., that the reaction of the economy to six years of below-average inflation cannot be correctly determined by adding up twelve copies of the reaction of the economy to two quarters of below-average inflation) must be modeled accurately if conditional projections with the model are to be accurate. But there is no logical distinction between using an accurate nonlinear model to project the effects of persistent or large policy changes and using an accurate linear model to project the effects of smaller, short-run policy changes. It is true that the nonlinear models appropriate to projecting the effects of large or persistent policy changes are likely to be complicated, and that the uncertainty about how the data should be interpreted is likely therefore to be larger in such cases. There may be plausible alternative identifying assumptions available that yield different conditional projections without conflicting with the data. Stating this another way, the role of untested subjective judgment (i.e., of "a priori theory") may be large. But this is to some extent true in any econometric policy analysis, and raises no new issues of principle.

There may be some policy issues where the simple rational expectations policy analysis paradigm – treating policy as given by a rule with deterministic parameters that are to be changed once and for all, with no one knowing beforehand that the change may occur and no one doubting afterward that the change is permanent – is a useful approximate simplifying assumption. To the extent that the rational expectations literature has led us to suppose that all real policy change must fit into this internally inconsistent mold, it has led us onto sterile ground.

5   Conclusions

It should be clear that, though the model of Section 3 is specially rigged, what is crucial to the rigging is the information structure. Whenever a policy authority makes imperfectly predictable choices (because it observes a noisy information variable, while the public finds the government's information variable redundant), we will reproduce the identifying assumptions justifying the form of econometric policy evaluation that is valid in this model.

In more complicated models, identification of the structural relation connecting policy actions to the private economy's reaction is likely to be less easy than it is here. Within the context of models that (like the model of this paper) yield a stationary linear structure while policy varies, different assumptions about the source of the variation in policy could make reaction unidentifiable or could lead to a need to identify it by use of techniques close to those of standard simultaneous equations theory. Examples of identification techniques that work directly with a VAR reduced form appear in Blanchard and Watson (1984) and Litterman (1984).

The generic version of the point made by this paper is as follows: We can ordinarily expect that accurate conditional projections of the effects of policy choices will be useful to policy makers; we can expect that there will be autonomous variation in policy in the data, so that statistical estimation will be valuable in preparing such conditional projections; and the identifying assumptions required to bring the data to bear in forming the projections will be much less than a complete behavioral interpretation of each equation in the probability model – in fact, not even requiring separation of expectational dynamics from other dynamics.

REFERENCES

Blanchard, Olivier, and Mark Watson. 1984. "Are Business Cycles All Alike." Discussion paper, National Bureau of Economic Research.
Cooley, Thomas F., Stephen F. LeRoy, and Neil Raymon. 1984. "Modeling Policy Interventions." Discussion paper, University of California–Santa Barbara and University of Missouri–Columbia.

Kydland, F., and E. Prescott. 1977. "Rules Rather than Discretion: the Inconsistency of Optimal Plans." *Journal of Political Economy* 85: 473–93.

Litterman, R. L. 1984. "The Costs of Intermediate Targeting." Discussion paper, Federal Reserve Bank of Minneapolis.

Lucas, Robert E., Jr. 1976. In Karl Brunner and Alan Meltzer (eds.), *The Phillips Curve and Labor Markets*. Amsterdam: North-Holland.

Roberds, Will. 1985. "Policy Analysis under Stochastic Replanning." Working Paper No. 278, Research Department, Federal Reserve Bank of Minneapolis.

Sargent, T. J. 1984. "Vector Autoregressions, Expectations, and Advice." *American Economic Review* 74: 408–15.

Sims, C. A. 1975. "Exogeneity and Causal Orderings." In *New Methods in Business Cycle Research*. Federal Reserve Bank of Minneapolis.

———. 1982. "Policy Analysis with Economic Models." *Brookings Papers on Economic Activity* 107–64.

———. 1984. "Solving Stochastic Equilibrium Models 'Backwards'." Discussion Paper No. 206, Center for Economic Research, University of Minnesota.

Theoretical issues in the foundations of monetary economics and macroeconomics

Pricing and the distribution of money holdings in a search economy, II

Peter Diamond and Joel Yellin

The circular flow of purchasing power is a staple of introductory economics. Yet it scarcely appears in recent theoretical work. Examples of explicit modeling of the circular flow are Lucas (1980) and our (1985b). In these models, stochastic expenditure patterns and limited investment and borrowing opportunities result in a distribution of holdings of fiat money. This analysis focuses on the determinants of prices as well as the distribution of money holdings. In the absence of analyses of richer menus of financial assets, it seems more appropriate to think of these models as reflecting the finance constraint of Kohn (1981) rather than the money constraint of Clower (1967).

In the model, we distinguish two groups of agents – workers and capitalists. There is a Walrasian labor market and a sequential search retail market where prices are set by capitalists. There is a circular flow of money with workers holding money while waiting for stochastic purchasing opportunities and capitalists simply transfering money between markets (mail float).

Our assumptions are strong; they enable us to solve the model explicitly in the steady state. The model economy has a unique steady-state uniform price equilibrium in which the greater the efficiency of the search process in the retail market, the higher the levels of nominal and real wages. Whether the nominal price increases or decreases with search speed depends on the other parameters. With an increase in the speed at which funds are transferred between markets, there is an increase in the nominal price, nominal wage, and real wage.

The model described below differs from the one in our 1985b paper by the introduction of a lag in the transfer of money from the retail market to the labor market. As in our (1985b), our use of search and price setting

Research supported by the National Science Foundation.

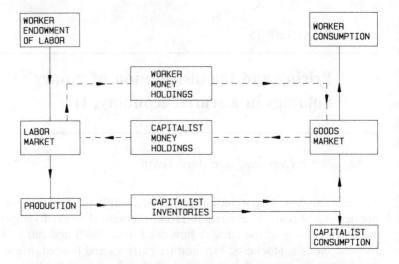

Figure 1. Schematic flow diagram depicting monetary model analyzed in text. Labor market is Walrasian. Goods market is mediated by random search technology that allows transactions at Poisson intervals. In each transaction, a worker purchases a commodity bundle of unit size. Capitalists hold money for a Poisson distributed lag time. Solid arrows are physical flows; dashed arrows indicate money flows.

differs from Lucas (1980), who assumes Walrasian retail markets and random preferences.

1   Description of model

Our model economy is pictured in Figure 1. It is peopled by two classes of agents, workers and capitalists. Each worker receives a flow of labor endowment at unit rate. He sells his labor services to capitalists on a labor market mediated by a Walrasian auctioneer.[1] Labor services are continuously compensated at a market-clearing rate w. A worker thus receives money wages at the rate w, and labor services flow to capitalists at a rate proportional to the total number of workers in the economy. We assume there are sufficiently large numbers of workers and capitalists that each group may be considered to form a continuum. We assume N workers per capitalist; we normalize the continuum of capitalists to 1. We assume further that there is a fixed aggregate quantity of money and no credit.

---

[1] There is no difficulty in principle in making the entire model non-Walrasian by introducing search and long-term contracts in the labor market.

The economic environment of capitalists is as follows. Capitalists hire workers on the labor market and employ them to produce goods continuously. Labor is the only productive factor. A unit of labor produces a unit bundle of goods with no delay. We assume that all capitalists are identically situated, that there are no direct inventory carrying costs, and that capitalists have no retail price reputations.

Capitalists use their inventories in two ways. First, they consume them continuously at a per capita rate c set by lifetime utility optimization rules described below. Second, they offer them for sale in the retail market at a price p per unit bundle. This price is also set in the optimization process. We assume that each retail transaction results in the purchase of a single bundle of goods. Retail revenues are transferred to the labor market to purchase labor services. However, the money transfer process takes time and is stochastic. In particular, we assume that the dollars from each transaction move between markets with a lag that is Poisson distributed with parameter a. This lagged flow can be viewed as a consequence of a simple post office. That is, at the time of each sale, the cash revenues from that sale are placed in an envelope and mailed to the capitalist. The lag in delivery of mail results in a mail float. Rather than assuming a discrete determinate lag, we make the convenient Poisson assumption for the distribution of delivery lags. Because there are many workers per capitalist, the aggregate flow of money into the labor market for each capitalist is taken to be determinate and equal to a multiplied by the stock of money in transit, m_c.

We assume retail trade is mediated by a random search technology that enables workers to search for and locate consumption opportunities. Such opportunities come at times set by a Poisson process with an endogenous arrival rate. Each consumption opportunity entails the possibility of purchasing a unit bundle of the consumer good at a price p that is set by capitalists. There is no credit; to make a purchase a worker must hold money in amount at least equal to p. We picture each bundle of inventory as available for purchase at a separate retail outlet.[2] A successful purchase by a worker is followed by consumption of the proceeds and results in a fixed gain of utility. Workers cannot buy more than one unit at a time.

We assume that workers' preferences are described by the expected present discounted value of utility of consumption, with a strictly positive discount rate. Because we consider only uniform price equilibria, no worker ever encounters a price sufficiently high to give him an incentive

---

[2] In a more realistic (but also more complicated) formulation, one would consider the distribution of inventories over the set of retail outlets of a single capitalist.

314   Peter Diamond and Joel Yellin

to wait for a better price. Given these simple time preferences and the lack of credit, in a constant-price equilibrium workers make every possible purchase. In particular, purchase opportunities are taken whenever a worker's money holding exceeds the retail price p.[3]

Two accounting identities are fundamental to the model. First, let T be the rate at which retail transactions occur, per capitalist. The money holdings of capitalists grow from retail sales and shrink from the payment of wages. In steady state with constant wages, capitalists spend the proceeds of retail sales as soon as they reach the labor market. In a steady state with constant money holdings, the wage bill of each capitalist is equal to his retail revenue:

$$dm_c/dt = pT - wN$$
$$= pT - am_c = 0. \tag{1.1}$$

A second identity describes the growth of capitalists' inventories. Let the inventory of commodity bundles per capitalist be x. Inventories grow at the rate am_c/w, per capitalist, due to production by labor hired with the (cash) proceeds of previous retail sales. Inventories shrink at the rate T due to retail sales and also as the result of capitalists' consumption of their own inventory. Therefore, we have the accounting relation for per capitalist flows,

$$dx/dt = -c - T + am_c/w. \tag{1.2}$$

Subject to constraints (1.1) and (1.2), capitalists set prices and choose consumption levels to maximize $\int e^{-rt}u(c)\,dt$, the integral of discounted utility. We describe the first-order conditions for the capitalists' choice problem below.

Our search model of the retail market leads to specification of the retail transaction rate T in terms of the money distribution and the total inventory. Let $F(m)$ be the distribution of workers' money holdings. Then the fraction of workers with money sufficient to consummate a purchase is $1 - F(p)$. In the simplest random search, the search technology enables the random pairing of a worker with a single commodity bundle. The transaction rate per capitalist is therefore

$$T = hN[1 - F(p)]x, \tag{1.3}$$

the product of the search efficiency h, the number of workers actively searching for consumption opportunities $N[1 - F(p)]$, and the total number of commodity bundles x in commerce. In this picture, in equilibrium each worker experiences an arrival rate b of consumption opportunities

[3] Out of steady state, a worker's choice problem depends on his beliefs about future prices.

equal to the retail transactions rate per worker actively engaged in search. Using (1.3), we therefore write

$$b = \frac{T}{N[1-F(p)]} = hx. \tag{1.4}$$

Thus, workers' money holdings obey a stochastic process. They increase continuously at the wage rate w. They decrease in jumps equal to the retail price p subject to the condition that no individual's money holdings can become negative. Jump times are set by a Poisson process whose arrival rate b is proportional to the total inventory in the market and the efficiency of the search technology. Let $f(m)$ be the equilibrium probability density of workers' money holdings. With the assumptions above, workers' equilibrium money holdings satisfy

$$wf'(m) = hx[f(m+p) - \theta(m-p)f(m)]. \tag{1.5}$$

The left-hand side of (1.5) represents the inflow of money wages, with the distribution of money holdings shifting to the right at rate w. The right-hand side represents the net outflow due to retail transactions, with some of those holding $m+p$ jumping to a holding of m while some of those holding m jump to a holding of $m-p$ if and only if $m \geq p$.[4] The solution of the difference-differential equation (1.5) is given in Section 2.

2   Equilibrium money holdings

The methods developed in our (1985a) enable us to solve (1.5) for the equilibrium distribution of workers' money holdings and to assert that the solution thus obtained is unique. We note first that it is a property of the model described in Section 1 that workers with sufficient funds are able to spend more rapidly than money is received. Formally, in equilibrium we have the inequality between endogenous quantities

$$w < bp. \tag{2.1}$$

Condition (2.1) is required for logical consistency. If this inequality does not hold then there is unlimited growth of the workers' stock of money, and this contradicts our assumption that the money stock is fixed.

Given (2.1), the arguments in our (1985a) tell us that the asymptotic distribution of money holdings is uniquely given by

$$F(m) = (b/wk)[1-F(p)][1-e^{km}+km] \quad m \leq p, \tag{2.2a}$$

$$F(m) = 1-[1-F(p)]e^{k(m-p)} \qquad\qquad m \geq p, \tag{2.2b}$$

---

[4] The symbol $\theta(x)$ denotes the Heaviside (unit step) function, which is 1 for positive x and 0 otherwise.

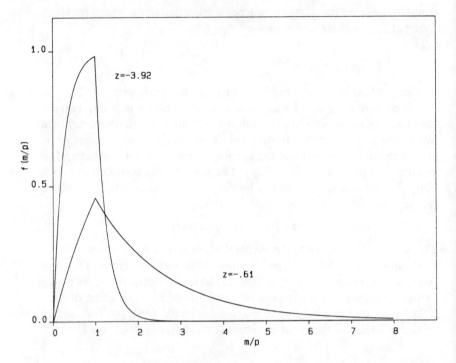

Figure 2. Probability density of money holdings defined by equation
(2.2). Note the flattening and extension of the right-hand tail as z increases. For the two densities shown, $1-F(p)$ is equal to 1/4 and 3/4.

where k is the unique real negative root of

$$wk = b(e^{kp}-1) \tag{2.3a}$$

and

$$1-F(p) = \frac{w}{bp} = \frac{e^{kp}-1}{kp}. \tag{2.3b}$$

By direct substitution, one verifies that (2.2) solves (1.5). Apart from
scale, (2.2) defines a one-parameter family of distributions.[5] It is convenient to follow our (1985b) and use pk as the parameter. We denote pk
as z and show the density of money holdings for two different values of z
in Figure 2.

As pointed out above, we assume there is a continuum of individual
workers, and therefore that there is no uncertainty regarding the aggregate distribution of money holdings. Then the asymptotic equilibrium

[5] We could use w/bp as this parameter as in our (1985a).

probability distribution for a single worker engaged in the stochastic trading process is also the asymptotic equilibrium distribution of money holdings over all workers in the economy.

We gain insight into the economics of the stochastic process governing workers' money holdings by relating the elasticity of demand in equilibrium to the parameters of the money distribution. Basic to our search model is the assumption that workers sample suppliers one at a time. Thus, in a uniform price equilibrium, workers are willing to pay (if able) at least a little more than the going price for the opportunity to make an immediate purchase. Because workers cannot spend more than they possess, in the neighborhood of the equilibrium price the demand curve for each capitalist is given by the distribution of workers' money holdings multiplied by the number of buyers that come in contact with his inventory. In particular, the demand curve in equilibrium, at a price level m near p, is proportional to the fraction of workers, $1 - F(m)$, holding at least the money level m. We may therefore define the elasticity of aggregate demand as

$$z = d \log[1 - F(m)]/d \log m \mid_{m=p}. \tag{2.4}$$

From (2.2),

$$z = pk. \tag{2.5}$$

From (2.3b) we can relate z to the parameters of the stochastic process, w, b, and p. Because monopolists do not set prices where demand is inelastic, only values of z less than -1 are of interest here.

If we compute the mean money holding per worker $\bar{m}_w$ implied by (2.2), we find

$$\bar{m}_w/p = 1/2 - 1/kp = 1/2 - z^{-1}. \tag{2.6}$$

As already stated, the number of workers and the nominal money stock m_0 are assumed to be fixed exogenous quantities. Thus, clearance of the money market implies

$$m_c = m_0 - N\bar{m}_w = m_0 - Np(1/2 - z^{-1}). \tag{2.7}$$

3   Capitalist behavior

It remains to examine the choice problem of capitalists. Each capitalist is big enough not to face uncertainty. We view capitalists as consuming continuously at a rate c out of their own inventories, maximizing the present discounted value of the utility of their own-consumption streams, with a positive utility discount rate r. Then, with the accounting relations (1.1) and (1.2) and the transactions technology (1.3) in mind, each capitalist optimizes by monitoring the time paths of price and inventory. In optimizing, capitalists are aware that the equilibrium distribution of money holdings satisfies (1.5). However, they assume that their own price-setting behavior does not affect workers' money holdings. Because there is random matching with no price reputations, capitalists cannot alter the rate of meeting between workers and goods for sale. In any meeting, a price sufficiently in excess of the prices charged elsewhere will not result in a sale even if the worker has sufficient money. However, we are looking for a uniform price equilibrium. Thus, we can solve the capitalists' problem ignoring this constraint since all capitalists are solving the same problem and will set the same price. Formally, the capitalists' choice problem is therefore

$$\max_{x,p} \int_0^\infty e^{-rt} u[c(t)]\, dt \tag{3.1}$$

subject to

$$dx/dt = -c - hN[1-F(p)]x + am_c/w,$$

$$dm_c/dt = phN[1-F(p)]x - am_c,$$

where we take $u(c)$ to be monotone increasing and concave, with $u'(0) = \infty$.

Eliminating c from the choice problem (3.1) and introducing a Lagrange multiplier λ, we form the Lagrangean

$$L = e^{-rt}[u[-\dot{x} - hNx[1-F(p)] + am_c/w]]$$

$$- \lambda[\dot{m} - phNx[1-F(p)] + am_c]. \tag{3.2}$$

Equation (3.2) yields the first-order conditions

$$e^{-rt}[-u'hN[1-F(p)] + \lambda phN[1-F(p)]] = \frac{d}{dt}[-e^{-rt}u']; \tag{3.3a}$$

$$u'F'(p) + \lambda[1-F(p) - pF'(p)] = 0. \tag{3.3b}$$

The auxiliary condition that determines λ is

$$\dot{\lambda} = (a+r)\lambda - u'a/w. \tag{3.3c}$$

Asymptotically, u', p, x, and λ are constant; therefore, in steady-state equilibrium we have the conditions

$$r = \left(\frac{gp}{w} - 1\right)hN[1-F(p)], \tag{3.4a}$$

$$F'(p) + \frac{g}{w}[1-F(p) - pF'(p)] = 0, \tag{3.4b}$$

where

$$g = \frac{a}{r+a}. \qquad (3.5)$$

The notation $F'(p)$ denotes the density dF/dm evaluated at $m = p$. Consistent with our assumption that there are many capitalists, we assume that capitalists take the distribution of money holdings as given. Thus, we do not differentiate $F(m)$ with respect to p, and the structural parameters of the money distribution do not enter into the first-order maximization condition.

Condition (3.4a) is analogous to the modified golden rule in optimal growth problems – the own marginal product of inventories is equal to the utility discount rate.

From the definition of z, (2.4), we can write the pricing equation (3.4b) as

$$1 - w/pg = [1 - F(p)][pF'(p)]^{-1} = -1/z, \qquad (3.6)$$

where, on the argument above, the elasticity z is taken to be less than -1. Equation (3.6) states that capitalists set the retail price p to maximize $(p - w/g)[1 - F(p)]$. The right-hand side of (3.6) is positive, and the real wage w/p is therefore less than the (unit) marginal product of labor times g. Observe also that the real wage is a decreasing function of the elasticity z. In our (1985b) we assumed no lag in the transfer of funds between markets. This corresponds to $a = +\infty$ and so $g = 1$ in (3.6).

4   Equilibrium conditions

We now show that the model described above has a unique steady-state uniform[6] price equilibrium. Consider the two Euler equations (3.4) for capitalist decisions, along with the money-market equation (2.7) evaluated in a steady state. With constant capitalist money holdings, we have $m_c/N = w/a$. Defining $\bar{m}$ as the total money supply per worker m_0/N, we can rewrite (2.7) as

$$\bar{m} = w/a + p(1/2 - 1/z). \qquad (4.1)$$

Using (2.3b) and (2.5) to eliminate $1 - F(p)$, we can write the optimal inventory condition (3.4a) as

$$\frac{r}{hN} = \left(\frac{e^z - 1}{z}\right)\left(\frac{pg}{w} - 1\right). \qquad (4.2)$$

Equations (3.6), (4.1), and (4.2) are three equations in three endogenous variables – p, w, and z.

[6] We have not considered whether there also exist equilibria with different prices in different transactions.

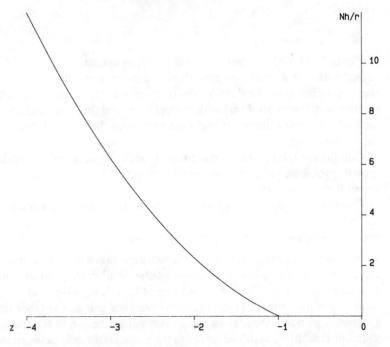

Figure 3. Equilibrium demand elasticity as a function of ratio of search speed to discount rate of capitalists.

Using (3.6) to eliminate $w/(pg)$ from (4.2), we derive the monotonic relationship between z and $r/(hN)$:

$$r/(hN) = (1 - e^z)z^{-1}(1 + z)^{-1}. \tag{4.3}$$

In Figure 3 we show the relationship between z and hN/r. As the search process speeds up without limit, the elasticity of demand grows indefinitely.

Using (4.1) and (3.6), we can solve for the wage and retail price in terms of the elasticity:

$$w = 2\bar{m}a(1 + z)/(2(1 + z) + (r + a)(z - 2)), \tag{4.4}$$

$$p = 2\bar{m}(r + a)z/(2(1 + z) + (r + a)(z - 2)). \tag{4.5}$$

In Figures 4a and 4b, we use (4.3)–(4.5) to show the behavior of the retail price and wage as functions of h. Note from (4.3) that z and h are inversely related. In particular, as h runs from 0 to values indefinitely large, $-z$ runs from 1 to values indefinitely large. Therefore, as h rises from 0, p moves monotonically from $2\bar{m}/3$ to $2\bar{m}(r + a)/(2 + r + a)$, w runs from 0 to $2\bar{m}a/(2 + r + a)$, and p/w runs from $+\infty$ to g^{-1}. Whether

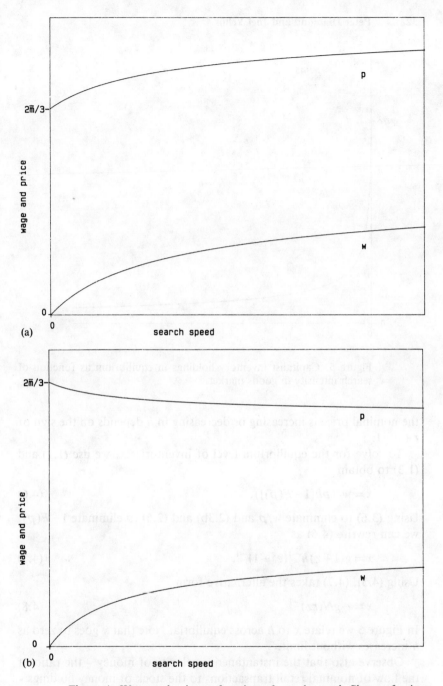

Figure 4. Wage and price as function of search speed. Shape of price curve depends on sum of Poisson parameter a and discount r. Figure 4a: $r+a>1$. Figure 4b: $r+a<1$.

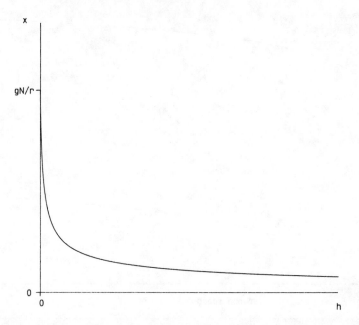

Figure 5. Capitalist inventory holdings in equilibrium as function of search intensity in goods market.

the nominal price is increasing or decreasing in h depends on the sign of $r+a-1$.

To solve for the equilibrium level of inventories x, we use (1.1) and (1.3) to obtain

$$x = w/(ph[1-F(p)]). \tag{4.6}$$

Using (3.6) to eliminate w/p and (2.3b) and (2.5) to eliminate $1-F(p)$, we can rewrite (4.6) as

$$x = g(1+z)h^{-1}(e^z-1)^{-1}. \tag{4.7}$$

Using (4.3), (4.7) takes the alternative form

$$x = -gN(rz)^{-1}. \tag{4.8}$$

In Figure 5 we relate x to h across equilibria. Note that x goes to zero as h increases without limit.

Observe also that the instantaneous velocity of money – the ratio of the flow of nominal retail transactions to the stock of money holdings – here takes the simple form [cf. (1.1)]

$$v = pT/m_0 = w/\bar{m} = 2a(1+z)/(2(1+z)+(r+a)(z-2))). \tag{4.9}$$

Money is held for three reasons in this model. Capitalists hold money while transferring it between markets. Workers hold money while they accumulate sufficient purchasing power to buy a unit of consumer goods. If supplies were instantly available, this would be the reverse of the usual Baumol–Tobin model of the transactions demand for money with continuous accumulation and discrete expenditures. Third, workers hold more than this minimal amount of money because of the stochastic arrival of purchasing opportunities.

There are two separate processes that involve lags. It takes time for capitalists to transfer money between markets, and it takes time for workers with sufficient purchasing power to find units of the consumer good to buy. If both processes occurred without lag ($a = h = +\infty$), the real variables in this economy would have the same values as in the Walrasian model with the same technology ($w/p = 1$, $x = 0$). The continuous convergence of real variables to their Walrasian values as the transaction processes speed up stands in sharp contrast to the discontinuity that occurs in similar partial equilibrium models of the retail market [Diamond (1971)]. The difference between these results arises from the endogeneity of demand in general equilibrium models in contrast to the exogenous demand in partial equilibrium models. As the retail search process speeds up, the distribution of money holdings changes, resulting in a greater elasticity of demand and therefore a lower markup over costs. In the limit, demand is seen as infinitely elastic, removing monopoly power in the retail market from the pricing equation.

For comparative steady states, we will vary the exogenous parameters h, a, and r. The speed of search in the retail market h enters (4.2), but does not enter the other equations explicitly. By influencing the distribution of money holdings, h affects p, w, and x monotonically as shown in the figures. In addition, w/p is monotonically increasing in h, as can be seen from (3.6) and (4.3).

The lag in the transmission of money between markets has two effects. First, it decreases the money supply available for workers' holdings. Second, it increases the costs of production, given the positive utility discount rate of capitalists. Thus it is not surprising that an increase in the speed a of money transmission between markets increases x, w, p, and w/p. To see this, observe that z is independent of a in (4.3) and differentiate (4.8), (4.4), (4.5), and (3.6) respectively with respect to a.

It remains to consider the effect of the utility discount rate of capitalists, r, on the steady-state position of the economy. From (4.3), z is increasing in r. Thus, from (3.6) and (4.8) we see that both w/p and x are decreasing in r. Similarly, differentiating (4.4) we see that the wage is decreasing in r. Differentiating (4.5), one finds that the sign of the derivative of the retail price with respect to r depends on the size of a, given the size of h/r. For sufficiently large a, p decreases with r; while for sufficiently small a, p is not monotonic in r. The utility discount rate enters the equations in two ways. The first way, involving $a/(r+a)$, reflects the greater cost of the lag in money transmission the greater is r. The second way, involving h/r, reflects the speed of the retail search process. The balance between these two ways determines the sign of the effect of r on p.

REFERENCES

Clower, R. 1967. "A Reconsideration of the Micro-Foundations of Monetary Theory." *Western Economic Journal* 6: 1-9.
Diamond, P. 1971. "A Model of Price Adjustment." *Journal of Economic Theory* 3: 156-68.
Diamond, P., and J. Yellin. 1985a. "The Distribution of Inventory Holdings in a Pure Exchange Barter Search Economy." *Econometrica* 53: 409-32.
　　1985b. "Pricing and the Distribution of Money Holdings in a Search Economy." Working Paper #370, Massachusetts Institute of Technology.
Kohn, M. 1981. "In Defense of the Finance Constraint." *Economic Inquiry* 19: 177-95.
Lucas, R. 1980. "Equilibrium in a Pure Currency Economy." *Economic Inquiry* 18: 203-20.

CHAPTER 16

The optimal inflation rate in an overlapping-generations economy with land

Bennett T. McCallum

Abstract: This paper is concerned with the optimal inflation rate in an overlapping-generations economy in which (i) aggregate output is constrained by a standard neoclassical production function with diminishing marginal products for both capital and labor, and (ii) the transaction-facilitating services of money are represented by means of a money-in-the-utility-function specification. With monetary injections provided by lump-sum transfers, the famous Chicago Rule prescription for monetary growth is necessary for Pareto optimality; but a competitive equilibrium may fail to be Pareto optimal with that rule in force because of capital overaccumulation. The latter possibility does not exist, however, if the economy includes an asset that is productive and nonreproducible – that is, if the economy is one with land. As this conclusion is independent of the monetary aspects of the model, it is argued that the possibility of capital overaccumulation should not be regarded as a matter of theoretical concern, even in the absence of government debt, intergenerational altruism, and social security systems or other "social contrivances."

1   Introduction

Most of the existing analyses of the optimal inflation rate[1] that have been carried out in models with finite-lived individuals have reached conclusions that seem to contradict the famous Chicago Rule for optimal monetary growth.[2] An exception is provided by McCallum (1983, p. 38), which

Paper prepared for the Austin, Texas conference of May 23–24, 1985 on New Approaches to Monetary Economics. I am indebted to Andrew Abel, Rao Aiyagari, Martin Eichenbaum, and John Whitaker for helpful discussions and to George Akerlof, John Taylor, and an anonymous referee for comments. Financial support by the National Science Foundation (SES 84-08691) is gratefully acknowledged.

[1] This issue, also referred to under the heading of the "optimum quantity of money," is of course concerned with the optimal *average* rate of inflation over an extended period of time. Consequently, it abstracts entirely from matters that concern cyclical fluctuations.

[2] An incomplete but representative list of examples includes Stein (1971), Helpman and Sadka (1979), Wallace (1980), Weiss (1980), Drazen (1981), and Woodford (1985).

325

suggests that analysis of overlapping-generations models is supportive of the Chicago Rule provided these models take account of the transaction-facilitating (i.e., medium-of-exchange) services of money.[3] More specifically, it is shown that, in a version of the Wallace (1980) model amended to reflect the existence of monetary transaction services, Pareto optimality of a stationary competitive equilibrium requires a rate of deflation equal to the marginal product of capital.[4] That particular model is one in which the marginal product of capital does not vary with capital intensity, however, and might consequently be judged inappropriate for analysis of this issue.[5] One leading purpose of the present paper, accordingly, is to re-examine the optimal inflation issue within a specification that incorporates a standard neoclassical production function with diminishing marginal productivity for both capital and labor inputs.

The investigation confirms that, with an overlapping-generations (OG) framework of the specified type, the Chicago Rule is indeed necessary for Pareto optimality. The analysis also indicates, however, that Pareto optimality may fail to obtain for a reason not considered in my previous discussion, namely, overaccumulation of capital. In particular, the steady-state net marginal product of capital (MPK) may be smaller than the rate of population growth, in the manner emphasized in the famous paper by Diamond (1965).[6] Because of this possibility, then, it is not valid to conclude that competitive equilibria will be Pareto optimal (in OG models with transaction-facilitating money) provided merely that the Chicago Rule prescription for monetary growth is obeyed.

---

[3] The main purpose of McCallum (1983) is to argue that those special overlapping-generations models (or other models!) that fail to take account of the transaction-facilitating services of money are highly inappropriate vehicles for monetary analysis, i.e., for analysis in which it is necessary to distinguish between assets that serve as a medium of exchange and those that do not. Further discussion of the issue is presented in McCallum (1986).

[4] This rule, which received its most famous exposition in Friedman (1969), was mentioned earlier by Friedman (1960, p. 73) and given a very clear statement by Marty (1961, p. 57). It has been termed the Chicago Rule by Niehans (1978, p. 93) and Weiss (1980). The discussion here and throughout the present paper assumes that monetary injections are made by way of lump-sum transfers to old agents.

[5] That a variable marginal product of capital is crucial in this context has apparently been suggested by Weiss (1980, p. 970).

[6] It has, of course, been pointed out by Barro (1974) that Diamond's result presumes the absence of operative intergenerational transfers. Throughout the present paper such an absence is taken for granted – not because I believe that to be a particularly realistic assumption, but in order to consider its implications for the optimality of the Chicago Rule. For the same reason, the possibility that population growth might be endogenous – as considered by Meltzer and Richard (1985) – is ignored. For an introduction to the concept of capital overaccumulation, see Burmeister (1980, pp. 57–74).

A second major purpose of the present paper, accordingly, is to show that the possibility of capital overaccumulation does not exist[7] if the economy in question is one that includes a positive quantity of an asset that is productive and nonreproducible – that is, in an economy with land. As this conclusion is independent of the monetary aspects of the model economy, and since all actual market economies do in fact include such assets, it follows that the possibility of capital accumulation should not be regarded as a matter of concern, even in the absence of government debt, intergenerational altruism, and social security systems or other "social contrivances."

The paper's emphasis on this last-mentioned result should not be interpreted as a claim that it has never before been recognized by an economist. In fact, there are brief passages in papers by Samuelson (1958, p. 481) and Stiglitz (1974, p. 139) that indicate recognition of the impossibility of capital overaccumulation.[8] But the point has received very little attention in the literature of monetary and macroeconomics, which includes various results that are overturned by its recognition. It would seem, accordingly, that some emphasis – as well as the exposition of an elementary proof – is warranted.

There are, of course, good reasons for being interested in analysis based on different assumptions than ours concerning taxes[9] and/or the optimality criterion.[10] However, both tradition and the inherent logic of economic analysis speak in favor of addressing the issue initially with the

---

[7] Even in the absence of intergenerational altruism, social security systems, and governmental debt.

[8] An ambitious recent paper by Tirole (1985), which is devoted primarily to an investigation of the possibility of asset-price bubbles, considers a version of the Diamond model extended to include rents. Much of the analysis assumes that the aggregate quantity of rent is exogenously fixed, an assumption that leads to some conclusions that do not pertain to an economy with a fixed stock of land. (Tirole's Proposition 2, for example, seems to be inapplicable to the economy described in the present paper.) In one place, Tirole mentions the possibility that rents could grow at the rate of population growth, in which case "a perfect foresight equilibrium must be efficient" (1985, p. 1979) – a conclusion that is similar in spirit to mine. He does not, however, consider a specification in which land, an asset fixed in total quantity, appears as a useful input to the productive process for aggregate output. Thus, his analysis provides no reason for believing that rents will tend to grow at the same rate as output – and in that sense does not include my result as a special case. A similar statement also applies to a much earlier but unpublished paper by Scheinkman (1980), which emphasizes the implausibility of capital overaccumulation. I am indebted to Olivier Blanchard for calling my attention to Tirole's paper.

[9] Helpman and Sadka (1980) assume that labor and capital returns are taxed at flat rates in a setting otherwise similar to mine.

[10] Notable discussions of the appropriate criterion have been provided by Samuelson (1967, 1968), Abel (1984), Calvo and Obstfeld (1985), and others.

Pareto criterion, and in a setting that is free of distortions due to income taxes and the like.

The organization of the paper is as follows. In Section 2 the basic monetary model – with a neoclassical production function but no land – is specified, and the conditions characterizing competitive equilibrium are derived. Next, in Section 3, conditions sufficient for a Pareto optimum are obtained and compared with those achieved as an automatic consequence of competitive behavior. In Section 4 the model is extended to recognize the existence of land, and the Pareto optimality analysis is conducted. Finally, some general conclusions are offered in Section 5.

2   An OG model with money

As indicated above, our object is to consider the optimal money growth issue in an OG model with a specification that reflects the transaction-facilitating services of money and, consequently, that asset's distinctive role as a medium of exchange.[11] For reasons argued at length in McCallum (1983), it is my judgment that this can be accomplished more satisfactorily by means of a specification of the money-in-the-utility-function (MIUF) type than by available alternatives.[12] Actually, my argument is for a specification in which agents derive utility only from consumption and leisure, but in which an agent's shopping time necessary to obtain consumption goods is reduced by holding increased amounts of real money balances (up to some satiation level) so that larger balances enable him to consume larger quantities of goods and/or leisure. For present purposes, however, it will suffice simply to adopt a MIUF assumption,[13] keeping in mind that there is some quantity of real balances – presumably a function of planned consumption – that will result in a zero marginal utility for the services provided by those balances.

The first ingredient in our model, then, is a lifetime utility function for two-period-lived agents born in t, which we write as

$$u(c_t, x_{t+1}, m_{t+1}). \tag{2.1}$$

Here c_t is consumption when young, x_{t+1} is consumption when old, and m_{t+1} is real money balances (after transfers) at the start of old age. It is

---

[11] An extensive discussion of the issue in an OG model in which "money" does not provide transaction-facilitating services to its holders is given by Wallace (1980).

[12] Cash-in-advance models amount to a special case of shopping-time or MIUF models. For a useful recent discussion of some ways of recognizing the transaction services of money, see Feenstra (1985).

[13] Related analysis focusing explicitly on the shopping-time specification has been conducted by Park (1986).

assumed that u has first partial derivatives u_1, u_2, u_3 and second partial derivatives u_{11}, u_{22}, u_{33}, satisfying $u_1 > 0$, $u_2 > 0$, $u_3 \geq 0$, $u_{11} < 0$, $u_{22} < 0$, and $u_{33} \leq 0$. It is also assumed that Inada-like properties pertain to consumption when young and old, so that agents will always choose positive amounts of c_t and x_{t+1}, but that u_3 can be driven to zero for some value of m_{t+1}, denoted $\hat{m}_{t+1}(c_{t+1})$. These agents are endowed with one unit of labor when young, which they supply inelastically, and none when old.

The second main ingredient of the model is a production function

$$y_t = f(n_t, k_t) \tag{2.2}$$

that is accessible to old persons. Here y_t is output by an old person in t, n_t is the number of manhours that he employs in t from young persons, and k_t is the quantity of capital that he saved when young (in period $t-1$). It is assumed that f is homogeneous of degree one and entirely well-behaved: $f_1 > 0$, $f_2 > 0$, $f_{11} < 0$, $f_{22} < 0$, and Inada properties prevail.

The agents described by (2.1) and (2.2) live in an ongoing economy where the rate of population growth is v; where there are competitive markets for labor, output, capital, and loans; and where the only governmental activity is the injection of lump-sum monetary transfers to old agents. The real quantity of such transfers to an old person during period t is denoted v_t. Therefore, if we let P_t be the money price of output and let M_t be the nominal money stock per old person after transfers in period t, then the government budget identity can be written in per-old-person terms as

$$v_t P_t = M_t - (1+v)^{-1} M_{t-1}. \tag{2.3}$$

Furthermore, if μ_t denotes the rate of growth of the aggregate money stock, so that $1 + \mu_t = (1+v)M_t/M_{t-1}$, we also have

$$v_t = \frac{(1+\mu_t)M_{t-1} - M_{t-1}}{(1+v)P_t} = \frac{\mu_t m_{t-1}}{(1+v)(1+\pi_{t-1})}, \tag{2.4}$$

where $1 + \pi_t = P_{t+1}/P_t$ defines the inflation rate π_t. Note that the definitions of μ_t and π_t imply that in a steady state, with constant values of the growth rates of all variables, we would have $1 + \pi = (1+\mu)/(1+v)$.

In this setting, the behavior of a private agent born in t can be modeled by maximizing $u(c_t, x_{t+1}, m_{t+1})$ subject to the budget constraints faced when young and old. With w_t denoting the real wage in t, these constraints can be written as[14]

$$w_t = c_t + k_{t+1} + \xi_t, \tag{2.5}$$

---

[14] Strictly speaking, (2.5) and (2.6) should be written as inequalities. Throughout the paper, however, we shall simplify by using equalities when the conditions of the problem imply that they will hold as such in equilibrium.

330   **Bennett T. McCallum**

where ξ_t denotes real money balances held at the end of t, and[15]

$$f(n_{t+1}, k_{t+1}) + (1-\delta)k_{t+1} - w_{t+1}n_{t+1} + v_{t+1} + \xi_t P_t/P_{t+1} = x_{t+1}. \qquad (2.6)$$

Also relevant, of course, is the identity

$$m_{t+1} = v_{t+1} + \xi_t P_t/P_{t+1}. \qquad (2.7)$$

The first-order optimality conditions for this problem include (2.5)–(2.7) and the following:

$$u_1(c_t, x_{t+1}, m_{t+1}) = u_2(c_t, x_{t+1}, m_{t+1})[f_2(n_{t+1}, k_{t+1}) + 1 - \delta], \qquad (2.8)$$

$$u_3(c_t, x_{t+1}, m_{t+1})P_t/P_{t+1} = u_1(c_t, x_{t+1}, m_{t+1})$$
$$- u_2(c_t, x_{t+1}, m_{t+1})P_t/P_{t+1}, \qquad (2.9)$$

$$f_1(n_{t+1}, k_{t+1}) = w_{t+1}. \qquad (2.10)$$

These determine the agent's decisions regarding c_t, k_{t+1}, ξ_t, m_{t+1}, n_{t+1}, and x_{t+1} as functions of v_{t+1} and the prices faced parametrically.

For a condition of equilibrium, we also require (2.3) and the following equalities:

$$n_{t+1} = 1 + v, \qquad (2.11)$$

$$f(n_t, k_t) + (1-\delta)k_t = x_t + (1+v)c_t + (1+v)k_{t+1}. \qquad (2.12)$$

Here (2.11) equates demand and supply of labor (per old person) while (2.12) is the overall resource constraint, also in per-old-person terms. These two equations, in conjuction with (2.3) and (2.5)–(2.10), are adequate in number to govern the behavior of c_t, k_{t+1}, ξ_t, m_{t+1}, n_{t+1}, x_{t+1}, v_t, w_t, and P_t for an exogenously specified time path of the policy variable M_t (or μ_t).

For analysis of steady-state conditions, with a constant $\mu_t = \mu$, the foregoing system can be simplified to the following:

$$f_1(1+v, k) = c + k + \xi, \qquad (2.13)$$

$$f(1+v, k) + (1-\delta)k - f_1(1+v, k)(1+v) + v + \xi/(1+\pi) = x, \qquad (2.14)$$

$$\frac{u_1(c, x, m)}{u_2(c, x, m)} = f_2(1+v, k) + 1 - \delta, \qquad (2.15)$$

$$\frac{u_3(c, x, m)}{u_2(c, x, m)} = [f_2(1+v, k) + 1 - \delta](1+\pi) - 1, \qquad (2.16)$$

[15] The possibility of making loans to (or borrowing from) other individuals of the same generation is not made explicit in (2.6) because the equilibrium quantity of such loans will be zero for each individual, as they are all alike. The existence of an (inactive) loan market is assumed, however, and justifies the form of condition (2.8), which implies that the (common) real rate of return on capital and loans is taken exogenously by each individual.

$$m = v + \xi/(1+\pi), \tag{2.17}$$

$$v = \frac{\mu m}{(1+v)(1+\pi)}, \tag{2.18}$$

$$1 + \pi = (1+\mu)/(1+v). \tag{2.19}$$

These determine c, k, x, ξ, m, v, and π as functions of the money stock and population growth rates μ and v.

3   Conditions for Pareto optimality

Our next step is to derive conditions relating to the attainment of Pareto optimality and to determine what inflation rate will permit these to be satisfied. Analytically, our approach will be to maximize the utility of a member of one generation subject to constrained values of the utility of members of all later generations, as well as the social feasibility requirements. Supposing that this calculation is made at date $t = 1$, the Pareto problem is then to maximize $u(c_0, x_1, m_1)$ subject to

$$u(c_t, x_{t+1}, m_{t+1}) = u_t^* \quad t = 1, 2, \ldots, \tag{3.1}$$

where the u_t^* are unknown solution values, and to

$$f(1+v, k_t) + (1-\delta)k_t = x_t + (1+v)c_t + (1+v)k_{t+1} \tag{3.2}$$

for $t = 1, 2, \ldots$. To find conditions sufficient for optimality, we formulate the Lagrangean expression

$$L_1 = u(c_0, x_1, m_1) + \sum_{t=1}^{\infty} \theta_t[u(c_t, x_{t+1}, m_{t+1}) - u_t^*]$$

$$+ \sum_{t=1}^{\infty} \lambda_t[f(1+v, k_t) + (1-\delta)k_t - x_t - (1-v)c_t - (1+v)k_{t+1}]. \tag{3.3}$$

For simplicity, let us introduce the notation $u_{jt} = u_j(c_t, x_{t+1}, m_{t+1})$ and $f_{jt} = f_j(n_t, k_t)$. The implied first-order conditions for $t = 1, 2, \ldots$ are then as follows:

$$\theta_t u_{1t} - \lambda_t(1+v) = 0, \tag{3.4a}$$

$$\theta_t u_{2t} - \lambda_{t+1} = 0, \tag{3.4b}$$

$$\theta_t u_{3t} = 0, \tag{3.4c}$$

$$\lambda_{t+1}[f_{2t+1} + 1 - \delta] - (1+v)\lambda_t = 0. \tag{3.4d}$$

In addition, we have (3.1) and (3.2) plus

$$u_2(c_0, x_1, m_1) - \lambda_1 = 0, \tag{3.5a}$$

$$u_3(c_0, x_1, m_1) = 0, \tag{3.5b}$$

and the transversality condition[16]

$$\lim_{t \to \infty} \lambda_{t+1} k_{t+2} = 0. \tag{3.6}$$

All of these would more appropriately be expressed as two-part Kuhn–Tucker conditions, reflecting the nonnegativity of most of the model's variables, but our assumptions on u and f are adequate to ensure that positive values will be relevant and that the simpler equalities can be used.

To determine whether the foregoing conditions will be satisfied by a competitive equilibrium, we refer back to equations (2.5)–(2.12). Doing so, we immediately see that the only possibilities for failure involve (3.4c), (3.5b), and (3.6). For the first of these to be satisfied, it must be the case – as we see from equations (2.8) and (2.9) – that P_t/P_{t+1} equals $f_{2t+1} + 1 - \delta$. That requirement can be re-expressed as

$$\frac{P_t - P_{t+1}}{P_{t+1}} = f_{2t+1} - \delta, \tag{3.7}$$

which is, of course, precisely the Chicago Rule prescription that the rate of deflation be equated to the (net) marginal product of capital.[17] Condition (3.5b) will obtain, moreoever, if the Chicago Rule held in the past – and otherwise dictates the value of M_1.

Thus we see that inflation at the Chicago Rule rate is necessary for Pareto optimality. Because the discussion of Weiss (1980) might appear to deny this, a brief word of explanation may be useful. The basic point is that Weiss's assumptions concerning the utility function imply that u_{3t}, the marginal service yield of real money balances, is strictly positive for all values of m_{t+1}. Thus the possibility of monetary satiation is precluded by assumption, with the consequence that Weiss's model is one in which no Pareto optimal equilibrium can exist. That this aspect of his specification makes Weiss's model inapplicable to issues regarding Pareto optimality has been recognized by Abel (1984) – whose own optimality criterion is more demanding – and by Park (1986).

It cannot be concluded, however, that a policy of creating money and inflation in accordance with the Chicago Rule is *sufficient* for Pareto optimality, for that rule does not guarantee satisfaction of the transversality condition (3.6). A simple way of seeing that point is to rearrange (3.4d) as follows:

---

[16] That the transversality condition and first-order conditions are jointly sufficient for optimality in a setting such as this is well known from the work of Weitzman (1973) and others. The first-order conditions are also necessary.

[17] That the deflation rate is here measured as $(P_t - P_{t+1})/P_{t+1}$ rather than $(P_t - P_{t+1})/P_t$ is an unimportant manifestation of our discrete-time framework.

$$\lambda_{t+1} = \frac{(1+\nu)\lambda_t}{f_{2t+1}+1-\delta}.$$ (3.8)

Consider, then, the limiting behavior of λ_t as the system approaches a steady state with a constant value of $k_{t+1} = k$. Clearly, if the steady-state k is such that $1 + \nu > f_2 + 1 - \delta$, then the transversality condition (3.6) will not be satisfied and the possibility of Pareto nonoptimality will be introduced. In fact, in this case the economy's parameters are such that the competitive equilibrium leads to a steady state with capital overaccumulation, so the equilibrium will not be Pareto optimal despite adherence by the monetary authority to the Chicago Rule prescription. This "market failure" is, of course, the same as that featured in the analyses of Diamond (1965), Cass and Yaari (1967), and Phelps (1966).

4   Extension to an economy with land

Reflection upon the nature of the capital overaccumulation phenomenon suggests, however, that a crucial feature of reality has been omitted from the model at hand. In particular, the reason for the phenomena's possible occurrence is simply that, as expressed by Cass and Yaari (1967, p. 251), "at efficient rates of interest consumers may want to hold more real assets than are available in the existing capital stock" (plus, in the present case, the real money stock). But in an economy with land – a nonreproducible, nondepreciating, and productive asset – this possibility cannot obtain, for the real exchange value of land can and will be as large as is needed to accommodate desired private saving at an efficient rate of interest.

To demonstrate the validity of this claim, we now modify the model of previous sections by changing the per-capita production function to

$$y_t = f(n_t, k_t, \ell_t),$$ (2.2')

where ℓ_t is land employed by a producer (an old agent) in t and where f is again homogeneous of degree one and well-behaved. In addition, it is assumed that the economy (i.e., f and u) is capable of attaining a unique steady state and that its dynamics are such that this steady state will be approached as time passes.[18]

With this modification, the budget constraints for an agent born in t become

---

[18] These assumptions make the situation with respect to existence, uniqueness, and stability similar to that presumed by Diamond (1965, p. 1134). Some comments on these assumptions will be provided in Section 5. With a fixed total stock of land, the assumed possibility of a steady state comes close to a requirement that f is Cobb–Douglas, a fact mentioned in a different but related context by Solow (1974). Steady-state analyses of real economies with land have been conducted by Meade (1968).

$$w_t = c_t + k_{t+1} + \xi_t + q_t \ell_{t+1} \tag{2.5'}$$

and

$$f(n_{t+1}, k_{t+1}, \ell_{t+1}) + (1-\delta)k_{t+1} - w_{t+1}n_{t+1}$$
$$+ v_{t+1} + \xi_t P_t/P_{t+1} + q_{t+1}\ell_{t+1} = x_{t+1}, \tag{2.6'}$$

where q_t is the real price in period t of a unit of land. The private optimality conditions then become (2.5'), (2.6'), and (2.7')[19] plus

$$u_{1t} = u_{2t}(f_{2t+1} + 1 - \delta), \tag{2.8'}$$

$$u_{3t} P_t/P_{t+1} = u_{1t} - u_{2t} P_t/P_{t+1}, \tag{2.9'}$$

$$f_{1t+1} = w_{t+1}, \tag{2.10'}$$

and also

$$u_{1t} = u_{2t}(f_{3t+1} + q_{t+1})/q_t. \tag{4.1}$$

For competitive equilibrium, we require satisfaction of (2.5')–(2.10'), (4.1), the government budget constraint (2.3), and the following three supply-equals-demand conditions:

$$n_{t+1} = 1 + \nu, \tag{2.11'}$$

$$f(n_t, k_t, \ell_t) + (1-\delta)k_t = x_t + (1+\nu)c_t + (1+\nu)k_{t+1}, \tag{2.12'}$$

$$\ell_{t+1} = \ell_0/(1+\nu)^{t+1}. \tag{4.2}$$

The last of these expresses an equality between the quantity of land demanded and supplied per old person, with ℓ_0 the land-to-old-person ratio in period 0. The eleven mentioned equations determine (for a given path of M_t or μ_t) the values of c_t, k_{t+1}, ℓ_{t+1}, n_{t+1}, ξ_t, m_{t+1}, x_{t+1}, v_t, w_t, P_t, and q_t.

Next we turn to the Pareto problem. In the present case it should be clear that the relevant Lagrangean expression is

$$L_1 = u(c_0, x_1, m_1) + \sum_{t=1}^{\infty} \theta_t [u(c_t, x_{t+1}, m_{t+1}) - u_t^*]$$
$$+ \sum_{t=1}^{\infty} \lambda_t [f(1+\nu, k_t, \ell_0/(1+\nu)^t)$$
$$+ (1-\delta)k_t - x_t - (1+\nu)c_t - (1+\nu)k_{t+1}], \tag{4.3}$$

and that the first-order and transversality conditions are as follows:

$$\theta_t u_{1t} - \lambda_t(1+\nu) = 0, \tag{4.4a}$$

$$\theta_t u_{2t} - \lambda_{t+1} = 0, \tag{4.4b}$$

---

[19] Here (2.7') is simply a new label for equation (2.7).

$$\theta_t u_{3t} = 0, \tag{4.4c}$$

$$\lambda_{t+1}[f_{2t+1} + 1 - \delta] - (1+v)\lambda_t = 0, \tag{4.4d}$$

$$u_2(c_0, x_1, m_1) - \lambda_1 = 0, \tag{4.5a}$$

$$u_3(c_0, x_1, m_1) = 0, \tag{4.5b}$$

$$\lim_{t \to \infty} \lambda_{t+1} k_{t+2} = 0. \tag{4.6}$$

As in Section 3, it is easy to see that the Chicago Rule condition

$$\frac{P_t - P_{t+1}}{P_{t+1}} = f_{2t+1} - \delta \tag{4.7}$$

must hold, and also that the behavior of λ_t can be expressed as

$$\lambda_{t+1} = \frac{(1+v)\lambda_t}{f_{2t+1} + 1 - \delta}. \tag{4.8}$$

But the latter can now, in view of (4.1), alternatively be written as

$$\frac{\lambda_{t+1}}{\lambda_t} = \frac{(1+v)q_t}{f_{3t+1} + q_{t+1}}. \tag{4.9}$$

Because the economy approaches a steady state, the limiting behavior of λ_{t+1}/λ_t can be deduced from the limiting behavior of the right-hand side of (4.9). To the evaluation of that expression we accordingly turn our attention.

In a steady state y_t/k_t must be constant, with the values of the denominator and numerator each proportional to $(1+v)^{(\alpha-1)t}$, where α is a positive fraction such that aggregate (*not* per-capita) output grows according to $(1+v)^{\alpha t}$.[20] The steady-state condition also requires that factor shares be constant,[21] so from the capital share expression $f_{2t}k_t/y_t$ we see that f_{2t} – that is, the marginal product of capital – must be constant. The share of land, by contrast, is $f_{3t}\ell_t/y_t$, from which we deduce that f_{3t} grows in the steady state according to $f_{3t} = f_{30}(1+v)^{\alpha t}$. Finally, with n_t constant, the labor-share expression $f_{1t}n_t/y_t$ implies that $w_t = f_{1t}$ grows at the same (negative) rate as y_t – that is, that $w_t = f_{1t} = f_{10}(1+v)^{(\alpha-1)t}$.

Continuing with the implications of steady-state growth, we refer to equation (2.12'), the economy's overall resource constraint. Because the left-hand side grows like $(1+v)^{(\alpha-1)t}$, so must each term on the right-hand

[20] If the production function is Cobb–Douglas with factor exponents of α_1, α_2, and α_3 (for n_t, k_t, and ℓ_t, respectively), then α would be equal to $\alpha_1/(\alpha_1 + \alpha_3)$.

[21] This requirement stems from the same arithmetic fact that necessitates the constancy of y_t/k_t: namely, that for two terms and their sum all to grow at constant rates, those rates must be equal.

side – which implies that c_t/x_{t+1} is constant with numerator and denominator each growing like $(1+\nu)^{(\alpha-1)t}$. Inspection of (2.5′) or (2.6′) then indicates that the product $q_t\ell_t$ must grow like $(1+\nu)^{(\alpha-1)t}$, which in turn implies that q_t behaves in the steady state according to $q_t = q_0(1+\nu)^{\alpha t}$.

From the foregoing, then, we can write the steady-state value of the right-hand side of (4.9) as

$$\frac{(1+\nu)q_0(1+\nu)^{\alpha t}}{f_{30}(1+\nu)^{\alpha(t+1)}+q_0(1+\nu)^{\alpha(t+1)}} = \frac{(1+\nu)^{1-\alpha}q_0}{f_{30}+q_0}, \qquad (4.10)$$

where $(1+\nu)^{\alpha t}$ has been canceled from the latter expression. But we also know that $k_{t+1}/k_t = (1+\nu)^{\alpha-1}$ in the steady state. Consequently, the steady-state behavior of $\lambda_{t+1}k_{t+2}$ is given by

$$\frac{\lambda_{t+1}k_{t+2}}{\lambda_t k_{t+1}} = \frac{q_0}{f_{30}+q_0}. \qquad (4.11)$$

But with $f_{30} > 0$, as assumed, the right-hand side of (4.11) is a positive fraction, which implies that the limiting behavior of $\lambda_{t+1}k_{t+2}$ is to approach 0 as $t \to \infty$. This guarantees that the transversality condition (4.6) is satisfied. Thus all sufficient conditions for Pareto optimality are satisfied by the competitive equilibrium in the economy under discussion, provided only that the money growth rate is such as to produce the Chicago Rule rate of inflation that induces satiation in real money balances.[22, 23]

5   Conclusions

The foregoing line of argument is straightforward enough that a summary should be redundant. Instead, we conclude with a few observations on the assumptions utilized and then on the significance of the main result.

Throughout the foregoing discussion, it has been implicitly assumed that the economy under consideration does not benefit from technical progress. It would appear, however, that a simple modification of the proof employed would remain applicable in the presence of technical progress, so long as the latter is of a type that will accommodate a steady state. What then of the assumption that steady-state growth is feasible? It is my guess that this condition too is unnecessary for the result, but this is at present only a guess – I do not have a line of attack to propose for the more general case.

[22] This statement presumes that the Chicago Rule inflation rate held in the most recent period so that the *initial* stock of real money balances induces satiation.

[23] That the steady-state value of the net marginal product of capital must exceed the rate of growth can be seen, incidentally, by noting from (2.8′) and (4.1) that $f_{2t}+1-\delta = (f_{3t}+q_{t+1})/q_t$ and then deducing that the steady-state value of the right-hand side of the latter is $[f_{30}+q_0(1+\nu)^\alpha]/q_0 > (1+\nu)^\alpha$.

Mention should perhaps be made of the possibility of multiple solution paths,[24] which may obtain even under conditions implying a unique steady state. In a very useful and somewhat neglected paper, Calvo (1978) has shown that multiple solutions – bubble paths converging to the steady state – are possible in a model with land but no capital or money, and it seems clear that similar solution paths would also be possible in the model of Section 4. As long as these paths approach a steady state, however, their existence will not invalidate our argument.[25]

As for the significance of our results, the main point regarding monetary theory is simply that the insights expressed in the Chicago Rule are applicable even to economies without infinite-lived agents. It could be added – at the risk of belaboring the obvious – that the Rule would remain applicable if the economy's money paid interest; however, the optimum would then require not a zero nominal rate of interest on nonmonetary assets, but rather a nominal rate equal to that paid on money.

In terms of the capital accumulation issue, our result – that overaccumulation is precluded by the presence of land – can readily be seen to obtain whether or not the economy is one with a medium of exchange. Consequently, it suggests that conclusions of a nonmonetary type requiring the possibility of overaccumulation should be reconsidered (at best).[26] As a prominent example, consider the argument developed in the final sections of Samuelson's original OG paper (1958, pp. 476–82). Evidently, these sections are intended to suggest that Samuelson's OG model provides analytical support for the notion that social compacts or "contrivances" – over and above the existence of markets – are apt to be necessary to avoid Pareto suboptimality in laissez-faire economies that go on indefinitely.[27] That this suggestion is not overturned by relaxation of the assumption that all goods are highly perishable is implied by Diamond's

---

[24] Some analysts would probably contend that bubble solutions should be accorded more emphasis than this statement implies. I would suggest, however, that bubble phenomena and the possibility of capital overaccumulation are distinct subjects that can best be understood in isolation. In particular, it would seem appropriate to discuss the overaccumulation possibility first under the assumption that bubble paths are excluded from consideration. [They are, of course, absent from the analysis of Diamond (1965).]

[25] For a much more complete discussion of multiple solutions in OG models the reader is referred to Tirole (1985). The reader should note, however, that Tirole's definition of bubbles (and market fundamentals) differs, in the case of Wallace (1980)-style OG models, from terminology previously employed by many authors – including McCallum (1983, p. 15). Consequently, some of Tirole's conclusions must be interpreted carefully.

[26] Here I take it for granted that no one would wish to argue that actual economies possess no assets with the properties of land. For many issues, of course, it is convenient and not misleading to ignore such assets in the analysis. But for issues relating to overaccumulation, recognition is apparently essential.

[27] In economies for which, in Samuelson's (1958, p. 482) words, "every today is followed by a tomorrow."

338   **Bennett T. McCallum**

(1965) demonstration that inefficient steady-state equilibria may exist in his model, a result that is in this respect a generalization of Samuelson's. But the analysis of the present paper indicates that this type of inefficiency – capital overaccumulation in a competitive economy free from tax distortions – requires the assumed absence of assets like land, an assumption that seems decidedly counterfactual and analytically inappropriate.

REFERENCES

Abel, Andrew B. 1984. "Optimal Monetary and Fiscal Policy in Overlapping Generations Models." Working Paper, Harvard University.
Barro, Robert J. 1974. "Are Government Bonds Net Wealth?" *Journal of Political Economy* 82: 1095–1117.
Burmeister, Edwin. 1980. *Capital Theory and Dynamics.* Cambridge: Cambridge University Press.
Calvo, Guillermo A. 1978. "On the Indeterminacy of Interest Rates and Wages with Perfect Foresight." *Journal of Economic Theory* 19: 321–37.
Calvo, Guillermo A., and Maurice Obstfeld. 1985. "Optimal Time-Consistent Fiscal Policy with Uncertain Lifetimes." Working Paper No. 1593, National Bureau of Economic Research.
Cass, David, and Menahem E. Yaari. 1967. "Individual Saving, Aggregate Capital Accumulation, and Efficient Growth." In K. Shell (ed.), *Essays on the Theory of Optimal Economic Growth.* Cambridge, Mass.: MIT Press.
Diamond, Peter A. 1965. "National Debt in a Neoclassical Growth Model." *American Economic Review* 55: 1126–50.
Drazen, Allan. 1981. "Inflation and Capital Accumulation under a Finite Horizon." *Journal of Monetary Economics* 8: 247–60.
Feenstra, Robert C. 1985. "Functional Equivalence Between Liquidity Costs and the Utility of Money." Working Paper, Columbia University.
Friedman, Milton. 1960. *A Program for Monetary Stability.* New York: Fordham University Press.
1969. *The Optimum Quantity of Money and Other Essays.* Chicago: Aldine.
Helpman, Elhanan, and Efraim Sadka. 1979. "Optimal Financing of the Government's Budget: Taxes, Bonds, or Money?" *American Economic Review* 69: 152–60.
Marty, Alvin L. 1961. "Gurley and Shaw on Money in a Theory of Finance." *Journal of Political Economy* 69: 56–62.
McCallum, Bennett T. 1983. "The Role of Overlapping-Generations Models in Monetary Economics." *Carnegie-Rochester Conference Series on Public Policy* 18: 9–44.
1986. "Some Issues Concerning Interest Rate Pegging, Price Level Determinacy, and the Real Bills Doctrine." *Journal of Monetary Economics* 17: 135–60.
Meade, J. E. 1968. *The Growing Economy.* Chicago: Aldine.
Meltzer, Allan H., and Scott F. Richard. 1985. "Debt and Taxes with Endogenous Population, or Why Public Social Security Systems Are Prone to Crises." Working Paper, Carnegie-Mellon University.
Niehans, Jurg. 1978. *The Theory of Money.* Baltimore: The Johns Hopkins University Press.

Phelps, Edmund S. 1966. *Golden Rules of Economic Growth.* New York: W. W. Norton & Co.

Samuelson, Paul A. 1958. "An Exact Consumption-Loan Model of Interest with or without the Social Contrivance of Money." *Journal of Political Economy* 66: 467–82.

1967. "A Turnpike Refutation of the Golden Rule in a Welfare-Maximizing Many-Year Plan." In K. Shell (ed.), *Essays on the Theory of Optimal Economic Growth.* Cambridge, Mass.: MIT Press.

1968. "The Two Part Golden Rule Deduced as the Asymptotic Turnpike of Catenary Motions." *Western Economic Journal* 6: 85–9.

Scheinkman, Jose. 1980. "Notes on Asset Trading in an Overlapping Generations Model." Working Paper.

Solow, Robert M. 1974. "Intergenerational Equity and Exhaustible Resources." *Review of Economic Studies* 41: 29–45.

Stein, Jerome L. 1971. *Money and Capacity Growth.* New York: Columbia University Press.

Stiglitz, Joseph E. 1974. "Growth with Exhaustible Natural Resources: The Competitive Economy." *Review of Economic Studies* 41: 139–52.

Tirole, Jean. 1985. "Asset Bubbles and Overlapping Generations." *Econometrica* 53: 1071–1100.

Wallace, Neil. 1980. "The Overlapping Generations Model of Fiat Money." In J. H. Kareken and N. Wallace (eds.), *Models of Monetary Economics.* Minneapolis: Federal Reserve Bank of Minneapolis.

Weiss, Laurence. 1980. "The Effects of Money Supply on Economic Welfare in the Steady State." *Econometrica* 48: 565–76.

Weitzman, Martin L. 1973. "Duality Theory for Infinite Horizon Convex Models." *Management Science* 19: 783–9.

Woodford, Michael. 1985. "Interest and Prices in a Cash-in-Advance Economy." Working Paper.

CHAPTER 17

Some unsolved problems for monetary theory

Neil Wallace

In this paper, I discuss two policy questions which I regard as unresolved: Should interest be paid on money and should currency provision be in the hands of the government? An affirmative answer to the first question stands as one of the few widely accepted general results of monetary theory. My discussion is intended to cast doubt on it. There is no widely accepted answer to the second question; some have asserted that currency provision is a public good while others have asserted that currency provision should be left to the market. My discussion of currency provision will not provide a resolution. Instead, I will discuss a way of formulating the question that seems to offer some hope for resolving it.

1   Payment of interest on money

The casual statement on the case for paying interest on money is familiar. Real balances are produced at zero social cost. In an equilibrium in which the real yield on other assets exceeds that on money – or, more generally, in which the marginal rate of substitution between future consumption and present consumption exceeds the real return on money – individuals face a positive alternative cost of holding money. Given the zero social cost, this positive alternative cost implies that too little money is being held. Payment of interest on money removes the positive alternative cost. I focus on one aspect of this casual statement: How does an equilibrium arise with a real return on money less than the relevant intertemporal marginal rate of substitution?

In order for a model to have such an equilibrium it must contain something that prevents individuals from borrowing at the real return on money. Obviously, if individuals can freely borrow at the real return on money

I am indebted for financial support to the Federal Reserve Bank of Minneapolis and to the National Science Foundation under grant NSF/SES-8308594 to the University of Minnesota. All views expressed are solely my own.

by issuing liabilities (forms of inside money) that are perfect substitutes for (outside) money, then such an equilibrium cannot come about. We are all familiar with the usual ways of ruling out such perfect substitution. Money-in-the-utility-function models rule it out through the assumption that money in the utility function is outside money, not the sum of outside and inside money with individuals free to issue inside money. Cash-in-advance (Clower-constraint) models rule it out by a similar identification of the objects that qualify as cash. It is ruled out in a more straightforward manner in a model like Bewley's (1983) in which it is simply assumed that there are no private credit instruments.

For appraising the payment of interest on money, it is desirable to be more explicit about what prevents individuals from borrowing at the real return on money. Explicit assumptions about what prevents individuals from so borrowing are likely to have implications for the feasibility of tax-financed payment of interest on money, and for the feasibility of other policies for dealing with the seeming nonoptimality that accompanies a real return on money lower than the relevant marginal rate of substitution. I will illustrate this by describing a formulation (that is more explicit than the models just mentioned) about what prevents individuals from borrowing at the real return on outside money. In this formulation, the feature that prevents private borrowing makes feasibility of tax-financed interest on money questionable. And, in it, if tax-financed interest on money is feasible then so are other policies that seem at least as desirable.

An overlapping-generations model without private borrowing

This is a stationary, one-good-per-date, pure exchange model of two-period-lived overlapping generations. Each person cares only about his own lifetime pattern of consumption, according to a twice differentiable and strictly quasiconcave utility function which implies that consumption at each date is a normal good. There is diversity in tastes and endowments within generations but no diversity across generations. Endowments are positive and the diversity within generations is such that there is someone for whom the marginal rate of substitution at the endowment is less than unity (h in Figure 1) and someone else for whom it exceeds unity (h' in Figure 1). Finally, suppose that those who are in the second period of their lives at the initial date, the initial old, own in the aggregate one unit of fiat outside money.

Such settings are usually analyzed under the assumption that nothing prevents individuals when young from borrowing at the real return on outside money. I want to make a different assumption, namely that indi-

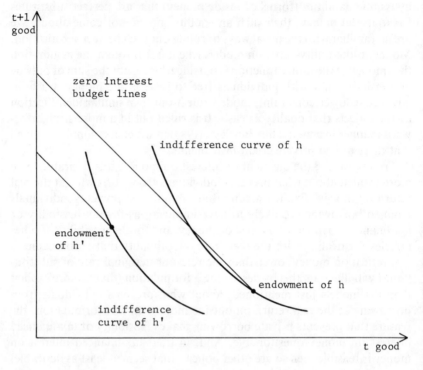

Figure 1

viduals cannot borrow at any return because they cannot credibly commit themselves to repay when old. Although young people know they will receive an endowment of the good when they are old, I assume that they cannot commit this as collateral on a loan and that nothing prevents old people, whether or not they have borrowed, from consuming their endowment and hence from reneging on any loan.

As I will now show, this model displays some features that seem to justify the prescription to pay interest on money. Thus, no nonintervention equilibrium is Pareto optimal. Also, there exists a nonintervention equilibrium with a positive and constant value of fiat money, one with a gross real return on money equal to unity. There also exists an interest-on-money scheme (financed by lump-sum taxes payable when old) that gives rise to a Pareto optimal equilibrium. The model, however, also displays features that should make us doubt the prescription. Lump-sum taxation payable when old seems inconsistent with the inability of people to commit income when old as collateral on a loan. Although there exists an interest-on-money scheme (financed by lump-sum taxes payable when young) that supports an optimal equilibrium, such schemes require that the tax rate levied on an individual depend on the individual's saving propensity. Finally, the distributional consequences of any stationary interest on money equilibrium – relative to the stationary monetary nonintervention equilibrium – cast doubt on the desirability of such schemes.

To prove that no optimal nonintervention equilibrium exists, one simply notes that optimality requires equality of marginal rates of substitution for all members of generation t. Under our assumption that individuals cannot borrow, this requires a real gross return on money no smaller than the maximum marginal rate of substitution at the endowment, denoted r^*. Because r^* is assumed to exceed unity, this requires a return that exceeds and is bounded away from unity for all t, or (equivalently) a minimum positive rate of appreciation of money. Because the real value of money is bounded by the sum of first-period endowments for a generation, a constant in this model, such appreciation cannot occur as an equilibrium.

That a positive and constant-value monetary equilibrium exists follows from the assumption that the marginal rate of substitution of some person is less than unity at the endowment (e.g., person h in Figure 1). The relevant equilibrium condition can be expressed as follows. First, for each h in generation t, let $s^h(r, v)$ be the utility-maximizing choice of $w_1^h - c_1^h$ (saving) subject to

$$c_1^h + c_2^h/r \le (1-v)(w_1^h + w_2^h/r), \tag{1.1}$$

$$c_1^h - w_1^h \le 0, \tag{1.2}$$

where (c_1^h, c_2^h), the vector of arguments of h's utility function, is h's consumption when young and when old, respectively; (w_1^h, w_2^h) is the corresponding vector of pretax endowments of h; v is a tax rate levied on wealth; and r is the gross real return faced by h. Note that constraint (1.2) is the version of the no-borrowing restriction implied by the assumption that any taxes are payable when old. The positive and constant equilibrium value of money is simply $\sum s^h(1, 0)$, where the summation (and all those below) is over the members of a single generation. Our assumption about diversity guarantees that the sum is positive.

In order to prove that there exists a v that supports an optimal equilibrium, first note that the normal goods assumption implies that with positive taxation payable when old, the marginal rate of substitution at the posttax endowment is smaller than at the pretax endowment. Thus, at any return $r \ge r^*$ and positive tax rate, everyone wants to save so that there exists a triplet (r, v, p) that satisfies $r \ge r^*$, $v \in (0, 1)$, $p > 0$, and

$$\sum s^h(r, v) = p, \tag{1.3}$$

$$(r-1)p = v(rW_1 + W_2), \tag{1.4}$$

where W_1 is the sum of endowments when young in a generation and W_2 is the corresponding sum when old. Equation (1.4) is the condition that interest payments (the left-hand side) be equal to tax revenue (the right-hand side). One way to prove that such a triplet exists is to show that for any $r \geq r^*$, there exists a $v \in (0, 1)$ that satisfies

$$(r-1) \sum s^h(r, v) = v(rW_1 + W_2). \tag{1.5}$$

Existence of such a v is implied by three facts. First, with $r > 1$, the left-hand side of (1.5) exceeds the right-hand side at $v = 0$. Second, there exists a v large enough but less than unity for which the right-hand side exceeds the left-hand side [essentially because $\sum s^h(r, v) < W_1$]. Third, both sides of (1.5) are continuous functions of v. That any such $(r, v(r))$ implies a positive p from (1.3) follows because $r \geq r^*$ implies $s^h(r, v(r)) > 0$ for all h. This, in turn, implies equality of marginal rates of substitution and Pareto optimality, because $r^* > 1$.

We now discuss features that call into doubt the prescription to pay interest on money in this model.

I have shown that with lump-sum taxes payable when old, it is easy to support an optimal equilibrium. However, such taxing seems to contradict the assumption that people cannot commit themselves to repay debts. If the government can enforce taxes payable when old, why can't it enforce debt repayment?

Taxes payable when young would not seem to suffer from the same enforcement problem, but as I now indicate, such tax schemes are subject to other difficulties. Above, I showed that an optimal equilibrium exists by showing that there are high enough returns and corresponding supporting taxes so that constraint (1.2) is not binding for any person. With taxes payable when young, each person faces constraint (1.1) and a more stringent version of (1.2), namely

$$c_1^h - w_1^h \leq -v(w_1^h + w_2^h/r), \tag{1.2'}$$

which is equivalent to $c_2^h \geq w_2^h$ if (1.1) holds with equality. In terms of Figure 2, for a given return and tax rate, constraint (1.2') requires that each person choose to be northwest of point s', while constraint (1.2) only requires the person to choose to be northwest of point s. It is easy to produce innocent examples for which there does not exist a steady state with a uniform tax rate, with taxes payable when young and with (1.2') non-binding.[1] Although there exist vectors of tax rates which support a steady state with (1.2') not binding, the tax rates must vary across people and

---

[1] One example has a common utility function given by $c_1^h c_2^h$ so that the choice of c_2^h subject only to (1.1) is

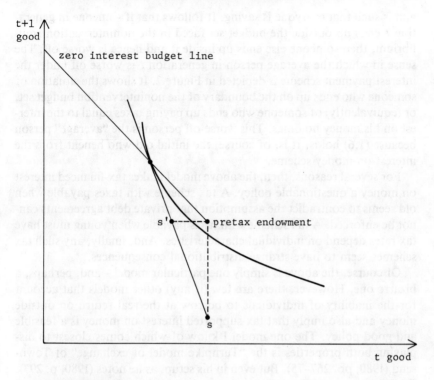

Figure 2

must be such that relatively high-saving people pay relatively high taxes, while still regarding those taxes as lump-sum. Obviously, the informational requirements for such taxing are substantial.

Regarding distributional consequences, at least some people in each generation other than generation 0 are worse off under any stationary optimal interest-on-money equilibrium than under the nonintervention equilibrium. Indeed, in a sense, the average member of each such generation is worse off. This follows from the fact that the interest-on-money equilibrium satisfies feasibility with equality,

$$\sum [c_1^h + c_2^h - (w_1^h + w_2^h)] = 0, \tag{1.6}$$

$$c_2^h/w_2^h = [1-v(r)]r(w_1^h/w_2^h)/2 + [1-v(r)]/2 \le [1-v(r)]r(w_1^h/w_2^h)/2 + 1/2.$$

In this case, the solution for $v(r)$ from (1.5) is

$$v(r) = [(r-1)/(r+1)](rW_1 - W_2)/(rW_1 + W_2),$$

a function of r and aggregate endowments only. If follows that $[1-v(r)]r$ is bounded above for all r by $2(W_1+W_2)/W_1$. Therefore, if $w_1^h/w_2^h < W_1/2(W_1+W_2)$ for some h, then $c_2^h/w_2^h < 1$ for that h, which violates (1.2').

and is such that everyone is saving. It follows that if someone in generation t ends up outside the budget set faced in the nonintervention equilibrium, then someone else ends up inside it and hence is worse off. The
sense in which the average person in generation t is worse off under the
interest payment scheme is depicted in Figure 2. It shows the situation of
someone who ends up on the boundary of the nonintervention budget set,
or (equivalently) of someone who ends up paying taxes equal to the interest on his money holdings. This worse-off person is the "average" person
because (1.6) holds. It is, of course, the initial old who benefit from the
interest-on-money scheme.

For several reasons, then, the above model makes tax-financed interest
on money a questionable policy. A tax scheme with taxes payable when
old seems to contradict the assumption that private debt agreements cannot be enforced. A tax scheme with taxes payable when young must have
tax rates depend on individual characteristics. And, finally, any such tax
schemes seem to have strange distributional consequences.

Of course, the above is simply one particular model – and, perhaps, a
bizarre one. However, there are few (if any) other models that account
for the inability of individuals to borrow at the real return on outside
money and also imply that tax-supported interest on money is a feasible
and good policy. The one model I know of which comes closest to dis-
playing both properties is the "Turnpike model of exchange" of Townsend (1980, pp. 267–75). But even in his setup, as he notes (1980, p. 297),
the feature – an extreme form of spatial and informational separation –
that rules out private borrowing makes one uneasy about the feasibility
of tax schemes for supporting interest on money.

2   Currency provision

Here I discuss an approach to studying currency provision. The goal of
such study is ultimately to answer questions of the following sort: Should
currency provision be a government activity? And, if so, how should it be
managed? Armed with a theory that addresses such questions, we might
hope to appraise the U.S. coinage act of 1792, which (among other things)
created a government mint, set up a denominational structure, directed
the mint to issue coins to those depositing gold and silver bullion at the
mint with no expense to the depositor, and yet made no provision for replacing worn coins with new coins. We also might hope to appraise the
current system of currency provision under which, for example, ten $1
bills exchange for one $10 bill despite the obvious production-cost dis-
crepancies, and under which worn units of currency are exchanged for
new units despite the cost of making the replacement. (The latter policy

is currently coming under pressure because of the large demand for new or almost new units of currency arising from the use of automatic teller machines.) We might also be able to better interpret the fairly general view that some economies have suffered from an inadequate currency. It is claimed, for example, that during the Colonial period and during periods in the nineteenth century, the United States suffered a shortage of small-denomination currency [see Hanson (1979) and Timberlake (1978, Chapter 9)]. It is also claimed that England during the nineteenth century suffered from a currency that was badly worn [see Jevons (1918)].

As these comments suggest, issues about currency provision arise both in (what we may loosely call) fiat money systems and in commodity monetary systems. That being so, it may be helpful to interpret the following discussion in the context of commodity money systems and, in so doing, avoid the additional complications that must be faced in studying fiat money systems.

I want to approach the study of currency provision in commodity money systems by using suggestions, made repeatedly, about the properties of objects that render them suitable as commodity monies. Among the suggested properties are: divisibility, durability, portability, and recognizability. However, I want to use this kind of list in what may be a new way. I want to treat the listed properties both as conjectures about properties that permit an object to play a prominent role in exchange, and as conjectures about properties that a decentralized system, a laissez-faire system, will in some sense misproduce – underproduce or overproduce. Naturally, even to discuss such possibilities requires that these properties not be too freely available in the environments or models we use. Indeed, even aside from the welfare economics objective, these suggestions about properties of commodity monies make no sense in environments where all objects share these properties to an unlimited degree – are perfectly divisible, durable, portable, and recognizable. Thus, for example, if we want to study divisibility then we had best start out with a model where not everything is divisible already, and where making things more divisible is costly. Also, in order to give the conjectures a chance, we want to have an environment in which there is conceivably some nontrivial role for media of exchange. Obviously, studying Robinson Crusoe alone on his island will not do. Before I discuss some features of a candidate model, I want to express (in a loose way) why one might be willing to entertain the possibility that a decentralized system misproduces some of the listed properties.

Consider divisibility and imagine a world in which the production of anything that is durable (say, a coin) costs more in resources than one slice of bread, bread being nondurable. It would then seem that, if there is only private coinage production, one would never observe a coin that exchanges for as little as one slice of bread. Could this also be a world where it would be convenient to have coins that exchange for as little as one slice of bread - convenient in the sense that people would be willing to be taxed to provide a subsidy supporting the production of a stock of such coins? If so, then we would have an instance of underproduction of small-denomination currency. Notice that in this loose kind of story, coins differ from other durable goods because it is posited that the services people get from coins depend upon what they exchange for. One modeling challenge is to determine whether something like this story can be made to emerge as an implication of a coherent environment or model.

My own thinking about candidate models takes as its point of departure the model of Harris (1979). Harris's model is one of pure exchange, where the resources or endowments consist of stocks of nondepreciating durable goods that yield services in proportion to the amounts held. Time is discrete and there are a large number of infinitely lived people, each of whom maximizes the expected value of discounted instantaneous utility, where instantaneous utility at date t depends upon the vector of services from the vector of durable goods carried over from date $t-1$ to date t. The special feature of the model - and the one that attracts me to it - is that people meet pairwise and randomly at each date. This pairwise random meeting pattern is treated by Harris as ruling out all trades except spot trades in durables between people meeting at a date. Treated that way, Harris's model is as conducive to a role for media of exchange as any setup I can imagine. However, to use the Harris model for the purposes I have in mind, it must be amended.[2]

All of Harris's durable goods are endowed to an infinite degree with those properties that make objects suitable as commodity monies; in particular, they are all perfectly divisible, durable, portable, and recognizable. Thus (for example) if we want to study divisibility, we must at least have a model where some or all durable goods are initially indivisible to a degree, and where there are costly technologies available for making things more divisible.

Unfortunately, I have not progressed beyond this very loose way of formulating questions about currency provision. Nevertheless, even this very preliminary discussion is suggestive both about directions to pursue and about how far we have to go. Moreover, I think there is considerable hope for progress along these lines. The conjecture that properties such

[2] One should also impose some version of rational expectations, which Harris failed to do. To accomplish this, subjective views about future trading possibilities must be endogenous - not exogenous as in Harris's formulation - and consistent with what agents know about other agents.

as divisibility, durability, and recognizability are particularly important for frequently traded objects still seems to be a good one. And now our modeling capabilities are such that we can actually study the role of such properties.

3   Concluding remarks

The two policy problems I have discussed – payment of interest on money and government currency provision – seem very different. I chose to discuss the first because it is often taken to be a solved problem. I chose to discuss the second because it seems so fundamental: An answer to it will not only determine whether some governmental role is desirable – the alternative being some sort of competitive money system – but will identify what that role ought to be. Certainly, the second problem subsumes the first, in that any model allowing us to analyze the government's role in the financial system will also have implications for whether there should be an interest subsidy on some or all of the assets in the model.

REFERENCES

Bewley, Truman. 1983. "A Difficulty with the Optimum Quantity of Money." *Econometrica* 51: 1485–1504.
Hanson, John R., II. 1979. "Money in the Colonial American Economy: An Extension." *Economic Inquiry* 17: 281–6.
Harris, Milton. 1979. "Expectations and Money in a Dynamic Exchange Model." *Econometrica* 47: 1403–19.
Jevons, W. Stanley. 1918. *Money and the Mechanism of Exchange.* New York: Appleton.
Samuelson, Paul A. 1968. "What Classical and Neo-classical Monetary Theory Really Was." *Canadian Journal of Economics* 1: 1–15.
Timberlake, Richard H., Jr. 1978. *The Origins of Central Banking in the United States.* Cambridge, Mass.: Harvard University Press.
Townsend, Robert M. 1980. "Models of Money with Spatially Separated Agents." In J. Kareken and N. Wallace (eds.), *Models of Monetary Economies.* Federal Reserve Bank of Minneapolis.

CHAPTER 18

Externalities associated with nominal price and wage rigidities

John B. Taylor

Arguments in favor of economic policy intervention are usually based on the existence of *externalities*. This mode of argument, long a tradition in microeconomics, is relatively new to macroeconomics. In the 1960s, for example, when Milton Friedman outlined in *Capitalism and Freedom* the pros and cons of government policy in many areas of economics, he centered his discussion around the existence of externalities in every area *except* macroeconomics.

Ever since the start of research on the microfoundations of macroeconomics in the early 1970s, many studies have attempted to correct this omission by casting proposals for macroeconomic policy in an externality framework. The vast majority of these studies has been concerned with externalities that relate to whether the natural or average rate of employment is inefficient. Few have been concerned with whether the observed fluctuations in employment around the natural rate are inefficient. In his 1972 book *Inflation Policy and Unemployment Theory,* Edmund Phelps summarized over a dozen externalities, all suggesting that the natural rate of employment is inefficient and higher than the optimum level of unemployment. Phelps mentioned externalities due to imperfect competition, information spillovers about conditions in the labor market from employed to unemployed workers, overpricing of labor due to lemon problems, failure to incorporate the value of self-respect from a good job, external effects of on-the-job training and experience, and income taxes that discriminate in favor of leisure. More recently, efficiency wage theories

This is a revised version of a paper presented at the monetary conference at Austin, Texas in May 1985. The research has been supported by a grant from the National Science Foundation at the National Bureau of Economic Research. I am grateful to Russell Cooper, Ellen McGrattan, Robert Hall, Kenneth Singleton, Joseph Stiglitz, Martin Weitzman, and participants at seminars at UC–Berkeley and Washington State University for useful comments and discussions.

based on shirking with costly monitoring of employee behavior or on turn-over costs have also shown that the natural rate is inefficient. [See, for example, Calvo (1979), Shapiro and Stiglitz (1984), and Yellen (1984).] Trading externalities as developed by Diamond (1982) also show that the natural rate is inefficient. These types of inefficiencies are now being ex-amined and applied by many researchers [See Katz (1986) for a review.]

Although recent progress on formally incorporating externalities into macroeconomics has clearly been significant, this emphasis on the ineffi-ciency of the natural rate seems misplaced from the point of view both of empirical experience with macroeconomic policy and much macroeco-nomic theory. In modern macroeconomic theories that incorporate both price–wage rigidities and rational expectations, the natural rate is viewed as approximately invariant to monetary and fiscal policy, and the assumed goal is to reduce the size and duration of the fluctuations in the economy around the given natural rate. [See, for example, Fischer (1977) or Phelps and Taylor (1977).] One of the central reasons that the economy departs from the natural rate for prolonged periods is the existence of nominal wage and price rigidities that prevent the economy from adjusting quickly to disturbances. But these wage and price rigidities are temporary; they lead to temporary fluctuations in employment, not to permanent under-employment. Eventually the economy tends to return to the natural rate of unemployment, and (on average) unemployment is equal to the nat-ural rate.

Although there are many models of macroeconomic fluctuations based on temporary nominal wage and price rigidities, there has been little dis-cussion of how policy proposals to stabilize fluctuations in these models should be related to externalities. Are these fluctuations inefficient from a social point of view? If not, where are the externalities? This is in con-trast to the relatively large amount of research on the efficiency of the natural rate.

The aim of this paper is to describe how a significant part of economic fluctuations can be interpreted as due to an externality directly associated with nominal wage and price rigidities. It argues that the externality is actually an implicit property of many existing macro models with wage and price rigidities, and explores ways – meant mainly to be suggestive for future research – to make the externality more explicit in these mod-els. The paper concludes by arguing that many policy proposals – such as indexing wages to inflation, legislating profit sharing, or even instituting incomes policies (including tax-based incomes policies) – can be viewed as attempts to deal with this externality; but all are either ineffective or cause other problems.

1   The empirical nature of price and output fluctuations

Empirical evidence on the relationship between output fluctuations and price and wage fluctuations underlies my view that price and wage rigidities are an important aspect of the theory of economic fluctuations. I begin therefore with a brief review of the empirical evidence. I focus on the experience of the major industrialized countries during the last thirty years. The variables that I focus on are (1) the output gap y defined as the percentage deviation of real output from the natural rate of output, the latter measured as a piecewise linear trend, and (2) the inflation rate p measured as the rate of change in the output deflator. The output–inflation data are based on annual observations for seven countries – Canada, France, Germany, Italy, Japan, the United Kingdom, and the United States – for the period from 1954 through 1984. I summarize the observations on these two series using simple bivariate vector autoregressions and their moving-average representations.

Table 1 reports the autoregressions for the seven countries, and Figure 1 plots the moving-average representations as calculated directly from the coefficients of these autoregressions. For annual data, two lagged values are sufficient to eliminate serial correlation of the residuals. I compute the moving-average process without orthogonalizing the error process in the estimated autoregressions. As described in Taylor (1980b, 1986), I find this approach leads to transformations of the vector autoregressions that are easier to interpret. However, the same general patterns in the moving-average coefficients are observed if one orthogonalizes the error process.

There is a striking similarity among the moving-average representations in the seven countries, as a glance at the general shapes in Figure 1 makes clear. The first row of plots gives the effect of an output shock on output (yy), the second row of plots gives the effect of an output shock on inflation (py), the third row gives the effect of an inflation shock on output (yp), and the last row gives the effect of an inflation shock on the inflation rate (pp).

Of course, both output and inflation are persistently moved by their own shocks in all the countries, as can be seen in the first and fourth rows. The pattern is much like the pattern for the United States noted in my previous work [Taylor (1986)]. However, what is more interesting and relevant for the role of price and wage rigidities in these fluctuations are the second and third rows, which show the dynamic cross-interaction between inflation and output in the different countries. In the United States the effect of output shocks is to increase inflation, while the effect of inflation shocks is to decrease output. In other words, the intertemporal cross-correlation between inflation and output shocks reverses sign when

Table 1. *Autoregressions for inflation and output, 1954–84*

Dependent variable	Lagged dependent variables				
	$p(-1)$	$p(-2)$	$y(-1)$	$y(-2)$	σ
Canada					
p	.798	−.062	.261	−.073	1.92
	(4.5)	(−.4)	(2.4)	(−.6)	
y	−.225	.165	.809	−.011	3.46
	(−.7)	(.6)	(4.1)	(−.05)	
France					
p	.591	−.101	.311	−.101	2.60
	(3.6)	(.7)	(1.8)	(−.9)	
y	−.137	−.189	.890	.142	2.98
	(−.7)	(−1.1)	(4.6)	(.6)	
Germany					
p	.852	−.235	.071	−.079	1.13
	(5.6)	(−1.6)	(1.6)	(−1.7)	
y	−1.020	1.085	.967	−.226	4.90
	(−1.5)	(1.7)	(5.0)	(−1.1)	
Italy					
p	.829	.088	.165	−.042	2.28
	(3.8)	(.37)	(1.3)	(−.28)	
y	−.437	.030	.872	.153	3.26
	(−1.4)	(.1)	(4.1)	(.7)	
Japan					
p	.740	−.193	−.166	.188	3.37
	(2.4)	(−.7)	(−.7)	(1.0)	
y	1.000	−.174	.432	.270	4.70
	(2.3)	(−.5)	(1.4)	(1.0)	
United Kingdom					
p	.790	.084	.746	.249	2.60
	(2.4)	(.5)	(3.4)	(.8)	
y	−.127	.083	.782	.006	2.46
	(−.6)	(.6)	(3.8)	(.0)	
United States					
p	.751	.096	.283	−.054	1.16
	(3.6)	(.5)	(2.9)	(−.5)	
y	−1.063	.772	.862	.024	2.26
	(−2.6)	(2.0)	(4.5)	(.1)	

Note: p = inflation rate, y = output gap, σ = std. error (percent).

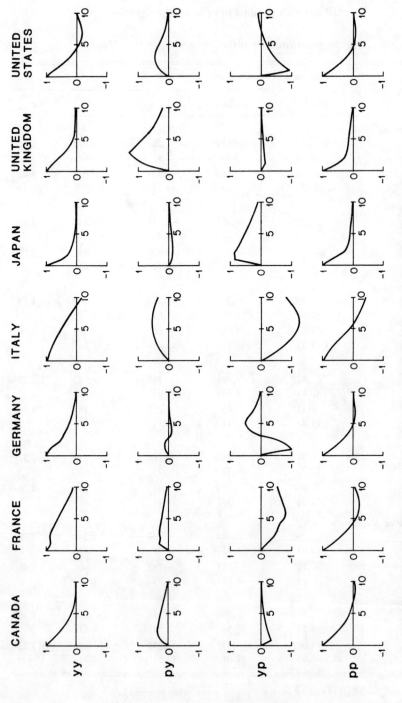

Figure 1. Moving-average representations computed from autoregressions reported in Table 1.

we switch variables. Figure 1 indicates that the same pattern seems to exist in most of the other countries; the only exception is Japan. Save this one exception, the reverse cross-correlation is apparently a central part of economic fluctuations.

A simple two-part theoretical explanation for these reverse cross-correlations is based on the existence of wage and price rigidities. The explanation goes as follows: (1) positive deviations of output from the trend level represent periods of excess demand during which prices and wages tend to be bid up gradually, and then raise the inflation rate with a lag; and (2) increases in inflation are not completely tolerated by policy makers, so that such increases result in less than fully accommodative policies that cause the economy to go into a recession after a lag. Less than fully accommodative policies could occur with monetary tightening in the face of inflation shocks, but fiscal policy could also be used. The story is similar in the case of shocks of the opposite sign: Decreases in output eventually cause declines in inflation, and decreases in inflation eventually cause increases in output.

Particular realizations of these cross relationships are well known in these industrialized countries. For example, the increase in inflation in the late 1960s and during the two oil shocks in the 1970s all led to recessions. More recently, in early 1986 a surprise decline in inflation – due largely to reductions in the price of oil – was expected to lead to continued high growth rates or real output despite the disruptions which the price change had in certain areas. In fact, most economic forecasters raised their forecast of world economic growth. These are all examples of the negative effect of inflation on output when inflation is dated prior to output.

On the other hand, inflation fell soon after the recessions in the 1970s and early 1980s. These are examples of the positive effect of output on inflation when output is dated prior to inflation.

It is not much of an exaggeration to say that all the significant fluctuations in the macroeconomy during the last thirty years have been due to these relationships between output and inflation. If so, then the intertemporal cross-correlations between inflation and output documented in Figure 1 are a crucial part of macroeconomic behavior that cannot be ignored. In Section 2 I argue that an important externality associated with wage and price rigidities is manifested in these correlations.

It may appear surprising that the same general explanation based on wage and price rigidities can apply in so many countries when we know that there are differences between the countries in their wage-setting institutions and macroeconomic policies. In fact, the differences – contract length, indexing, degree of accommodation by the monetary authorities – would affect the length of the lags rather than the signs of the coefficients

356   John B. Taylor

Of the seven countries, the one that is most different from the others is
Japan, where wages are apparently set in a synchronized fashion rather
than being staggered as in the other countries. Of course, this may be one
reason why the empirical observations are so different in Japan.

Are these correlations consistent with other business cycle theories –
such as the real business cycle theories described by King and Plosser
(1984)? There are many structural explanations of any reduced-form correlation, but in my view the above explanation is still more complete than
alternative business cycle theories. It is clearly beyond the scope of this
paper to discuss all alternative theories. To my knowledge, however, de-
scriptions of real business cycle theory do not attempt to deal with the
timing relations between inflation and output that I documented and emphasized above. In principle, the negative relation between inflation and
output could be due to shifts in the production function, rather than to
the tightening of monetary policy. However, focusing on one example, it
is hard to think of a productivity shock that could have led to the large
recessions in 1981–82. Moreover, shifts in productivity per se do not generate the Granger prior relationship between inflation and output. For
the Granger causality one needs to rely on other explanations – based
perhaps on expectations.

2   The nature of the externality: an illustrative example

The nature of the externality associated with nominal wage and price rigidities is fairly easy to explain informally; indeed, except for a change in
terminology and emphasis, the basic idea has been around since the beginning of macroeconomics as a field. I start with an early statement of
the idea from Milton Friedman, since I referred to his research as an example of the tendency not to mention externalities explicitly in macroeconomics. Consider Friedman's (1948) analysis of the implications of
wage rigidities for his famous proposals for monetary and fiscal policy.
When there are wage rigidities, he writes,

let there be a substantial rise in the wage of a particular group of workers as a consequence either of a trade-union action or of a sharp but temporary increase in
the demand for that type of labor or a decrease in its supply, and let this higher
wage rate be rigid against downward pressure. Employment of resources as full as
previously would imply a higher money income, since, under the assumed conditions of rigidity, other resources would receive the same amount as previously,
whereas the workers whose wage rate rose would receive a larger amount if fully
employed . . . . The only escape from this situation [of unemployed resources] is
to permit inflation.

If the increase in inflation is prevented then there must be a decline in output and employment.

When the wage rate of a group of workers increases, there will tend to be an increase in the overall level of wages. Firms, whether competitive or imperfectly competitive, will raise their prices accordingly. If the money supply is unchanged then this increase in wages and prices will reduce the real supply of money in the economy; real output necessarily falls. The fall in output associated with a fall in real money balances is consistent with any reasonable model of aggregate demand, whether based on a simple quantity equation, a full ISLM apparatus, or a model in which a reduction in real money affects real output by reducing the amount of intermediated credit. Note that if the money supply is increased in response to the exogenous wage shock, then there will be an increase in inflation. Only if real money balances are held constant will a decline in employment below full employment be avoided.

In fact, the mechanism bringing about the decline in overall employment in Friedman's 1948 model is fiscal policy rather than monetary policy. In Friedman's 1948 framework, the tightening of aggregate demand occurs because the higher level of nominal income increases taxes – the tax system is progressive – but government spending does not change. The increase in the government budget surplus is a drag on the economy. This story contrasts with the case where the money supply is fixed and the increase in prices reduces real balances, raising interest rates and thereby causing investment demand and output to fall. The end result is the same.

This is an externality because the workers who increase their wage do not take account of the influence of their actions on the overall price and wage level. Changes in the overall price level in turn affect the economy unless they are nullified by the policy makers. The workers therefore ignore the fact that they cause a drop in the overall level of employment that occurs as the central bank does not accommodate the increase. The wage rigidities create an interdependency in the economy. If workers could coordinate their wage setting, with some cutting their wages so that the overall wage level does not increase, then the adverse effects could be avoided. Competition rules out such coordinated wage setting, however.

It is important to emphasize that this externality is an economywide phenomenon, involving the interaction among markets. If one looks only at one market (say, the labor market), it is indeed difficult to see why the externality would exist. The implicit-contract work of Azariadis (1975), for example, suggests that even with wage rigidities the labor market will be operating efficiently. Looking at only one market ignores the fact that the externality occurs because of interdependencies throughout the economy. Short of collectively instituting an economywide auction market for all goods, there is no way to avoid this interdependency. The group of workers whose wage rate rose substantially suffers only part of the reduction in employment. Because the drop in employment is economywide, even though it is temporary much of it falls on other workers, and the market provides no way to make compensation.

3   Externalities in a model with nominal wage setting

Consider a model where there are no externalities and where prices and wages are perfectly flexible – set by a central auctioneer. For concreteness suppose that the economy consists of two types of workers whose employment (n_1 and n_2) is used in producing goods according to the production function

$$y = f(n_1, n_2). \tag{3.1}$$

Suppose that each type of worker has a utility function

$$U_1(y_1, n_1), \qquad U_2(y_2, n_2), \tag{3.2}$$

where y_1 and y_2 are consumption of the single good by each type of worker. Note that I have not included consumption of type-1 workers in the utility function of type-2 workers. This would be an obvious externality unrelated to wage and price rigidities. Let the nominal wage rate for each type of worker be x_1 and x_2, and let the price of output be p.

If the workers and the representative firm take wages and prices as given and maximize profits and utility, and if prices and wages are such that demand equals supply, then the equilibrium values of n_1, n_2, x_1/p, and x_2/p are given by the solution to

$$f_1 = x_1/p, \qquad f_2 = x_2/p; \\ U_{1n}/U_{1y} = -x_1/p, \qquad U_{2n}/U_{1y} = -x_2/p, \tag{3.3}$$

with y given either by the production function (3.1) or by total income. Let the solution values be y^* for total output and n^* for total employment.

In this model, with no externalities, the competitive equilibrium clearly is efficient. From a macroeconomic perspective this competitive equilibrium corresponds to the "natural" rate of employment and output. In other words, the natural rate of employment n^* and the natural rate of output y^* are efficient. Note that the absolute level of nominal wages and prices is undetermined.

Now consider the possibility of economic fluctuations. I assume that these fluctuations arise as the economy moves from one long-run equilibrium in the above model to another long-run equilibrium. Suppose there are shocks to production or to utility in this simple competitive economy. If the shocks are permanent then the economy will eventually settle down to a new equilibrium. This new equilibrium will also be efficient. But we are interested in the fluctuation in the economy as it moves away from the old equilibrium and toward the new one. The fluctuation will depend on the mechanism through which prices and wages are adjusted.

Suppose that nominal wages (x_1 and x_2) and the price are set by different decentralized decision makers. Assume also that there is a desire to keep the average price and/or wage from drifting too far away from some target. That is, x_1, x_2, and p are each under the control of a different agent, but there is a common goal of maintaining price stability; that is, keeping $(p+x_1+x_2)/3$ near some target. Alternatively the goal could be to maintain p near some target; we choose the average of wages and prices to emphasize that all nominal price and wage decisions generally enter into the aggregate target. In order to have a determinate aggregate target, it is necessary to have at least one of the wages or the price (or an average of the three) enter the model. There are many ways this could be done. For example, real money balances could be entered into the production function or the utility functions. A more direct approach, which incorporates the policy reactions described in Section 1, is to assume that policy makers keep demand for goods away from the natural rate according to the rule $y = y^* - a(m - M/(p+x_1+x_2))$, where M is the money supply and where a and m are positive constants. In other words, total demand for output is directly controlled by the monetary authorities in such a way that the economy is at the natural rate only if $p+x_1+x_2 = M/m$, where M and m are set by the monetary authorities. There is no need to be specific at this point about the mechanism through which the monetary authorities do this. Note that when total production is greater or less than y^*, employment could be determined by some employment rule through which (for example) employment is reduced or increased proportionally for each type of worker according to the ratio y/y^*. We also leave open the explicit nature of this employment rule.

In this situation, employment and therefore utility will be affected by the overall price level. There is of course an overall average price–wage level (M/m) that will make output equal to the natural rate. But the decentralized price and wage setters have aims other than targeting the overall price level – namely, adjusting relative wages and real wages to values appropriate to the new optimal allocation. And if they do not coordinate their wage and price setting then they will not be able to keep the average price–wage level equal to M/m at all times, nor the level of output and employment equal to the natural rates. The lack of coordination in price and wage adjustment clearly generates an externality. This externality is quite general and exists for a whole range of possible price and wage decision rules (for example, staggered wage setting and marginal-cost pricing), except for those in which prices and wages are determined by a central auctioneer and are perfectly flexible.

The existence of this externality seems consistent with the empirical observations mentioned in Section 1. The increase in inflation that leads to recessions corresponds to the increase in $p + x_1 + x_2$ that leads to a decline in y relative to y^* in the model. More specifically, the increases in oil prices in the 1970s represented part of a relative price shift that – under the existing wage–price setting system – led to an increase in the overall price level that was not fully accommodated by the monetary authorities and that therefore led to a recession. Similarly, the decline in oil prices in 1986 should lead to a worldwide boom.

The wage and price setting system that currently exists in the United States and in many other countries can be viewed as a practical substitute for a world in which prices are perfectly flexible and determined by a central auctioneer. This substitute involves seemingly infrequent changes in wages and prices, made by decentralized decision makers. It is not clear whether these infrequent changes are the result of adjustment costs, or whether they have evolved because the overall system would work less well with more frequent changes. The actual wage–price system (as distinct from the imaginary auctioneer) now appears to be fairly effective in allocating resources. But it also leads to the externality that we have mentioned. An unresolved question is whether the externality is a necessary part of the allocative mechanism. For example, does the degree of monetary accommodation – the extent to which the relative wage increase leads to an increase in overall inflation or a drop in output – influence the size of the relative wage increase? In Taylor (1981) it was shown, in a particular staggered-contract model, that more accommodation leads to smaller relative price variability. This reduced variability could hinder the allocative effects of the initial wage increase.

4   Is it a pecuniary or technological externality?

An important distinction is sometimes made between pecuniary and technological externalities [see Scitovsky (1954)]. Pecuniary externalities per se are not a cause of inefficiency. They occur as a result of a change in tastes or production, and a consequent change in prices, that move the economy from one equilibrium to another. Greenwald and Stiglitz (1986) make the distinction this way: Technological externalities occur when "the action of one individual or firm directly affects the utility or profit of another," while pecuniary externalities occur "when one individual's or firm's actions affect another only through effects on prices." For example, if there is a permanent change in people's tastes away from butter to margarine, workers employed in making butter will be paid less in the new equilibrium than they were in the old equilibrium. There appears to be an externality, in that the people who change their tastes have an effect on the well-being of butter manufacturers and their employees that they ignore when they make their taste change. Yet both equilibria – the one before the taste change and the one after – can be Pareto efficient, in which case there is no externality in the usual (or technological) sense of the word. Except for distributional considerations there is no reason for policy intervention in the case of pecuniary externalities, as is clear from this example.

Is the externality that we discussed in Sections 2 and 3 a pecuniary externality? I have argued that it is not. But there is a superficial similarity in that individuals affect each other through prices. The shock that called for a change in wages in Friedman's example of downward wage rigidities was a change in a utility or production function, but the actions of individuals or firms did not directly affect the utility or production function of others. The natural state of the economy could be Pareto efficient in this example. If so, after wages and prices have fully adjusted the economy would be back in a Pareto efficient situation. In the case of wage and price rigidities, however, the externality occurs during the transition from one possibly Pareto efficient equilibrium to another. The externality is in the price adjustment process itself, not directly in the conventional utility or production functions. People do not take account of the fact that their actions have adverse effects on the behavior of the economy as it passes between equilibria. The externality is quite different from the traditional types of externalities that have nothing to do with slow wage and price adjustment, but it is nevertheless more than a purely distributional pecuniary externality.

Recently, Akerlof and Yellen (1985), Blanchard and Kiyotaki (1985), and Mankiw (1985) have shown that price and wage rigidities, which occur simply because workers or firms have a *small* cost of adjusting prices and wages, can lead to *large* welfare losses in the economy as a whole. These "near rational" price decisions have impacts on other agents in the economy because there are other sources of inefficiency in the economy – for example, monopolistic competition. Hence, there is a similarity with the pecuniary externality mechanism mentioned above: Pecuniary externalities can have welfare effects if there are other sources of inefficiency in the economy. The externality that I describe in this paper is conceptually distinct from the mechanism described by Akerlof and Yellen (1985), Blanchard and Kiyotaki (1985), and Mankiw (1985). The externality in this paper would exist even if there were no other distortions or nonconvexities in the economy. Here it is the lack of coordination in achieving an aggregate price–wage target in any economy where nominal wage and price decisions are decentralized, combined with a social desire for stable aggregate price–wage, that generates the externality.

5   Reform proposals

Many macroeconomic policy changes and reforms that have been proposed can be interpreted as ways to eliminate the externality associated with nominal wage and price rigidities. In this section we briefly review three proposals: indexing, incomes policies, and the profit-sharing proposal made by Weitzman (1985).

Indexing

Indexing can be thought of as a way to facilitate movements in the overall level of wages and prices while not interfering with the relative wages or real wages. If wages were more responsive to changes in prices, then the overall level of wages and prices could adjust more quickly without real effects on output. With wages fully indexed to prices, a reduction in the money supply could reduce the average level of wages and prices toward a target level, with little or no change in output. The externality associated with wage rigidities would effectively be reduced.

As Fischer (1977) and Gray (1976) have shown, however, indexation can hinder the adjustment of the economy to changes in productivity or tastes that require changes in the real wage or in relative wages. In terms of the model discussed above, indexing wages x_1 or x_2 to prices p prevents real wage adjustments. Indexing wages x_1 to other wages x_2 prevents relative wage adjustments. Thus, the imposition of indexing to alleviate the externality associated with wage rigidities can have harmful side effects. Indexing does not appear to be a satisfactory solution to the externality problem, because it interferes with relative- and real-wage adjustments that must occur if resources are to be allocated efficiently when tastes or technologies change.

Incomes policies

Wage and price controls – as well as tax-based incomes policies – have frequently been proposed and sometimes used in the United States and other countries. These policies can also be interpreted as a way to eliminate the externalities associated with wage and price rigidities discussed above. In terms of our discussion in Section 3, the theoretical idea behind wage and price controls is to prevent the average level of wages and prices from rising without using restrictive monetary and fiscal policies. Relative price changes of the type mentioned earlier could take place, but by controlling the overall inflation rate the controls effectively force other wages to be reduced, or not increase as much.

In practice, however, wage and price controls do not seem to have worked very well. It is difficult to control the overall level of prices without having an impact on relative prices. As our discussion above makes clear, coordinating wage and price decisions of individual decision makers would necessarily interfere with the price-adjustment mechanism and thereby probably interfere with the allocative role of the price system.

Profit sharing

A recent proposal by Weitzman (1985) is to replace the current price–wage adjustment system with a profit-sharing system. One of the stated aims of Weitzman's proposal is to reduce the size of economic fluctuations. Is the proposal effective in eliminating the externality discussed in this paper? Two aspects of profit sharing need to be considered. First, profit sharing has characteristics similar to indexing: When there is a drop in demand that causes prices and profits to fall, wage payments are automatically reduced. Thus, as with indexing, the overall level of wages and prices falls more quickly in response to a monetary contraction and with a smaller effect on output. A disadvantage of profit sharing is also similar to indexing: Changes in labor productivity may require a change in the profit share going to workers. Just as indexing keeps the real wage from changing, profit sharing keeps the labor share from changing. Of course it would be possible to change the parameters of a profit-sharing plan, but the same could be said for an indexing formula.

A second aspect of profit sharing is that it would change the demand for labor. As Weitzman emphasizes, firms paying less at the margin to hire workers will want to hire more workers. How does this increased demand for labor fit into the general discussion of externalities discussed in this paper? In order to answer that question, a less general framework than the one introduced above is clearly necessary. For this purpose I look at the staggered wage-setting model that I have used in earlier work [Taylor (1980a)]. Consider the following variables and notation: The money supply is m, the price level is p, the average wage rate is w, the contract wage is x (set in any period by a subset of the workers), and real output is y; all these variables are measured in logs. Note that the notation in this section is different from the previous sections.

Aggregate demand is given by

$$y = b(m - p).   \tag{5.1}$$

We assume that there is a natural or potential level of output, normalized to be $y = 0$.

We will consider two economies – one based on wage payments and the other based on profit sharing. In the wage-payment case, prices are assumed to be a markup over the wage. The price equation, in log form and omitting constants, is simply

$$p = w.   \tag{5.2}$$

Note that, in the long run, output $y = 0$; so the price level and therefore the wage w must equal m in the long run. In the short run, the wage is given by a staggered wage-setting equation

$$x = .5(w^e + w^e_{+1}) + c(y^e + y^e_{+1}),   \tag{5.3}$$

where x is the contract wage set by workers in a given period. The superscript e represents the expectation of the variable. I look only at the case where wage decisions last two periods. (Note that the subscripts on x now represent the period rather than the type of worker.) The average wage is given by $w = .5(x + x_{-1})$. The behavior of the model is much like that described in Section 2 or 3. When there is an increase in the wage of one group of workers [equation (5.3) is shocked], a fixed money supply leads to a contraction of output. Alternatively, an accommodative monetary policy leads to a larger increase in the overall wage and price level, and a smaller drop in output. The externality associated with the nominal rigidities are just as in the earlier example.

Now consider the case of Weitzman's share economy. Rather than being paid a fixed wage rate x, workers are paid a lower fixed wage x^f plus a share x^s of the profits of firms. The parameters x^f and x^s are taken as parameters of the profit-sharing contract. The vector $x' = (x^f, x^s)$ replaces the single parameter x (the contract wage) in the standard wage model.

How will prices be determined in the profit-sharing case? Weitzman assumes that prices – at least in the short run – are set as a markup over the fixed-payment part of the profit-sharing contract. In terms of the notation introduced so far, this implies the following analogy with equation (5.2):

$$p = v,   \tag{5.4}$$

where $v = (x^f + x^f_{-1})/2$ is the average of the wage portion of the profit-sharing contract in this period and the previous period. [As we discuss below, prices will adjust to a value that is not given by equation (5.4) in the long run.]

We now need to explain the determination of the pair x'. The most straightforward assumption is that pair x' is determined in the same way that the single wage x is determined in the wage model; that is, through equation (5.3). Workers would prefer a profit-sharing contract with a high x' much as they would prefer a wage contract with a high x. The market would then determine the overall level as represented by the pair x'. In attempts to bid workers away from other firms in good times, firms would bid up the contract x' relative to the other firms' contracts. Conversely, in bad times (with high unemployment) workers would be less willing to bargain for a contract with an x' much higher than the prevailing x'. In normal times, it is reasonable to expect that workers and firms would set profit-sharing contracts that were about equivalent to the prevailing level of contracts. These considerations that go into the determination of the profit-sharing contract are identical to those that go into the simple wage contract. Consequently, a reasonable profit-sharing determination equation for x' is again equation (5.3).

Weitzman is not specific about how the wage parameters would adjust, except that they will converge to values for which the economy will operate at the same long-run equilibrium as under the pure wage system. This long run will also imply a different value for p than given in equation (5.4); as the pay parameters adjust, the price level will adjust to give the same level of real balances as in the pure wage economy.

In the profit-sharing economy, the equations are (5.1), (5.3), and (5.4), with x' replacing x in equation (5.3) and with p adjusting upward (slowly perhaps) to cover total wage payments. The behavior of the profit-sharing economy and the wage economy is therefore very similar, *as long as part of the profit-sharing system entails a fixed wage component,* however small. The reasons could be the same as those listed by Friedman (see Section 2). Suppose, for example, that it is the result of a strong trade union action: The trade union of one group of workers receives a big increase in its profit-sharing contract. Unless there is an offsetting decline in the terms of the other group of workers this will increase the demand for money – more will be needed to pay workers in the form of wages. The increase in the demand for money will result in a loss of output unless it is accommodated by the central bank. In sum, the externalities of the wage system continue to exist in a profit-sharing system.

6   Concluding remarks

The aim of this paper has been to describe the externality existing in macroeconomic models of economic fluctuations that are based on nominal price and wage rigidities. The general description does not rely on any one specific model of wage and price determination. Three elements of any model are crucial for the externality, however: (1) wages and prices are set in nominal terms by decentralized decision makers, (2) there is a common desire for stability of the aggregate price–wage level, and (3) the monetary system is able to make total demand for production and employment differ from the efficient levels whenever the aggregate price–wage level is off target.

The paper also briefly examined three policy proposals that can be interpreted as attempts to deal with this externality. All three – indexing, incomes policies, and profit sharing – do not seem to alleviate the welfare loss associated with the externality without creating other problems. Apparently, more detailed and explicit models of nominal wage and price adjustment are necessary before we can say how other types of proposals [such as "more-or-less accommodation" of monetary policy as in Taylor (1980a)] are likely to deal more effectively with the externality.

REFERENCES

Akerlof, George A., and Janet L. Yellen. 1985. "Can Small Deviations from Rationality Make Significant Differences to Economic Equilibria?" *American Economic Review* 75: 708–20.

Azariadis, Costas. 1975. "Implicit Contracts and Underemployment Equilibria." *Journal of Political Economy* 83: 1183–1202.

Blanchard, Olivier, and Nobuhiro Kiyotaki. 1985. "Monopolistic Competition, Aggregate Demand Externalities, and the Real Effects of Nominal Money." Working Paper No. 1770, National Bureau of Economic Research.

Calvo, Guillermo. 1979. "Quasi-Walrasian Theories of Unemployment." *American Economic Review, Papers and Proceedings* 69: 102–7.

Diamond, Peter. 1982. "Aggregate Demand Management in Search Equilibrium." *Journal of Political Economy* 90: 881–94.

Fischer, Stanley. 1977. "Long Term Contracts, Rational Expectations, and the Optimal Money Supply Rule." *Journal of Political Economy* 85: 191–205.

Friedman, Milton. 1948. "A Monetary and Fiscal Framework for Economic Stability." *American Economic Review* 37: 245–64.

———. 1962. *Capitalism and Freedom.* Chicago: University of Chicago Press.

Gray, J. 1976. "Wage Indexation: A Macroeconomic Approach." *Journal of Monetary Economics* 2: 221–35.

Greenwald, Bruce C., and Joseph E. Stiglitz. 1986. "Externalities in Economies with Imperfect Information and Incomplete Markets." *Quarterly Journal of Economics,* to appear.

Katz, Lawrence. 1986. "Efficiency Wage Theories: A Partial Evaluation." In Stanley Fischer (ed.), *The Macroeconomics Annual.* National Bureau of Economic Research.

King, Robert, and Charles Plosser. 1984. "Money, Credit and Prices in a Real Business Cycle." *American Economic Review* 74: 363–80.

Phelps, Edmund S. 1972. *Inflation Policy and Unemployment Theory.* New York: W. W. Norton.

Phelps, Edmund S., and John B. Taylor. 1977. "Stabilizing Powers of Monetary Policy under Rational Expectations." *Journal of Political Economy* 85: 163–90.

Scitovsky, Tibor. 1954. "Two Concepts of External Economies." *Journal of Political Economy* 17: 143–51.

Shapiro, Carl, and Joseph Stiglitz. 1984. "Equilibrium Unemployment as a Worker Discipline Device." *American Economic Review* 74: 433–44.

Taylor, John B. 1980a. "Aggregate Dynamics and Staggered Contracts." *Journal of Political Economy* 88: 1–24.

1980b. "Output and Price Stability: An International Comparison." *Journal of Economic Dynamics and Control* 2: 109–32.

1981. "On the Relation between the Variability of Inflation and the Average Inflation Rate." In K. Brunner and A. Meltzer (eds.), *The Costs and Consequences of Inflation,* pp. 57–85. Carnegie Rochester Conference Series on Public Policy, Vol. 15.

1986. "Improvements in Macroeconomic Stability: The Role of Wages and Prices." In Robert J. Gordon (ed.), *The American Business Cycle: Continuity and Change.* University of Chicago Press (for the National Bureau of Economic Research).

Weitzman, Martin. 1985. "The Simple Macroeconomics of Profit Sharing." *American Economic Review* 75: 937–53.

Yellen, Janet. 1984. "Efficiency Wage Models of Unemployment." *American Economic Review, Papers and Proceedings* 74: 200–5.